CW01301623

David Gascoyne was born in 1916 in Harrow, Middlesex, and educated at Salisbury Cathedral School and the Regent Street Polytechnic, London. His first collection of poetry, *Roman Balcony and Other Poems*, was published when he was sixteen, and in 1933 Cobden-Sanderson brought out his novel *Opening Day*. Both books are remarkable achievements for an adolescent, and they were followed by the equally striking poetry collections *Man's Life Is This Meat* (1936) and *Hölderlin's Madness* (1938), which established his reputation as one of the most original voices of the 1930s. Gascoyne was among the earliest champions of Surrealism: in 1935 his *A Short Survey of Surrealism* was published, and in the next year he was one of the organisers of the London International Surrealist Exhibition. From this period, and during his time living in France in 1937-39, date his friendships with Dalí, Max Ernst, André Breton, Paul Eluard and Pierre Jean Jouve. As well as becoming internationally celebrated as a poet – especially after publication of his *Poems 1937-1942*, with its Graham Sutherland images – Gascoyne became highly regarded as a translator, notably of the leading French Surrealists.

After the war Gascoyne again lived in France (1947-48 and 1953-64), partly in Paris and partly in Provence. He consolidated his reputation with *A Vagrant and Other Poems* (1950) and with *Night Thoughts* (1956), commissioned by Douglas Cleverdon for BBC Radio. His *Collected Poems*, published by Oxford University Press in 1965, were reprinted six times. Enitharmon Press published a substantial volume of *Selected Poems* in 1994, and in 1996 his *Selected Verse Translations*.

David Gascoyne now lives with his wife, Judy, at Northwood on the Isle of Wight. He has recently been made a Chevalier dans l'Ordre des Arts et Lettres by the French Ministry of Culture for his lifelong services to French literature.

DAVID GASCOYNE

Selected Prose
1934–1996

Edited by Roger Scott

with an introduction by
Kathleen Raine

London
ENITHARMON PRESS
1998

First published in 1998
by the Enitharmon Press
36 St George's Avenue
London N7 0HD

Distributed in Europe
by Littlehampton Book Services
through Signature Book Representation
2 Little Peter Street
Manchester M15 4PS

Distributed in the USA and Canada
by Dufour Editions Inc.
PO Box 7, Chester Springs
PA 19425, USA

Text © David Gascoyne
Introduction © Kathleen Raine
Preface © Roger Scott

ISBN 1 900564 01 7
ISBN 1 900564 06 8 (limited edition of 50
numbered copies, signed by
David Gascoyne, Kathleen Raine and Roger Scott)

British Library Cataloguing-in-Publication Data.
A catalogue record for this book is available
from the British Library.

Set in 10pt Bembo by Bryan Williamson, Frome,
and printed in Great Britain by
The Cromwell Press, Wiltshire

DAVID GASCOYNE: SELECT BIBLIOGRAPHY

Poetry
Roman Balcony and Other Poems (London: Lincoln Williams, 1932)
Man's Life Is This Meat (London: Parton Press, 1936)
Hölderlin's Madness (London: Dent, 1938)
Poems 1937-1942 (London: Editions Poetry London, 1943; reprinted 1944, 1948)
A Vagrant and Other Poems (London: John Lehmann, 1950)
Night Thoughts (London: André Deutsch, and New York: Grove Press, 1956; Paris: Alyscamps Press, 1995)
Collected Poems, edited by Robin Skelton (London: Oxford University Press & André Deutsch, 1965; reprinted 1966, 1970, 1978, 1982, 1984)
Penguin Modern Poets 17, with Kathleen Raine and W. S. Graham (London: Penguin Books, 1970)
The Sun at Midnight: Poems and Aphorisms (London: Enitharmon Press, 1970)
Three Poems (London: Enitharmon Press, 1976)
Early Poems (Warwick: Greville Press, 1980)
La Mano del Poeta, bi-lingual selection of poems, edited by Francesca Romani Paci (Genoa: Edizioni S. Marco dei Giustiniani, 1982). Awarded the Premio Biella-Poesia Europea 1982
Five Early Uncollected Poems (Leamington Spa: Other Branch Readings, 1984)
Collected Poems 1988 (Oxford University Press, 1988; reprinted 1988)
Extracts from 'A Kind of Declaration' & Prelude to a New Fin-de-Siècle (Warwick: Greville Press, 1988)
Tankens Doft, selection of poems, edited by Lars-Inge Nilsson (Lund: Ellerströms, 1988)
Miserere: poèmes 1937-1942 (Paris: Granit, 1989)
Three Remanences (London: privately printed, 1994)
Selected Poems (London: Enitharmon Press, 1994)
Encounter with Silence: Poems, 1950, introduction by Roger Scott (London: Enitharmon Press, 1998)

Prose
Opening Day (novel; London: Cobden-Sanderson, 1933)
A Short Survey of Surrealism (London: Cobden-Sanderson, 1935; London: Frank Cass & Co., 1970; San Francisco: City Lights Books, 1982)

Thomas Carlyle (London: Longman, Green & Co., 1952; reprinted 1963, 1969)
Paris Journal 1937-1939, with a preface by Lawrence Durrell (London: Enitharmon Press, 1978)
Journal, 1936-37 (London: Enitharmon Press, 1980)
Journal de Paris et d'ailleurs, 1936-1942, translated by Christine Jordis (Paris: Flammarion, 1984)
Rencontres avec Benjamin Fondane (Cognac: Arcane 17, 1984)
Collected Journals, 1937-42, introduced by Kathleen Raine (London: Skoob Books Publishing, 1990)
Lawrence Durrell (London: privately printed, 1993)
The Fire of Vision: David Gascoyne and George Barker, edited and introduced by Roger Scott (London: privately printed, 1996)
Selected Prose 1934-1996, edited by Roger Scott, with an introduction by Kathleen Raine (London: Enitharmon Press, 1998)

Translations
Salvador Dalí, *Conquest of the Irrational* (New York: Julien Levy, 1935)
Benjamin Péret, *A Bunch of Carrots: Twenty Poems* (London: Roger Roughton, 1936; trans. with Humphrey Jennings; second edition published as *Remove Your Hat*, 1936)
André Breton, *What is Surrealism?* (London: Faber, 1936)
Paul Eluard, *Thorns of Thunder*, Selected Poems edited by George Reavey (London: Europa Press & Stanley Nott, 1936; trans. with Samuel Beckett, Denis Devlin, Eugène Jolas, Man Ray, George Reavey and Ruthven Todd)
Collected Verse Translations, edited by Alan Clodd and Robin Skelton (London: Oxford University Press, 1970)
André Breton and Philippe Soupault, *The Magnetic Fields* (London: Atlas Press, 1985)
Benjamin Péret, *Remove Your Hat and Other Works* (London: Atlas Press, 1985; trans. with Martin Sorrell)
Pierre Jean Jouve, *The Unconscious, Spirituality, Catastrophe* (Child Okeford: Words Press, 1988)
Three Translations (Child Okeford: Words Press, 1988)
Poems of Milosz (London: Enitharmon Press, 1993)
Pierre Jean Jouve, *The Present Greatness of Mozart* (Birmingham: Delos Press, 1996)
Selected Verse Translations, edited by Alan Clodd and Robin Skelton, with an introduction by Roger Scott (London: Enitharmon Press, 1996)

CONTENTS

Select Bibliography	5
Acknowledgements	10
Preface	11
Introduction	14

★

Section 1

STATEMENTS ON POETRY/THE POET'S MISSION
The Future of the Lyric Imagination	25
A Kind of Declaration	35
Departures	44
David Gascoyne in Interview	47

RESPONSES TO QUESTIONNAIRES
Answers to 'An Enquiry'	54
Authors Take Sides on the Spanish Civil War	56
A Comment on Auden	57
Authors Take Sides on the Falklands	58
On the State of Poetry	63

Section 2

ESSAYS
French Poetry of Today	71
Poetry and Reality	74
Note on Symbolism	77
Léon Chestov	79
Thomas Carlyle	94
A New Poem by Pierre Jean Jouve: 'Language'	115
The Sun at Midnight	119
My Indebtedness to Jouve	125
The Poet and the City	126
Meetings with Benjamin Fondane	133
The Most Astonishing Book in the English Language	140

INTRODUCTIONS AND PREFACES
Friedrich Hölderlin 155
Poets of Tomorrow 163
Kenneth Patchen 164
A Little Anthology of Existentialist Thought 171
Benjamin Fondane 174
T. S. Eliot 182
Roland Penrose 186
Benjamin Péret 189
Novalis and the Night 199
Elizabeth Smart 207

Section 3

MEMOIRS AND OBITUARIES
Self Discharged 215
David Wright 228
Antonia White 232
Tambimuttu 237
Geoffrey Grigson 240
Edgar Morin 245
S. W. Hayter 250
Julian Trevelyan 252
Salvador Dalí 254
Eileen Agar 259
PL Editions and Graham Sutherland 263
Lawrence Durrell 270
George Barker 274

Section 4

REVIEWS
Some Recent Art Exhibitions 285
Henry Miller 287
F. T. Prince 290
Denis Roche 294
Marcel Jouhandeau 299
Angelos Sikelianos 306
Jeremy Reed 315
Julien Green 318

Vincent van Gogh	323
Lawrence Ferlinghetti	326
Humphrey Jennings	332
John Cornford / Christopher Caudwell	337
Pierre Jean Jouve	343
Vernon Watkins	349

Section 5

WRITINGS RELATING TO SURREALISM
Paul Eluard	355
Paul Eluard / Hugh Sykes Davies	356
Two Surrealist Film Scenarios	
Procession to the Private Sector	357
History of the Womb or Nine Months' Horror	373
Louis Aragon	376
René Char	381
André Breton and Philippe Soupault	386
Archives du Surréalisme	399
Francis Picabia	404
Gala Eluard	427
Leonora Carrington	431
Max Ernst / Man Ray	436
André Breton	446

Section 6

ADDITIONAL UNCOLLECTED WRITINGS
Blind Man's Buff	457
Chorus	460

ACKNOWLEDGEMENTS

The Enitharmon Press is most grateful to the
Trustees of the Elephant Trust for a grant
which has made it possible to publish this book.
The publisher also wishes to acknowledge the support, advice
and hospitality of Kathleen Raine, Judy and David Gascoyne;
the generous editorial assistance given by Alan Clodd and
Marco Livingstone; and the devoted, energetic and scholarly work
of the book's compiler and editor, Roger Scott.

EDITOR'S NOTE

The editor would like to record his gratitude for the
friendship, unfailing help and kindness shown by
David Gascoyne, Stephen Stuart-Smith and Alan Clodd
throughout the making of this book.

NOTE ON THE TEXT

All the texts have been edited for consistency
in accordance with current editorial practice.
London is the place of publication of books
cited in the essays or in the footnotes
unless otherwise stated.

PREFACE

*'There neither is, nor can be, any **essential** difference between the language of prose and metrical composition.'*
Wordsworth: Preface to the **Lyrical Ballads**

Those who cherish the mature poetic achievement of David Gascoyne following his early forays into Imagism then Surrealism, and the lapidary quality of his translations, will also recall the extraordinary impact of the revelatory *Journal 1936-37* and *Paris Journal 1937-1939*,[1] discovered in Notebooks and issued in print so late in his career. However, this first publication of his *Selected Prose 1934-1996*, including many contributions inaccessible for too long in 'little magazines', and some pieces never published before is, in its breadth and vision, likely to astonish even those who consider that they enjoy a close acquaintance with his work. These items range from statements about poetry, answers to questionnaires, essays and reviews, to memoirs and obituaries of fellow poets, friends, writers, artists, together with writings about Existentialism, Surrealism and Alchemy, and two Surrealist film scenarios.

Reviewing Gascoyne's *Paris Journal 1937-1939*, 'a rich masterpiece – the authentic record of the anguished growth of a young poet towards self-hood', in 1980[2] Alan Young finds it 'unique in modern English literature.' He suggests, legitimately, that Sartre's *La Nausée* 'comes closest to its humanizing despair in French writing', and adds parenthetically, ('I do not now over-estimate Gascoyne's powers of self-analysis and profound metaphysical anguish by this comparison).' Young believes that confirmation of that journal's 'uniqueness' lies in the fact that, 'despite his knowledge of the French language, of French life and letters, Gascoyne is essentially an English artist; his problem is the shaping vision of the English language within English culture.'[3] Young considers in conclusion that 'There is really no mystery in the fact that such hard-won self-discovery also produces deep human compassion and genuine art.'

---

[1] Enitharmon Press, October 1980, and August 1978 respectively. In 1991, Skoob Books Publishing brought out the *Collected Journals 1936-42*, publishing for the first time the entries from New Year 1940 to 1942, and a long 'Afterword' by the author.
[2] *P.N. Review* 14, Vol. 6, No. 6, p. 65.
[3] Ibid.

He is referring specifically to the poem 'Pietà', but Gascoyne may be said to bring that 'deep human compassion and genuine art' to his prose as well as to his poetry. Often self-deprecating, he is generous in his assessment of others, never rancorous or bitter about those he has met, known and loved in the memoirs, obituaries or reviews, where he astutely balances the subjective and the objective. His writing has gravitas, and the sensitivity he first displayed at seventeen years of age in his only novel, *Opening Day* (1933). Commenting on that work which preceded the ground-breaking *A Short Survey of Surrealism* by some two years, Philip Gardner has pointed to the 'polish and efficiency of its prose' and 'the combination of self-absorption and unsentimental detachment which characterises Gascoyne's later work';[4] Julian Symons, too, has acknowledged the operation of 'a remarkably detached eye.'[5]

In the light of his impressive and consistent life-time's achievement as a prose writer in such a variety of forms and modes, Gascoyne's own comments about himself early in his career in an unpublished section from his *Journal 1936-37*, headed simply 'Myself',[6] are both poignant and pertinent. There are affinities here, as elsewhere, with the Baudelaire of *Mon Coeur mis à nu*. What begins as a free-association exercise becomes a moving but excoriatingly honest attempt at self-analysis, almost two years before he started attending sessions with Pierre Jean Jouve's psychoanalyst wife, Blanche Reverchon.[7] Gascoyne writes at one point

> There is a marked antithesis in my work between poetry and prose. At present, I feel that I am not really a poet but that the content of my work will always be chiefly poetic. I feel that the side of my work which deals with criticism, 'character', morals, philosophical ideas, politics, etc., has not been sufficiently developed. I know I have considerable imagination, but have recently realised that I exploit it far too easily. I have never been able entirely to make up my mind whether I really want to become a good poet or a good novelist, (or philosopher – critic – moralist – politician);

---

[4] 'David Gascoyne' in *British Poets 1914-1945* (Detroit, Michigan: Gale Research Co., 1983), p. 148.
[5] Review of *Journal 1937-1939*, in *The Sunday Times*, 3 September 1978.
[6] Dated Monday, 18th January 1937 (in an orange Notebook). Beginning with the heading 'Mother', with an interpretation of the piece that follows, Gascoyne goes on to examine 'Work', 'Sex', and 'Money', ending with a 'Balance: Summing Up'. There is no entry in the published *Journals* between 13.1.37 and 19.3.37.
[7] The first session is reported in the entry 22.X.38. However, he did visit Antonia White's analyst in what must have been February 1937, according to the note written on 13 March.

I have always wanted to be both, but this does not seem practically possible; I have an idea that unless I decide one way or the other, I shall never succeed at anything. But perhaps I am really intended to synthesise the two [. . .]

During the years that have followed this painful exercise, David Gascoyne has demonstrated the extent to which he would develop not only in terms of his outstanding achievement as a poet and translator, but also, beyond the self-doubt expressed in 1937, as an elegant, meticulous writer of controlled, reflective prose (with its occasional echoes of Henry James), in which rhythm is given due attention. Gardner has indicated, too, Gascoyne's ability to 'handle abstract terms (those big words so distrusted by Hemingway) with such felicity and conviction'.[8] Now, in this remarkable collection, we can appreciate for the first time the sheer volume, range and quality of the harvest of more than sixty years, during which he has suffered long periods of writer's block and three breakdowns. Gascoyne has referred to the manic depression, schizophrenia and paranoia from which he hopefully declared himself to be completely recovered in 1979. The very fact that he felt able to make this assertion then, and that now in 1998 we have been able to edit and present this selection of his prose work in this his 82nd year, is due in very large measure to the vital — and revitalizing — influence and devotion of his wife Judy since their marriage in 1975, after which he began to write and travel again following a loss of confidence and self-esteem.

It seems appropriate, in conclusion, to extrapolate Philip Toynbee's words from his very approving review in 1978 of *Paris Journal 1937-1939*, where he speaks of Gascoyne 'describing some scene or person with a brilliant and percipient clarity which reminds us, if we had begun to need the reminder, that this is a writer of outstanding talent.'[9]

ROGER SCOTT
University of Northumbria
January 1998

---

[8] Op. cit., p. 148.
[9] *The Observer*, Sunday 20 August, p. 22.

INTRODUCTION

It has long been my belief that David Gascoyne is our last poet whose work has the quality of major poetry; and by 'last' a judgement is implicit on a materialist civilization in its terminal phase, which has declined to a point at which this country is no longer capable of producing or sustaining major poetry, nor is the expectation of readers fitted to recognize it.

I use the term 'major poetry' in an exact sense – a sense in which it was still acknowledged by my generation (I was born in 1908). I doubt whether the words carry any meaning for most present-day readers and writers of verse. There are still some few good minor poets but major poetry is I believe different not in degree but in kind from anything being produced at this time. Major poetry is, in the first place, concerned with great themes and universal issues which are the concern of humanity as a whole in terms of the poet's time and place. Homer, Dante, Shakespeare, Blake, Wordsworth and Shelley, and in my own lifetime Rilke, Eliot, Pound, David Jones and Yeats write in terms of history, politics and cosmology in the light of the Imagination. The poet's personal life is subsumed in a shared collective experience. Our secular world has ceased to be aware of what can only be called higher levels of mind and thought – of what at other times has been known as 'inspiration', whose voice is not the poet's personal voice except insofar as he participates in the shared human world for which he is empowered to speak. A major poet is one who has transcended, or should one say sacrificed, his personality to the universal Imagination.

The second mark of a major poet is full knowledge of the significant events, ideas and currents of thought of his world, not merely by observation but by participation. The poet bears witness to the blood-stream of history. He participates also in the record of the experience of the human imagination from time immemorial, whatever has deeply engaged the mind and spirit, whether in books or in those other records of the arts and thoughts of humanity. Journalists may have witnessed the same events, scholars read the same books, but the poet *lives* them.

The third mark of a major poet is of course inspiration itself. Whoever or whatever the Inspirer may be is a matter of terminology – the Muse, the Unconscious, the Angel, the Holy Spirit or Universal Self – inspiration remains a reality which illuminates the personal mind with a fuller and clearer vision, a fuller knowledge, a clearer understanding of the true nature of things. Most poets are privileged with this vision occasionally, but a few live habitually in this enlightened state. In this sense poetry is a sacred language – another concept meaningless in terms of secular values. Indeed one may say that a secular culture is not capable of producing great poetry. The English language of the modern Western and westernized world lacks the scope by virtue of which Sanskrit, Hebrew and Arabic are deemed 'sacred' languages – that is to say capable of communicating meaning on the levels of the sensible world, the worlds of feeling, intellectual, and spiritual experience. English has never been in this sense a 'sacred' language, nor has any European language (Greek or Latin) produced 'prophetic' poetry in the sense of the Hebrew prophecies, the Holy Qur-an, or the Bhagavad Gita, although our greatest poetry has touched a level not far short of these – Yeats includes Shelley's *Prometheus Unbound* among his 'sacred books' and Blake called himself a 'prophet'. In the absence of the state of visionary illumination there may be skilful and clever verse or personal expression of feelings and judgements (which seem to fulfil the expectation of the modern reader of verse) but not the full range of major poetry.

From the outset David Gascoyne has been gifted with imaginative vision not intermittent but habitual. His life has been a total commitment to the task of the poet. He has been engaged politically, culturally and spiritually in the great events of his time, and for this reason his prose writings here collected form an unique record of the great currents flowing through Europe in this century. He writes as a participant in the political and cultural events of France (where he has often lived for long periods); early and briefly he joined the Communist Party and was for a short time a reporter on the Spanish Civil War. His translations from both French and German (Hölderlin and Novalis) poets are outstanding for their empathy with the poets themselves. He is deeply read in the philosophy of Heidegger and other German philosophers of the Imagination. He has brought to events both great and small his ever-vigilant imaginative attention, a kind of angelic clarity of insight. He has read everything, it seems, written by all those, famous or obscure, whose work formed a part of the violent, tragic, yet creative expression of the Europe of his time, discerning the significant and the significance of every expression of that living current. This material, both published and unpublished, or retrieved from obscure sources by his devoted editors, has a dimension of history.

★ ★ ★

The Surrealist writer Philippe Soupault once said to me, 'David is not an English poet, he is a French poet writing in English'. It is true that David made for France as soon as in his late teens he had enough money to pay his fare to Paris, and that he there met the writers and painters of the Surrealist movement, of which he became a member; but he never became an expatriate writer in the sense of Lawrence Durrell or Henry Miller (both of whom he knew and admired). It is true that the creative mainstream at that time was flowing in France (in the arts) and in German philosophy, but David strongly disowns Soupault's judgement. He is, he would claim, an imaginative patriot, formed by the rich heritage of English poetry. As a boy he was a chorister at Salisbury cathedral, and the sober beauty of Anglican chant, of the Book of Common Prayer and the King James Bible, the silent presence of the great Gothic cathedral and its precincts must have been among the deep influences that held David's heart, finally, to England. A later influence was Geoffrey Grigson, editor of *New Verse* and author of the first book on Samuel Palmer that discerned the genius of that most English of visionary painters, *The Valley of Vision*, who for some years was David's mentor.

The Imagination was, first and last, central to David's genius, and André Breton's contribution to the opening of the 'unconscious' regions of the mind (which was to be the most important creative discovery of this century) was remarkable, and charismatic. The Surrealist movement attempted to ally itself to officially Marxist materialist Communism, making overtures to Stalin for recognition from Moscow (which was never granted). Aragon and Eluard became members of the Communist party, but Breton opposed this move, saying – according to David Gascoyne – that he was 'not only a Communist Surrealist but also a Catholic Surrealist'. Breton himself, anticlerical as he was, was above all a Surrealist and the Surrealist way of life anticipates Jung's much later theory of 'synchronicity', the a-causal, so to say magical, coincidences of events which seem to reveal some unknown laws at work for those who open themselves to imaginative experience. Those engaged in surreal living practised the writing of automatic poetry as a way of exploring hitherto unknown regions of the mind; as did David himself in the first excitement of this newfound way of experiencing. Breton himself, with his medical training, contributed no less to the exploration of regions of the Imagination than did Freud and the depth psychologists – indeed the explorations of regions of psyche is the proper sphere of the arts rather than the sciences, to which Surrealism has made its rich contribution, mainly in the work of Breton and in the paintings of Ernst, Dalí and Magritte. No poet who had encountered the powerful influence of Breton could fail to undergo its transforming power. Some of David's own 'automatic' poems written at this time have real beauty.

Herbert Read and Roland Penrose introduced Surrealism into

England through the Surrealist Exhibition of 1936, the same year as the outbreak of the Spanish Civil War which so engaged the imagination of a young generation in England, many of whom joined the International Brigade. Humphrey Jennings and Julian Trevelyan (who had been living in Paris) were active in this memorable movement; but Surrealism and the more extreme gesture of the 'absurd', Dada, never took on in England although not without influence on Mass-Observation, initiated by my husband Charles Madge and Humphrey Jennings. In the same way as the French Revolution influenced, but did not engage, the English Romantic poets, so Surrealism in England remained a style (mainly taken up by fashionable commercial advertising) and not a way of life or an insight into realms of the unconscious mind and an inspiration of art. Even Humphrey Jennings, in his few poems and his great compilation *Pandaemonium*, was concerned with the revealing 'image' not the exploration of inner states. In many ways Surrealism was an after-shock of the French Revolution inspired by the same impulse to destroy and overturn the existing order, of which the Russian and Spanish revolutions were also repercussions. David was deeply and passionately engaged in the political involvement of the French imagination and its determination to overturn 'bourgeois' society. This deep current of hatred and desire to destroy the heritage of the past stemmed from a spiritual malaise not shared in England to the same extent.

It was only when many years later I visited India for the first time that I realized the greatness of Mahatma Gandhi's contribution to the world of non-violence as a political weapon. In fact Shelley had already in *The Masque of Anarchy* and in his earlier poem *The Revolt of Islam* given expression to this revolutionary idea which had influenced Gandhi. Gandhi's grandson, Ramchandra Gandhi the philosopher, pointed out to me that India has never had a revolution. Only then did it occur to me that revolutions are a malady of Western civilization, not the glorious signs of progress we Europeans tend to see them as. India has had wars between states and kingdoms, has undergone invasions and conquests, and the missionary zeal of Islam and Christianity, without at any time breaking the continuity of the great river of Indian civilization from time immemorial to the present. India's great epic battle of Kurukshetra was in defence of the rule of *dharma* against disruptive forces of the kind that inflamed the French imagination from the Revolution to Rimbaud and *Ubu Roi*. The zeal with which Europe has devoted itself to political subversion can be seen, in the light of other cultures, as the mark of an immature civilization. It is notable that the other great movement of thought of the twentieth century has come from Eastern civilizations, and India especially.

Oriental ideas seem to have played no part in David Gascoyne's imaginative life, so completely did he identify himself with the European experience. But within a few years he had come to see the inadequacy of Surrealism: he could never have accepted the *nihil* at the heart of atheism, and a stronger influence on David's early years in Paris proved to be the Christian (but anticlerical) poet Pierre Jean Jouve. David was expelled by the Surrealists because in his noble poem-sequence *Miserere* he invokes a 'Christ of revolution and of poetry' – religion was totally unacceptable to official Surrealism. David's subsequent – and no less revolutionary – vision was not so much a 'Christ of revolution and of poetry' as a revolution of Christ and of poetry. Throughout his mature writings he has proclaimed the Resurrection of Christ. We are living, David has understood, through the experience of Christ's entombment, in the hope and anticipation of Resurrection. The words 'apokatastasis' and 'palingenesia', much in use among German Romantic philosophers at the end of the nineteenth century, appear often in David's writings.

David's Christ, like Blake's, is the 'divine humanity' in all humankind, the spirit of Imagination and of prophecy. In this sense the truth of Christianity (or of the teaching of Jesus Christ which is not at all the same thing as the power organization of the Church) has much in common with the 'liberty, equality, fraternity' of the French Revolution as this spilled over into *'Surréalisme au service de la révolution'*. David remained passionately anti-fascist. While he saw the poet as speaking for his time and place as a voice prophetically inspired, he also entertained the idea that poetry might one day become a common language written by everyone. This faith in the divine Presence shared by all at heart is nobly expressed in his radio play *Night Thoughts*, first performed on the Third Programme of the BBC in December 1955. For all the darkness he has traversed in his life David Gascoyne has never lost his faith in the redemptive power of the Imagination; palingenesia will come, 'But alas! our generation walks in night, dwells as in Hades, without the Divine' – with these words from Hölderlin he prefaces *Night Thoughts*.

★ ★ ★

The most significant imaginative experience of the twentieth century has surely been the discovery and exploration of mental regions beyond what had hitherto been regarded as the boundaries of consciousness. This has by no means been the work only of the depth psychologists, and has taken many forms. In the wide diversity of David's interests one can see his concern with those regions of the Imagination as a common theme – the irrational affirmations of Surrealism with its openness to synchonicities and magical events, and the practice of automatic writing opening a door to an order beyond the common daily mind. In the attunement of attention to surreal events of the kind Breton describes in his novel *Nadja*, Surrealism as a way of life was imaginatively intoxicating, especially so to a young poet for whom a new world was suddenly opened. Europe had long ceased to possess a culture which included invisible worlds that had existed for Christendom before the Renaissance and to some degree before the French and industrial revolutions. Now into the void of spiritual illiteracy the discoveries of Freud threw a first uncertain light. Freud, a materialist, offered no larger context within which his 'unconscious' could be comprehended, seeing these contents as mainly material repressed from consciousness. Jung was later to discover structure and order within the psyche but Surrealist imagery had meanwhile developed its own style and rhetoric. Breton, who was trained in medicine, certainly made a contribution, in the exploration of the surreal, no less important than did Freud's psychoanalysis. David wrote much 'automatic' verse during his period with the Surrealists and poetic inspiration and prophecy was his lifelong concern – the frontiers of madness in Hölderlin, Novalis's deep penetration of the nocturnal regions on the borders of death.

A long paper on a turn of the century American work of dubious yet not entirely meaningless 'prophecy' is the subject of a long essay: *OAHSPE: A New Bible* was discovered by David while browsing in Watkins' bookshop in Cecil Court, and became for a time (shortly after the end of the war) a virtual obsession, at once fascinating and repellant. Whatever we may think of such 'prophetic' material, it comes from somewhere. Mediumship is a 'reality': are these communications messages to be taken to heart? David was himself to become the recipient of such 'messages', which spilled over into what our society calls madness. It was in his long experience of 'madness' in the Berghöltzli mental asylum that Jung made his most profound discoveries about the nature of psyche. David himself ventured into those unmapped regions and paid a heavy price, himself confined for a time in a mental hospital. Yet he writes most perceptively about *OAHSPE*, with clarity and insight. David's poems are of great formal beauty, Imagination imparting to his work not chaos but (as in all art) order and structure. Henry Corbin's writings on the 'imaginal' were not available at that time, and David became the victim of his own openness to regions within or beyond the common daily mind. The breaking beyond the bounds of consciousness was clearly a necessary work in this century, a liberation at once frightening and dangerous when undertaken in the cultural ignorance of the modern West. But 'inspiration' is and has always been the domain of poetry, and to this work David was at all times committed.

David at a very early age knew Antonia White, whose book *Frost in May* contains a meticulous account of a period of madness, and her very beautiful piece of writing, *House of Clouds* he particularly admired. The Church itself has always been well aware of the thin line between inspired prophetic vision and chaotic insanity; but whatever the real or imagined 'dangers' these little-known regions of mind exist and have in this century once more forced themselves on our recognition. Far removed from Surrealist revolutionary subversion, mocked by the left-wing poets of the Thirties, Yeats was deeply engaged in mediumship, the study of magical techniques, and his work *A Vision* is just such a 'communication' as *OAHSPE* claimed to be. Yet no critical judgement could have been clearer than that of the great poet who writes of 'a vast image out of *spiritus mundi*' the 'rough beast its hour come round at last' that 'slouches towards Bethlehem to be born'. The Magical Society of the Golden Dawn with which Yeats worked for many years was rooted in the Western esoteric tradition, but the most important influence on Yeats and his friend George Russell ('AE'), and it may prove in retrospect the most profound influence of all in reversing the materialist premisses of this century, has been the 'oriental philosophy' and India in particular. My generation was all but totally ignorant of Indian philosophic works, and this mainstream so far as I know played no part in David Gascoyne's exploration of the inner worlds. It was with the European experience and quest that he totally identified himself, politically, spiritually and culturally.

I have often wondered what would have become of India's great and honoured saint, Ramana Maharshi, had he been born in England. As a schoolboy he followed a sudden and irresistible impulse to seek enlightenment. Stealing a few rupees from his aunt's purse (most of which he later returned) he set out for the holy hill of Arunachala. He discarded his clothes, meditating in temple precincts, developing sores, bitten by insects, surviving on offerings of food from people used to wandering holy men and pilgrims, persisting until the Goddess answered his prayers. Indian culture supported his spiritual quest and to this day his ashram draws pilgrims from all over the world. Perhaps David's experience is the answer – attempting to deliver his prophetic message to Buckingham Palace he was arrested by the police, confined in a mental institution where he was treated with drugs and therapy until such time as he conformed to 'normal' standards. David made himself a 'vagrant', as the title of one of his books testifies, refusing to live by values other than those of his vision of a transfigured world. If David has retained that vision and his faith in humankind's ultimate redemption, it is no thanks to the prevailing culture of our nation. David feels that he has failed to deliver his prophetic message and perhaps one has to say that he is a major poet, *manqué*: but that does not make him a minor poet. Nor is his silence that of an abandonment of his calling, rather it is the eloquent silence into which a great poet has fallen in a time and place that 'dwells as in Hades, without the Divine'.

The writings in this volume will astonish readers by their range, by the number of books he has read and the total engagement of his attention in his reading of them, by the scope and depth with which he has lived the dark and fragile European imaginative experience of his time. In his life no less than in his works he has borne witness to those values in whose service he has paid so high a price. A more civilized future may read with gratitude and follow the clues he offers through the labyrinth of our dark century, awaiting in Hades, like David himself, 'the Sun at Midnight'.

KATHLEEN RAINE

1

STATEMENTS ON POETRY/ THE POET'S MISSION

★

RESPONSES TO QUESTIONNAIRES

THE FUTURE OF THE LYRICAL IMAGINATION

The title of my lecture is *The Future of the Lyrical Imagination* and I have come here to talk particularly on the subject of Poetry, but I believe that before I start on my main theme I should first say that two entirely different worlds are today engaged in the fiercest conflict: on the one hand, the world of metaphysics, idealism, religion, rationalization, the morality of castration and restraint, ego-inflation and mediocrity – on the other, the world of dialectical super-materialism, the liberation of man, new perspectives, physical delight, profound belief in the future, endless possibilities.

In a word, we are witnessing, and to a greater or lesser degree taking part in, the conflict between on the one hand, exploitative capitalism fast becoming Fascism and on the other, Communism.

Now, since the subject of this talk is Poetry, the question we must ask, having made that very necessary preliminary statement, is: what is the relation of Poetry and of poets to this gigantic conflict, and what part do they play in it?

It is difficult not to become confused at this point. You will no doubt want to ask me to begin with: what is my definition of poetry, do I believe in the necessity of propaganda-art, and so on. My attitude will, I hope, become clear as I continue. First of all let me say that the most satisfactory answer I know of to the question about Poetry's relation to the political struggle is that of the great Surrealist poet Paul Eluard: 'All poets worthy of the name,' he says, 'are fighting the system of exploitation side by side with the workers. For true poetry is the camp of those who are fighting for the deliverance of Man.'

My own favourite definition of poetry is also Eluard's: 'Caprice, contradiction, violence, – they are poetry; in other words, poetry is a perpetual struggle, life's very principle, the queen of unrest.'

Let me say straightaway that I do not for one moment agree with the dictums of Cecil Day Lewis concerning revolutionary poetry. Though understanding quite as clearly as he does the urgent necessity of realizing

---

Lecture given to the Oxford Union, December 1936. Previously unpublished. Transcribed by Alan Clodd from D.G.'s Notebooks (Deposit S121, vols. 7 and 13) in the British Library.

that the class struggle is the one important determining factor in the world today, I do *not* believe that the poet should try to confine his legitimate means of expression, his legitimate subject-matter, within the rigid confines of propaganda verse. I do *not* believe that the poet should try to write verse plays about Noah's Ark with Noah representing Stalin.

Before I go on to develop my argument, let me read you two contrasting poems.

> Exhibit A: Dylan Thomas [. . .]*
> Exhibit B: Julian Bell [. . .]

The existence of the first is completely justified by the fact that it is poetry, and gives us something that only poetry can give us.

The existence of the second is only justified by its theme. But its theme could have been stated very much better in prose, and gains nothing at all by being forced into verse form. The second poem, in fact, is not, strictly speaking, a poem at all. It is two-thirds dead. While the first is a vital organic whole, that lives on in the mind of the reader and enriches him.

The great Lautréamont in his extraordinarily sane and balanced thesis on poetry wrote:

> A philosophy exists for the sciences. It does not exist for poetry.
> I do not know of any moralist who would make a first-rate poet.

Yet many of the younger poets of today are to a greater or lesser degree attempting to assume the function of a moralist. Particularly is this true of W. H. Auden. Think of *The Dog Beneath the Skin*. I should say quite definitely that it is a morality play. Auden seems to me a man divided against himself. In some of his best poems this inner division seems to resolve itself into synthesis. I think 'The Witnesses' is a poem in which this synthesis of the poetic and anti-poetic occurs.

One can state with a considerable amount of certainty that lyricism – lyrical thought – the lyrical impulse – is nothing more or less than *uncontrolled thought*. Or rather, perhaps, thought that escapes from the conscious control of the reason and proceeds on its own way and of its own impulse, so that the poet is afterwards surprised to find what he has written. And that, in the end, is what the idea of 'inspiration' (the Poet-Muse relationship) boils down to. In the light of the discoveries of modern psycho-analysis there is really no mystery about it at all. I should say that anyone possessing a reasonable amount of imagination and innate sensi-

---

* Indicates here and elsewhere that the titles of the poems were not included in the draft.

bility to language can attain, with practice, to the state of mind necessary to this kind of thought, this kind of writing.

The lyrical poetry that is the product of uncontrolled thought has little in common with descriptive, moralistic or propaganda poetry. One may call the former, 'poetry-activity-of-the-mind'; and the latter, 'poetry-means-of-expression'.

Of the two poems I read just now, I should say that the poem by Julian Bell represents a fair example of 'poetry-means-of-expression', and the poem by Dylan Thomas an example of 'poetry-activity-of-the-mind'.

To further illustrate what I mean by 'poetry-activity-of-the-mind', I will read a few miscellaneous poems which illustrate the principles of lyrical or uncontrolled thought.

First, and this is merely by the way, I will read four curious lines that I found recently at the end of a poem by the seventeenth-century parson, George Herbert. [. . .]

And here is a group of poems by three young English poets, all of whom are aged roughly twenty:
'The Passion' by Clifford Dyment
'Signs' by Kenneth Allott
'Flora and Fauna of the Lunar Passages' by Ruthven Todd.
Finally, a group by three French Surrealist poets:
'One for All' by Paul Eluard
[. . .] by Benjamin Péret
'The Free Vision' by André Breton

I insist that 'poetry-activity-of-the-mind' is superior *as poetry* to 'poetry-means-of-expression'. I am persuaded that 'poetry-activity-of-the-mind' is the true end towards which all the most vital poetry of the past has been progressing, and that it provides the largest number of possibilities for the future – that is to say for *post-revolutionary society*.

In what sense is lyrical poetry revolutionary? Surely all true, living poetry is today in a certain sense, revolutionary. It is difficult to imagine a state of society more hostile to the very existence of poetry than twentieth-century capitalist society. Everything under capitalism now is the most violent contradiction to poetry. It is not difficult to see how the status quo depends for its continuation on the production of a state of mind absolutely inimical to poetry. One might say that bourgeois education was a state machine for crushing and destroying the last ounce of the imagination that every child is born with. (That remark, unfortunately, is an excessive simplification. Bourgeois education has many more unpleasant functions to perform than that. Nevertheless, the destruction of natural imagination is even so a very important function of capitalist pedagogy.)

Extremely relevant here is the following quotation from that altogether remarkable and inspiring book with such a banal and inadequate title – *The New Road to Progress* it is called – by the American psychologist Dr Schmallhausen. He says:

> It has become necessary to distinguish sharply between education and enlightenment; the one is content to look backward, the other, out of its creative discontent, looks forward. What is great in our age – in literature, drama, social philosophy, psychological wisdom, moral transformation, human idealism – is inspired by the radical and revolutionary potentialities of life newly rediscovered. That is why Soviet Russia fascinates and provokes the whole contemporary world. In a nutshell: life has become desperately real; education continues to be flagrantly unreal.

'Life newly re-discovered' – life perpetually re-discovered, re-created anew – that is the very essence of poetry, as I conceive it.

As for bourgeois education, – let us take just one single example – the teaching of poetry, in our board schools, elementary schools, council schools, private schools, public schools, secondary schools – the method is fundamentally the same in every one of them. The same old stodgy collections of the worst and most uninspired poems in the language, a large percentage of them mediocre verses saturated with the spirit of bombastic militarism and imperialism, the same old soppy little rhymes that are fondly imagined to be suitable for children – the same absurd footnotes and dry-as-dust quotations. (How many children had Lady Macbeth? Who was the Lady of the Lake?) You know the kind of thing – the same sickening routine of learn-by-heart and paraphrase – Well, with all that, it is positively a wonder to me that anyone at all manages to pass through their schooldays and still retain the least affection for poetry. It is not surprising for a moment that the vast majority of people loathe and detest it.

Why is this so? Why should bourgeois education distort and mangle the true spirit of poetry; why should it thwart and stifle the genuine imaginative and lyrical impulse that so many children quite naturally possess?

Because bourgeois culture has never at any time felt genuine poetry to be at all a comfortable bedfellow. It prefers to treat poets as madmen during their lifetime and after their death it more often than not proceeds to beatify them and to misinterpret everything they ever wrote, to treat them as misunderstood saints. It happened to [de] Sade and to Blake, it happened to Baudelaire, to Rimbaud, it is happening to Lawrence.

No – true poetry has never been the ally of bourgeois academic culture. If the spirit of poetry is, as Eluard says, 'a perpetual struggle, life's very principle, the queen of unrest', how can it be reconciled with a system whose aim is to make men passive, docile, complacent and smug? The adventuresome mind must be crippled as early as possible, lest it discover the unsavoury truth that man is criminally exploited for profit by his more fortunate fellows, and that 'family', 'patriotism', 'religion' and 'democracy' are all just so many props that hold this gangster system together.

It is sometimes said that poetry provides at best but a retreat from reality. I believe that the confusion evident in such a point of view is the product of over-simplification. For poetry is a reflection of the real, a transformation of it, perhaps, but not, like 'religion', a distortion and disguise of it. Granted, however, that there is a certain amount of truth in the contention; we must then admit that that in itself presupposes the hostility of poetry, not to reality *qua* reality but to the realities produced by the existing social order.

'If, under the existing form of society,' writes Tristan Tzara, the onetime Surrealist poet, 'poetry constitutes a *refuge*, an *opposition*, to the ruling class, the bourgeoisie', – in the future society, when the economic antagonism of classes will have disappeared, poetry will no longer be subjected to the same conditions. The poet (I am forced to use this unsatisfactory term for want of another name, for already it is true that the old terminology is no longer adequate for the new content) – the poet, then, takes refuge in the domain of poetry because he associates his opposition to the capitalist class with his opposition to the form of thought known as 'controlled', which is the progenitor of science, of present-day civilization, made use of by the bourgeoisie. [Schmallhausen, pp. 202-3]

Just as labour in a socialized society is nothing more than what we understand as such today, just as the proletariat when no longer exploited loses the significance we now accord it, so perhaps one may predict that poetry, losing all but its name in following its historic necessity, will become part of a collective mental activity (such as the dream is now) in accordance with the nodal line of proportionate relationships, and that under this form Lautréamont's formula: 'Poetry, made by all', will become a reality.

It is lamentably true that poetry today is written, read and appreciated by an extremely small and limited number of people. This, as we have shown, is simply another symptom of the disease called capitalism. A conscious attempt to write down to the masses, to simplify poetry's inherent complexity of subject-matter and treatment, in order to reach and influence a wider public – as Day Lewis, Auden and many others are doing today – is doomed to failure. The revolutionary poet who makes this attempt is deserting his historical role in the development of poetry.

Let us put it like this: the poet today is separated from the masses by a high, thick wall made of prejudices, misapprehensions and ignorance. This wall is deliberately constructed by capitalism. The part of the poet is *not* to climb over this wall to the other side, for in doing so he must inevitably leave his treasure behind him. The part of the poet is to do everything in his power to bring about the collapse of the wall. And the wall's demolition can only be brought about by proletarian Revolution.

Yet again: a considerable part of Marx's *Das Kapital* is devoted to demonstrating how the transformation of quality into quantity is brought about, and vice versa. Can this law be equally well applied to poetry as to economics? I believe it can. The advent of Communist society will bring about the transformation of the minute section of the population who understand and appreciate poetry today, into the vast majority. In other words, Communism will elevate the masses to an intellectual level at which the appreciation of poetry will be a common right, a natural affair. For poetry will then no longer be in contradiction with life. I believe that nothing distinguishes man from the brute more than the exercise of the imagination.

Dr I. A. Richards once wrote: 'Poetry will supersede religion.' Though seldom much in sympathy with Dr Richards' dictums, I feel that there is profound truth in this remark.

'Religion,' says Schmallhausen, 'has prevented the mind from being human. And since religion has been the main ingredient in education, religion has also been responsible for keeping the mind from developing its mentality. The State as a device for exploitation and suppression has co-operated successfully with the Church in making the mind inhuman and moronic.'

Religion as it is today is undoubtedly a part of the vested interests. Yet long long years ago in pre-capitalist society, it did, perhaps, perform a positive function for humanity. The mature mind, once liberated from an exploitative system that has need of religion's soporific comfort, no longer requires it. The positive function that religion once performed was the exercise and training of man's spirit: it provided a balance and complement to the rationalizing and logical functions of the mind.

Now it is in the domain of science that the rational and logical functions play the greatest part today. And proletarian society has the greatest possible need for science. Indeed, as it can be proved, Communism is the one and only hope for scientific progress. Capitalism in its Imperialist stage, fast becoming Fascism, is forced more and more to commit sabotage on science, to cancel by degrees all scientific progress and to fall back into the most contemptible metaphysical idealism. Science is revolutionary.

Does the logical and reasoning side of the mind still need a balance and a complement? Yes, a rich, fully integrated, balanced conception of life, a proletarian attitude to life, is one that gives fullest scope to both the material and the spiritual. While Religion today constitutes nothing more than the opposition of idealism to materialist and scientific progress, Science and Poetry go hand in hand. 'Poetry will supersede Religion' as a natural and necessary complement to the reasoning faculty of the mind.

I see every reason to believe that poetry will play an immensely important part in the new humanizing re-education of post-revolutionary society.

In post-revolutionary society, scientific progress will no longer be confronted by the barrier of sabotage and ideological reaction that is being set up by the ruling classes today. And as science advances – I am speaking now of technical science, or more strictly, technology, – it is obvious that the amount of labour necessary for the comfortable subsistence of society will become proportionately less and less. Man will at last be free to indulge his *sacred right to fertilizing idleness*. No longer will circumstance force him to work to eat to work to eat to work . . . More and more leisure will be his to enjoy and make use of. 'The sacred right to idleness' is a phrase that sounds very much like a counter-revolutionary slogan during the present epoch of social reconstruction in the U.S.S.R. which might well be called the Stakhanovite epoch. But no serious student of history would dispute its rightness as applied to the future.

It is not Utopianism to predict that simultaneously with the increase of communal leisure for the classless society, will begin a period of intellectual and cultural expansion unlike anything the world has ever seen before.

It may now perhaps be easier to see the importance of the conception: 'poetry-activity-of-the-mind'. It has always seemed to me that Poetry is by no means restricted to the printed page. I believe that Poetry is destined to break all its bounds and to become a sort of supreme expression of the communal imagination, uniting and surpassing all the other arts. At this point I am going to give you four quotations from widely different sources, all of which indicate the direction that I believe Poetry is destined to take:

1. Lautréamont: 'Poetry should be made by all, not one.'
2. I. A. Richards: 'Poetry will supersede religion.'
3. Herbert Read: 'Art will then become life.'

And fourthly a somewhat longer quotation, this time from the Surrealist André Breton:

Surrealist poetry painting and construction from now on permit the organisation of perceptions of an objective tendency. These perceptions, by their very tendency to appear objectively, present a profoundly disturbing and revolutionary character in so far as they call forth imperiously, from exterior reality, something to correspond to them. One can predict that to a very large extent this something *will be*.

It is, of course, dialectically impossible to predict precisely what forms this by now quite clearly defined tendency will take in the future classless society. But I hope I have succeeded in demonstrating that this tendency does exist and is bound to become of increasing importance.

I might add something as to the social function that will be performed by 'poetry-activity-of-the-mind'. The social function of 'poetry-means-of-expression' is quite clear; one might say that it was specially designed to play a social function. There is some question as to whether 'poetry-means-of-expression' will survive; at present the possibility of its survival seems far greater than that of 'poetry-activity-of-the-mind'. I personally believe that they will both continue to develop side by side, gradually modifying one another until finally there will be no distinction between them.

The useful and important function that 'poetry-activity-of-the-mind' would perform in post-revolutionary society would be in the nature of *sublimation*. This concept, *sublimation*, is among the most important of the discoveries of bourgeois psychoanalysis. Without wishing to go into the question of the relationship of Freud to Marx, it is necessary before proceeding further to assert that the present-day role of psychoanalysis, devoting itself almost entirely to the diagnosis and cure of the neuroses of individual members of the upper and middle classes, is a reactionary one. The psychoanalysts, because of their inability to understand that the only way to cure neuroses is to wipe away the entire social system in which they occur, stand in the same relation to psychology as Major Douglas and Co. to economics. As John Strachey has very wisely pointed out: 'Freud is the last great bourgeois thinker unable to overcome his class limitation.'

But to return to the concept of *sublimation*. This is a sort of psychic transformation process by means of which wishes become symbols, inhibited emotions become sources of energy, impulses become constructive forces; the principal idea on which the concept is based being that everyone is endowed with a certain amount of primitive psychic energy, and that when this energy cannot find its natural outlet, it will create another outlet for itself elsewhere. It is obvious that in a fully communized society, inhibitions of impulse tend to become greater rather than less. What is to become of all the pent-up natural energy that communal conditions of living will produce? The process of sublimation will to a very large extent find new and constructive channels of outlet quite easily and naturally.

Let us take an example. Sadism. Sadism can provisionally be divided into two parts:
(a) verifiable perversion of instinct caused by known defects in the moral and ethical environment created by the bourgoisie, and
(b) hypothetical, a latent human impulse, primarily destructive, connected with what is vaguely known as the death-instinct.

There is a certain confusion here. What I mean is that a revolution in social conditions would to a very large degree remove the causes of Sadism as a sexual perversion; while what would remain of Sadism as a latent human impulse of destructive character would then be open to *sublimation*. Geoffrey Gorer in his splendid book, *The Revolutionary Ideas of the Marquis de Sade*, does in fact describe how already in Russia the sublimation of latent human Sadism has been brought about. He describes the construction of the Dneiperstroi Dam as a feat of 'constructive Sadism'.

Apart from wide-scale feats of construction of this kind, there will still be plenty of material requiring sublimation in post-revolutionary society, especially during the period of ever-increasing leisure. The suggestion that I am leading up to is that 'poetry-activity-of-mind' will be an ideal medium for bringing about the sublimation of anti-social impulses. Just as in the case of the individual, for whom the nightly dream performs the function of sublimation of unresolved conflicts and inhibited impulses of his private life, so in communal society, 'poetry-activity-of-mind' provides the widest possible scope for the playing out of mass inhibitions and anti-social fantasies. (What forms these inhibitions and fantasies will take under [a] classless society we cannot, of course, predict.)

At the same time, Poetry would be fulfilling its true aim – that of completely humanizing and liberating the spirit of mankind, and giving significant meaning to universal leisure.

It is easy enough, however, glibly to talk of the classless society. In case my discourse is going a little too far into the domain of the optimistically hypothetical, let us return to a final consideration of the poet's position here and now.

What is the poet to do who believes that the real future of poetry lies in 'poetry-activity-of-mind' rather than with 'poetry-means-of-expression'? I believe that he must continue his researches on the one hand, and do all he can to fight for the revolution and against reaction on the other. If he does not take part in the political struggle he becomes an empty and meaningless figure; if he does not carry on the tradition of 'poetry-activity-of-mind', the future society may be deprived of the highest development of the highest of all the arts.

There is plenty of ideological work to be accomplished. It still remains for some particularly penetrating mind to rescue the discoveries of Freud in the name of dialectical materialism. It still remains to rescue the most vital works of the art and literature of the past in the name of proletarian culture. It still remains for someone to write a revolutionary poem in which the word 'comrades' does not appear in every verse. It still remains to formulate a theory of revolutionary poetry that will also be a revolutionary theory of poetry.

A KIND OF DECLARATION

This is an imaginary interviewer (I.I.) interviewing David Gascoyne . . . Written by David Gascoyne for *Temenos* I (1980).

I.I. – What would you as an Englishman like to say to those attending an international gathering of poets?

D.G. – Above all I should like to quote from one of Wordsworth's sonnets on National Independence and Liberty (1803):

> We must be free or die
> Who speak the tongue which Shakespeare spake . . .

and I would then say that I hoped that today this might well be declared by fellow poets throughout the world if transposed in the form of 'who speak the tongue that Dante spake, that Lorca spake, that Camoens spake, that Villon spake, that Pushkin and Blok spake, that Hölderlin spake, that Parmenides and Seferis spake', and so on.

(I must interrupt myself at this point just to add that if I had completed the quotation, it might have tempted me into a completely irrelevant digression concerning faith and morals ('those which Milton held' in Wordsworth's words), an engrossing topic involving Poetry and Revolution (the English and Puritan one to begin with) as well as religious and ethical problems and their relation to this particular preoccupation of mine; but I must leave further consideration of such a possibility for some quite different occasion.)

I.I. – Do you believe that the poet should be politically committed and that this should influence his writing?

D.G. – While still in my 'teens I was a Communist. I have read a good deal of Hegel, Marx and Engels, and would still describe myself as a convinced and unrepentant socialist, but it would strike me as tactless to try to introduce a discussion of political principles on an occasion of this kind.

I.I. – Then you do not believe that poetry can be expected to serve as a sort of propaganda?

D.G. – Certainly not. But on the other hand, I decidedly believe that all poetry of any significance does and should provide propaganda of a certain kind.

Temenos I (1982), ed. Kathleen Raine, pp. 155-69. Also in Michel Rémy, *David Gascoyne, ou l'urgence de l'inexprimé* (Presses Universitaires de Nancy, 1984), pp. 146-55.

I.I. — *Kindly elucidate.*
D.G. — The poetry I refer to as being of true significance is not simply that which is authentic. As Peter Levi has observed, 'in minor modern poetry the experience may be genuine yet the language is not, and it is nothing but authentic language that can express reality in a poem'. The kind of poetry I am thinking of is that which is capable of arousing in the reader that sense of astonishment and wonder at being alive and at the mysterious multiplicity of reality such as has been believed by many thinkers to be the beginning of all true philosophy; and it is in favour of such an experience of wonder that the poetry I mean may be described as constituting a kind of propaganda.

I.I. — *Is one to suppose that poetry and philosophy are very closely interrelated in your mind?*
D.G. — Indeed they are, and if what I have called significant poetry has content, as of course it is bound to have, then whether the subject be everyday life, the inner life, people or places, the greatness or beastliness of men or the beauty or industrial degradation of Nature, whatever in fact the subject, and there is one to be found I believe in even the best 'Surrealist' poem, then the poem's content will almost certainly prove to be capable of philosophical interpretation, as Heidegger has to my mind conclusively demonstrated in his Hölderlin commentaries and in 'On the Road to Language'; though I should never wish to appear dogmatic about any particular interpretation of any given text. In fact it might be said that the importance of a poem may on one level be gauged by the number of possible interpretations to which it is liable to give rise.

I.I. — *Does not philosophical poetry tend to lead the poet into too great a use of abstraction and to an elitist abstruseness?*
D.G. — There are two distinct questions to be elucidated here, and I have not the time or space to deal adequately with either. Firstly, as I said somewhat baldly in a recent poem, 'Whales and Dolphins': 'A poem should avoid abstraction and / all forms of private declaration of belief'. One of the most important realizations of modern poets in nearly all the countries about whose poetry I know anything at all has been that one must convey whatever content one has to express (and without more than merely ephemeral content, poetry is hardly worth the trouble it takes to write it, though it may give a certain temporary pleasure to both writer and a superficial type of reader) in as concrete and freshly vivid a way as one is capable of finding. The present condition of all language, overtly poetic or otherwise, is critical, as one would expect in a world-situation of ever-increasing extremity. The avoidance of cliché and inauthentic, unspontaneous diction is a challenge that must be faced every time pen is put to paper. Abstruseness is certainly to be avoided as far as possible, and only

a poet positively determined to be labelled cerebral could possibly think of it as an infallible indication of poetic excellence. On the other hand, difficulty in understanding a poem is often something that has to be wrestled with, and the resultant increase of insight in the reader, both into the 'meaning' of the poem and into himself, may prove to be ample compensation to him for his effort. Something of the same sort might incidentally be said in passing about the supposed difficulty of some of the most rewarding and therefore important modern music: once one has familiarized oneself with frequently extreme dissonance and other of the more recent musical innovations, one will surely find one's capacity to appreciate and enjoy music greatly extended. To revert to poetry, were you to enquire what I myself would now try most to aim at achieving supposing I should be able to look forward to producing a handful of new poems to add to those of mine that have already been published, I should answer, I think, concision, terseness, immediacy and 'newness' (never mere novelty). At my age, I doubt very much whether I shall ever be able to achieve this, judging from the poem I referred to just now, which happens to be a 72-line effort produced in response to a request for a contribution to an anthology in aid of the Greenpeace Foundation, and it is ostensibly concerned with Whales and Dolphins, while managing also to contain about half-a-dozen quotations (including one from Kathleen Raine). An interviewee should never lose the opportunity for a little self-advertisement . . .

Should you now wish to lead me back to an attempt to make a purely personal statement about poetry, as apart from the kind of generalizations which are apt to sound glib, I think I ought to begin by saying that ever since 'coming-of-age' at least, and I'm not at all sure when exactly this was, I have been preoccupied in one way or another with the apparent conflict between a concern for Truth, regarded as something ever to be sought for in this life but which one can never be certain of having found without the gift of that ultimate faith for which, if one is granted its achievement, Truth is a Person, and the pursuit of poetry, which Pascal, for instance, regarded as a probably frivolous diversion from what should be our most constant and overriding concern. One cannot know what Pascal would have made of the suggestion of George Herbert (admittedly no Jansenist) that:

> A verse may find him who a sermon flies,
> And turn delight into a sacrifice.

At the same time, the aphoristic form, of which Pascal is surely one of the great masters (by accident, as it happens, since the *Pensées* are no more than notes for a lengthy treatise), may be regarded as being very closely related to that of poetic expression, if one accepts as one of poetry's many possible definitions that it is the distillation of essences. Certainly other outstanding aphorists have been poets, Lao Tsu, Novalis, Coleridge, Blake, Baudelaire, and Nietzsche (the latter more a philosopher than a poet, but who did write some, I understand, not inconsiderable poetry) to name but a few. Poetry and Truth, then, may be seen as contradictory concerns. Pilate's question may have always seemed like a jest, but to me it is rather a philosophical one. (Nowadays it is thought rather funny to ask 'What is Man?') We are familiar with Keats' answer to the question: I have always found it highly questionable. Christianity is quite as disturbing as it may be consoling. Truth is undeniably sometimes hideous, as the suffering not only of Christ but of innumerable ordinary human beings, not to speak of children and animals, about whose sufferings we have only recently begun to be adequately aware, should make obvious.

It may be safely assumed that I do not 'believe in' astrology; but being a Libran, I am undoubtedly given to weighing up the pros and cons; so I will once more say here that 'at the same time' Heidegger, not my principal *maître à penser*, though I have already referred to him, seems to me to be at least partially right in asserting that the essence of Truth is freedom. And I believe that although we are always declaring our love of it and professing our willingness to die in defence of it, as to which I said at the outset that I hoped modern poets of all countries would agree with Wordsworth's sentiments as expressed in a famous sonnet, I also happen to believe that the majority of us are *frightened* of freedom and employ an enormous amount of ingenuity in avoiding, by means of verbal camouflage, casuistry and a variety of other forms of self-deception, ever having to exercise the free will we are always arguing about and which I believe we do indeed possess.

Here again I find myself in danger of being led away into too long a digression, this time on the subject of fear. It is certainly a key-word in any sort of analysis of the contemporary situation, and above all in existential thought about it. The distinction has been drawn, first by Kierkegaard and then by Heidegger, each in his own different way, between dread, fear and anxiety. That this is the Age of Anxiety has by now for long already become a cliché of the kind I observed earlier one has to keep trying to avoid. But that fear is a predominant factor in the condition of the modern psyche is an inescapable fact. Fear of what? It is difficult to draw up any list of a precise length, or to name the fears we are prone to in order of pre-eminence or intensity, but if I might be permitted to make reference to something written some time ago by myself, in *Night Thoughts* I referred to the fear of fear itself, of failure, of uncertainty and loss, of change, of strangeness and strangers, fear of Love, which is perhaps the most basic and which sometimes adopts complicated forms of which at least one is familiar to most of us, and 'the exhausting fear of Death and Mystery'. I might well have included the fear of being oneself, of recognizing and accepting in oneself the capacity for cruelty, destructiveness and violence; but I concluded my catalogue in that particular passage with fear of Nothing, absolutely Nothing. In this I was no doubt influenced by Heidegger's 'What is Metaphysics?', which I first read in Henry Corbin's pioneer French translation before the War and which made a deep impression on me. 'Nothing – how can it be for science anything other than a horror and a phantasm?' asks Heidegger. But, as he goes on to demonstrate later in the lecture, it is not merely science and scientists who have such a horror of Nothing that they will not allow it to be alluded to, but it is something of which everyone may be supposed to have some sort of experience, specifically in a rarely encountered but ultimately unavoidable form of boredom, that now universal malady of industrialized man. At this point Heidegger draws the distinction already referred to between fear and 'dread'. 'Dread differs absolutely from fear . . . We are always afraid of this or that definite thing . . .' Obviously I cannot give a detailed summary of the lecture here, but will conclude by saying that the essential point to be made is that in a peculiar state of boredom, we have an 'uncanny' feeling of indifference and of the withdrawal of 'what-is-in-totality', which leaves us with nothing to hold on to but nothingness. 'Dread reveals Nothing'. And the philosopher significantly concludes in his Postscript that it is those who are most courageous who are the readiest to undergo the experience of dread in which is revealed the Nothing which, according to him, is the basis of all Metaphysics, a domain in which ordinary logic has to be 'suspended', and in fact altogether abandoned.

Believers are told that the fear of God is the beginning of Wisdom. Those who are still brave enough to call themselves Christians believe in a God they have been brought up to address as our Father. A loving Father is not terrifying. There is puzzle and paradox in all this, and a kind of declaration concerning poetry is not the place to enter into a theological discussion. But what I have been trying to lead up to is some expression of what, in my belief, constitutes perhaps the most important function of poetry in the world at present, and here theology of *some* kind is highly relevant. I believe that it is for poets first and foremost to testify to the existence of something the lack of which, all the evidence today would seem to show, is everywhere beginning to be felt and recognized, and that is, to employ *faute de mieux* one more already hackneyed and inadequate expression, the dimension of the Transcendent. And as one might expect of a critical historical situation, it is, thank heavens, actually producing in poetry a response which shows an awareness of this lack and of the need to express the general longing for a way to fill it. Two lines from the last stanza of a poem by Dannie Abse, who is a full-time doctor and a 'sceptical' humanist as well as a poet, strike me as typical of the kind of feeling that haunts more and more poets who do not feel they have been gifted with the grace of faith in anything more than mortal humanity:

> There are moments when a man must sing
> of a lone Presence he cannot see.
> . . . .
> There are moments when a man must praise
> the astonishment of being alive,
> when small mirrors of reality blaze
> into miracles; and there's One always
> who, by never departing, almost arrives.

And while I am making quotations, perhaps this is the place for one from George Steiner's 'Tolstoy or Dostoievsky', which is relevant both to what I have just been saying and to a point I tried to make earlier:

> In works of art are gathered the mythologies of thought, the heroic efforts of the human spirit to impose order and interpretation on the chaos of experience. Though inseparable from aesthetic form, philosophic content – the entry of faith or speculation into the poem – has its own principles of action. There are numerous examples of art which moves us to performance or conviction through its proposal of ideas. To these modes contemporary critics, with the exception of the Marxists, have not always been attentive.

I.I. – *With reference to your last quotation, 'let's leave politics out of this!'*
D.G. – I thought perhaps you might raise that objection. But I began by making an avowal at the outset to the effect that I am still a convinced socialist, and if such a thing as Communism with a human face were honestly possible I think I should be a Communist – no doubt as an unorthodox one as I am an unorthodox Christian, if anything. At the same time, I would always sympathize with anyone's objection to the modern passion for labelling a group or an individual once and for all with some handy reference tag. But I'm afraid that for me 'political issues' in the broadest sense can no longer be left out of account in any sort of attempted summary of what will most urgently be demanding poets' attention in the 1980s. An obvious implication of what I have tried to say already is that 'man does not live by bread alone'; and I am certain that Marxists are going to have to face this fact sooner or later, if they are not already doing so. The great importance attached to 'culture' by the Soviet bloc is evidence of their increased realization of this; though one may well ask what sort of culture can exist where there is no

official recognition of the existence of authentic spirit. Yet while it may be as well to remember that the Russian Orthodox Church is still officially tolerated and allowed to carry on performing public ceremonies of worship, even attracting ever-growing congregations, 'according to certain sources' it should also be borne in mind that it is precisely in Russia (still 'Holy' at heart, I believe, though in this case I am thinking most particularly of the Baptists) and in her satellite countries that true Christianity of the kind that requires martyrdom, if necessary, is most likely to be found. The artistic impulse and what Teilhard de Chardin, who was by no means wholly hostile to the original ideals of Communism, has defined as the need to worship and the knowledge of how to do this are both essentially subversive in the Soviet countries at present.

I.I. – If you are going to bring politics into your 'declaration', may I remind you of Yeats's words:

> We have no gift to set a statesman right;
> He has had enough of meddling who can please
> A young girl in the indolence of her youth
> Or an old man upon a winter's night.

D.G. – Apart from retorting that it was not very long after writing these words that Yeats himself became a Senator, and that I have the greatest respect for the point of view of many poets, such as C. H. Sisson, for instance, who firmly believe that Yeats was right about this question, I should like to say that unless we make up our minds about what is actually happening, socially and economically, in the world at this moment, and as to *which side* we are on (much though I may approve of the late André Breton's designation of the word 'engagement' as ignoble), and moreover attempt not only to declare our position but to try, however impotently, to actually *do something* about it, it may happen before the middle of the next century that there are no more young girls or old men left in the world to be pleased by our magical and mellifluous utterances, all record of which will of course have been destroyed in the final conflagrations.

I.I. – Does this mean that you are ultimately pessimistic about the chances of human survival?

D.G. – Not ultimately. I think we are in grave danger and that it is natural to the human species to react to danger in the interest of self-preservation. I also believe that most of society is psychologically or spiritually sick and that Freud's concept of the death-wish is not without considerable factual foundation; though I would agree with those who consider that to think of mankind as turning into a mass of lemmings is exaggerated. But having on at least three occasions definitely crossed the perilously thin dividing line between sanity and derangement, I think I can claim to know what evil is like, and if what we are at present menaced by can conceivably be described as an evil and destructive demiurge, then I think I dare say, without bravado and hoping not to appear ostentatious, that I have experienced evidence of the existence of some such force intimately and directly, this experience being a factual one, however 'merely subjective'. I do not understand this force. My own experience of it might seem to suggest that I am liable to be tempted into something like manicheism; yet I have always fought shy of heresies, at least in theory. Shakespeare at his darkest, however, suggests that his views concerning the power or powers controlling the universe, or at least men's destinies, were far from orthodox. What I can state positively is that I have been brought face to face with evil *in myself;* and while I know I cannot exactly be described as a common man, certainly not as a model of normality, I do not regard myself as being at all exceptional in this respect, though perhaps not everyone consciously realizes to what extent they are capable of cruelty, violence and destructiveness.

I.I. — You have already said that you did not intend to allow yourself to wander into a discussion of theological questions, but here you go again. I thought that in any case you had some sort of reputation as being a Christian poet. If you are one in fact, one might have expected your outlook to be ultimately optimistic?

D.G. — I would never claim either to have the least leaning to theological didacticism, being suspicious to begin with of all dogma, notoriously a pretext for strife and divisiveness; or to be a representative of contemporary Christian poetry. But I have received the benefit of a conventional Christian upbringing, and still believe, in fortunately still recurrent moments of certain conviction, in the unprecedented occurrences of the Incarnation and in the meaningfulness of the term Resurrection. At the same time, perhaps as a Chestovian existential 'thinker', Original Sin (Knowledge) and the Fall of Man are undoubted facts for me. The question we seem to be facing, as we enter the 1980s, is whether or not we can collectively come once more to believe in the Redemption, and thus be able to exclaim, if Original Sin *is* Knowledge, much of which (Technology) increaseth (as we now know only too well) sorrow, 'O felix culpa!' As regards optimism, I once noted in a little book of would-be aphorisms tentatively entitled *Blind Man's Buff* that optimism and pessimism are no more than the complementary lenses of a pair of (non-rose-tinted) spectacles required by our innately myopic vision when in search of an 'outlook'.

I.I. — You do not wish to bring your 'declaration' to a conclusion by making any further observations on the subject of Technology?

D.G. — In relation to the problems of the modern poet, you mean?

Frankly, so much has been said by so many people on this particular topic of late that I do not feel that I have much to add that would be of interest, beyond pointing out that I only wish that it were possible to make it understood that when one declares oneself, as I do, critical of, indeed militantly against, the complete subservience of not only the intellectual Establishment but of even minimally educated people to the virtually despotic hegemony of empirically scientific rationalism, one is not necessarily anti-rational, and that in arguing that Logic is inadequate, one is not urging the abandonment of logic. All one asks for is a general recognition of the imperfections of a wholly rationalist, therefore also as a rule (outmodedly) materialist, utilitarian and scientifically optimistic view of the world and the current crisis it is undergoing. In the same way one, that is to say I personally, would like to hear from some of the official representatives of religion, i.e. Churchmen, some acknowledgement of the fact that until very recently our Christianity has all too often been in practice a travesty of the original precepts of the Gospels, and the usual interpretations of Christ's teaching far too comfortable and over eager to be acceptable to Caesar, in spite of the old label 'opium of the people' having long been recognized as out of date.

I.I. – And you still maintain that such concerns are part of the poet's business?

D.G. – Not of *all* poets maybe; but whether we like it or not we are all 'members one of another', and it is coming increasingly to be grasped that the era that has already begun is essentially that of Convergence. Everything seems to be in the balance, polarization is intensifying in every domain and each problem is seen to be becoming less and less capable of being considered apart from every other one. Not for the first time, let me say that 'at the same time', I happen to believe less and less in the possibility of saying anything of significance adequately or conclusively, and that to attempt to do so is to risk losing oneself in the quicksands of discursive verbosity, digressiveness and one-sidedness. George Steiner, already quoted, has also remarked in *After Babel* that 'The concept of the "lacking word" marks modern literature'; and that 'Goethe and Victor Hugo were probably the last major poets to find that language was sufficient for their needs'. To attempt to put what is probably in the last resort inexpressible would appear to be not simply absurd, for absurdity can be creative, but futilely useless. Beyond a certain point, the more one tries to express what one feels it to be urgent to try to say at least something about, the less one manages to communicate. To testify to the truth insofar as one is capable of doing so may perhaps be something one should be prepared even to die for, if necessary; but one should not delude oneself that any single individual can satisfactorily or definitively formulate The Truth about anything.

DEPARTURES

In the Spring of 1947, the French poet Pierre Jean Jouve came to this country and delivered a lecture entitled *L'Apologie du poète* in Oxford and London. This was immediately after what can now be seen as a significant turning-point in the development of modern French poetry: the emergence of poetry of Resistance. The gist of this brief message to Michael Horovitz and the readers of *New Departures* is that the poetry of today and of the unforeseeable future must, it appears to me, now be regarded as Resistance poetry if it is to be taken seriously. At the same time, I would point out that there exists in England a quasi-traditional resistance to real seriousness which is as much liable to affect poets as it is to dominate the outlook of supposedly more 'ordinary' citizens.

Jouve opened his recently reprinted discourse (*Le temps qu'il fait*, 1982) by saying that Elizabeth Barrett Browning's phrase referring to the poet as the sayer of essential things was one that had recurred to him throughout his life. In a country still intellectually determined to a great extent by the kind of thinking classifiable as logical positivist empiricism, which treats with ridicule the supposition that the concept of essence has meaning, it follows that what the poet says, if it is about essential things, will commonly be regarded as being devoid of serious foundation and relegated to the domain of harmless musings or mere word-spinning of a more or less agreeable kind. This then is the situation in which poets of today ought first to realize that they are in effect Resistants, militant defenders of their right to express their reactions to what they conceive to be the essential features of the world into which they have been born, against an attitude which tends to rob their work of its greatest justification.

There is a more immediate reason to liken the poetry appropriate to our coming fin-de-siècle to that produced in France in particular during the mid-century Occupation of that country by a power representing the most naked embodiment known to date of Nihilism. In 1947, Jouve observed that poetry had then recently become the subject of the kind

---

New Departures 15 (1983), ed. Michael Horovitz, p. 56. Also in Michel Rémy, *David Gascoyne, ou l'urgence de l'inexprimé* (Presses Universitaires de Nancy, 1984), pp. 143-5.

of attention it could well have done without, that of theorists debating the merits or defects of committed poetry. Such theorists, Jouve remarked, were generally not themselves poets, which accordingly made their theories so much the more authoritarian. He went on to say: 'Since Poetry is always a direct or indirect mirror of the times, a great part of the world's pain has found an issue in Poetry, which has brought once more into evidence the formidable problems of the relation between Poetry and politics, between the poem and action, – the problems of "conviction", as Baudelaire defined them.' Jouve added that he would first humbly admit that we do not know what Poetry is, and that every poem, if it is a true one, remains a mystery. The question referred to above is unavoidably related to that of content. However impossible it may be to define poetry adequately, and however mysterious the nature of a poem, we can say with some certainty that the original etymologically derived meaning of a poem was approximately a *making*, a vessel made of words. It depends on the poet whether its contents be trivial, ephemeral, topical or of permanent value.

Until recently, it had become customary to assume that the attention paid to a poem should primarily be directed to the skill and adequacy of its construction, and that what it was intended to communicate was only of ancillary interest. But most poets will by now have realized that the making of any poem implies a series of word-by-word decisions, conscious or subliminally determined, and that all these decisions will have been fundamentally influenced by the amount of serious thought he has been in the habit of giving to himself, the nature of poetry, and his experience of life and the state of the world in general. The poet is finally responsible for the type of content of the poem he makes and will only have made full use of his gift if he has cared sufficiently about communicating something more than the purely aesthetic pleasure afforded by the appreciation of an ingeniously and competently made verbal object.

The last thing I want is to appear to be making the arrogant suggestion that poets should be writing in any other way than that which spontaneously occurs to them. If I choose to think of our time in terms of a metaphor such as the World's Midnight, and thus risk seeming to be inclined to the speciously melodramatic, that is my own affair. I would only submit that it has become increasingly difficult to ignore the blatant contemporary reality of violence, aggressive hostility, terror, dehumanization, polarization, explosive disruption and all the other all too familiar phenomena presented to us daily as evidence of what such words must inadequately be used to express. How can any of us ever suppress some longing to depart from such an overtly catastrophic ambience and from the nihilistic hegemonies of power, self-interest and autonomously proliferating technology – or avoid expressing, however indirectly, some symptom of this longing in the poems we manage to produce?

When Michael Horovitz invited me to participate in one of his *Poetry Olympics* events at The Young Vic towards the end of 1981, I decided to translate and read a text by the still little-known visionary poet René Daumal. It so happens that the poet by whom Daumal and his friends of *Le Grand Jeu* group were most inspired was Rimbaud[1]. To accompany and illustrate the preceding prose, I append the following poem by Rimbaud, written a century and a decade ago, which gives amazingly prophetic voice to the feelings still leading to all desire for radical new departures:

DEPARTURE

Seen enough. The vision has been encountered in every air.
Had enough. The murmur of towns in the evening, and in the
sunshine, and always.
Known enough. The halts of life. – O Murmurs and Visions!
Departure in new affection and noises!

By way of conclusion, I would say that, more surely than responsibilities begin in dreams, departure, unlike escape or evasion, is the result of deliberate resolution.

---

[1] Translated by Professor Roger Little, from the appendix to *Rimbaud: A Critical Introduction*, by C. A. Hackett (Cambridge University Press).

DAVID GASCOYNE IN INTERVIEW

'I am a poet who wrote himself out when young and then went mad.'

David Gascoyne is a very tall, slightly stooped figure. When I went to visit him recently in his home on the Isle of Wight he had just got back from a conference in Luxembourg and was suffering from a cold. We sat by the fire with his black and white cat called Jeffrey.

Collected Poems 1988 brings together work from over half a century and I began by asking him whether he found any themes which ran all through his poems? He immediately answered: 'The hollowness of the world without a spiritual dimension.'

Did he think of himself as a religious poet?

'I suppose I cannot deny that I am one. I was brought up as a Protestant, though my parents were agnostics. When I was eight I became a chorister at Salisbury Cathedral. We went to Matins and Evensong twice a day except Wednesday and Holy Communion as well as Matins on Sundays. Then when I went to London and began to read everything I could get hold of – Marx, Freud, Spengler – I became an atheist, or thought I was. I also became a member of the Communist Party when I was nineteen, because I thought that was the best way to struggle against Mosley who seemed to be in the ascendant at that time and because friends of mine were members and teased me into being one. But after I had been to Barcelona and seen how the Communists treated everyone else on the left I soon became disillusioned. My disillusion was really because I realized pretty early that man cannot live by bread alone and when the masses go home from their demonstrations and find themselves alone in the dark, all they have to fall back on is what was scornfully described by the party line philosophy as "mere subjectivity". I could never accept that subjectivity was "mere". I believe that man has a soul and I still believe that Keats's "Life is a vale of soulmaking" is a wonderful definition.'

I reminded him that he recorded in his *Journals* that André Breton accused him of having become a Roman Catholic.

'The line in "Miserere": "Christ of revolution and poetry" was shocking perhaps to very orthodox Christians and also to anti-religious

---

Interview by Lucien Jenkins in *Stand*, Vol. 33, No. 2 (Spring 1992), pp. 20-25.

French intellectuals who have been violently opposed to the Catholic Church since before the French Revolution. The Surrealists were, you might say, religiously anti-religious. I have actually seen Benjamin Péret spitting at a *curé* on a bus because he thought it was his duty. He would have reproached himself if he had not done so. I came to feel that the Surrealists had based themselves on Jacobins, they were all French Revolutionary figures – Saint-Just, or Danton.'

What had he found in French poetry that he could not find in English poetry?

'*Poésie* cannot be translated by the English word poetry. Since the middle of the nineteenth century there is the mantic idea of poetry. There is a poem by Victor Hugo called "Ce que dit la bouche d'ombre", the mouth of shadow; the poet is a mask, through whom words from beyond come. Baudelaire is an example and Rimbaud and Mallarmé.'

David Gascoyne's 'Miserere' has an epigraph from Jouve, a poet for whom he has an enduring admiration and whom he has translated.

'When I became dissatisfied with Surrealism, by chance, wandering along the *quais*, I discovered in a secondhand bookseller's box a copy of *Poèmes de la folie de Hölderlin* translated by Pierre Jean Jouve and Pierre Klossowski, the brother of the painter Balthus. I discovered not only Hölderlin but Jouve. I began to read his poetry and his novels. A bookseller-librarian noticed that I was taking out books of Jouve and reading them with enthusiasm and mentioned that Jouve was a client of hers and that if I came in on next Thursday afternoon, she would introduce me to him. Jouve asked me to visit him and I began to go to his Thursday evenings. His wife was a Freudian analyst. At these evenings not only literary and philosophical friends of Jouve came, but also a lot of Blanche Reverchon's patients, which was not very orthodox. Although Jouve was not a member of the Surrealist group – he didn't frequent them at all – there was the connection that he too used the unconscious as a source of poetry. But at the same time there was a spiritual dimension which is lacking in Surrealist poetry.'

David Gascoyne has referred to Jouve as the greatest poet he has known. How had Jouve influenced his own poetry?

'The poems after "Miserere" are all strongly influenced by Jouve. Even the poem which was originally titled "To Benjamin Fondane" and which is now "I.M. Benjamin Fondane", because at the time I wrote it was before he was arrested and sent to Auschwitz and then to the gas chambers at Birkenau and I didn't know it until after the war. Jouve uses the material that the Surrealists used. His poetic art is the cultivation of spontaneity to obtain contact with the unconscious. He would not have known what he was going to write when he sat down to write. I think too that Blanche confided in him a lot of the material of the analyses that she conducted. Some of his poems were published in a Surrealist art review* because of this subject matter: it was obviously material out of the depths of the unconscious, sexual and obsessive. It was only Jouve who had the idea of spirituality and the erotic force being interconnected: the esoteric idea, the Smaragdine Tablet of Hermes Tristmegisthus, the saying that that which is above is as that which is below for the creation of the One Thing. That is to say, the finally unified world in which spirit and matter are no longer seen as in contradiction, and reason and imagination are no longer opposites, nor subjectivity and objectivity. That was the idea of the Surrealists: Breton says this many times, especially in the Second Manifesto. That was what appealed to me in Surrealism, the attempt to overcome the contradictions between all these aspects of reality. Industrial, scientific, imperialistic society thrives on these contradictions in which you have Either/Or instead of And.'

But surely the Surrealists celebrated conflict, rather than working for reconciliation of opposites?

'The Surrealists claimed to be based upon dialectics and the whole idea of dialectics, as developed by Hegel particularly, is that in order to bring about synthesis you have to carry the opposites to extremes, to bring about a conjunction – this is alchemical as well as dialectic thought – the fusion or reconciliation, the final reunification if you like, is brought about by pushing things to extremes rather than by reconciling them in a superficial – insincere – way.'

So how had the Surrealists become involved with the Communist Party: surely they weren't natural allies? After all, what about socialist realism?

'They wanted poetry to be in the service of humanity, they wanted to bring about a revolution of consciousness, which they thought should be an integral part of The Revolution – *Le Surréalisme au service de la révolution*. They had the very democratic idea that poetry can be done by everybody. But the Communist Party wouldn't have anything to do with them and there was a complete break. Finally Aragon went over to the Communist Party and submitted to the directive that poetry had to be written for the proletariat, socialist realism and all that, and Breton became a Trotskyist and in fact got to know Trotsky quite well.'

And his own involvement in what was then Harry Pollitt's Communist Party?

'I belonged to a cell in Twickenham and went to a few meetings there: perfectly ordinary people who were dissatisfied with the Labour

---

* Editor's note: Three poems in *Minotaure*, No. 6 (1935).

Party, suburban people, partly working class, partly middle class clerical types. I took part in more than one procession in London's East End to demonstrate against Mosley. I sold the *Daily Worker* outside the bus station in Hounslow on a few occasions. I think I really believed in it. At the end of the war I suppose I voted Labour. I read Marx and Engels quite seriously at one time, but I felt there was something lacking.'

David Gascoyne knew a number of Surrealist painters and his work of the Thirties includes the poems dedicated to Dalí and Magritte.

'When I wrote the name of René Magritte at the top of the page I didn't try to describe any of his pictures, I just sat down and wrote about the sort of subjects that he would paint. The Dalí poem is again not a description of a painting but an attempt to use his kind of mythologizing. But it is a very brief period in my life, belonging to the Surrealist Movement, writing Surrealist poetry. I disliked the label "Surrealist Poet" which was hung around my neck for years and years, long after I had stopped writing automatically.'

David Gascoyne's verse is very strongly visual. In 'The Gravel Pit Field' the poem gazes intently at a small area of landscape, considering it in brilliantly lit detail.

'The visual sense is very strong for me. I might describe myself as a scopophile, a voyeur. John Cowper Powys describes himself as a scoptophile in his astonishing *Autobiography*.'

Gascoyne is known as a poet having strong connections with France, but wasn't there also some influence from American poetry?

'At one time I regularly received books from Miss Steloff of the Gotham Book Mart in New York. Before the war I used to go to see Norman Cameron almost every weekend and he introduced me to the poetry of Hart Crane, John Crowe Ransom and Allen Tate. When I was in Paris in 1933 at the age of seventeen one of the books I bought from Sylvia Beach was Wallace Stevens's *Harmonium*. I found something in American poetry that was more exciting than English poetry. Anthony Rudolf introduced me to the poetry of George Oppen. I've always liked the poetry of William Carlos Williams but I think Oppen in his way is quite as good as Williams. That is poetry which neither scans in a conventional way nor has a traditional form but is nevertheless extremely subtle metrically and has its own internal form. I have written a few sonnets, there's one called "From Morn to Mourning" and another one called "The Uncertain Battle". Then there are certain poems which have their own form: that is to say I discover the first stanza and then I repeat the form. But I've never written "Free Verse" –' (he pronounces the words contemptuously), '– in which so much contemporary verse is like prose cut up into lines more or less arbitrarily.'

When people think of the Thirties they often think first of Auden and his circle. David Gascoyne wrote at the time of feeling a 'great gap' between his work and theirs: does he still feel it?

'I was very stupid about MacNeice when I was young, I appreciate him now. His work is one of the best poetic documents of the mid-twentieth century. "The sunlight on the garden hardens and grows cold": an observation put into language which sounds as though it has always been there.'

Gascoyne repeated the quotation. 'It's perfectly appropriate and it sounds so good.' He had also known William Empson. 'In Empson's poetry words are put together like wonderful carpentry, so that you feel that every word belongs to every other word. Empson was unusually sensitive to words and meanings; a word to Empson was like an onion.' And Auden? 'Well, I admired Auden very much, liked his poetry and read it continually. Auden wrote a strange book called *The Orators*, which shows the strong influence of having read Saint-John Perse, very much a mantic poet — *"bouche d'ombre"* again. My poem "The Conspirators" is not exactly Audenesque but it is an attempt to write a narrative poem which was not out of key with the kind of poetry Auden was writing. And that poem of mine "Farewell Chorus"[1]. It's Thirties political poetry by someone who has read and loved Guillaume Apollinaire.'

Had he felt, being involved with the Communist Party, a duty to write political poetry?

'I think in the *Journals* you can find the pricking of conscience that one ought to write politically. At the end of the summer of 1935 in Paris there was the huge Congress of Intellectuals for the Defence of Culture against Fascism, with writers from all over Europe and America. Theodore Dreiser was there, Thomas Mann was there, Henri Barbusse and Aragon, all discussing what the writer should do. Everybody had a questioning attitude. Even Dylan Thomas: "Five Fingers" and one or two others were political.'

He had written in his *Journals* 'I belong to Europe before I belong to England': was this a matter of 'influence', or something more than that?

'Apart from Auden and Spender, the other English poets of my generation were not so much interested in European poetry. Eliot of course was a European poet. He translated Saint-John Perse and was very concerned that *The Criterion* should be an organ of European, not just English or American, culture. I was very bad at French at school. But then I read Arthur Symons on the 1890s writers who were keen on writers like Baudelaire and Verlaine, and even Rimbaud is mentioned. On the

---

[1] 1939, first published in *Partisan Review*.

way home from school I would go down the Charing Cross Road and visit Zwemmer's and buy back numbers of *transition* and *La Révolution surréaliste*. Then I began to want to read Rimbaud, Mallarmé, Baudelaire and so on in the original. I had a copy of Aloysius Bertrand's *Gaspard de la Nuit*.'

Had he, I asked, kept up with contemporary British poetry?

'Well, I try to. But you have to remember that I was, as it were, dead for about ten years. I never was much one for the Fitzrovia crowd. Drinking half pint after half pint (which was all one could afford in those days) never appealed much to me. Then I missed The Movement, you see. When I came back from Vancouver Island I was able to write *Night Thoughts* and then I dried up. I went to live in France – in Paris in the winter and Aix-en-Provence in the summer – and at that time I read a lot of detective stories, as well as Saul Bellow and *Lolita*. But I wasn't reading very much contemporary English poetry then. The poets younger than myself whom I knew best were David Wright and John Heath-Stubbs. I like and appreciate the poetry of John Heath-Stubbs, although there is a certain English quality which I much dislike: urbanity. I prefer extremism, things which are on the margin, really: I still like Dada because it is anti-literature.'

And younger poets?

'I never was an enthusiast for the poetry of Larkin: I find it dreary and depressing. Obviously accomplished, but accomplishment is not enough. If I were younger I think I would feel an affinity for the poetry of Tony Harrison. His "V" when it was broadcast created a sensation, like *The True Confession of George Barker*. Everyone was very indignant at all the fucks, but I thought it was a very serious poem and I admired it. When he recites it himself I find his particular kind of chanting almost as off-putting as Yeats's way in a previous generation. But I admire and respect Tony Harrison – and his translations, I think, are superb. Christopher Logue's translations from Homer, *Kings*, and his previous book *War Music*, I think are excellent.' He also respects Geoffrey Hill's work. 'I read his *The Mystery of the Charity of Charles Péguy*; I admired it very much.'

He wrote his book, *The Sun at Midnight*, after he had come out of hospital.

'I had been mad in France once and I was about to go mad in England. I was quite embarrassed about it afterwards when I became a little more sane: having *The Sun at Midnight* published was like being dragged through the street in one's underclothes. I was on the verge of going off my head. I tried to get into Buckingham Palace, you know, one morning at half past eight. A guard at the gates wouldn't let me in so I slapped his face. I was seized and interrogated, but they were surprisingly polite to me. All the time there was a second self which retained complete lucidity, recording it all.'

But the attempt to get into Buckingham Palace was not his first episode of madness. 'I still have not written the story of what happened to me in Paris in 1964. I tried to get into the Elysée to see de Gaulle. I was set upon in the entrance to the Elysée Palace.' He chuckled, wheezing slightly from his cold. 'I tried to explain that I had a mission to see de Gaulle. These *Babus*, great big tough men, four of them, began to close in on me and I began to struggle and you know, when you're in that state you become extremely strong and have an amazing influx of violence. I was taken to the nearest *gendarmerie* and I was kept there for the whole afternoon. Two people from the British consulate came to try to get me out and to save me and I slapped their faces. I found myself in hospital in a strait-jacket. They finally said I must go back to England but on no account to live alone.' So, in his early forties, Gascoyne went to live with his parents on the Isle of Wight. 'My parents were very sweet but I had the terrible feeling that they must think I was a complete failure. My *Collected Poems*, the first edition, came out in 1965 and I thought, "Thank goodness, at least I have got this to show them." Then my father died and I had acute depression. I went off my head in London.'

There is a whole subculture associated with the idea of the *poète maudit*: did he feel that there was a real link between his history of mental illness and his creativity? He answered slowly, choosing his words carefully.

'It's difficult to say. The root cause of my mental breakdown was a severe and prolonged amphetamine addiction.'

Did he see that as the only cause? Again he answered carefully and rather quietly.

'Probably not the only cause. To me, poetry is a mysterious gift of putting words together in a certain way. Poetry is like a substance, the words stick together as though they were magnetized to each other. I am a poet who wrote himself out when young and then went mad. I tried to write poetry again and succeeded to a certain extent but it is not the same as the poetry I wrote before.'

I reminded him of what he had said at the beginning about the hollowness of the world without a spiritual dimension. He nodded and ended the interview by citing Hölderlin, saying: 'The poet's job is to go on holding on to something like faith, through the darkness of total lack of faith, what Buber calls the eclipse of God.'

ANSWERS TO 'AN ENQUIRY'

AN ENQUIRY

1 Do you intend your poetry to be useful to yourself or others?
2 Do you think there can now be a use for narrative poetry?
3 Do you wait for a spontaneous impulse before writing a poem; if so, is this impulse verbal or visual?
4 Have you been influenced by Freud and how do you regard him?
5 Do you take your stand with any political or politico-economic party or creed?
6 As a poet what distinguishes you, do you think, from an ordinary man?

DAVID GASCOYNE'S ANSWERS

1 This question is particularly difficult to answer, because I do not really understand how contemporary poetry can be *useful* to anybody. There are poets, who feel they must write poetry, and there are readers, who feel they would like to read poetry. Is one to understand that *useful* means: useful in joining these two groups together?

My own poetry is not useful to me, in the ordinary sense of the word, except as an occasional sort of elaborate diary or as a means of making money. Which last, as we all know, is absurd. I always hope that my poems are useful to someone in some way, but I don't suppose they are, so I leave it at that.

2 I do not feel that there is any use at all for the kind of pastiche narrative poem that is associated with Eliot, Pound and Bottrall. Nor very much use for the poeticized historical narrative, such as MacLeish's *Conquistador*. What might be useful now would be a poem expressing the ever-rising feeling of crisis, anxiety and panic; a poem that would treat this feeling in a loose, universal and epic sort of way. I mean a poem narrating the contemporary Zeitgeist of Europe, or even of the World.

New Verse 11 (October 1934), pp. 11-13.

3   Immediately before writing a poem I experience a very satisfying inner fusion. Often I have to wait for a long time for this feeling. Sometimes I have an idea and feel 'This will make a good subject for a poem,' but unless all the rest of the feeling, which might be described as energy or enthusiasm, accompanies the initial idea, I know that I am not yet ready to write the poem, or that it is not worth writing.

The impulse that I experience is neither verbal nor visual, but a mixture of both together with something else besides.

4   I have never been directly influenced by Freud in my poetry, but I have been indirectly influenced by him through the Surrealists. To give oneself up at any time to writing poems without the control of the reason is, I imagine, to have in a way come under the influence of Freud. I no longer find this navel-gazing activity at all satisfying. The Surrealists themselves have a definite justification for writing in this way, but for an English poet with continually growing political convictions it must soon become impossible.

5   My political feelings are not yet sufficiently developed or matured for me to be able to answer this question, beyond saying that I have the strongest possible sympathy with left-wing revolutionary movements.

6   I believe that the poet is distinguished from the 'ordinary man' by his attitude towards experience. This attitude, as far as I am concerned, is one of continual expectancy, which may at times become a state of hyperæsthesia. At the same time I am very doubtful as to whether the 'ordinary man' exists at all. Everyone probably has some sort of attitude towards experience, though perhaps neither so constant nor so consciously developed as that of the poet.

AUTHORS TAKE SIDES ON THE SPANISH WAR

One would have to be devoid of the most elementary feelings for decency and justice in order to preserve an attitude of indifference towards the inhuman gangster warfare being waged by Fascism against the people of Spain and their elected Government.

Authors Take Sides on the Spanish Civil War, published by the *Left Review* (1937), no pag.

A COMMENT ON AUDEN

There is such a thing as lyrical complacency, lyrical irresponsibility. It would be a great deal better for poetry, for both its readers and its writers, if nine out of every ten contemporary poets became silent. W. H. Auden is one of the rare exceptions.

The traditional wisdom of the poet is that of one who stands outside; it is 'unfairly' won; and, though vaguely comforting, impractical. As soon as the purely lyrical poet becomes implicated in real life, he loses this wisdom, to find that what he has learnt through struggle, instead of grasped through intuition, he cannot write about. W. H. Auden is one of the rare exceptions.

One has only to compare such widely varied poems as 'A Bride in the '30s', 'Casino', and 'Spain', for instance, with the efforts of most of Auden's contemporaries to deal critically and constructively with other people's problems, or even with their own, to see that strength of character and depth of experience are inseparable, ultimately, from important poetry. Without them, poetry may be ravishingly beautiful, but *merely* decorative, *merely* lyrical.

'Sixteen Comments on Auden', *New Verse* 26-7 (Auden Double Number, Nov. 1937), pp. 24-5.

AUTHORS TAKE SIDES ON THE FALKLANDS

THE QUESTIONS

Are you for, or against, our Government's response to the Argentine annexation of the Falkland Islands?
How, in your view, should the dispute in the South Atlantic be resolved?

AUTHORS TAKE SIDES ON THE FALKLANDS

On returning yesterday (7 June 1982) from a five-day trip to Paris, I found your questionnaire awaiting me. Fortunately the time at present at my disposal for answering the two very clear-cut questions to which you request an answer is limited, since the whole Falklands issue has been for me personally from the outset murky, to say the least, and I should otherwise have been tempted to run on in my usual prolix fashion, trying to make clear the least nuances of my reaction. Had I been asked to reply either to the questionnaire regarding the Spanish Civil War,[*] or that sent out by you in 1966 to elicit reactions to the war in Vietnam, my answers would have been brief and categorical. I hope and trust my left-wing principles have not become woolly with the passing of time, but concerning what is at this moment taking place in the S. Atlantic, I still find myself in a to a certain extent divided state of mind, although my initial reaction, during at least the first three weeks of the conflict, was one of cold, simmering fury. The keyword I would have then chosen as pre-eminently applicable to our unvigilant government's reaction to the Argentine's takeover of what the French, for instance, have always known as *Les Malouines*, was 'ineptitude', a term I should still precede with the qualification 'colossal'.

Living in the Isle of Wight as I have now for many years, I had been for some time not altogether unaware that just across the Solent, at Southampton, an Argentine office was established with the express purpose of purchasing arms from us, something which they apparently

---

Authors Take Sides on the Falklands, ed. Cecil Woolf and Jean Moorcroft Wilson (Cecil Woolf Publishers, 1982), pp. 37-43.

[*] Editor's note: See page 56.

continued to do without the least difficulty up until less than two months before the junta's attack; nor, as has been pointed out by allegedly seditious spokesmen, did any government official then ever make any reference to the detestable nature of repressive Latin American regimes, certainly not to the blatantly fascist Argentine one. All such regimes, no doubt, were tacitly regarded as providing at least a temporary check to the ever-lurking threat of Soviet-inspired subversion. The scandal of the debilitated laxness of our once much-vaunted Intelligence Service is too obvious to mention. The muscle-flexing televised announcements of just what we were intending to do and just how we would carry out our intentions with which during the latter half of the second month of the conflict the BBC and, possibly more moderately, ITN regaled us appeared flagrantly to contradict the maxim with which we were once so familiar, according to which dangerous talk costs lives, and were tantamount to releasing information one would have considered surely to be classified as secret to the world at large and especially, of course, to the doubtless highly gratified Argentines' vigilant Intelligence Services.

Here I must admit that, although initially much in sympathy with the stand, now seen never to have stood a chance, adopted by Tony Wedgwood Benn and Dame Judith Hart, there came a moment when whatever residual element of 'pragmatism' remains ingrained in my outlook told me that once this 'unfortunate adventure', as even the most sympathetic elements of the French press have more than once qualified it, was embarked on, involving the impulsive despatch of as massively imposing a task force as we could muster, then it was simply futile to continue insisting on the pursuit of 'international negotiations' under the umbrella auspices of the UN, so patently stuck in interminable sessions of confused blah-blah predestined to checkmate. Not without some reluctance, I yielded to what has surely been a very widespread feeling: now that our government's operations have irrevocably started, let's get the whole thing done with as fast as possible, with the minimum of bloodshed and loss of life on both sides. Yesterday evening's BBC 'Newsnight' programme, however, undertook a discussion of the serious possibility of a prolonged war of attrition. 'If only the Argentines,' observed a typical military interviewee, 'would have the decency to call it a day and lay down their arms, many lives might still be saved'; yet he seemed realistic enough to be prepared to admit they would be unlikely to behave in so conveniently gentlemanly a fashion.

Despite having been all my life of a resolutely left-wing political tendency, I think I may justly claim also to have been since coming of age properly patriotic. I should be proud to think that my kind of patriotism might be considered not dissimilar to that of my friend the late Humphrey

Jennings. Perhaps my favourite London statue is that of Nurse Edith Cavell in the Charing Cross Road, with inscribed at its base her terse last words: 'Patriotism is not enough'. Unfortunately our national idea of decency, admirable though it may be, is not now enough either. Though we now know Dr Johnson's dictum to the effect that patriotism is the last refuge of scoundrels to have been too often misquoted, surely true love of one's country is rather something that entails lucid auto-criticism and the desire to be able to be honestly proud, without complacency or chauvinist self-deception, of the genuinely good characteristics and actions of the nation into which one happens to have been born. Though probably the majority of French people, for instance, still consider our counter-offensive against Argentina to have been fundamentally justifiable, and many are obviously embarrassed by the French origin of the execrated exocet, at least one reputable daily paper has drawn attention to the tendency of our media to exaggerate *(gonfler)* the least *(les plus minces)* details concerning adolescent Argentinian vandalism and seemingly arrogant cockiness, and to a certain repetitious self-righteousness in our communiqués. This is not to suggest that the reports and propaganda emanating from Buenos Aires are not immeasurably more mendacious and distorted than our own; but one would wish there to be observable a total contrast between the treatment of the continually changing situation by the press controlled by a typical fascist military dictatorship and its reporting as undertaken by those purporting to give voice to the views of a true democracy. To someone like myself, who for at least fifty years has tried, in however insignificant or ineffectual a way, to further international understanding and the recognition of European cultural unity, the risk we now run of alienating our continental neighbours by adopting a course of behaviour that might only too easily be mistaken for a reversion to the casual superiority and unquestioning self-assurance typical of our empire-building colonialist era at its apex is, to put it mildly, perturbing.

Another question raised by the present conflict that is closely connected with the factitious patriotism too frequently encouraged by our media is that concerning the compassion most sections of society naturally feel for the young men who have lost or are still risking their lives in atrocious conditions very far from home, 'in the cause of freedom', as most of them no doubt keenly believe, and as we must all trust they will eventually turn out in fact to have been doing. When President Reagan seeks to reassure us that what they are fighting for down there is not 'real estate' but rather the noble cause of demonstrating that aggressive invasion of territory will always meet with inflexible resistance, it is difficult for anyone with a retentive sense of the history of this century not to remember the quasi-sacred principle that took the form of our duty to defend brave little Belgium against the unprovoked aggression of the last of the Kaisers in 1914, a cause that led vast numbers of young men to lay down their lives for it with enthusiasm, while ten years later an equally vast number of survivors came to regard their sacrifice as having been futile and vain. How long will it be this time before people will sadly or bitterly be wondering 'where have all the flowers gone?' The natural compassion just alluded to, moreover, is apt to be modified in the most detrimental way if one draws a parallel with, for instance, the recent utterances of M. George Marchais when he seized the obvious opportunity to denounce the 'imperialist powers' for once more using the young men at their disposal as 'cannon fodder', especially if one happens to be aware that this political leader not long ago caused such offence by his unmistakably antisemitic remarks that numbers of his most intelligent followers resigned from the Party of which he remains the head. Opportunism of this description has recognizable counterparts here; but wherever it manifests itself it is at the present time doubly dangerous because it is so apt to encourage the apathetic disillusionment with *all* political parties and their actions that would appear to represent today the gravest danger facing what we believe to be authentic democracy.

During my brief recent stay in Paris, I was fortunate enough to have the opportunity of conversing for an hour or so with a distinguished writer (one of *les Quarante* in fact) whose name I have no inclination to drop but whose love of our country and most things English is among his marked characteristics. He declared himself grieved and concerned by the situation in which the British find themselves at the moment, but more particularly anxious about the long-term outcome of the conflict, whatever that may turn out to be. He also expressed to me the view, with which, though a younger and less privileged observer, I find myself wholly in accord, that the bleakest factor in all public affairs today is the absence of any figure of sufficient stature to inspire wholehearted international admiration and confidence, the ubiquitous presence, in other words, of seldom more than mediocre representative officials. Incompetence in diplomacy, in strategy and in statesmanship appear to have become endemic in the field of international relations. Is it not also astonishing how few supposedly responsible British politicians appear to have more than the most elementary notion of the nature of the Latin-American temperament with its legitimate idiosyncrasies, all contributing to the varied but closely related cultural traditions of those countries originally colonized by Spain and Portugal? It seems to me not entirely irrelevant to speculate how many of the public men who have been most vocal during the past sixty or so days are at all familiar with the works of

Conrad, Hudson or Cunninghame Graham, for instance. Even some acquaintance with the writings of Prescott would surely assist the development of some degree of understanding of the historical background of that part of the Western hemisphere that has lately been brought to the forefront of world attention.

At this point, realizing that despite having written about the subject of your questionnaire at inordinate length I do not appear to have taken any definite stand with regard to it, I must quench my explanatory verbal flow. Just in case you should find, understandably enough, that this contribution to your dossier is too long to print as it stands, I now append a short poem which you might care to use in place of the preceding pages. It was hastily written on the day mentioned in the title and revised the day after. The rather feeble pun contained in the title refers to the quite insignificant fact that I have seldom written what are generally known as 'occasional poems'. It is clearly a non- or apolitical poem, and is distanced from the burning Falklands issue by the use of a deliberate form, which is that of a verbal square made of 144 syllabic units, as follows:

> Rare Occasional Poem
> May 13th 1982

> The 'Thought for the Day' that was broadcast this morning
> Told us Crisis means Judgement. But who is the Judge?
> You may or may not feel that one can exist.
> Judgement can signify verdict, decision or
> Fate, among other things. Yesterday, Fatima:
> Priest tried to stab Pope. There was one more announcement
> That a new Incarnation of Christ will appear
> On TV before June has ended; by which time
> Perhaps the dense fog which at present surrounds us
> Will have somewhat dispersed, thus revealing at least
> Whether fervour for fatherland, freedom or force
> Have prevailed in the South Atlantic, – or foresight.

ON THE STATE OF POETRY

Dear

    Agenda is preparing a special issue on the current state and role of poetry in the United Kingdom and Ireland. We would be grateful to receive your reflections or comments – up to five hundred words.
    We append a few famous/infamous remarks which may stimulate a response.
    Comments or replies for publication should reach us by October 2nd 1989.
    Thank you.
    Yours sincerely,

William Cookson   Peter Dale
enc.

Poet, what is it you do?
                                                         Rilke.

Literature is a form of permanent insurrection and recognizes no straitjackets. Every attempt to change its angry, ungovernable nature will fail. Literature may perish but it will never conform.
                                        Mario Vargos Llosa.

There is a great deal of shallow nonsense in modern criticism which holds that poetry – and this is a half-truth that is worse than false – is essentially revolutionary.
                                                  Allen Tate.

A writer is another kind of government.
                                              Solzhenitsin.

Poetry is truth seen with passion.
                                                Yeats.

The arts are a chief means of communication with the dead. Without communication with the dead a fully human life is not possible.
                                                Auden.

Poetry is at bottom a criticism of life.
                                                Arnold.

'On the State of Poetry', *Agenda* 27, No. 3 (special issue, 1989), pp. 3-5 and 31-5.

All poetry is of the nature of soliloquy.
                                            J. S. Mill.

   . . . Sure a poet is a sage;
A humanist, physician to all men . . .
                                            John Keats.

All poets are liars.
                                            Plato.

Poets are the unacknowledged legislators of the world.
                                            Shelley.

He who thinks that all art [skill] will make anything fit to be called a poet finds that the poetry which he writes in his sober senses is beaten hollow by the poetry of madmen.
                                            Plato.

The poet's job is to define and yet again define till the detail of surface is in accord with the root in justice.
                                            Ezra Pound.

Poetry is responsible. It's a form of responsible behaviour, not a directive. It is an exemplary exercise.
                                            Geoffrey Hill.

Poetry is no more language than the landscape is paint.
                                            Karl Shapiro.

By the time I came of age in the 1930s, I had become familiar with most of what was then twentieth-century poetry: Pound, Eliot, the Imagists and the poets associated with Harold Monro, his Bookshop, Chapbooks and Chatto anthology; and was excited by the emergence of Auden, Spender, MacNeice – *New Signatures* and *New Country*. I continued to read the new work of living poets with curiosity and varying degrees of appreciation until I reached my thirties. I should add that I had first begun to read Baudelaire, Rimbaud and Mallarmé in the original while still in my teens, and went on to become familiar with the work of most contemporary French poets, the Surrealists in particular, as well as with the translations then available of such outstanding Europeans as Rilke, Pasternak, Maiakovski, Ungaretti and Lorca. And I read modern American poetry, from Whitman to the early Lowell, with on the whole greater enthusiasm than contemporary English poetry aroused in me. By the age of forty I had begun to read poetry, classic or recent, less and less frequently, so that by the time the so-called Movement was under way I was scarcely reading new poetry at all. During the last decade, however, I hope I have read sufficient recent English and Irish poetry to enable me to acquire a fairly broad view of the present state of poetry *chez nous*.

A lifelong Francophile, I have repeatedly observed that *poésie* cannot adequately be translated by the word 'poetry'. During the past century most (or at least a significant number of) French poets have been signally concerned with *la parole*, another word lacking a satisfactory equivalent in English. If I refer to this, it is not in order to indicate a personal preference for a foreign conception of poetry, but rather to suggest what it is that, broadly speaking, is *not* going on at present in English-language poetry. It seems to me that at the root of the implicit difference between the approach to poetry of our compatriots who write it and that of those who are writing it in many other languages is a concern with or indifference to the question of *ontology*. In other words, I surmise that the poets most frequently acclaimed with either rapture or more reserved appreciation by Anne Stevenson on the one hand and Peter Porter on the other are probably inclined to regard the very word 'ontology' with mistrust or distaste.

As I write this, I have just been reminded by Radio 3 that Emily Dickinson, whose voice is still for many readers acceptably 'modern', wrote poetry mainly concerned with 'nature, love, death and eternity'. As long as there are poets who deal with these themes with an individual voice and personally forged vocabulary, I thought, poetry will continue to fulfil a perennial function. But then it occurred to me that *eternity* can no longer be regarded as a 'buzz-word' for the majority of poets writing in English today. On the other hand, if one's going to be flippant, one may as well refer to *ontology* as the 'buzz-word' of a number of prominent French poets and the critics who write about them.

The trouble with an enquiry such as that instigated by the present issue of *Agenda* is that it tends to oblige one to make unavoidably sweeping generalizations and necessarily personal evaluations. Nevertheless I will risk observing that much of what is often designated 'post-modernist' poetry seems to be particularly concerned with shoring up fragments against its (the poets'/the age's) ruins, rather than with providing a convincing answer to the notorious question as to whether poetry is possible after Auschwitz. Symptomatic of this shoring up against ruin (presumably above all against the imminently obvious bankruptcy of the Judaeo-Christian tradition) is the noticeable increase of poems about poetry and poets, of allusion to supposedly key cultural figures ancient and modern, and of the use of quotations with or without brackets, embedded in the text or serving as epigraphs. In, for instance, Michael Schmidt's 1983 Carcanet anthology, *Some Contemporary Poets of Britain and Ireland*, which includes work by eighteen contributors, one can find at least twenty-five examples of the current dependence on what might be termed cultural iconography, ranging from Jeremy Taylor to Coleridge, from Pieter de Hooch to Stubbs the Victorian RA, from Vivaldi to Satie, and from Keats to Rupert Brooke. The celebratory recreation in poetry of what George Steiner might call talismanic figures representing moments of Western cultural history has been going on, of course, at least since Browning (cf. his Paracelsus, Sordello, Andrea del Sarto, to name but a few); and the frequent incorporation of fragmentary quotations is one of the features that made *The Waste Land* the most provocative, glossed and influential poem of the 1920s; while quotations from a vast number of sources, American, European and Chinese, ancient and contemporary, pivotal and trivial, are intrinsic to the fabric of Pound's *Cantos*, illustrating like multiple verbal collages the vision they promote of history winding towards its conclusion at the end of what has hitherto been known as Civilization.

Collections by younger poets produced since 1983 by Penguin, Carcanet, OUP and Bloodaxe have often confirmed the view that a main present poetic tendency is to salvage the most memorable items from the endangered museum of past literary and artistic achievement. Since the same date there can have been few finer long poems indicative of the present state of human affairs (to reflect which will ever, to my mind, be the primary function of poetry) than Geoffrey Hill's *The Mystery of the Charity of Charles Péguy*. It is prefaced by a quotation from Péguy that complements the vision of history to be discerned in the *Cantos*:

> *Nous sommes les derniers. Presque les après-derniers. Aussitôt après nous commence un autre age, un tout autre monde, le monde de ceux qui ne croient plus à rien, qui s'en font gloire et orgueil.*

This epigraphical passage is undated, but was obviously written prior to 1914 and published presumably in one of the *Cahiers de la Quainzaine* that Péguy persisted in writing and publishing throughout the decline of the ill-fated, ineptly named *belle époque*. In an appended note, Geoffrey Hill refers to Péguy as 'one of the great souls, one of the great prophetic intelligences, of our century'. The poem which he offers as his 'homage to the triumph of his "defeat" ' is part narrative, part meditation, and embodies not only an impeccably researched and imagined historical background to the subject but an insight into the essence of Péguy's impassioned message to his contemporaries and a mostly unheeding posterity. This is hardly the place to comment further on an in every way exceptional work, the style of which has some affinity with and to my mind surpasses that of the early Robert Lowell (NB: specifically Catholic faith is an issue irrelevant to Hill's purpose in this poem). In the 9th section, however, occurs a passing reference to Rimbaud (unnamed) that immediately confirmed my earlier belief that Hill is aware of and writing about what may well be the most crucial question facing poets of the present *fin-de-siècle*:

> 'Je est un autre', that fatal telegram,
> floats past you in the darkness, unreceived.

That 'fatal telegram' has, it so happens, been received and decoded with his customary rare percipience by George Steiner in *Real Presences* (subheaded *Is there anything in what we say?*), one of the few recent works of its kind that can be considered 'required reading' for all those concerned with the quandaries of language, especially as used by poets, at the present time. Limited space prohibits attempted summary of Steiner's cogent exposition of the implications of Rimbaud's momentous phrase, which he regards as central to the 'deconstruction' that is the most distinctive feature of what has come to be known as postmodernism. The fragmentation inherent in quotation referred to earlier is a prominent aspect of such deconstructuralism (to employ a rebarbative term typical of the latest New Criticism), as is the identity problem respecting authorship to be found in the employment of pseudonyms and personae by many representative modernist poets such as Pound and Pessoa.

George Steiner's latest book also has exceptional pertinence to any consideration of poetry at the end of the 1980s on account of its courageously unequivocal statement that 'any thesis that would, either theoretically or practically put literature and the arts beyond good and evil is spurious'. Steiner continues: 'The archaic torso in Rilke's famous poem says to us: "change your life". So do any poem, novel, play, painting, musical composition worth meeting.' Early last October, a weekend newspaper quoted in its 'Sayings of the Week' column an observation by John Ashbery: 'There is the view that poetry should improve your life. I think people confuse it with the Salvation Army.' I was reminded by this witticism of Rilke's archaic torso, and wondered whether the difference between change and improvement could be dismissed as merely a matter of semantics. I was led on to ask myself whether the concept of poetry as a vehicle for the expression of spiritual activity is in fact destined to become as archaic as the torso of Rilke's poem.

The poetry of today's younger English-language practitioners frequently displays admirable technical skill, verbal virtuosity and a wide range of cultural reference; but it seems to be suffering from a surfeit of brilliance and urbanity, and in danger of foundering in the shallowness that results from the habit of avoiding the ultimately profound in case it should make one appear embarrassingly portentous. At the same time there appears to be no effort being made to revive the tradition of Swift and Pope; one might think contemporary society worthy of satire of a somewhat higher order of savagery and wit than that still purveyed by *Private Eye*, for example. The appearance of a worthy successor to Edgell Rickword, the neglected subject of an excellent new study by Charles Hobday[1] would be propitious and duly welcome.

Despite all the hopeful signs of change and increased tolerance and humanity in Eastern Europe, I cannot resist feeling sympathy with the topical relevance of the words of Robinson Jeffers quoted by Colin Falck at the end of his Introduction to the 1987 edition of Jeffers' *Selected Poems*[2]:

> The spirit that flickers and hurts in humanity
> Shines brighter from better lamps; but from all shines.
> Look to it: prepare for the long winter: spring is far off.

---

[1] Charles Hobday, *Edgell Rickword: A Poet at War* (Manchester: Carcanet, 1989).

[2] Robinson Jeffers, *Selected Poems*. The Centenary Edition edited by Colin Falck (Manchester: Carcanet, 1987).

2

ESSAYS, INTRODUCTIONS AND PREFACES

FRENCH POETRY OF TODAY

'I accustomed myself to simple hallucination,' wrote Rimbaud in 1873. 'Then I expressed the sophistries of my magic by means of the hallucination of words!' That is why Rimbaud is always taken to be the first of modern French poets. Today there is scarcely a French poet writing who has not in some manner accustomed himself to this 'simple hallucination'. Since Baudelaire (and it would be possible to cite even further antecedents) poets have proceeded ever deeper and deeper into those regions below the active, conscious mind where, according to more than one school of thought, all poetry has its source. The history of French poetry since the middle of the nineteenth century is the record of the gradual percolation of the *irrational* element into creative writing.

In a letter to a friend, Rimbaud once wrote: 'If that which comes down *from there* has form, I will give it form: if it has no form I will leave it formless.' This idea, of course, has been subject to infinite variations. Some poets have preferred to cast their mould beforehand and then to pour into it, more or less at random, whatever came into their heads. Some, of a lesser order, have taken pains that no form whatever should be apparent in their work. Others create, quite consciously and with the aid of the strictest logic, word-systems whose chief appeal is to the unlogical strata of the mind, as Mallarmé and Valéry have done. Then there are the adherents to the sewing-machine-umbrella-operating-table theory; Lautréamont's famous phrase has been an excuse for hundreds of incoherent poems. The practitioners of this aesthetic claim that as between two opposing poles an electric spark is produced, so with the junction of two or more entirely unrelated images a spark of pure poetry can be obtained. The poems of André Breton and, more especially, Tristan Tzara are packed with these hydra-headed images. Breton's latest collection of poems, for instance, is entitled *The White-haired Revolver*.

The Surrealist movement began almost exactly ten years ago with the publication of Breton's *Manifeste du surréalisme: poisson soluble* in 1924. For more than three years before that it had been gradually evolving out of the moral chaos of the Dada movement. In 1922 a semi-Dadaist paper called *Littérature* had published an article entitled *L'Entrée des Mediums*, containing automatic writing and trance-utterances by Robert Desnos,

---

Everyman (31 August 1934), pp. 234, 251.

René Crevel and others, which was the beginning of perhaps the most important of Surrealist activities. A history of the movement from then until the present day, an account of its personalities and its productions would fill a long and extremely diverting book. Surrealism has produced more than one fine painter; a philosophic-theorizer, André Breton, whose writings are among the most interesting of modern times; the most sensational film ever produced, *L'Age d'or*; and at least one first-rate poet, Paul Eluard. A year or two ago a number of Surrealists, headed by Louis Aragon and Maxime Alexandre, broke away from the strict discipline of Breton's leadership and joined the Communist Party proper, with which, of course, they had had all along the greatest sympathy. This was the result of 'L'Affaire Aragon', which arose out of a dispute following the legal prosecution of Aragon early in 1932 for 'inciting to murder' and 'provoking insubordination in the army' in his poem 'Le Front Rouge', which appeared in the first number of *Literature of the World Revolution*, a revue published in Moscow by the 'International Union of Revolutionary Writers'. *Le Front Rouge* was published last year in an English translation by the American poet, e. e. cummings. It is a wild appeal to the French proletariat to revolt and to smash the old shams and hypocrisies of the bourgeois regime, in the form of an account of a train journey to the Soviet State of the future.

Poems containing entirely *undirected* thought have been written by Maxime Alexandre, Jacques Baron, Joë Bousquet, Robert Desnos, Georges Hugnet, Benjamin Péret, Pierre Unik, Roger Vitrac and others. Everything depends on the degree of the poet's sensibility; the uncontrolled thoughts of one not a poet set down on paper do not make a poem. The poet commences with the first image that comes into his head, follows it with another, continues, reaches a climax, finishes off. It is precisely the simple psychological game of free-association, only controlled by a poetic mood or rhythm. The driving force of this poetry, it is claimed, is the *libido*; Jung is sometimes quoted in defence of this theory. So the poem becomes a dream in words, and can be interpreted as such, which probably accounts for the large percentage of erotic images, and images of violent death, blood, fire and so on, that they contain.

The poems of Paul Eluard cannot easily be placed in this category. He is never crude, never violent, always musical; the shocks that he gives us are always pleasant shocks. Image follows image in a limpid stream, forming a rich and moving synthesis, something more than a mere pattern of emotive words. Of the work of lesser poets one often feels that theirs is simply a spate of words without beginning or end. But examine these seven lines of Eluard:

> A ce souffle à ce soleil d'hier
> Qui joint tes lèvres
> Cette caresse toute fraîche
> Pour courir les mers légères de ta pudeur
> Pour en façonner dans l'ombre
> Les miroirs de jasmin
> Le problème du calme.

The greatness of his gift makes the words seem to follow one another in an inevitable sequence, creates an atmosphere with which, unlogical and remote though it is, we seem to find ourselves familiar. It is sometimes said of Eluard that he has written of love better than anyone since Baudelaire, and that is a just tribute.

Of the older contemporary French poets (Max Jacob, Blaise Cendrars, Valéry Larbaud, Ribemont-Dessaignes) much could be written; modern French poetry is not nearly as widely known in England as it deserves to be. Though I am chiefly concerned here with more recent work, there is one great individualist who cannot be passed over without mention, Saint-John Perse, whose poem *Anabase* has been introduced to English readers in a translation by T. S. Eliot. His influence has been very wide, and those affected by it include W. H. Auden and Archibald MacLeish.

'At dawn we shall enter splendid towns,' said Rimbaud, but French poetry has not yet reached them. It has gradually taken possession of extraordinary territories, each more startling than the last, but now it is to be seen that it is impossible to go any further in that direction. In the near future we expect to see a new start made. The long trek back to Reality will begin, a reality that a new and stronger generation will be able to face without taking refuge in the fascinating phantasies of the subconscious.

POETRY AND REALITY

D.G. *refers to an article written by John Mair, 'Sense and Abstraction', published in the first number of* The Literary Review.

... He went on to describe in some detail the main features of what constitutes, in fact, the great crisis in Poetry today, this crisis being the product of the acute contradiction apparent in the formula: Poetry: Reality, – just as the general social crisis of today is the product of the acute contradictions within the system under which we are at present.

The curious thing is that the Surrealist poets whom Mr Mair quotes as having attained 'the final escape, the last solitary mountain', – far from being politically disinterested or 'opposed to material determinism, communal construction, or both', were among the first European writers of bourgeois origin to turn to Communism – and to adopt, integrally, the philosophy of dialectical materialism.

As long ago as 1925, the Surrealist poets (and artists) were among the signatories of the manifesto entitled *La Révolution d'abord et toujours*, in which the following words occurred: 'Nous ne sommes pas des utopistes: cette Révolution nous ne la concevons que sous sa forme sociale. S'il existe . . . de l'individu.' Remember, this was some years before the appearance of the so-called 'left-wing' English poets – Auden, Spender, Day Lewis – some years before the 'conversion' of M. André Gide (or of M. Edgell Rickword).

This was not just a passing mood of intellectual revolt: the revolutionary political attitude of the Surrealists is inseparably bound up with their attitude to poetry. André Breton in his recent book *Position politique du surréalisme*, writes: 'Notre collaboration à l'Appel à la lutte du 10 février 1934, conjurant pour nous de "tour d'ivoire".'

No, it really cannot be said that because certain poems are not about strikes, factories, the armaments camp, – or whatever, the authors of such poems are therefore 'unwilling or unable really to face the concrete facts of the world in which they live.' The truth is that rather than constituting

---

Literary Review (May 1936), pp. 6-8. It has not been possible to obtain a copy of this issue; the text of the article has been reconstructed from D.G.'s Notebook Add. MS 56040 in the British Library.

a refuge or retreat from reality, such poems are written in opposition to, or in defence of the existing conception of the real.

An attempted definition of poetry from the point of view of a Surrealist poet is the following, by Paul Eluard: – 'Caprice, contradiction, violence, – they are poetry; in other words, poetry is a perpetual struggle, life's very principle, the queen of unrest.' If this is so, how then can poetry ever be reconciled with a system, one of whose chief aims is to make men passive, docile and smug? That is what I mean when I say that Surrealist poetry constitutes not a *retreat* from, but an *assault* on the current conception of reality. The poet whose work is devoted to achieving a more complete freedom for the imagination, to discovering the complicated, startling and poetic relationships that exist between all *things* (images), cannot be indifferent to the social system in which he lives, a social system doing everything in its power to thwart him in his endeavour to create a richer and more lively universe – not for himself alone, but for everyone who has eyes to read and imagination to comprehend with. 'Poetry should be made by all, not one.' [Lautréamont: quoted in D.G.'s Notebook Add. MS 56042]

Dylan Thomas, for instance, is such a poet. Is he politically indifferent, opposed to communal construction, unconcerned with the affairs of the real world? – 'I take my stand,' he says, 'with any revolutionary body that asserts it to be the right of all men to share equally and impartially, every production of man from man and from the sources of production at man's disposal, for only through such an essentially revolutionary body can there be the possibility of a communal art.' [*New Verse*, 11]

The answer of Paul Eluard is even clearer: 'All poets worthy of the name are fighting the system of exploitation side by side with the workers. For true poetry is the camp of those who are fighting for the deliverance of man' – such instances could be multiplied indefinitely.

The imaginatively inventive poet is the iconoclast par excellence. The unshackled imagination, expressed via poetry, is opposed to all fixity of forms, all permanent stability of concepts, all stereotyping of images.' (The new number of *Cahiers d'art*, devoted to the recent work of Picasso* – poet in words, now, as well as in paint – makes this very clear, particularly in the article by Christian Zervos, 'Fait social et vision cosmique'.) That is why the Nazis, in their frantic attempts to turn men into brutes, in order to perpetuate a form of society now played out have found it necessary to suppress many other things, all manifestations of an 'advanced' or 'experimental' order in poetry and in art. Nothing distinguished man from the brute so much as the exercise of his imagination.

---

* Editor's note: 'Picasso 1930-1935' (Paris: Editions Cahiers d'Art, 1936).

The position, as I see it, is this: The poet today is separated from the masses by a high, thick wall, made of prejudice, misapprehension and ignorance. The wall is deliberately constructed by the existing order. The part of the poet is *not* to climb over the wall to the other side, as certain poets seem to be trying to do at present, by 'writing down to the masses' (though this attempt can be of no avail, and is doomed to failure, since the number of readers for anything labelled 'poetry' at all is at present strictly limited), simplifying their work and thus eliminating from it all that is authentically poetic – curious, capricious, complex), for in doing so he must inevitably leave his treasure behind him. The part of the poet is to do everything in his power to bring about the collapse of the wall, and the wall's demolition can only be accomplished by proletarian revolution.

A considerable part of Marx's *Das Kapital* is devoted to demonstrating how the transformation of quality into quantity is brought about, and vice versa. Can this law be equally well applied to poetry as to economics? I believe it can.

The revolution has no need of poetry, but poetry has great need of the revolution.

NOTE ON SYMBOLISM

It sometimes happens that one is given the power with which to extract a symbol from the incoherent welter of existence. The origin of this power is mysterious. And to the Reason, equally mysterious, and therefore suspect, is the nature of the satisfaction which such a symbol can afford the mind.

The symbol in question may be as simple as a polished stone, of clearly defined outline and unambiguous significance; and likewise, it may be labyrinthine in its complexity, and subject, even within the limits of a single identity, to constant metamorphosis.

The symbol has subjective objectivity. It may be described as reflection, precipitate, crystallization, image talisman, and so on, according to the disposition of its creator, or of its beholder; but it escapes all final definition.

The function of the symbol being unavoidably associated both with poetry and with the dream, it can never be given complete distinction. It may legitimately be defined in terms both of poetry proper and of 'unorganized' dream; yet the essential function of the symbol, considered as an absolute, surpasses that performed by either of these phenomena.

The symbol is a bridge between subjective reality of personal experience and the objective reality of the Spirit. When poetry or dream can be said to be controlled by a dynamism of spiritual, as distinct from merely somatic or unconscious mental, origin, then this control must be exercised by means of the intervention of the symbol.

To the 'pure' Reason, the Spirit can never be more than hypothesis, but, at the same time, it transcends the Reason, having often been known to attain a degree of independent consciousness of itself strong enough to enable it to suspend at will, without doubt or retrospection, the rational jurisdiction of the Super-ego.

When Reason banishes the Spirit, as it is apt to do when it confuses spiritual intuition with the blind and wishful suppositions of the physical instincts, or when it supposes its absolute authority to be threatened by

---

'Note on Symbolism: its role in metaphysical thought', *Poetry Quarterly*, Vol. 8, No. 2 (Summer 1946), pp. 86-7. Also in Michel Rémy, *David Gascoyne, ou l'urgence de l'inexprimé* (Presses Universitaires de Nancy, 1984), pp. 141-2.

forces which it cannot 'understand', Man immediately begins to lose his ancient sense of mission and of purpose on the earth. The increasingly apparent futility of his existence becomes a source of constantly augmented torment to him; and in order to bring the incomprehensible suffering of this existence to the only end that unredeemable futility is fit for, he hastens to prepare a final orgy of destruction for himself and all his works. For Man cannot endure for long the constant imminence of the aimless Void which is concomitant with denial of the Spirit.

The Spirit can return to life only through the secret channel of our inmost individuality. Each man must undertake alone and in silence the task of creating a new spiritual reality with which to fill the Void forever underlying objective and empirical reality's changing and uncertain surface.

The Void itself cannot be apprehended except by means of a symbolic expression (self-contradictory representation). By realizing such a term of reference we can free ourselves from the terrible non-existence implicit in the negation of the Spirit; for we then become aware of being able to choose between this non-existence and the possibility of a negation of the negation. Thus may the Spirit's awareness of itself and of the predicament which threatens it be revived within us. Not until then will it become possible once more to attribute a tolerable human reality to our life on the earth; which still remains, in spite of all the compendious clear-cut explanations of Science and Reason, the most absolutely mysterious and inspiring subject-object for the contemplation of God's Poetic Imagination.

LEON CHESTOV

'Qui voudra suivre *Chestov?'* BENJAMIN FONDANE

I

As far as it is possible to judge, there exists at present among the intelligent reading public in England only a dim and confused conception of the significance of Existential Philosophy and its situation in relation to the rest of contemporary thought. It is unlikely however that the confusion that reigns here in people's minds with regard to this philosophic movement is anything like the dense and inextricable confusion regarding it that must by this time have become general in France. Intellectual discursivity, having sensed the menace to itself that a proper understanding of the essential thought of the philosophers who may rightly be described as existential would represent, seems to have found the topic of *Existentialisme* more stimulating than any other to have cropped up in France for a long while and to have set about muddling the crucial issues involved with a dogmatizing polemical gusto such as is fortunately seldom equalled on this side of the Channel. Here, stifling our resentment at being as usual about a decade behind the intellectual development of the rest of Europe, we generally miss the real point, pass on garbled accounts of what it is all supposed to be about and are wearily deprecating in our comments on it.

When I refer to Existential Philosophy, I should like it to be quite clear from the start that I do not mean this expression to be understood to designate the philosophy associated with the movement headed by the brilliant ex-professor, publicist and playwright Jean-Paul Sartre. If one would form a just estimate of the distance that separates Sartre's *Existentialisme* from the kind of thought that in what I am going to say I shall refer to as existential, one should try to imagine Pascal writing a poetic novel about the gulf that he felt to be yawning at his side all the time towards the end of his life. Existentialism is the post-experimental

---

'Léon Chestov: After Ten Years' Silence', *Horizon* 118 (October 1949), pp. 213-29. Also in David Gascoyne, *Journal 1936-37* (Enitharmon Press, 1980), pp. 127-44.

intellectual exploitation of the experience of existing. The kind of philosophy that I wish to discuss is actual spiritual activity. Not all that goes on within man is what the Marxists call 'mere reflection'.

Frequently heard and familiar enough though the names of the representatives of Cartesian Existentialism have become, it is extremely seldom that anyone refers to the one great modern thinker who can justly be described as a representative of authentically existential philosophy, Léon Chestov. For every mention of Chestov's name during the ten years that have passed since his death, there have been I should imagine at least five hundred references to Jean-Paul Sartre. While it would be untrue to say that Chestov remains quite unknown in this country, since three books of his have been translated and published here[1] – *Anton Chekov and Other Essays*, with an introduction by Middleton Murry, in 1916, *All Things are Possible*, introduced by D. H. Lawrence, in 1920, and in 1932, introduced by Richard Rees, *In Job's Balances*, a book uniting in one volume several representative short works – it is still necessary to say that this great, profoundly disturbing Russian thinker, whose message for the present time is quite as significant as his friend Berdyaev's, is unjustly neglected and his importance altogether underestimated.

Léon Chestov, exiled after 1920 by the Soviet Politbureaucratic revolutionaries to whom his philosophy was insufficiently optimistic to be useful to their purposes, was a Voice Crying in the Wilderness his whole life long. *Vox Clamantis in Deserto* is the sub-title of one of his last works, *Kierkegaard and Existential Philosophy*, published in French translation a year or two before the first appearance of Sartre, who has always resolutely ignored him, though the world described with such long-drawn-out repugnance in his own imaginative works is certainly a desert. It is not surprising, however, that Chestov's voice has remained inaudible to one who has declared, during a discussion of the epistemological foundations of Existentialism, that the Absolute is in Descartes. The Absolute that is to be found in Descartes's Cogito is absolute self-sufficiency, and if this produces a desert, Sartre's superb intelligence can still reign supreme in it and immediately reduce to silence all voices crying 'Prepare ye . . .'.

---

[1] *Anton Chekov and Other Essays*, Modern Russian Library (Dublin and London: Maunsel & Co. Ltd., 1916).

All Things are Possible (The Apotheosis of Groundlessness), authorized translation by S. S. Koteliansky (Martin Secker, 1920).

In Job's Balances: On the Sources of the Eternal Truths, translated by Camilla Coventry and C. A. Macartney (J. M. Dent & Sons Ltd., 1932).

Coming as the most recent successor of two or three of the most original and significant thinkers of the nineteenth century – Kierkegaard, Nietzsche, Dostoievsky – Chestov may be considered to have made it possible at present to think of Existential Philosophy as such, that is to say to see it as a distinct current of thought with special distinguishing characteristics and central preoccupations, with a task and destiny to fulfil in the history of the spiritual crisis of Western man in the present age. The *Existentialisme* of Sartre does not belong to this current of thought. It is a perversion of the thought that inspired Kierkegaard and Dostoievsky (the Knight of Faith and the Underground Man) based on a typically French Cartesian misunderstanding of the essence of the special contribution of these solitary individualists to European philosophical speculation. Heidegger's position in relation to this situation is a quite special one, which I cannot begin to discuss here, but it should not be confused with Sartre's, simply on the supposition that they are both 'atheists', as innumerable facile vulgarizers and subtle casuists have attempted to do during the last five or ten years. What critics really mean when they state, as for instance Mr J. V. Langmead-Casserley does in a recent book, *The Christian in Philosophy* (Faber), that 'in writers like Heidegger and Sartre we are confronted by an existentialism which is specifically atheist', is simply that the assumption of these philosophers is that contemporary man is not a conscious believer in God. To assume this does not make one an atheist; and when Sartre does also announce himself as being specifically an atheist, this is a professional naïveté on his part. The now universal state of human existence cannot be said to be one of continual, profound, everyday faith in the living God. To have real faith in God is not at present natural to man in the world. To be a wholehearted and practically consistent believer is to be an exception to the normal condition of man in the twentieth century. It is the universal, *a priori* condition of human existence that is the subject existentialism undertakes to describe, to begin with, and the exceptions can only have significance in relation to a 'normal' or 'ordinary' state that has been first properly defined and analysed. It becomes clear after the initial examination of the ordinary state of man's existence has been made that there exists in it a tendency towards something else, which is ordinarily resisted in ways which Heidegger in particular subjects to detailed analysis. This something else is the state which results from a change of the 'ordinary' state of existence into a more highly developed state. The state of the conscious and deliberate atheist and the state of the authentic Christian both represent a higher development of existence than that of the ordinary. The only thing that any existentialist philosopher could be said to set out to convert anyone to is responsible choice. The important point that

Sartre misses is that neither belief nor disbelief can be taught to anyone, and atheism, as soon as it becomes specific, is a belief: a belief in the non-existence of the spiritual dimension of reality, resting on a refusal to recognize that there is a Ground of Being.

II

'Socrates spent the month following his verdict in incessant conversations with his pupils and friends. That is what it is to be a beloved master and to have disciples. You can't even die quietly,' wrote Léon Chestov in 1905, thirty-four years before his own death. 'The best death is really the one which is considered the worst,' he wrote: 'to die alone, in a foreign land, in a poor-house, or, as they say, like a dog under a hedge.'

Chestov did not die in a poor-house, but otherwise he may be said to have achieved this ambition. His only disciple in 1939 was the Roumanian-born Jewish poet and philosopher, Benjamin Fondane, who was destined to a death in the gas-chambers at Birkenau six years later. At the end of his life, Chestov was resigned to being neglected or mischievously misinterpreted by his contemporaries, who if ever they referred to him, did so to pour scorn on his crazy 'anti-rationalism', being unable to observe that few thinkers in the history of philosophy have had so realistic a respect for the power of human reason, even though this was a respect tempered by a realization of its limitations and of its hypnotic influence over those whom it enslaves. He did not want disciples – he did not even want to have pupils or a class of students, which for a philosopher in these days is rare. He believed philosophical activity to consist in absolutely undivided truth-seeking, and this he could not reconcile with telling people they need seek no more, should they happen also to be seeking Truth, but simply attend his classes and pay attention while he told it them, the proper fee at the end of the term, and the maximum amount of lip-service to the importance of his ideas. To adopt the role of a teacher of this kind, would then have been altogether in contradiction with the inner position, the adoption of which is a necessary prerequisite of Existential Philosophy, properly so-called. It is perfectly extraordinary how this simple fundamental distinction which makes Existential Philosophy *existential*, is still so universally and completely ignored, particularly by professors.

It was not unintentially that in introducing Léon Chestov I began by referring to his death. In Chestov's philosophical writings the thought of death is like a constant groundnote; death was to him a starting-point as well as the ultimate goal for speculative thought. The first and most indispensable prerequisite for whoever would undertake the task of philosophy was for Chestov not the rational faculty or cogitative power, but courage. All advances in the realm of human thought are the result of victory over fear. The justification of Socratic doubt, which questions the foundedness of all commonly accepted truths as a matter of discipline, is in the realization that we are ever apt to use our faculty of rational thinking less for the purpose of arriving at the truth than for that of protecting ourselves from fear of the unknown.

Chestov addressed his philosophy not to a class of passive students, but to an individual reader, his interlocutor. With regard to the fruitfulness of the normal master-pupil relationship, or what has become in the modern world the normal relationship between teacher and taught, he was from the very beginning completely sceptical; but if he had not had some faith in the possibility and efficacy of communicating real philosophic thought he would hardly have continued to the end of his life to publish books in which an interlocutor is continually stimulated to reconsider the views of other great philosophers as well as his own views of them.

Chestov in many of his works leads his interlocutor through a careful and penetrating analysis of certain of the writings of Tolstoy, Dostoievsky and Chekhov to the possible recognition of the startling and difficult fact that there exist certain situations and states, such as have to be passed through at least once by all who are mortal, wherein a man may suddenly have to admit that the ordinary, reassuring truths and assumptions upon which we all base our everyday life and which it might well seem outrageous even to question publicly, are no longer able to satisfy him, but seem to the contrary to have been simply the easily available, conventionally legitimized means whereby men commonly stupefy themselves so as to continue to be able to remain fast asleep even when wide awake and busily occupied in carrying on very competently their no doubt highly important and altogether worthwhile daily affairs.

For most of us, this moment of dislocation, of panic, of abrupt unfamiliarity and questionableness of everything hitherto regarded as certain, is throughout our whole lives postponed, evaded, and its possibility and implications absolutely denied and ignored. But as Chestov took pains to make vivid to his interlocutor, with the approach of death, this moment may become increasingly difficult to postpone. For it is in part the moment of fully recognizing the truth of the fact of Death itself, and of its immense enigmatic significance for the whole of the human life that leads to it.

It would be a great mistake to regard Chestov's preoccupation with Death as a gloomy aberration or morbidity; it is in fact a thoroughly normal and healthy preoccupation for a philosopher and it is the ordinary current attitude to the darker aspect of reality that is morbid. It is generally far too easily forgotten today, in discussions of modern philosophy, that there have been in the history of thought few definitions of philosophy's purpose which more deserve serious attention, the attention of our second thoughts, than the Platonic-Socratic 'preparation in view of death'. Most modern philosophers, restlessly haunted by the ambition of succeeding in the enterprise of making philosophy an important department of the imposing edifice of Materialist Science, or rather the indispensable epistemological handmaid of an authoritative world-hegemony of laboratory and classroom workers and mathematicians, do not care, it would seem, to be reminded of this supposedly nonsensical formulation of the purpose of speculative thought; indeed, they seem unanimously to take it for granted that we should all be inarticulately resigned to being dead already.

In this respect, Heidegger's philosophy is an exception; in it the way all men regard Death most of the time they are alive, or rather the quasi-universal Western educated habit of evading real seriousness – and an appearance of seriousness is more than almost anything else made to serve to facilitate this evasion – has been treated as the subject of a rigorous, detailed analysis. For Heidegger, resolution-in-view-of-death is an experienced reality that is to be regarded as the necessary foundation of all human life having personal authenticity. Until we have undergone the realization that comes with a moment of the kind I tried to describe just now, we shall be all the time as it were running away from our true self, unable to accept life in its complete seriousness, continually anxious to keep always to the most superficial level of experience where everything is a matter of course and nothing new or difficult ever disturbs the unexceptional monotonously humdrum normality of a mediocre existence.

Martin Heidegger, in making the analysis to be found in *Sein und Zeit* of everyday banality and the inauthentic conception of death that is based on hearsay and clichés and not on a profound personal realization, was partly inspired originally by a story of Tolstoy's, *The Death of Ivan Ilyitch*. It happens that this story was among the later writings of Tolstoy that Chestov examines at some length in his book *The Revelations of Death*, in an essay entitled 'The Last Judgement'. The moral to which Chestov's reflections on Tolstoy's greatest short story led him, he has expressed in what seems to me a rather more cogent form than that given it in that essay, in another of his writings, 'Revolt and Submission', where he says:

> Despite his reason man is a being subject to the power of the moment. And even when he seeks to consider all things *sub specie aeternitatis*, his philosophy is usually *sub specie temporis* – indeed, of the present hour. This is why men reckon so little with death, as

though death did not exist. When a man thinks on his dying hour – how do his values and standards change! But death lies in the future, which will not be – so every one feels. And there are many similar things of which one has to remind not only the common herd but also the philosophers who know so much that is superfluous and have forgotten, or have never known, what is most important.

After I had been reflecting quite recently on these words of Chestov and was beginning to plan the present dissertation, I happened idly to pick up an anthology of old English poetry, and on the page at which I opened it, this is the poem I found:

> A good that never satisfies the mind,
> A beauty fading like the April showers,
> A sweet with floods of gall that runs combined,
> A pleasure passing ere the thought made ours,
> An honour that more fickle is than wind,
> A glory at opinion's frown that lowers,
> A treasury that bankrupt time devours,
> A knowledge than grave ignorance more blind,
> A vain delight our equals to command,
> A style of greatness, in effect a dream,
> A swelling thought of holding sea and land,
> A servile lot, decked with a pompous name
> Are the strange ends we toil for here below
> Till wisest death makes us our errors know.

Several of the fourteen lines of this sonnet of Drummond of Hawthornden seem to me to refer specifically to illusions which today as much as ever are particularly influential, illusions of the kind which without our being in the least aware of it may colour and modify the whole of our outlook, fundamental ideas and behaviour, with the result that we become unreal human beings, maladapted to the real world we live in, absurdly confident of our sanity, common sense and grip on things, all the while being objectively no more than inefficient bunglers, wasters, and self-deceivers.

Those who are familiar with Kierkegaard's life and thought will recall that his real career as a serious philosopher with a great vocation did not begin until he had gone through the experience of what he called 'the great earthquake'. Now there is no doubt that this terrible and profoundly effective experience which forced upon him certain essential realizations about himself which it may be he could not have reached by any less drastic way, was a crisis precipitated by the death of his father.

Thus, it may be said, then, that Existential Philosophy as we know it today had its origins in the death of the philosopher's father. There is a deep connection between this fact and the truth expressed by Chestov in another passage from the work I quoted from just now in which he says:

> As soon as man feels that God is not, he suddenly comprehends the frightful horror and the wild folly of human temporal existence, and when he has comprehended this he awakes, perhaps not to the ultimate knowledge, but to the penultimate. Was it not so with Nietzsche, Spinoza, Pascal, Luther, Augustine, even with St Paul?

There cannot be for the Christian any reality in Christ's resurrection unless he really believes in it. Not very long after Kierkegaard's campaign against the high-toned insincerity of the Churches representing the social acknowledgement of God's reality in the clever, busy, highly respectable bourgeois world of the mid-nineteenth century, Nietzsche proclaimed to European thinking men, who had succeeded in banishing all real religious consciousness from everyday life completely, 'God is dead!'

When he has comprehended this, man awakes, perhaps not to the penultimate knowledge, but to the prepenultimate. I believe that the ultimate, or penultimate knowledge will be found to be the beginning of all really transparent apprehension of the world which scientific knowledge decomposes. This is because I have the faith of a Christian and really believe in the truth and presently imminent reality of the Resurrection, so far as I understand it.

> The ancients, to awaken from life, turned to death. The moderns flee from death in order not to awake and take pains not even to think of it. Which are the more 'practical'? Those who compare earthly life to sleep and wait for the miracle of the awakening, or those who see in death a sleep without dreamfaces, the perfect sleep, and while away their time with 'reasonable' and 'natural' explanations? This is the basic question of philosophy, and he who evades it evades philosophy itself.

III

It might be said that philosophy as Chestov envisaged it was, instead of being as it is supposed to be, a part of one's education, a subject studied in a course having its place in the curriculum of a university, a necessary *antidote* to one's education. Philosophy in this sense – truly Existential

Philosophy, which aims, not at making as complete and rational a discursive exposition as possible of the purely conceptional problems of existence, but at launching individuals into a more fully conscious and authentic real existence of their own, is really the beginning and foundation of a second education, one that continues throughout the lives of all of whom it might ultimately be said that they attained anything like wisdom. To begin with, it brings one to the realization that the knowledge of the world, of man, of history, of reality, with which one has been equipped by one's education, the picture one has of the reality which is the contingent context of one's life, is only a structure of more or less ready-made and on the whole passively accepted *ideas*, corresponding to the objective real world with a degree of accuracy that no one could ever hope to calculate.

The most outstanding characteristics of Chestov's philosophy are its anti-idealism and its anti-rationalism. Now both these expressions require immediate modificatory definition. Chestov was not a disbeliever in the invisible, not anti-metaphysical in the sense in which the Logical Positivists are anti-metaphysical. Philosophy can never dispense with ideas or with the use of the rational faculty. But a self-critical philosophy can become conscious that the individual thinker's ideas are necessarily only approximate and partial reflections not to be confused with what they reflect, and that the Reason with the deificatory capital R is only a collective reflection of the individual's faculty of thinking rationally re-reflected in the minds of individuals.

Idealism in the sense in which Chestov's philosophy understands the word is thinking which treats ideas as though they were the completed final end-product of thinking, whereas they can for the existing individual never be more than the means by which he thinks, convenient approximate reflections from which the thinker should continually re-detach himself and what they reflect.

To some extent, everyone is an idealist, in the sense of the word which I have been attempting to define. Undoubtedly everyone has an idea of the world we live in which is only a very approximate, and to a large extent second-hand, hearsay idea of it, and just as undoubtedly we rely on this idea that we have cultivated and allowed to grow up in our minds and come to accept it just as though it really corresponded to the actual world in its unknowable objectivity. And unless we are continually conscious of the difference between knowing a thing and thinking one knows it before having had an opportunity to do so, we are thus in danger of becoming secured against reality, which *in reality* is inevitably mysterious, being only very incompletely knowable through any one individual's experience, unaccountable in fact and perhaps still full of astonishing surprises and things of which we had never dreamed. It is only too easy to become comfortably secured against reality in this way, secured against it by an ideal reality which a kind of universal tacit agreement among us allows us to regard as identical with the only true reality, though the reason we tolerate it as a substitute is that it is what we call normal, average, safe, readily accountable, domesticated in fact to fit in with our own ordinarily egotistical purposes.

Only with a full realization of the extent to which we are all idealists of this kind, only, that is to say, with a proper realization of our actual state of Socratic ignorance, for which there can be no *a priori* truths until we have found out what they are for ourselves, can the autocritical habit of mind indispensable to a genuine philosopher begin to develop.

Anti-idealism is the result of a realization of how fatally easy it can always be to confuse an idea of a thing that one has in one's mind that came to be there as the result of our having read or been told something about someone or something, with an idea that we might have developed of the same thing if we had actually experienced knowledge of it ourselves. We remain very largely ignorant of the extent to which our knowledge is in reality knowledge of the knowledge of others. Education fosters this sort of confusion and ignorance, unless a conscious anti-idealism enables us to be continually on our guard against it. We cannot possibly do without the knowledge of others, but it is most useful to us when we are fully conscious that it is not the result of our own experience when we remember it. As soon as we become aware of the extent to which we are conditioned by and dependent on ideas, we become perceptibly more realistic and objective; at the same time we become more open-minded, tolerant, pacific and co-operative. We cease to think of ourselves as the elect, to whom the last word on our special subjects has been specially divulged by grace of the goddess of Reason; for an orderly but after a while dusty permanent model scheme of basic assumptions for referring to about Everything, we exchange a new habit, that of having a thorough spring-clean and stocktaking of all our ideas regularly at not-too-long intervals.

It may be that Chestov himself nowhere expresses what I have called his anti-idealism in quite the bald form in which I have presented it; it may be, too, that what I have said either reveals the quintessence of Chestov, or is, to the contrary, a misrepresentation of him resulting from my having used Chestov's name merely as a cover under which to pass off some idea or attitude of my own. If the latter were actually the case, I might still argue with a grain of truth that in this I had at least given an illustration of Chestov's method. At any rate, Chestov did himself express quite clearly enough the anti-idealism I have spoken of, in the following words:

Even the blind, one would think, must arrive at the conviction that matter and materialism are not the crucial issue. The most deadly enemy of the spirit everywhere is not inert matter, which in fact, as the ancients taught, and as men teach today, exists not at all, or only potentially as something illusory, pitiable, powerless, suppliant to all — the most deadly and pitiless enemies are ideas. Ideas, and ideas alone, are that with which every man must do battle who would overcome the falsehood of the world.

I think I may add here, that he who would overcome the false materialist philosophy which has so often been denounced as the real reason for the present situation in our relations with Léon Chestov's native land, the philosophy of the Communist intellectuals leading the great Party which claims to represent the toiling Russian masses, the philosophy which drove Chestov into exile after 1920, will be unable to get very far until he sees that Materialist Idealism, which does not yet realize that it ought truly to be thus so-called, confuses reflection and reflector. Certainly, there cannot be a reflection without a reflector for it to be seen in, but it is a naïve and fatal error to confuse the two on account of their being inseparable in living experience, although easily separable in reflected or theoretical experience by the (immaterial) experimenter.

It might also be added that Christian philosophy properly so-called is anti-idealist in just the sense I have been discussing, or otherwise can be only a quasi-Christian philosophy, as most philosophies since Christ, with the possible exception of such philosophy as might in a certain sense be called Socratic, have inevitably been. 'The Sabbath was made for man and not man for the Sabbath' is the classic maxim which might serve as the type for an authentically Christian anti-idealism.

For a Christian existential philosopher, all we highly rational, educated men are in reality all we still to a very large extent ignorant and unconscious men, just as all we respectable citizens are in reality all we miserable sinners.

'For we must disrobe ourselves of all false colours, and unclothe our Souls of evil Habits,' says Thomas Traherne, in *Centuries of Meditation*:

> All our Thoughts must be Infantlike and clear; the Powers of our Soul free from the Leaven of this World, and disentangled from men's conceits and customs. Grit in the eye or yellow jaundice will not let a Man see those Objects truly that are before it. And therefore it is requisite that we should be as very Strangers to the Thoughts, Customs and Opinions of men in this World, as if we were but little children.

And Kierkegaard tells us very much the same thing, in an entry in his *Journals*:

> *Truth is naked.* In order to swim one takes off one's clothes – in order to aspire to the truth one must undress in a far more inward sense, divest oneself of all one's inward clothes, of thoughts, conceptions, selfishness, etc., before one is sufficiently naked.

This attitude of continual auto-criticism, which I have characterized as Anti-Idealism, is recognizably the same as that which Chestov expresses in the following passage from his *All Things Are Possible*:

> There is no mistake about it, nobody *wants* to think. I do not speak here of logical thinking. That, like any other natural function, gives man great pleasure. For this reason philosophical systems, however complicated, arouse real and permanent interest in the public provided they only require from man the logical exercise of the mind, and nothing else. But to think – really to think – surely this means a relinquishing of logic. It means living a new life. It means a permanent sacrifice of the dearest habits, tastes, attachments, without even the assurance that the sacrifice will bring any compensation.

IV

What superficial commentators have unanimously described as 'anti-rationalism' and even 'irrationalism' in Chestov, is really nothing of the sort, but a necessary implication of his anti-idealism and a result of his unusual objectivity of mind, or what amounts to the same thing, of his highly auto-critical habit of thought (prior to the actual approximate formulation of his thought in writing, that is to say). A thinker who is above all aware of his own ignorance and uncertainty, who is not deceived by his ability to discover and repeat impressively sounding formulae into supposing that he has solved a problem and said the last word on a subject, who is constantly asking questions, and questioning where it is the rule to see nothing questionable, will not be satisfied for long with the criteria which simple-minded rationalists regard as the sole supreme arbiters of their thought. This does not mean that he must therefore despise Reason or logic; it simply indicates that he is not limited by the common confusion between what man has discovered, and what he has invented for purposes of convenience, in his mind.

No. 267 of Pascal's *Pensées* may relevantly be quoted here: 'The last proceeding of reason is to recognize that there is an infinity of things which are beyond it. It is but feeble if it does not see so far as to know this. But if natural things are beyond it, what will be said of supernatural?' Also No. 272: 'There is nothing so conformable to reason as this disavowal of reason.'

The individual human reason becomes more rational as a result of losing its idealist awe of the Cartesian Goddess of Reason, who is never satisfied until everything has been reduced to clarity and distinctness, even if by artificial means; in recognizing its inevitable limitations and in liberating itself from the delusory self-sufficiency of the Cartesian cogitator, reason transcends itself and can become reintegrated with the creative imagination.

In a previous quotation, Chestov asks whether real thinking does not mean a relinquishing of logic. That he means by this an emancipation from complete dependence on logic is obvious from the following passage from the same book (*All Things Are Possible*):

> To discard logic as an instrument, a means or aid for acquiring knowledge, would be extravagant. Why should we? For the sake of consequentialism? i.e. for logic's very self? But logic, as an aim in itself, or even as the *only* means to knowledge, is a different matter. Against this one must fight even if he has against him all the authorities of thought beginning with Aristotle.

Existential Philosophy cannot be understood unless it is seen to be a protest and a struggle, fighting against not only Aristotle, but also against, for instance, Descartes, Spinoza, Hegel, Spencer, Husserl and Carnap. Its objectively critical attitude to the notion of Pure Reason and its refusal to make itself dependent on any predetermined method or criteria is related to its preoccupation with the problem of Original Sin and the hypothesis that the present condition of man is a fallen and not a supernatural one. Since man began to become civilized, his condition has been necessarily an unnatural one. Reason, the use of which has led to the progressive development of human civilization, is nevertheless not an entirely unmixed blessing. It is the blessing promised to Eve by the serpent and comes from the tree of which the fruit is death and limitation, not life and freedom. Existential Philosophy is a struggle for liberation. With it, an essentially Christian philosophy, as distinct from a nominally and superficially Christian philosophy, enters the history of Western thought. This is true even of Nietzsche, if not of the whole of Nietzsche (in whom the 'will to stupidity' and the 'will to power' not infrequently come into stultifying conflict), at least of that part of his thought which still remains creatively valuable; for Christianity had become by Nietzsche's time so profoundly self-contradictory on account of the predominance of pagan ethical principles in European thought surviving even Luther and the Reformation (the Renaissance and the secularization of classical learning putting back with one hand what the Lutheran Reformation had taken away with the other) that the genuinely Christian liberation in thought had to assume the guise of Anti-Christ. It is Nietzsche's greatest fault and weakness that he failed to understand this situation and his relation to it anything like as fully as he might have done.

Chestov is of all the great existentialist philosophers – the others are Pascal, Kierkegaard and Nietzsche – the one who is most necessary to a true understanding of the significance of existential philosophy in general and of its role in the crisis of modern thought. He is the philosopher of Tragedy and of Paradox; a seeker after the 'one thing needful', a solitary thinker whose despair does not counsel us to come to terms with defeatist resignation, but can inspire in those capable of it the violence with which alone is the Kingdom of Heaven to be taken. His message is just that which is needed as a corrective to the dispassionately impotent, science-seduced teaching of present-day British Academic philosophy. 'The don is the eunuch,' as Kierkegaard wrote in his *Journals*, 'but he has not emasculated himself for the sake of the Kingdom of Heaven, but on the contrary, in order to fit better into this characterless world.' Chestov never made the slightest attempt to fit in with the characterless modern world; perhaps that is why he has been so largely ignored by the intellectual representatives of this world till now; but it is also the reason why one can be confident that he will eventually be heard nevertheless, for such thinking as his is for modern philosophy increasingly 'the one thing needful'.

'Power without wisdom is dangerous,' Bertrand Russell went so far as to admit in a broadcast talk not long ago, 'and what our age needs is wisdom, even more than knowledge. Given wisdom, the power conferred by science can bring a new degree of well-being to all mankind: without wisdom, it can only bring destruction.' This would appear to indicate a belated readiness on the part of an authoritative representative of scientifically aspiring materialist Thought to turn at last to the consideration of what Unamuno has called 'the most tragic problem of philosophy', or at least to concede that scientific thought and wisdom are two quite different things, since they became separated by the University dictatorship of the professoriat, which exiles human subjectivity and silences the private feelings of the individual's heart. The utterances of Bertrand Russell in view of the crisis of contemporary society should be compared with the answer of the old professor to the young student whose personal crisis drives her to seek his wise advice in Chekhov's *A Dreary Story*.

Supposing the philosophers who speak in the name of scientific materialism do gradually become aware of their lack of wisdom, and begin to try to become philosophers in the true sense of the word (the etymological definition is 'one who loves wisdom'), where are they to turn? Existential Philosophy does not give itself out to be wisdom; though it looks rather as though Sartre, for instance, would have no objection to the public making use of his philosophy as though it were. Existential philosophers may be said to be in general agreement, however, with Pascal's saying: 'I can only approve of those who seek with lamentation'. Should anyone turn to Chestov for wisdom, this is what he has to say to him:

> Although there have been on earth many wise men who knew much that is infinitely more valuable than all the treasures for which men are ready even to sacrifice their lives, still wisdom is to us a book with seven seals, a hidden hoard upon which we cannot lay our hands. Many – the vast majority – are even seriously convinced that philosophy is a most tedious and painful occupation to which are doomed some miserable wretches who enjoy the odious privilege of being called philosophers. I believe that even professors of philosophy, the more clever of them, not seldom share this opinion and suppose that therein lies the secret of their science, revealed to the initiate alone. Fortunately, the position is otherwise. It may be that mankind is destined never to change in this respect, and a thousand years hence men will care much more about 'deductions' theoretical and practical, from the truth than about truth itself; but real philosophers, men who know what they want and at what they aim, will hardly be embarrassed by this. They will utter their truths as before, without in the least considering what conclusions will be drawn from them by the lovers of logic.

In case the end of this passage should seem to lend itself to any ambiguity, I think I may add that it is unlikely that Chestov, in speaking of 'real philosophers', was thinking of the representatives of bourgeois materialism, thinkers who also certainly 'know what they want and at what they aim', i.e., knowledge, i.e., power.

THOMAS CARLYLE

Just as the individual man may aspire to become something, so does the age; and this is what it aspires to: it would build up the established order, abolish God, and through fear of men cow the individual into a mouse's hole – but this is what God will not have, and He employs the exactly opposite tactics: He employs the individual to provoke the established order out of its self-complacency.

SØREN KIERKEGAARD, *Training in Christianity*

In January 1836, two years after first taking up residence in Cheyne Row in Chelsea, Thomas Carlyle wrote in his *Journal*:

> I thought to-day up at Hyde Park Corner, seeing all the carriages dash hither and thither, and so many human bipeds cheerily hurrying along, 'There you go, brothers, in your gilt carriages and prosperities, better or worse, and make an extreme bother and confusion, the devil very largely in it. And I too, by the blessing of the Maker of me, I too am authorized and equipped by Heaven's Act of Parliament to do that small secret somewhat, and will do it without any consultation of yours. Let us be brothers, therefore, or at most silent peaceable neighbours, and each go his own way.

He went his way, and did indeed accomplish his secret somewhat; and at this distance it appears to be anything but small. Now his statue is to be found on the Chelsea Embankment; and at Westminster, almost as much a monument to Carlyle as to the only Christian dictator known to History, outside the House of Commons, stands the statue of the man whom Carlyle succeeded in persuading Englishmen to reconsider and duly to honour, Oliver Cromwell.

From early manhood to old age, Carlyle was aware of a vocation, a duty, and responsibility: to bear witness to the Divine nature of the true man, and to speak and write the Truth as far as it lay in him to do so, and thus to transmit the message of God to man in his generation. To

---

Thomas Carlyle, Supplement to British Book News No. 23, published for the British Council & the National Book League by Longmans, Green & Co. (1952).

the sophisticated modern reader, this will seem an odd and outmoded solemn way of speaking; but unless one realizes that this was indeed how Carlyle himself conceived his life's task, and that it is to just this exceptional seriousness that his writing owes its strength, one will not be likely to form anything like a just estimate of Carlyle's importance. If there is anything that ought more than another thing to be said at present, halfway through the twentieth century, about the importance of Carlyle, it is that he is more than a great Victorian writer, he is one of our great national prophets, and as such, a writer whose message is still full of import to living men and women. For the time being, his situation is much the same as that of another great Victorian prose writer, Ruskin; if either of them is referred to, it is often for the purpose of drawing attention to the pitiable or distasteful nature of his character and private life; what interests modern critics seems to be far less what they had to say than the unsuccessful nature of their marriages.

The ideal unread Carlyle of today, the popular image of him, that is to say, by which his reality is hidden from most people at present, is a dyspeptic, irascible old man in a dressing-gown, an egoist alternately cruel and indifferent to his too clever wife, and an early prophet of Fascism and the cult of the Superman.

Instead of attempting an argued refutation of such unverisimilitude, let me quote a remark made by Leigh Hunt, who for many years was a close neighbour of the Carlyles: 'I believe that what Mr Carlyle loves better than his fault-finding, with all its eloquence, is the face of any human creature that looks suffering and loving and sincere'; which is not the sort of thing that is likely to be said about any man unless there is a very good reason for it. Elizabeth Barrett Browning, in a letter to a friend written in 1851, said of Carlyle: 'It is difficult to conceive of a more interesting human soul, I think. All the bitterness is love with the point reversed.' And another revealing couple of sentences are two of his own, from a letter to his wife written after a period of stomach and domestic trouble (two kinds of trouble which really were practically synonymous for Carlyle): 'Nay, to tell you the truth, your anger at me . . . was itself sometimes a kind of comfort to me. I thought, "Well, she has strength enough to be cross and ill-natured at me; she is not all softness and affection and weakness".'

The fact, which must be mentioned before I proceed further, that there are *two Carlyles*, has been the subject of a distinguished book of criticism by Mr Osbert Burdett; and I say the fact advisedly, for it seems to me that this is not a matter merely of one critic's speculative theory. There are two Carlyles almost as indubitably as there are two Hegels, two Wordsworths. What factor should be pointed to as having been most responsible for the transition from the first to the second, it is a delicate matter to decide, as this transition cannot be precisely dated. London, which was irresistible to him, and which he could never leave for long after the move from Scotland in 1834, did something to him, no doubt, and something more than weary, exasperate, and sadden him. His own eventual success may have done something to him, besides intensifying his sense of the hypocrisy of Britain in the Crystal Palace Age. His mind did not grow weaker, but much sorrow seems to have benumbed it; and perhaps, after all, much though the determining influence on his work of his digestive and nervous systems has been exaggerated by journalists, it was the Fiend Dyspepsia that finally eroded the keen edge of his thought, and led him to resort increasingly often to the reiteration of his own formulae. Before leaving the subject, one can but ask whether the influence on Carlyle's life of his friendship with Lady Harriet Baring, or rather, with the Ashburtons, since Lord Ashburton, Lady Harriet's husband, remained also his close friend until his death, may not have had something to do with the change. The Seer of Craigenputtock and the Sage of Chelsea, though one and the same man, are not, whatever it was that transformed the one into the other, one and the same thinker; nor can it be said that half a lifetime's experience of life in the British capital, not without many encounters with *le beau monde*, contributed any notable addition to the Sage's wisdom.

Carlyle's first important book, one of the most astonishing first books by any author of genius of the nineteenth century, was entirely conceived and written on his native heath. And in *Sartor Resartus* we may find as disillusioned a picture of the true nature of early Victorian society – in the chapter in which an Irish family meal, and an English aristocrat's (or parvenu's? this is not specified) toilet, are shown us in contrasting tableaux as illustrative of the vast yawning chasm that at that time separated the social extremes – as any of the lurid cartoons to be found in the *Latter-Day Pamphlets* or later writings. There crept into his later analyses of what was wrong with society at least one fundamental error that vitiates a good deal of what he had to say on this subject during the second half of his life: the quasi-Manichean notion of a God who loves 'good citizens' and detests criminals.

Thomas Carlyle was one of the sternest critics of the nineteenth century's special pride, the rise and progress of Democracy, yet he himself was one of the most striking examples of a kind of triumph which is thought to be one of Democracy's chief justifications. The son of a Scots house-builder and contractor, of simple working-class family, Carlyle early in young manhood became the translator and personal friend of undisputably the greatest and most influential man in Europe, Goethe;

and in his old age Queen Victoria sought to make his acquaintance as having himself become one of the most influential great men of her reign. In his early life he and his wife lived in what were then called 'the most straitened of circumstances'; before he died his writings, not one of which was ever influenced by the least monetary consideration, had made him a wealthy independent man, able to contribute anonymously to many philanthropic causes. His life is an irreproachable example of the achievement of the Hero as Man of Letters.

Before he died, Carlyle had already become the Grand Old Man of Victorian Literature, the 'Sage of Chelsea', and it is this figure of him, as represented in the famous Whistler portrait, that has remained in the popular imagination ever since. One of the ways in which the reading public protects itself from dynamic influences is that of prematurely canonizing the disturbing genius, and circulating a picturesque legend about him accompanied by some poster-like pictorial image and an easily memorized cliché, slogan, or quotation. Acquaintance with this superficial epitome-effigy dispenses one from the effort of reading the collected works of the writer thus represented, whose living essence from then on is hidden from view and becomes less and less known to posterity.

One of the most frequently repeated of modern misunderstandings of Carlyle's is the idea that, because he was a critic of Democracy and an admirer of Heroes, he must have been one of the thinkers who prepared the way for Totalitarianism, along with Houston Stewart Chamberlain and the Comte de Gobineau. This is a disgraceful misunderstanding, and could only have grown so common in a society which had ceased to know any longer what it means to *believe* in anything higher than self-interest and the necessity for compromise. It is one of the many prevalent mild forms of insanity to believe that one's critics are always one's enemies. If what they say is true, they are on the contrary one's best friends. What Carlyle loathed and detested, and denounced so fervidly, was not the Democracy we know now that we really do want to achieve and perpetuate, but the early nineteenth-century misconception masquerading under that name. If the last hundred years have witnessed a very considerable transformation in the popular understanding of what is meant by Democracy, and at least it is certain that no one today really believes that it means *laissez-faire*, then Carlyle is certainly one of the writers whom we have to thank most for the change.

The thing that Carlyle had to tell the society of his time was that it had departed from Truth and Sincerity, and that the materialist ideal of profit and prosperity which, with the newly-laid-down railways and the ever more triumphant progress of industrial development on every hand, was whirling everyone away towards a future of entirely delusory glory, was a base and ungodly ideal. How vehemently and how repetitively he said just this, and in what accents of tremendous, reverberative denunciation and admonition!

Unhappy Workers, unhappier Idlers, unhappy men and women of this actual England. We are yet very far from an answer, and there will be no existence for us without finding one. 'A fair day's-wages for a fair day's-work': it is as just a demand as Governed men ever made of Governing. It is the everlasting right of man. Indisputable as Gospels, as arithmetical multiplication-tables: it must and will have itself fulfilled; – and yet, in these times of ours, with what enormous difficulty, next-door to impossibility!

For the times are really strange; of a complexity intricate with all the new width of the ever widening world; times here of half-frantic velocity of impetus, there of the deadest-looking stillness and paralysis; times definable as showing two qualities, Dilettantism and Mammonism; most intricate obstructed times! Nay, if there were not a Heaven's radiance of Justice, prophetic, clearly of Heaven, discernible behind all these confused world-wide entanglements, of Landlord interests, Manufacturing interests, Tory-Whig interests, and who knows what other interests, expediencies, vested interests, established possessions, inveterate Dilettantisms, Midas-eared Mammonisms – it would seem to every one a flat impossibility, which all wise men might as well at once abandon. If you do not know eternal Justice from momentary Expediency, and understand in your heart of hearts how Justice, radiant, beneficent, as the all-victorious light-element, is also in essence, if need be, an all-victorious *Fire*-element, and melts all manner of vested interests, and the hardest iron cannon, as if they were soft wax, and does ever in the long-run rule and reign, and allows nothing else to rule and reign – you also would talk of impossibility! But it is only difficult, it is not impossible. Possible? It is, with whatever difficulty, very clearly inevitable.

(*Past and Present*, Bk. I, Chap. 3)

When I described Carlyle as a great 'national prophet', I was not using the term in any loose sense. Three of Carlyle's books are entirely devoted to a kind of writing that is very exactly to be described as prophetic. In *Chartism* (published in 1840), in *Past and Present* (1843) and the *Latter-Day Pamphlets* (1850), Carlyle addresses the British nation and presents a vision of History, an exposure of the reality underlying present appearances and an evocation of the collective Future, at once terrible and yet to the eye of faith wonderfully hopeful. All three books are written in a prose that has much, except metre, in common with poetry, and rising in many passages to a dithyrambic pitch. With the exception of certain books of Ruskin's, particularly *Unto this Last* (1862), there is nothing else in Victorian prose literature comparable to these works. Among general works of literature of the nineteenth century, only a few, such as Whitman's *Democratic Vistas*, Kierkegaard's *The Present Age* and *Attack on 'Christendom'*, certain pages of Baudelaire's prose, certain portions of Nietzsche's writing, may be said to belong to the same sort of category.

Today it would seem more difficult than ever to understand immediately what Carlyle meant by the term Hero. During the last twenty-five years the world has witnessed such a huge preposterous travesty of the Heroic idea and had such a ghastly revelation of the true nature of Humbug-heroism in the rise and fall of the Nazi and Fascist movements that one would have thought men would not be likely to fall a-worshipping any sort of Hero again for a long while to come. But large numbers of the world's population apparently feel no shame in bowing the knee to dictators of wide diversity; and I hardly dare assert of so large a number of people that they all ought to be blushing.

As long as one refrains from actually reading with care *On Heroes, Hero-Worship and the Heroic in History* it is easy to remain convinced that the subject is one most suited to adolescence. After reading the book, it is still possible to feel that Carlyle's conception is a little confusing and does not seem to have been firmly grounded on a clear preliminary definition. Plenty of definitions are thrown out during the course of the six lectures, but there is nothing to indicate a recognition of the fact that Heroism is essentially a matter of narrative, not of a man's feats or character. Men do not become Heroes during their own lifetime; or if they do, seldom survive the transient adoration of their contemporaries, certainly not if they themselves seek for or approve of it. Carlyle himself failed to recognize Abraham Lincoln as the one man among his contemporaries who might truly be thought worthy to be described as a man of the same mould as the Lord Protector of our former Commonwealth.

The six lectures on Heroes were first delivered in May 1840. If since then they had been read as often as they have been referred to, we should no doubt have heard a great deal less about Carlyle the prophet of Fascism. The epithet is far less appropriate to him than it is even to Nietzsche. To begin with, it is quite clearly the Divine Right of Kings that modern dictators have attempted to reappropriate to themselves, and Carlyle's favourite hero, it should constantly be remembered, was *not* Charles I, but the common man who was forced by his Puritan conscience to assume national leadership in defence of civil liberty *against* autocracy. None of Carlyle's heroes (unless it be Napoleon, about whom his enthusiasm is but lukewarm) bears the slightest resemblance to any twentieth-century national political figure, with the possible exception of Mr Winston Churchill. As all honest thinking people must have realized long ago, the ideology of Fascism is completely without intellectual integrity, and its ideals are pompous imitations; and the Democracies, in refusing any longer to recognize the usurped authority of the Dictators and allying themselves with all men in Europe who revolted against their tyrannous regime, were actually assuming the heroic responsibility of resisting Falsehood and taking up arms in the defence of Truth, or rather of the faith that Truth exists. The Democracy that Carlyle attacked with such bitterness and pertinacity no longer existed in the Europe of the 1930s except in those countries where the worship of Shams had become compulsory.

The book cannot, I think, be regarded as by any means one of Carlyle's best, though after *The French Revolution* it is probably the most famous. It is unweariyingly repetitive and uninterruptedly exhortative and picturesque, and it must be admitted that its manner may make it a little difficult to assimilate much more than half a hero at a time. While on the subject of Carlyle's style, however, I think I should say that the modern reader is just as likely as a Victorian to find it fascinating, and a most exhilarating change from the blandly correct or casual manner of nine out of ten modern authors; or on the other hand, to find it exasperating, a portentous rumbling and intolerable bore. In my opinion, the reader who finds himself in the latter case is to be pitied; but I will say no more on this subject, which since Carlyle first appeared in print, has occasioned more than enough inept, quite styleless comment.

As Cromwell may be said to have been Carlyle's favourite Hero, Boswell may be cited as an example of his idea of the Hero-worshipper. A good deal of the following passage from his concluding lecture, on Johnson, might be thought to apply today almost equally well to Carlyle himself:

> Johnson's Writings, which once had such currency and celebrity, are now, as it were, disowned by the young generation. It is not wonderful; Johnson's opinions are fast becoming obsolete: but his style of thinking and of living, we may hope, will never become obsolete. I find in Johnson's Books the indisputable traces of a great intellect and great heart: – ever welcome, under what obstructions and perversions soever. They are *sincere* words, those of his; he means things by them. A wondrous buckram style, – the best he could get to then; a measured grandiloquence, stepping or rather stalking along in a very solemn way, grown obsolete now; sometimes a tumid *size* of phraseology not in

proportion to the contents of it: all this you will put-up with. For the phraseology, tumid or not, has always *something within it*. So many beautiful styles and books with *nothing* in them; – a man is a *male*factor to the world who writes such! *They* are the avoidable kind!

It will perhaps be only fair to let Carlyle himself have the last word on the subject of his lectures *On Heroes and Hero-Worship*. This is what he noted in his *Journal* after the last of the series had been delivered:

> Jane says, and indeed I rather think it is true, that these last two lectures are among the best I ever gave (she says the very best, but I do not think that); and certainly they have not done me nearly so much mischief as the others were wont. I feel great pain and anxiety till I get them done on the day when they are to be done; but no excessive shattering of myself to pieces in consequence of that.
>
> I got through the last lecture yesterday in very tolerable style, seemingly much to the satisfaction of all parties; and the people all expressed in a great variety of ways much very genuine-looking friendliness for me. I contrived to tell them something about poor Cromwell, and I think to convince them that he was a great and true man, the valiant soldier in England of what John Knox had preached in Scotland. In a word, the people seemed agreed that it was my best course of lectures, this. And now you see I am handsomely through it, and ought to be very thankful.

The three principal prophetic books of Carlyle are not the books of his most likely to attract the modern reader; and it is doubtful whether they are read today except by specializing students. This is a pity, for they all contain magnificent pages of writing, and are not wholly limited to the discussion of mid-Victorian problems. The title of the first, and the shortest, of these books, *Chartism* (1840), suggests that its interest is wholly early Victorian; and this may account for the fact that surprisingly few people seem to be acquainted with the magnificent vision and epitome of English history that it contains, a piece of writing only fifteen pages in length which would seem one of the most essential texts in all Victorian literature for the purposes of a national democratic Education.

When *Past and Present* first appeared in 1843, Emerson, in reviewing the book in *The Dial* called it 'Carlyle's new poem, his *Iliad* of English woes, to follow his poem on France, entitled the *History of the French Revolution* . . . it is a political tract, and since Burke, since Milton, we have had nothing to compare with it'. This monumental rhapsody of Gothic prose built in four parts – 'Proem', 'The Ancient Monk', 'The

Modern Worker', 'Horoscope' – is a series of rotatory ruminations on this theme (essentially the same as that 'God is Dead!' which is the theme of much of Nietzsche's): Man among the dark Satanic mills of Industrialism has lost his Soul, modern society is no longer bound together by the cement of living faith, human life devoid of spirit is only death and sordid nightmare!

> It is even so. To speak in the ancient dialect, we 'have forgotten God'; in the most modern dialect and very truth of the matter, we have taken up the Fact of the Universe as it is *not*. We have quietly closed our eyes to the eternal Substance of things, and opened them only to the Shows and Shams of things. . . .
> (*Past and Present*, Bk. III, Chap. 1)

This was the state of affairs he had already described in his previous book, *Chartism*:

> Alas, in such times it grows to be the universal belief, sole accredited knowingness, and the contrary of it accounted puerile enthusiasm, this sorrowfulest *dis*belief that there is properly speaking any truth in the world; that the world ever has been or ever can be guided, except by simulation, dissimulation, and the sufficiently dextrous practice of pretence. The faith of men is dead: in what has guineas in its pocket, beefeaters riding behind it, and cannons trundling before it, they can believe; in what has none of these things they cannot believe. Sense for the true and false is lost; there is properly no longer any true or false. It is the heyday of Imposture; of Semblance recognising itself, and getting itself recognised, for Substance. Gaping multitudes listen; unlistening multitudes see not but that all is right, and in the order of Nature. Earnest men, one of a million, shut their lips; suppressing thoughts, which there are no words to utter. To them it is too visible that spiritual life has departed; that material life, in whatsoever figure of it, cannot long remain behind. . . .
> (*Chartism*, Chap. 5)

Such is the state of affairs into which the writer who may be called prophet is sent. His function is to diagnose and understand the spiritual malady of the age, and to interpret the age to itself, by articulating, and not shutting his lips from, the thoughts which other earnest men suppress or leave unuttered. And the core and essence of his message is this: 'that Speciosities which are not Realities cannot any longer inhabit this world.'

> Alas, was that such new tidings? Is it not from of old indubitable, that Untruth, Injustice which is but acted untruth, has no power to continue in this true Universe of ours? The tidings was world-old, as old as the Fall of Lucifer: and yet in that epoch unhappily it was new tidings, unexpected, incredible; and there had to be such earthquakes and shakings of the nations before it could be listened to, and laid to heart even slightly! Let us lay it to heart, let us know it well, that new shakings be not needed. Known and laid to heart it must everywhere be, before peace can pretend to come. This seems to us the secret of our convulsed era; this which is so easily written, which is and has been and will be so hard to bring to pass. All true men, high and low, each in his sphere, are consciously or unconsciously bringing it to pass; all false and half-true men are fruitlessly spending themselves to hinder it from coming to pass.
>
> (*Chartism*, Chap. 5)

It is clear enough from this passage, surely, that the convulsed era that Carlyle wrote about is not yet over. In *Sartor Resartus*, an early book, he suggests that we may be at present but half-way through it. Adapting from Jean-Paul (two of whose *novellen* Carlyle translated) a term chosen by the German as the title of a book of his never translated into English, he refers many times both in *Sartor Resartus* and in *The French Revolution* to the *Palingenesia* or 'Phoenix Death-Birth of Human Society', and hints that this is a process which may be expected to last *three hundred years*! Louis-Claude de Saint-Martin referred to the French Revolution as 'an epitome of the Last Judgement', and if we take the French Revolution as the convulsive overture with which the whole Palingenesic era began, then we may still have a little less than a hundred and fifty years more of *Sturm und Drang* and indeed of all too realistically prophesied fire-consummation to look forward to before we 'find ourselves again in a Living Society, and no longer fighting but working'.

> For the rest, in what year of grace such Phoenix-cremation will be completed, we need not ask. The law of Perseverence is among the deepest in man: by nature he hates change; seldom will he quit his old house till it has actually fallen about his ears.
>
> (*Sartor Resartus*)

This conception of the Palingenesic nature of the Present Age is one of the key ideas to his whole work. It was this that led him to be drawn for a short while to the teachings of Saint-Simon, to whom he refers in passing in *Sartor Resartus*; though he followed the advice of Goethe, who wrote to him: 'From the St Simonian Society pray hold yourself aloof.'

In the same connexion, although there is no indication that Carlyle was acquainted with the writings of either of them, one might mention Ballanche and Fourier.

In his Inaugural Address on being installed as Rector of Edinburgh University, in 1866, Carlyle said: 'I need not hide from you, young Gentlemen, that you have got into a very troublous epoch of the world. . . .'

> Look where one will, revolution has come upon us. We have got into the age of revolutions. All kinds of things are coming to be subjected to fire, as it were: hotter and hotter blows the element round everything. . . . It is evident that whatever is not inconsumable, made of *asbestos*, will have to be burnt, in this world. Nothing other will stand the heat it is getting exposed to.

It was in *Chartism* that Carlyle delivered his stirring clarion-call on the subject of Education. It is difficult today fully to realize how great was the need for such a call, as difficult perhaps as it is nowadays to realize what was then, before the turn of the nineteenth century, the position of women in society. The situation both of women and of education has been vastly altered; but not so much so that we do not need to be reminded that they both still constitute a problem for the social conscience. Carlyle's words have lost none of their force, and may well serve to indicate what Britain's true greatness as an empire has lain in recognizing in some degree:

> To impart the gift of thinking to those who cannot think, and yet who could in that case think: this, one would imagine, was the first function a government had to set about discharging. Were it not a cruel thing to see, in any province of an empire the inhabitants living all mutilated in their limbs, each strong man with his right arm lamed? How much crueller to find the strong soul, with its eyes still sealed, its eyes extinct so that it sees not! Light has come into the world, but to this poor peasant it has come in vain. For six thousand years the Sons of Adam, in sleepless effort, have been devising, doing, discovering; in mysterious infinite indissoluble communion, warring, a little band of brothers, against the great black empire of Necessity and Night; they have accomplished such a conquest and conquests: and to this man it is all as if it had not been. . . .
>
> Heavier wrong is not done under the sun. It lasts from year to year, from century to century; the blinded sire slaves himself out, and leaves a blinded son; and men, made in the image of God, continue as two-legged beasts of labour; – and in the largest empire of the world, it is a debate whether a small fraction of

the Revenue of one Day (£30,000 is but that) shall, after Thirteen Centuries, be laid out on it, or not laid out on it. Have we Governors, have we Teachers; have we had a Church these thirteen hundred years? What is an Overseer of souls, an Archoverseer, Archiepiscopus? Is he something? If so, let him lay his hand on his heart, and say what thing!

(At this point, we might today just hear, through the mighty roar of world-wide ballyhoo, a distant voice affirming: 'I am Ezra Pound.')

Education is not only an eternal duty, but has at length become even a temporary and ephemeral one, which the necessities of the hour will oblige us to look after. These twenty-four million labouring men, if their affairs remain unregulated, chaotic, will burn ricks and mills; reduce us, themselves and the world into ashes and ruin. Simply their affairs cannot remain unregulated, chaotic; but must be regulated, brought into some kind of order. What intellect were able to regulate them? The intellect of a Bacon, the energy of a Luther, if left to their own strength, might pause in dismay before such a task; a Bacon and Luther added together, to be perpetual prime minister over us, could not do it. What can? Only twenty-four million ordinary intellects, once awakened into action; these, well presided over, may. Intellect, insight, is the discernment of order in disorder; it is the discovery of the will of Nature, of God's will; the beginning of the capability to walk according to that. With perfect intellect, were such possible without perfect morality, the world would be perfect; its efforts unerringly correct, its results continually successful, its condition faultless. Intellect is like light; the Chaos becomes a world under it; *fiat lux*. . . . According as there was intellect or no intellect in the individuals, will the general conclusion they make-out embody itself as a world-healing Truth and Wisdom, or as a baseless fateful Hallucination, a Chimæra breathing *not* fabulous fire!

Carlyle, the ardent, profoundly reverent and grateful pupil of Goethe, was one of his best translators and interpreters and became himself of all English writers of the nineteenth century indisputably the greatest Teacher. He believed that if he tried his utmost to communicate the truths he could most clearly see, that men, willingly or unwillingly, would listen to him, that they would recognize the truth insofar as he could succeed in communicating it to them, and that eventually they would be changed by it. His whole life was built on this faith; the gratitude of millions must have proved to him, had he lived till the end of the nineteenth century only, that it was not faith in an illusion. It was, in fact, faith in the essential *respectability*, in the stricter sense of the word, of the common man, insofar as the latter is still, in the strict sense of the word, an individual, which as a member of the crowd he is *not*.

Since Carlyle's challenge to the governors of England on the subject of Education in *Chartism* (1840), there have been ever increasing educational improvements of every description, ever vaster sums expended annually on the nation's education, or at least on the larger if not the best part of it, and yet the world still seems full of people whose education has not made them proud of it, and people whose education has made them proud of it for the wrong reasons; sufficiently full at any rate to make it seem that the masses are perhaps uneducable. But the majority of 'educated people' may be depended on to agree in principle that unless one has a proper respect for education and a sense of the true equality that it alone can bring, one can hardly be expected to be other than a pseudo-democrat.

The idea of literature being educational in intention seems today almost uncouth; but it has not always been so regarded. That literature requires a higher degree of education in the reader than the average man can at present be presumed to possess is quite a common assumption; and the display of considerable erudition is by some students thought not to be an incidental accompaniment of literary ability but invariably an indication of merit.

Carlyle's conception of literature is one that much needs reconsidering in these days. It is outlined succinctly enough in the following passages:

> Literature is but a branch of Religion, and always participates in its character: however, in our time, it is the only branch that still shows any greenness; and, as some think, must one day become the main stem.
>
> (*Characteristics*)

> Genius, Poet: do we know what these words mean? An inspired Soul once more vouchsafed us, direct from Nature's own great fire-heart, to see the Truth, and speak it, and do it; Nature's own sacred voice heard once more athwart the dreary boundless element of hearsaying and canting, of twaddle and poltroonery, in which the bewildered Earth, nigh perishing, has *lost its way*. Hear once more, ye bewildered mortals; listen once again to a voice from the inner Light-sea and Flame-sea, Nature's and Truth's own heart; know the Fact of your Existence what it is, put away the Cant of it which it is *not*; and knowing, do, and let it be well with you!
>
> (*Past and Present*, Bk. II, Chap. 9)

Beyond all ages, our Age admonishes whatsoever thinking or writing man it has: Oh speak to me, some wise intelligible speech; your wise meaning, in the shortest and clearest way; behold I am dying for want of wise meaning, and insight into the devouring fact: speak, if you have any wisdom! As to song so-called, and your fiddling talent, – even if you have one, much more if you have none, – we will talk of that a couple of centuries hence, when things are calmer again. Homer shall be thrice welcome; but only when Troy is *taken*: alas, while the siege lasts, and battle's fury rages everywhere, what can I do with the Homer? I want Achilles and Odysseus, and am enraged to see them trying to be Homers!

(*Life of Sterling*, Part III, Chap. 1)

Literature, when noble, is not easy; but only when ignoble. Literature too is a quarrel, and internecine duel, with the whole World of Darkness that lies without one and within one; – rather a hard fight at times, even with the three pound ten secure. Thou, where thou art, wrestle and duel along, cheerfully to the end; and make no remarks.

(*Past and Present*, Bk. II, Chap. 12)

But I say, have you computed what a distance forwards it may be towards some *new* Psalm of David done with our new appliances, and much improved wind-instruments, grammatical and other? This is the distance of the new Golden Age, my friend; not less than that, I lament to say! And the centuries that intervene are a foul, agonistic welter through the Stygian seas of mud: a long *Scavenger Age*, inevitable where the Mother of Abominations has long dwelt.

(*Latter-Day Pamphlet*, No. VIII, 'Jesuitism', August 1850)

Of Literature, in all ways, be shy rather than otherwise, at present! There where thou art, work, work; whatsoever thy hand findeth to do, do it, – with the hand of a man, not of a phantasm; be that thy unnoticed blessedness and exceeding great reward. Thy words, let them be few, and well ordered. Love silence rather than speech in these tragic days, when for very speaking, the voice of man has fallen inarticulate to man; and hearts, in this loud babbling, sit dark and dumb towards one another. Witty, – above all, O be not witty: none of us is bound to be witty, under penalties; to be wise and true we all are, under the terriblest penalties!

(*Latter-Day Pamphlet*, No. V, 'Stump-Orator', May 1850)

> And yet our Heroic Men of Letters do teach, govern, are kings, priests, or what you like to call them; intrinsically there is no preventing it by any means whatever. The world *has* to obey him who thinks and sees in the world. The world can alter the manner of that; can either have it as blessed continuous summer sunshine, or as unblessed black thunder and tornado, – with unspeakable difference of profit for the world! The manner of it is very alterable; the matter and fact of it is not alterable by any power under the sky. Light; or, failing that, lightning: the world can take its choice. Not whether we call an Odin god, prophet, priest, or what we call him; but whether we believe the word he tells us: there it all lies. If it be a true word, we shall have to believe it; believing it, we shall have to do it. What *name* or welcome we give him or it, is a point that concerns ourselves mainly. *It*, the new Truth, new deeper revealing of the Secret of this Universe, is verily of the nature of a message from on high; and must and will have itself obeyed.
>
> (*On Heroes and Hero-Worship*, Lecture V)

The convulsive era of which Carlyle wrote, as I said just now, is the same as that in which we are still living. These words, though written in 1831, have an astonishing topical present relevance:

> The doom of the Old has long been pronounced, and irrevocable; the Old has passed away: but, alas, the New appears not in its stead; the Time is still in pangs of travail with the New. Man was walked by the light of conflagrations, and amid the sound of falling cities; and now there is darkness, and long watching till it be morning. The voice even of the faithful can but exclaim: 'As yet struggles the twelfth hour of the Night: birds of darkness are on the wing, spectres uproar, the dead walk, the living dream. Thou, Eternal Providence, wilt cause the day to dawn!'
>
> Such being the condition, temporal and spiritual, of the world at our Epoch, can we wonder that the world 'listens to itself', and struggles and writhes, everywhere externally and internally, like a thing in pain? Nay, is not even this unhealthy action of the world's Organization, if the symptom of universal disease, yet also the symptom and sole means of restoration and cure? . . . Innumerable 'Philosophies of Man', contending in boundless hubbub, must annihilate each other, before an inspired Poesy and Faith for Man can fashion itself together.
>
> (*Characteristics*)

The message of Carlyle for the present generation is also particularly that which he articulated in his book on his friend John Sterling, a man who failed to become either an important poet or a religious reformer, but spent his life struggling to give expression to his desire for a wider recognition of true greatness and nobility, and was perhaps a figure representative of the purest idealism[1] of his generation.

> Old hidebound Toryism, being now openly cracking towards some incurable disruption . . . long recognized by all the world, and now at last obliged to recognize its very self, for an overgrown Imposture, supporting itself not by human reason, but by flunkey blustering and brazen lying, superadded to mere brute force, could be no creed for young Sterling and his friends. In all things he and they were liberals, and, as was natural at this stage, democrats; contemplating root-and-branch innovation by aid of the hustings and ballotbox. Hustings and ballotbox had speedily to vanish out of Sterling's thoughts; but the character of root-and-branch innovator, especially of 'Radical Reformer' was indelible with him, and under all forms could be traced as his character through life.
>
> . . . Piety of heart, a certain reality of religious faith, was always Sterling's, the gift of nature to him which he would not and could not throw away; but I find at this time his religion is as good as altogether Ethnic, Greekish, what Goethe calls the Heathen form of religion. The Church, with her articles, is without relation to him. And along with obsolete spiritualisms, he sees all manner of obsolete thrones and big-wigged temporalities; and for them also can prophesy, and wish, only a speedy doom. Doom inevitable, registered in Heaven's Chancery from the beginning of days, doom unalterable as the pillars of the world; the gods are angry, and all nature groans, till this doom of eternal justice be fulfilled.
>
> . . . We shall have to admit, nay it will behove us to see and practically know, for ourselves and him and others, that the essence of this creed, in times like ours, was right and not wrong. That, however the ground and form of it might change, essentially it was the monition of his natal genius to this as it is to every brave man; the behest of all his clear insight into this Universe, the message of Heaven through him, which he could not suppress, but was inspired and compelled to utter in this world by such methods as he had. There for him lay the first commandment; *this* is what it would have been the unforgivable sin to swerve from and desert; the treason of treasons for him, it were there; compared with which all other sins are venial!
>
> (*Life of Sterling*, Chap. 7)

---

[1] *Idealism*: in the loose and unphilosophical sense of the word, referring to ideal *aim*, not pure *idea*.

At first sight, I think it would not seem that this biography of a gifted young man who accomplished nothing, though he never ceased to be a seeker, were among the books of Carlyle's most likely to have interest for the modern reader. But it does contain the expression of an attitude towards established Religion which still, if anything even more than when it was written, is the attitude of a mature and *free* religious mind (and a religious mind that is not free is merely a superstitious mind).

> This battle, universal in our sad epoch, of 'all old things passing away' against 'all things becoming new', has its summary and animating heart in that of Radicalism against Church: there, as in its flaming core, and point of focal splendour, does the heroic worth that lies in each side of the quarrel most clearly disclose itself; and Sterling was the man, above many, to recognize such worth on both sides. Natural enough, in such a one, that the light of Radicalism having gone out in darkness for him, the opposite splendour should next rise as the chief, and invite his loyalty till it also failed. In one form or the other, such an aberration was not unlikely for him. But an aberration, especially in this form, we may certainly call it. No man of Sterling's veracity, had he clearly consulted his own heart, or had his own heart been capable of clearly responding, and not been dazzled and bewildered by transient fantasies and theosophic moonshine, could have undertaken this function [*i.e. that of the priesthood*]. His heart would have answered: 'No, thou canst not. What is incredible to thee, thou shalt not, at thy soul's peril, attempt to believe! . . . Elsewhither for a refuge, or die here. Go to Perdition if thou must, – but not with a lie in thy mouth; by the Eternal Maker, no!'

Commenting on a letter from France to himself from his friend Sterling, Carlyle writes as follows, giving a forceful indication of his attitude in maturity, towards all outward forms of religion in the modern world:

> Tholuck, Schleiermacher, and the war of articles and rubrics were left in the far distance; Nature's blue skies, and awful eternal verities, were once more around one, and small still voices, admonitory of many things, could in the beautiful solitude freely reach the heart. Theologies, rubrics, surplices, church articles, and this enormous ever-repeated thrashing of the straw? A world of rotten straw; thrashed all into powder; filling the Universe and blotting out the stars and worlds: – Heaven pity you with such a thrashing floor for world, and its draggled dirty farthing-candle

for sun! There is surely other worship possible for the heart of man; there should be other work, or none at all, for the intellect and creative faculty of man!

On another letter to him, from Rome, Carlyle makes even more scornful comment:

> It is surely fit to recognize with admiring joy any glimpse of the Beautiful and the Eternal that is hung out for us, in colour, in form or tone, in canvas, stone, or atmospheric air, and made accessible by any sense, in this world: but it is greatly fitter still (little as we are used that way) to shudder in pity and abhorrence over the scandalous tragedy, transcendent nadir of human ugliness and contemptibility, which under the daring title of religious worship, and practical recognition of the Highest God, daily and hourly everywhere transacts itself there. And, alas, not there only, but elsewhere, everywhere more or less; whereby our sense is so blunted to it; – whence, in all provinces of human life, these tears!

If these words are vehement, they are not more so than those which Carlyle had 'quoted' from a pseudonymous *alter ego* of his, whom he calls Crabbe, in the Seventh of the *Latter-Day Pamphlets* ('Hudson's Statue', 1 July 1850), on the subject of the 'so-called Christian *Clerus*' (he himself calls it 'a wild passage'):

> Legions of them, in their black and other gowns, I still meet in every country; masquerading, in strange costume of body, and still stranger of soul; mumming, primming, grimacing, – poor devils, shamming, and endeavouring not to sham: this is the sad fact. Brave men many of them, after their sort; and in a position which we may admit to be wonderful and dreadful! On the outside of their heads some singular headgear, tulip-mitre, felt coal-scuttle, purple hat; and in the inside, – I must say, such a Theory of God Almighty's Universe as I, for my part, am right thankful to have no concern with at all! I think, on the whole, as broken-winged, self-strangled, monstrous a mass of incoherent incredibilities, as ever dwelt in the human brain before. O God, giver of Light, hater of Darkness, of Hypocrisy and Cowardice, how long, how long!

These are not the words of an anti-religious man, but of a religious man of unusual earnestness; and they show that it is not altogether a vagary to associate Carlyle's name with that of Nietzsche: here, far more than in any supposed affinity of the Carlylian Hero with the Superman, may be perceived the real ground of any such connexion as there may be.

That Carlyle's attitude towards the rest of his fellow men had in it a certain amount of arrogance, his remark about Democracy: 'Twenty-seven millions, mostly fools', is sufficient indication; but it also contained such genuine humility and so clear a realization of the insignificance of the greatest man in relation to the inscrutable All, that he was ever incapable of the passionate self-assertiveness and dionysian *hubris* that carried Nietzsche off into his final madness. His religious radicalism is more adult and sane than that of the Prophet of Superman, while being healthier and less strained than the agonizingly scruple-tormented Kierkegaard's.

> The essence of all 'religion' that was and that ever will be is to make men *free*. Who is he that, in this life-pilgrimage, will consecrate himself at all hazards to obey God and God's servants, and to disobey the Devil and his? With pious valour this free man walks through the roaring tumults, invincibly the way whither he is bound. To him in the waste Saharas, through the grim solitudes peopled by galvanized corpses and doleful creatures, there is a lode-star; and his path, whatever those of others be, is towards the Eternal. A man well worth consulting, and taking note of, about matters temporal.

Today once more it is important to recognize in what Carlyle expresses in the passages quoted above the most essential part of his message as a religious man and a prophet. If anyone not really familiar with Carlyle's writings should be puzzled by remembering, in this connection, the often repeated expression 'Hebrew old-clothes', which recurs constantly throughout his works, he may be enlightened by these words from Martin Buber's outstanding work of exegesis of the Hebrew Prophets of the Old Testament: 'The leader-God . . . wants to root out of men's hearts the notion that it is possible to satisfy Him merely with worship and cult.'[1] And the word worship in this sentence is not to be confused, be it noted, with the meaning that Carlyle most often gives it; for Carlyle, worship was first and last the immediate reaction of *sincerity*, and without sincerity, nothing, nothing, that man, be he never so pious and never so highly consecrated and ordained, can either say or do, will ever be satisfying to God. But his own words can best tell us what Carlyle understood by the word Worship:

---

[1] Martin Buber, *The Prophetic Tradition* (Eng. trans., 1950).

> I will insert this also, in a lower strain, from Sauerteig's *Aesthetische Springwurzeln*. 'Worship?' says he: 'Before that inane tumult of Hearsay filled men's heads, while the world yet lay silent, and the heart true and open, many things were Worship! To the primeval man whatsoever good came, descended on him (as, in mere fact, it ever does) direct from God; whatsoever duty lay visible for him, this a Supreme God had prescribed. To the present hour I ask thee, Who else? For the primeval man, in whom dwelt Thought, this Universe was all a Temple; Life everywhere a Worship.'
>
> *(Past and Present*, Bk. III, Chap. 15)

The position of Carlyle in importance I would reckon to be somewhere about mid-way between two very great and extremely different men of the nineteenth century, Søren Kierkegaard on the one hand, and Walt Whitman on the other. All three alike are particularly to be distinguished as having at the basis of their work what Carlyle called 'an open loving heart'.

Both Carlyle and Kierkegaard were poets who wrote in prose. Both were anti-romantic romantics and anti-idealist Post-Hegelians. Both might well be called 'knights of faith'; both thought of themselves as 'witnesses to the truth', and suffered hostility and derision in consequence. Both were virtuosos of homilectic eloquence, who fully realized the vanity of all eloquence that fails to move the hearer's heart. Above all, it is in the way they both understood the fatal significance in the modern age of the disintegration of 'society' into 'coteries', 'swarmeries' and 'crowds', that the closeness of Carlyle's thought to Kierkegaard's should be seen. Every analysis of the modern crisis of civilization that fails to take account of Kierkegaard's and Carlyle's criticisms of the Crowd and of the anti-Christian spirit which invariably animates it (for it is always the Crowd that cries 'Give us Barabbas!'), is bound to lead to further misunderstanding of all present social problems.

In situating Carlyle between Kierkegaard and Whitman, I was thinking also of the pessimism and the optimism of Carlyle; on the one hand 'this British Hamlet from Cheyne Row, more puzzling than the Danish one' (as Whitman described him), and on the other the enthusiast whose vision of 'the divine idea of the world' and faith in the necessity of fire for the new-birth of the Phoenix enabled him to see 'before us . . . the boundless Time, with its as yet uncreated and unconquered Continents and Eldorados, which we, even we, have to conquer, to create. . . .'

It might well be considered that it is just this middle situation of Carlyle that makes him a writer with a message of special value to the present generation, if it could but be clearly disengaged from the misconceptions and misinterpretations that have long accumulated about his work, and which are partly the result of a sort of self-protective instinct in the many who do not wish to be confronted by the real significance of what the prophet has to tell them, and from those parts of Carlyle's writings which really are not of such immediate relevance to us now (and these would probably in all amount only to the lesser part of his work). By 'middle situation', I mean that in which it is possible to see that there is no genuine hope, except that which can survive a long and courageously searching look at the worst; only from this position, it would seem, can one see the worst, and still be able to see enough of the purposes of the Eternal to be able to live without wasting our potentialities.

Carlyle cannot be claimed either by the Left or by the Right. He was too faithful to his vision of 'the Divine Idea of the World' to be a partisan of any hard-and-fast ideology; more than heroism, he worshipped the Objective. This briefest of introductions to his writings has not attempted to give any idea of *The French Revolution* or to do justice to Carlyle's conception of History and the art of the Historian. Social and Literary Historians in general cannot yet be said to have done this fully either.

A NEW POEM BY PIERRE JEAN JOUVE: 'LANGUAGE'

Last spring, the *Mercure de France* published a new book of poetry by Pierre Jean Jouve: *Langue*, the fifth volume of his poetic work to have appeared since the end of the war. In the four previous volumes (*Hymne, Génie, Diadème,* and *Ode*), Jouve's poetic style has been seen to undergo a process of modification and renewal; the style of *Ode* was quite unlike that of anything that he had written earlier, while *Langue*, which is in a style that seems closely to resemble it, represents a still further phase of evolution, corresponding to the inner development of the poet in his struggle for spiritual significance.

It has been apparent for some time that the whole poetic work of Pierre Jean Jouve will eventually reveal itself to be constructed according to a consciously conceived plan. With the publication last year of the autobiographical commentary on his own writings called *En Miroir* (extracts from which appeared simultaneously in three different revues last February) and the broadcasting of a series of ten *entretiens* by the French radio last autumn, the monumental outlines of the structure which his work as a whole represents may become more easily distinguishable. In its entirety this work will soon consist of at least a dozen volumes of poetry, four volumes of prose fiction (all pre-dating 1935), and five or six volumes of essays.

In *En Miroir*, Jouve has written: 'My passion becomes involved only when confronted with an idea, a scheme, that is at once the same, and different.' There are a number of themes that are fundamental and recurrent throughout his entire production, and one may be sure that, however unfamiliar the style and imagery of his most recent poetry, most of these themes will be found to recur, though possibly in transmuted or augmented form, in the poems of the sequence called *Langue*. It contains altogether forty-one poems, and is divided into three main sections. The dominant theme may be defined as the *a priori* non-existence of a language in which the unknown may be expressed, and the struggle to create, which is at the same time the prayer to be granted, such a language; and thus we may say that the work has a certain essential similarity to

---

London Magazine, Vol. 2, No. 2 (February 1955), pp. 49-52.

Eliot's *Four Quartets*, although the latter is in most ways so very different in conception and style.

One of the most characteristic features of Pierre Jean Jouve both as a novelist and as a poet has always been his highly developed awareness of the Unconscious, of the guilt by which the Unconscious is dominated in all men, and of the struggle in the Unconscious of the instincts of life and death, which seem always to be locked inextricably together. Poetry, like the works of the great mystics, Jouve regards as proceeding from Eros, or rather, as representing the highest degree of sublimation of the erotic instinct (speaking, in the preface to *Sueur de sang*, for instance, of 'l'élévation à des substances si profondes, ou si élevées, qui dérivent de la pauvre, de la belle puissance érotique humaine'). In *Langue*, it is clear that what the poet is attempting is above all the conjuration of a new transport of sublimation by means of which erotic energy may be transformed into the power to give reality through articulation in language to a hitherto unknown spiritual dimension.

> Mais que baise, une seule fois, mon âme nue sur mon âme!
> Innovant les mondes nouveaux.

At the same time, the poem is philosophical in the specifically Socratic sense of being a meditation directed towards 'preparation in view of death'. An experience of the approach of death, and of an Orphic reconciliation with death resulting in a restoration to life of the loved one, is embodied in the substance of the poem, and it is this which provides the subject of what are certainly the most beautiful and most deeply moving pages of the whole text, in the passage which begins: 'Alors arriva d'un coup la face du Tonnerre.'

In the concluding poems of the sequence, the poet's voice attains to a tranquillity beyond desolation, and the principal theme of the whole is clarified in a last statement which is like the resolution at the end of a musical composition (the music-like structure of the work is another feature which it shares with the *Four Quartets*). The following in particular provides a key to the whole intention of *Langue*:

> At so many years' distance from the day of birth, with death distant by only a few days, after so many figures that appeared to rise and fall in the same sky of desire wherein disappointment and pleasure were both of the same shade of blue.
> after all the monotony befallen in the gardens – the distance that seemed so close at hand yet so remotely lost – and all the insecurity at the end – art in its repetitions altogether terrified to be alone amidst unbounded and bare space,

one seeks the meaning and the letter and the spirit: the meaning is dear to God: the meaning is what reaches the God-consciousness, and as a phrase resounds from the main vocable and rings through all the rest that are disposed on either side of it,
the word of life is only to be read in the absurd – imprinted within absolute Absurdity and shining there like love of which the forms are infinite.

At the present time it is reassuring to find that there can still exist in the world some poets entirely preoccupied, not with an art of agreeable diversion, but with an art that bears witness to the life of the spirit beyond and out of death.

The part of the poem quoted above is not a particularly difficult passage to render into English; but a good deal of *Langue* presents the translator with problems of almost insuperable difficulty. Solemnity of tone does not ever pass easily from one language into another; and invocation and apostrophe are apt to sound impossibly odd in translation. The following three poems, or subsections of the poem, happen to seem to lend themselves more readily than most of the rest of the text to recreation or transcription in an idiom which it is hoped is not too unlike either the poetic style of the original, or readable English.

I

During that moulting season of the formless final world
The conquerors held out still: alone and without horses either of plaster or of gold
And without money (lost in the sands and in the circuses, and on all fronts)
Without even a moist lance's oriflamme. And then what thrusts of troops that never moved!
Pure conquerors of ancient time – and all cathedrals in their train –
They awaited with their passion in the swarming towns of dwarfs
An extraordinary onslaught of empty emotion and explosiveness
Which might enable all to be recovered by the vitals that were losing all their blood.

II

Ah! the poet now writes only for the heavens' empty space
Pure blue that winter can no longer see! he writes in conjuration of the silence of the snows

Of the stifling of fallacious festal days! and in the lack and in the lacklustre it reveals, each line he writes is just as though he were not there (and his slim figure, dressed in the lights' glare, is just as though he were not there),
 And in his solitude devoted to that admirable, secret conjuration, behold him pleading his peculiar loves
 When none would undertake to risk love's courage in his stead:

 Then on the fabled winds' black shore, over the seaweeds' slumber, under nearly weightless whirling swells of fog,
  He seals the word up in the bottle of green glass,
  Bells of despair and horrible seawrack!
 He launches on the highest wave a bottle without action, force or aim, yet which one day
  The waves will wash up to love's level, beyond beauty, beyond glory, beyond day.

III

 Clear light of day! flow once more through the furrow you have worn upon the mortal avenues
  Gleam on the capitals and globes of stone, waken the sacred snakes,
  All men's activities! And mortal thought of mine pursue once more
  Your way towards hope's narrow zone, with great deliberate works in view:
  Both works and death before my eyes stand like glad monuments devoured by the sky's plants,
  Pure ruin well contented to be filled with its vast future and its natural love.

THE SUN AT MIDNIGHT

The Demonomination Question Today.
Personally (ever since a certain symbolic anti-racialist ceremonial vigil in front of the Lincoln Memorial recently – Spring, 1964), I shall always insist on being regarded as simultaneously a Jew, (– my name is David; and as a boy I was a Cathedral chorister, which meant that in consequence I had to listen to two lessons from the Old Testament nearly every day for six years, as well as sing the Psalms); a C. of E. protestant; *and* a pretty catholic Protestant. I may say also that I am a Christian Scientist – up to (or down to?) a point; (though I refuse to discuss just where I think this point is situated; apparently it does one no good to think about such things much anyway). I should also like to think of myself as a kind of Transparent Muslim, if that were possible . . . David X.

Trials and Temptations of the Humanly Faithful under Difficulties of their Own Invention. . . .
All my really intelligent friends, of whom there have fortunately for my own intelligence been a good many throughout my life, have suffered, and sometimes quite painfully, from much the same sort of strange and really ridiculous religious difficulties; and these were difficulties which in the final analysis may be said all to boil down to the same fundamental problem, which was indeed until quite recently a previously well-nigh insoluble one. The problem is as follows: How to *believe* such an obviously true and yet almost as obviously falsified tale (– dogma, or rigmarole, it simply depends upon your own habitual vocabulary)? And the answer is this: *It just wasn't rationally possible.* And it wasn't possible for the following three main reasons, *viz:* a) *It was really true*, and we didn't recognize the fact; b) we thought we *had* recognized the truth, and were at the same time encouraged to *believe* that we had by *all* our spiritual or rather, professional educators, the priesthood included; and c) the whole subject then most often became altogether too embarrassing a riddle of contradictions to be worth bothering to think about *seriously* any more.

Two Rivers, Vol. 1, No. 1 (Winter 1969). Editor's note: These extracts were not published in *The Sun at Midnight* (Enitharmon Press, 1970), as they were not included in that manuscript.

And this is the Real Joke of it all: The Truth actually *was* so very much more Rational *and* Wonderful than we could possible realize, with our own wonderful, for all that they were rationally limited, intellects, *the whole bloody time.*

And who can deny all that blood, – spiritual, intellectual and generally very *physical* blood indeed, at times like our own? And that was also always (– *symbolically*, mind you,) the blessed Blood of Our Lord Saviour Jesus Christ, – as of course you must know already, you've heard it enough times to be pretty sick of the world's favourite word for haemoglobin and its associate chemical substances, by now.

The Way of the Haut Monde; (or Sketch for a Character-Study: Portrait of a Strange, Lying and Transparent Step-Sister.)

(Needless to say, as usual, that the characters in this story are entirely imaginary and bear no relation to any living or dead person.)

This Tale is but one among innumerable others drawn from the unconscious depths of current Society. It concerns, to begin with, a Wicked Step-Sister's Brother-in-Arms and their Christian Bastard of a Father-in-Law, who loved his own monstrously misbegotten progeny so much that he married his brother-in-law's niece (*en second noces*) in order to save some of the rest of the family from comparative penury and thus at the same time ensure the inheritance necessary to preserve a great Anglo-Irish-American manufacturing (and 'collaborationist') family's rapidly vanishing share of the profits involved in an enormous international armaments swindle; so that their bogus, treacherous but at the time extremely well-known patronymous relation should be spared the universal loathing he would otherwise have inspired among all the true high-society people then surrounding a most loyal and magnanimous Monarch and his rather extraordinary but much-loved and truly beautiful Consort, on the occasion of a certain event that *might* still then have spared the world yet one more holocaust, an outcome in any event wellnigh inevitable, since the aforementioned Monarch's unjustly accused Second Cousin had already involved and compromised himself in a scandalous affair that had quite thrillingly convulsed more than half the élite of Europe with ambiguous emotions, and had then allowed himself to be more or less blackmailed into signing a hastily drawn-up document he never even gave a thought to properly reading through, and thus put himself almost completely into the power of one of his enemies' enemies' most powerful enemies.

Now at this point it is obvious necessary to draw a deep breath; and it should also be obvious that it is not permissible for me to continue any further for the moment, since hardly any remaining living person has ever had more than the merest inkling that anything has ever been otherwise than as everyone else has always been firmly convinced most other people had always thought it had been.

And such are and will (no doubt) to some extent long continue to be the ways of this – er, – World.

What it Can Mean to be Despised and Rejected.

We needn't go into the Biblical details of this particular story any more. In any case, the Scape-goat was a billy-goat, and not a turn-coat, and scape-goats have well-known traditional functions which always enable them to chuckle over their supposed grievances once they have safefully retired to their peaceful native wildernesses. But when it is a case of a *lady* goat, an animal of fundamentally gentle, amiable and sometimes even doting disposition – (have you ever looked a she-goat in the eyes?) – well, then I can leave the rest of the story to your no doubt tough modern imagination, if you've still got one.

The Approaching Abolition of Hang-Dog Diehards. (1964)

Approval of capital punishment necessarily implies a certain approval of the legal institution of Crucifixion. And who are the people who still do keep on so approving? Undoubtedly, a great many unconsciously guilty people who probably, in spite of their approval, would not much care actually to have to live with the hangman on mutually respectful or even on promiscuous terms. Such people are quite often apt to be convinced that they are orthodox Christians.

Dying *is* hard for diehards; which is why they are never very much inclined to think about any possible positive alternative to sentencing a few other human beings to death from time to time for a crime they are bound to feel themselves almost incapable of admitting to consciousness or hence of committing.

How long, O Lord, how long will it be before the United Kingdom becomes a fully and authentically civilized part of the world?

Can the Devil be Mocked?

There can be only little room for doubt that Moral Rearmament was an excellent thing to begin with; and it is unfortunate that it has rapidly become merely one more the many tedious forms of moral rearmament. (The Devil loves to spoil the best things, as we know). I can only suggest that its sincerest followers now rename it Moral Disarmament (and thus really fool the Devil). They might then start trying to find a good new group-name for Modern Pharasaism at its *Best*.

Half-hearted Neo-Lutheran Denunciation.

It would by now be impossible for the present generation further to exaggerate the claims to holiness and above all piety of the rather late Vicar, – of Christ, mind you, – Pius XII: the Prelate said by some to have had the key to the greatest power the Christian *Catholic* Church has ever known. The outrageous polemic stirred up by the bitter enemies of Christian Unity in Protestant, I should say in *Christian* Germany, represented by the pseudo-Christian or at least just possible partially Christian Protestant playwright Hochhuth, has left a pretty indelible impression in the minds of many a *true Christian* that the late good Pope of famous – world-famous and not in the least in-famous – memory, was, if anything, an even more timorous and prevaricating old diplomat than he appeared to a large number of non-Catholics to be even during his lifetime. Can even the true 'Vicar of Christ' on earth, even at this late date, have so little cared to remember the very elementary conception of Christian martyrdom? How many of the most deeply sincere Catholics and even many other ardent present-century followers of the Lord we equally share, let us admit, the Cross of, were perhaps cheated of the genuine halo of martyrdom by his apparently pusillanimous example? Well, anyway . . . He was *such a good man*, even were he only such and such a good man; though the point is really that if he was only such a good man as he may well be said to have been, apart from hagiography, then he may perhaps also be said to have been a bit of a pious *deputy* though not a fraud, to have dared accept his Supremely Holy Office.

One Ceremony at Least That Need Never be Repeated.

During the French Revolution, as Carlyle, the supposed prophet of proto-crypto-fascism, has taught us, a strange and remarkable ceremony was performed, under Robespierre's unconsciously inspired, satirical and artistic influence, in the Cathedral of Notre Dame in Paris, *la Ville Lumière*.

When a certain lady, an ex-actress and book-seller's cultured wife, was invited to play the part of God's Divine Fool, the Sacred Goddess of Reason, she gladly and very naturally accepted the role with the supreme approval of her possibly husband-frustrated intellect. And having first found the Stage beneath her, and then her educated, if not boring, elderly husband not quite up to her own high-minded standards of true free-thinking emancipation, she triumphantly ended up by finding the ancient custom-consecrated high altar of Mankind's previous and by then apparently outdated Deity under her bottom.

We need not suppose this to be a legend of 'realistic' significance; but fundamentally it is still a genuine historical fact that anyone who cares to may look up for him, or even herself, in any public library.

From what, or whom, do womenizers flee?
Tormented by dissatisfaction,
Till each lovely in turn then torments them
With the reproach of too much action?
The Psyche? She's a sort of woman too;
Or so it was traditionally said;
Though not a Circe nor a treach'rous whore.
Perhaps that's it. One answer's not in bed.

The Importance of Patience and of Being in Earnest.
This is a title that is bound to suggest the ever perennial topic of *Homosexuality*. A few years ago, I should undoubtedly have fought shy of bringing it up at all frankly. Nowadays, I rather suspect my sometimes malicious conscience of prompting me to make a clean breast of what I really believe to be the truth about it, and so get it off my chest. But I am not going to be so obliging, because I have never at all cared to be categorical about what is, after all, a pretty delicate and ambiguous subject of conversation. And my full confession would not in all probability prove sensational enough to be of engrossing interest to more than a small and oddly sane minority of people, anyway. – *Honi soit qui mal y pense*, shall we say?

Translation of a quotation from a popular survey of the various forms of contemporary madness, by the novelist Hervé Bazin, of *L'Académie Goncourt:* 'La Fin des Asiles' (Grasset, 1959):

> Absolute normality doesn't exist, and a good thing, too, because it would turn out to be deadly boring. Also dangerous: for if mental balance means proper adaptation, mental hygiene can do nothing to adapt man to the *abnormally normal* injustices of the society in which he lives. From this situation it is easy to see what should be the true relation between hygiene and morality . . .

The deeper spiritual meaning of Sodom is: shame of common humanity, neighbourly mistrust, and all-round mutual persecution (blackmail, etc., etc.). It is the City of imagined conspiracies. ('Confederacies', in Isaiah's sense of the word (VIII, 12).) Its true Ruler is despair of human Law; and disbelief in mortal compassion is its rule).

A Normal and Increasingly Common Objection.
Such a lot of modern literature nowadays is what would be called in a hospital socio-therapeutical work. Sartre, for example (*La Nausée* – early

period, and *Saint-Genet* – later development). But is it completely creative? Would a creative writing course, as in America, do the writer any good at his present age? It is difficult but fortunately not quite impossible to believe it. All the needed essentials are there, though not yet fully admitted to consciousness.

Of course, the world *is* a hospital, – as Eliot says.

Ratiocination is procrastination.

MY INDEBTEDNESS TO JOUVE

Adam has asked me to write a few words about the importance of the music of Mozart. At his request I have translated four of Pierre Jean Jouve's poems that attest most clearly to the tremendous veneration that this great poet felt for Mozart's music during the later part of his life, particularly during the period shortly before the last war when these particular poems were written, and when Jouve was preparing his remarkable prose analysis of the opera *Don Juan*.

I am proud to have been the translator of the introductory essay to Jouve's book *Grandeur actuelle de Mozart* (which first appeared in the N.R.F.) and to have been able to persuade Cyril Connolly to publish it in English in an early issue of *Horizon*.* It was to this essay that I owe my first mature appreciation of the true significance and exceptional greatness of Mozart, as like so many supposedly musical people in the Thirties, my idea of his music was very much the conventional one, in which the aspect of sunny charm and the pathos of prematurely carried-off genius combined to hide the profundity and sublimity that characterize the true Mozart.

I wish this note could be continued to the length of an essay of my own, though I have never had musicological pretensions and have none now, but happen to think that Michel Fano, Messiaen's pupil who collaborated with Jouve in writing two books of musically-technical and poetic analysis of Alban Berg's operas *Wozzeck* and *Lulu*, was right in believing that a music-loving poet can bring intuitive insights to the appreciation of a composer with whom he feels a special affinity, or to whom he is indebted, that are of more value than some of the stricter school of music critics would be likely to admit. But I know very well I could never hope to approach the quality of understanding and the beauty and aptness of language, that Pierre Jean Jouve achieved whenever he wrote about music.

Adam 422/424 (1980), pp. 52-3.

* Editor's note: Reprinted as *The Present Greatness of Mozart* (Birmingham: Delos Press, 1996).

THE POET AND THE CITY

There may have been a certain coincidence involved in the fact that on almost the same day that the Secretary-General engaged in organizing the Third European Poetry Festival wrote to invite me to take part in it and to send him beforehand, together with some of my poems, a few pages on the theme of *Le Poète et la ville*, a group of young people connected with the London School of Contemporary Dance were performing a staged, balletic version of a 'radiophonic poem' called *Night Thoughts* that I actually wrote as long ago as 1954 and which was broadcast by the BBC the following year. Naturally I was pleased that what I had tried to express then, which is much concerned with the scarcely avoidable image or metaphor of the City taken as representing the oppressive and dehumanizing environment of the typical Western man of today, should apparently still have enough relevant appeal to even a few members of a generation so much younger than my own to make them wish to use it as a vehicle to express their feelings about the present time. If I refer to this occurrence, I trust you will believe that I do so unprompted by complacency or motives of self-promotion, but rather to explain that it has encouraged me to restrict the present *essai* to a brief explanatory recapitulation of the essential subject of a work of mine originally conceived more than a quarter of a century ago.

The published text of *Night Thoughts* is preceded by an epigraph consisting of these words from Hölderlin: 'Aber weh! es wandelt in Nacht, es wohnt, wie in Orkus, / Ohne Göttliches unser Geschlecht . . .'* What follows is a triptych, beginning with a section devoted to the solitary 'Nightwatchers', followed by a phantasmagoric 'Megalometropolitan Carnival', and concluding with an 'Encounter with Silence'. All is overshadowed by the darkness consequent on what Martin Buber has termed the 'Eclipse of God'. The notion of God's apparent death actually goes back to the end of the eighteenth century, predating Nietzsche's famous

---

Cahiers sur la poésie 2 (Université de Bordeaux, 1984), pp. 135-43. First published in *Poëzie in De Stad – La Poésie dans la ville* – Actes du 3e Festival de Poésie à Louvain (Automne 1981), Leuvense Schrijversaktie (Cahier 30).

* Editor's note: 'But alas! our generation walks in night, dwells as in Hades, without the Divine . . .'

formulation, in Para. 125 of *Le Gai Savoir*, by over eighty years. My own use of it as an overall presupposition may be considered to constitute a reference to what, it seems to me, must by now appear an almost over-familiar conception. But if one's concern is to present a reflection of and on the actual human condition in as simple and immediately efficacious a way as possible to an audience of individuals unknown to one whose number could not be gauged with any certainty, one can hardly be much concerned with either the novelty or the familiarity of the view one is attempting to transmit through words and dramatic presentation, but only with one's own certainty that it truly corresponds to a fundamental metaphysical reality characteristic of the age one lives in because of knowing that one has oneself had actual experience of it.

Certainly there is little that is novel, either, about the equation of members of twentieth-century society with the denizens of what I have denominated 'Megalometropolis' in the second section of *Night Thoughts*. The prefix *mega*, of course, merely means inordinately vast (as in 'one million times'), that is to say in this case in comparison with the earliest conceivable conglomeration of dwellings, as briefly alluded to in this section in a reference to 'the primaeval City', imagined to have risen from the site of the original Forest, otherwise to be thought of as the Garden wherein grew the Tree of Knowledge, scene of the primal Fault or Fall from which has ultimately resulted the mechanized inferno full of confused and alienated masses which is the setting of the culmination of this section. It opens quietly, with a factually-based evocation of a great nocturnal modern City, in fact London, a few recognizable details of which are specifically mentioned in passing by the principal Narrator. The completely secularized and routine-controlled aspects of a contemporary capital, together with its unnaturally sprawling size, are suggested; and the introductory part of the second section concludes with a depiction, by hypnotically cadenced, alternating voices, of the deserted business-district, the city's effective axis, the description intended subliminally to imply the ethical emptiness at the core of our financially speculative and commerce-impelled world. Midnight has now passed and almost all the City's myriads are wrapped in separate yet collective slumber. At this point a transformation of content and tempo occurs. The city-dwellers having all fallen asleep, the principal Narrator announces:

'Enter the Dreams.'

Then, a second Narrator having briefly indicated a transition from externally real townscape to fantasy, the first invites the listener to

'Enter the Dream.'

Just as a view regarding spiritual night as attendant on the arid bankruptcy of unbelief dominates *Night Thoughts* as a whole, so my own qualified acceptance of C. G. Jung's concept of a collective Unconscious is a necessary presupposition for an insight into what I attempted to perform in the central section of it, that is to say: elaborate a purported dream that has to be thought of as that of an anonymous Everyman in imminent danger of becoming a soulless mass-man devoid of all individuality, although at the same time it must be borne in mind that personal identity has its roots in unconscious depths and is connected with the death associated with descent into the earth. It is not therefore to be considered the dream of anyone in particular, certainly not as a transcription of one of my own, since it was composed with a consciously controlled deliberation completely at variance with the approach necessary to produce the type of writing, i.e. orthodox Surrealist automatism, to cultivating which I once devoted a period of my youth. The dream episode I endeavoured to dramatize for the purposes of radio on this occasion is in fact an amalgam of a number of heterogeneous elements. I have already referred to subliminal implication, and this term should largely elucidate what I set out here to achieve: to arouse *rémanences* and association-clusters in the listener's memory and some deeper layer of consciousness connected with it. In order to accomplish this aim I employed fleeting, sometimes merely hinted, allusions to a fairly wide and disparate range of mythological symbols and archetypes, such as the prehistoric forest/garden already mentioned; the mandalaesque circus/square at the City's centre; the column in the middle of it that may also be a fountain; the entrance to the Underworld (ostensibly the Underground, the Metro, the Subway), which is described as 'the lair of the Labyrinth-Omphalos Boss', an expression involving an untranslatable pun (Boss=*boss/patron*), referring both to a stone lump, the navel, believed by the early Greeks to be positioned at the middle of the world and, obliquely, to both Minos and Pluto. Immediately under the earth's surface, the dreamer enters a nether city imaging the one above it as though in obverse, to which is appropriate a counterfeit day, bustling with hurrying crowds, concerning which Engels, were he writing today, would surely find words even more scathing than those he used in his mid-nineteenth century study of *The Working Class in Britain*:

> There is something distasteful about the very bustle of the streets, something that is abhorrent to human nature itself. Hundreds of thousands of people of all classes and ranks of society jostle past one another; are they not all human beings with the same characteristics and potentialities, equally interested in the pursuit of happiness? . . . And yet they rush past one another as though they had nothing in common or were in no way associated with one another.

At the beginning of this evocation of a city under ground, which from now on begins to reveal itself as increasingly infernal, I have taken care to introduce the image of Arcades, complete with luxury shopwindows, in recognition of its use by Rimbaud, in one of the *Villes* texts to be found in *Les Illuminations*, (possibly the most remarkable of all premonitory expressions of the specifically modern City myth):

> Sur quelques points des passerelles de cuivre, des plateformes, des escaliers qui contournent les halles et les piliers, j'ai cru pouvoir juger la profondeur de la ville! C'est le prodige dont je n'ai pu me rendre compte: quels sont les niveaux des autres quartiers sur ou sous l'acropole? Pour l'étranger de notre temps la reconnaissance est impossible. Le quartier commerçant est un circus d'un seul style, avec galeries à arcades. . . .

Here it would be possible to see an unconscious anticipation of the inexplicably sinister arcades that are a distinctive feature of so many of the early paintings of Chirico, and though these appear to belong to some small Mediterranean town, they too have surely contributed something to the modern City myth considered visually. And before leaving the subject of this myth, mention must be made of Fritz Lang's classic film of the mid-1920s, *Metropolis*, which must, though it never occurred to me at the time, have been at the back of my mind while I was planning this section of *Night Thoughts*: surely its powerful vision of enslaved masses toiling at giant machines in a vast underground City of the future, menaced by imminent disaster, is one of the most unforgettable achievements of the silent screen.

From the moment my anonymous dreamer begins his descent, the rhythm of the three Narrators' commentary becomes increasingly marked and accelerated. A certain satirical tone also should be perceptible in their account of his progress towards some unspecified appointment, through a labyrinth of staircases, passageways, escalators and corridors, while from time to time an onomatopoeically repetitious Chorus representing the sound of approaching train-wheels is heard intermittently. These Choruses end each time with words that make clear that a typical 'anxiety dream' situation is developing:

> The Damned are the Damned are the Damned are the Damned are The Day of Wrath the Atom Plan the Wrath to Come the Atom Bomb the Coming Day the Greatest Bang the Biggest Bomb the Wrath of God the World of Man the Day to Come the Bang the Bomb . . . (ad inf.)

At the same time, the Narrators recount the varied distractions that offer themselves to the harried throngs attempting to reach the trains, by reciting the contents of the posters and placards on the walls past which they have to hurry: they are solicited by the tasteless allurements of travel agents, the entertainment industry, monotonously overadvertised products, all presented as a rival Chorus of Publicity. This is ended by the first Narrator plainly stating that; 'The Sleeper came here on a Quest, to find that he is lost,' and designating his present environment as 'Latter Pandemonium', the 'Capital of every Pseudo-Super-City State.'

This is the juncture at which the climax and 'Carnival' proper of the episode is reached. Pandemonium, of course, is Milton's name for his Satan's subterranean City in *Paradise Lost*, and ought therefore, strictly speaking, to be distinguished from the Inferno of Dante's *Divine Comedy* as stemming from a Protestant as opposed to a basically Catholic system of theological cosmic reference. But as mentioned earlier, I have attempted no more than an amalgam of fractured mythic symbolism, for the use of which I could if necessary fall back on the old plea of poetic licence. There is, in any case, no space left in which to explore such niceties; though it should be observed that Carnival in Catholic countries marks the beginning of Lent, to be followed by Passion-week and the Resurrection of Easter, while elsewhere the term is now generally used indiscriminately to denote almost any sort of fancy-dress merrymaking.

A voice parodying a typical radio announcer giving a running commentary on some momentous occasion now ends by describing the arrival on the scene (Pluto Plaza) of 'a Very Important Person indeed', 'the Old Man himself'; and this caricature obviously conceals an 'archetypal' compound of at least three figures, Satan, the Devil and Mephistopheles. Satan, according to Hebraic tradition, means 'the adversary', while the Devil in his Mephistophelian role is essentially the preventor or negator: I have in fact presented him as playing the part of an opportunist seducer in the deceptively benevolent guise of a great public personage fulfilling an engagement to deliver a speech declaring 'endless Carnival to be left open to the Four Winds of Publicity, Gossip, Idletalk and Rumour'. He then ritually cuts a ribbon, *cordon* or cord, and calls on the Master of Spring Opening Ceremonies to take charge of the ensuing festive proceedings. The incognito Prince of Darkness's delegate thereupon utters an exhortatory oration in which he urges all those present to fling themselves with abandon into a masked-ball/fashion-show/rock 'n' roll-marathon/orgy during which all remaining sense of care or responsibility may be as forgotten as any sense of danger which might have arisen from the fact that the floor of the Plutonic ballroom is at the same time a skating-rink of black ice which may melt or collapse at any moment. Despite the increasingly loud pulsations of music, a Chorus of intermingling rapturous exclamations is now momentarily to be heard, composed of expressions all of which paradoxically refer (in English) to the reverse of the profane ('Divine!' – 'Out of this world!' – 'Heavenly!' – 'Adorable!', etc.) As Mircia Eliade pointed out, in a paper written in 1959, the reversal of roles and wearing of costumes (*travesti* = temporary transvestism) characteristic of the European Carnival tradition which has its origins in the fertility ceremonies of almost all early cultures, 'implies a total confusion of values, the specific sign of orgiastic ritual'. This muddled brouhaha of sophisticated clichés is abruptly terminated by the first Narrator's quoting two typically classical eighteenth-century couplets from a poem by Pope:

> Hell rises, Heaven descends, and dance on earth:
> Gods, imps, and monsters, music, rage and mirth,
> A fire, a jig, a battle, and a ball;
> Till one wide conflagration swallows all.

These quasi-eschatological lines by Alexander Pope are followed at once by the Voice of a mask, giving sincere utterance to the inward existential anguish hidden by the revellers' simulated 'mirth'. His speech is delivered to the accompaniment of a musical background in which, as specified by my directions, the traditional *Dies Irae* theme is distinguishable, intermingled with the equally traditional, though less ancient, melody known in England as *Girls and Boys Come out to Play*. This music (composed for the BBC production, incidentally, by Humphrey Searle, the sole English pupil of Webern) reaches the climax of its crescendo with a piercing, high-pitched trumpet blast, which at the same time represents the Last Trump and provides the sleeper with a reason to wake up and so escape the by now intolerable situation to which his dream has brought him. 'Sleepers, Awake!'

> The trumpet sounds, the curtain falls, the fabric strange dissolves
> And the familiar scene shows through: the darkened stage
> Which is the sleeper's bedroom; the familiar properties
> Of daily use arranged around the bed. The ordinary street
> Outside the window and its streetlights in the ordinary night.
> You awaken from the Pandemonium of your dream, the midnight carnival,
> And find yourself in the Dark City of the present day again.

The three Narrative voices now only require a few more quietly reflective lines to bring the central section of *Night Thoughts* to an end.

It may be objected that *la ville*, the town, the subject the poets invited to contribute to this compilation have been asked to write about, is not the City of mythical proportions I have attempted to evoke. Certainly most of the poets I know personally, by no means all British, have to spend some of their time in cities but prefer to live as much as possible in the country. The small town in which it is possible to participate to a certain extent in some sort of community life without feeling oppressed by a sense of stagnation is becoming increasingly rare. But perhaps the small country town is the ideal habitat for the poet. At any rate, as long ago as 1908, Miguel de Unamuno put the case for the small town in terms which, to me seem still persuasively valid:

> Very well then – he who has no sense of his own personality and is willing to sacrifice it on the altar of sociability, let him go and lose himself among the millions of a metropolis. For the man who has a longing for Nirvana the metropolis is better than the desert. If you want to submerge your own 'I', better the streets of a great city than the solitudes of the wilderness. It is not a bad thing now and again to visit the great city and plunge into the sea of its crowds, but in order to emerge again upon terra firma and feel the solid ground under one's feet. For my part, since I am interested in individuals – in John and Peter and Richard, in you who are reading this book – but not in the masses they form when banded together, I remain in the small town, seeing every day at the same hour the same men, men whose souls have clashed, and sometimes painfully, with my soul; and I flee from the great metropolis where my soul is whipped with the icy whips of disdainful glances of those who know me not and who are unknown to me. People whom I cannot name . . . horrible!

So I hope it will be considered only natural and not simply escapist that I decided to set the concluding section of *Night Thoughts* in the countryside and to call it *Encounter with Silence*. One of the central themes of the entire work is the ever-increasing danger for the urbanized and technologically-orientated man of today of being swallowed up in the unthinking and manipulable masses. 'But what should it profit a man to gain the whole world yet lose his own soul?' All those individuals who struggle to preserve their independence and essential humanity feel an instinctive solidarity with one another, as I believe contemporary poets do. Which was why I brought my 'radiophonic poem' to an end with the words:

> Greetings to the solitary. Friends, fellow beings, you are not strangers to us. We are closer to one another than we realize. Let us remember one another at night, even though we do not know each other's names.

MEETINGS WITH BENJAMIN FONDANE

[Benjamin Fondane was born in Rumania of German Jewish parents. He settled in Paris in 1923 where he published works of philosophy, poetry and literary criticism. He died in the gas chambers of Birkenau on 3 October 1944.]

My meeting with Fondane at a critical moment in my youth was both providential and decisive. The encounter really took place in the Reading Room of the British Museum, once frequented by Karl Marx, where at the end of 1935 and the beginning of 1936 I used to go to read everything available on Rimbaud, on whom I proposed to write a book as a sequel to a short work I had written on Surrealism.

Amongst the numerous books, mostly in French, with which the B.M. Library supplied me, was one which was probably its most recent acquisition on Rimbaud, Benjamin Fondane's *Rimbaud le voyou*. I had no need to look any further for other books about my favourite French poet for I had found just the book which revealed the Rimbaud I intuitively felt to be the true one, and who attracted me more than any other modern poet. But more even than that, in Fondane I found someone who explained to me why Surrealism no longer satisfied me as a means of poetic expression, nor as a means of revolutionizing human subjectivity, by the fundamental change in society which is necessary if we are to avoid another dictatorship as tyrannical and sterile as those which we have seen up to the present time.

I lost no time in writing a long letter to Fondane, care of his publishers, Denoêl and Steele.

21, Grove Terrace
Teddington,
Middlesex,
England
24.7.37

Dear Sir,
    I have not the least excuse for writing to you; I do not know you, and

---

Aquarius 17/18 (1986-7), pp. 23-9. Translated from the French by Robin Waterfield.

I am not amongst those who write casually to authors whose books they have read.

Nevertheless I feel a strong urge to communicate something to someone, I know that I shouldn't, but it is a desire which I have weakly yielded to. After all it may be of some interest to you to know how your ideas have decisively influenced the thought or should I say the inner life, of someone else.

When I was fourteen I read somewhere an article by an old literary hack of the 1890s, Arthur Symons, in which he wrote in a somewhat summary fashion about Arthur Rimbaud. At that time I had an unbridled taste for the exotic, and the unusual; black magic demonology, erotica, the drawings of Aubrey Beardsley, mystical and mysterious writers. I immediately recognized that Rimbaud was someone of interest to me. Although I could then scarcely read French, I bought his works and with the help of a friend who knew a little more French than I did, I started to translate them almost word for word. You will appreciate that this was for me, a most revealing and disturbing experience. (Phrases in *Illuminations* for example are perhaps more powerfully evocative and hallucinatory for someone who only partially understands French, than for a Frenchman. Soon after an English translation of the *Illuminations* was published which greatly helped my defective understanding.)

I still knew almost nothing about the 'true life' of Rimbaud. The following year an English magazine published a large special number on Surrealism.* This was the beginning of my acquaintance with the writings of André Breton, Eluard's poems and so on. As might be expected all this time I was writing poetry and experimenting with automatic writing and so forth. At sixteen I had 'the good fortune' to have a novel (extremely bad) in which I attempted to chronicle the difficulties of adolescence, accepted by a publisher.

I decided I wanted to be a poet or at least a writer. As I was making no progress at all in the school I was attending, which I found horribly boring, my parents agreed to my leaving. With the money which I had earned from the novel I have mentioned I made my first trip to Paris, where I met some of the frequenters of Montparnasse, artists like Max Ernst, Dalí, and others. . . . For me it was a heady adolescent ferment of ideas, ambitions, poetry, sexual experiences, all of which now seem to me quite unreal.

During the whole of this period I was very much taken up with Surrealist ideas. Surrealism really seemed to be the bomb which could break open to me this dull mediocre world. It was only later that I realized that

---

* Editor's note: *This Quarter*, 'Surrealist Number' (September 1932), guest editor André Breton.

this bomb was only to go off tomorrow, always tomorrow! In 1935 my publishers commissioned me to write a book on the Surrealist movement. I made another trip to Paris where I met Breton who made a great impression on me and Eluard whom I still like very much and Max Ernst and all the others. In the autumn my book was published and so here in England I met people interested in Surrealism. But do you know England?

It is a country where the meaning of revolt has never been understood, where everything is straight away reduced to banality. In England Surrealism was thought to be something artistic (with a vague revolutionary aspect which was forgotten as soon as possible). Last year there was an enormous International Surrealist Exhibition: can you imagine it, it was madly successful, chic, worldly, faintly shocking, 'amusing'.

I was so fed up that I almost at once joined the Communist Party, and for several months was immersed in political action. (This upset Breton whose politics, in any case, I always viewed with suspicion: Trotskyism as politics is 'artistic', unreal, quite unaware of the true nature of politics.)

In October I went with a friend to Barcelona, where I worked for sometime in the government propaganda department.

I spent a whole year writing my big book on Rimbaud. After a year during which I was reading everything I could find about Rimbaud I went to visit a friend George Reavey who lent me *Rimbaud le voyou*. I met Breton who was in London at the time and when he saw the book under my arm, he shook his head in his serious way and said, 'Oh that!, it is a book which is completely antagonistic to me.'

The first time I read it my mind was not open to what it could teach me. I was not ready to understand the things that I believe I understand today. As I have said I still believed in the possibility of finding what I was looking for, this non-existent solution? – in politics; I was soon disillusioned.

This past year has been for me a period of great inner struggle. I have tried to understand myself, I have undergone painful experiences and frustrations of all sorts – I leave you to imagine them, no doubt they are very usual. During all this time Rimbaud was very much in my mind. Thinking about him and trying to understand him it soon became apparent to me that of all possible interpretations yours was the only one that I could accept without reserve: I found that I had in me, something hard to define but to put it at its lowest, a great curiosity to know about the realm of the metaphysicians (I don't like this expression, and would like to find another). I read Pascal again avidly; then Dostoievsky, Papini and Baudelaire, Kierkegaard for the first time; Unamuno, Chestov (*All Things are Possible*) and much else besides.

All this took up all my time for several months. At first I accepted the position implicit in your book and in the thought of all these men, but without accepting it *in its entirety*, i.e. resisting it and believing also in something else. Only recently, in a period of solitude and great concentration, have I understood that there is no other way for me but to give myself completely and for ever, for how could one draw back, to despair. You can see that I am taking my first steps in this realm; but I have no doubt that it is where I belong. I am nearly twenty-one years old (but it is surely useless to ask whether I am too young for such knowledge, for one either *knows* or one doesn't). You must surely know about all this inner confusion and contradiction. One exists above all to discover why one should wish to live. For me it is because I believe the simple but frightening truth that I live in order to pass on information about something truly mysterious. So then do I yield to despair? If one believes that there is some value in the *cry* of suffering? But there, I am talking nonsense.

If only one could infect the spirits of a few others! Apart from the fact that all ambitions are ridiculous, isn't this the most malicious of all?

I hardly expect, dear Sir, an answer to this letter. I only hope that you will believe in my complete sincerity in writing to you and that you will excuse my very imperfect French.

Please accept my dear Sir my gratitude as well as my sincerest regards.

David Gascoyne

Fondane replied to my letter of admiration and unsolicited confidences with the greatest of tact, and I might add caring. I cannot say how much I regret having not been able to keep his letter, which I carried about in my pocket for years.* In an old notebook however I jotted down several phrases and I think I can still more or less faithfully reproduce the contents of his letter. He replied to me that seemingly we can never discover truth by our own efforts but that sometimes truth *lays hold of us*. 'God knows,' he wrote (and here I remember his exact words) 'if in following the path of Surrealism you were far off the mark . . .' With this letter which became for me as precious as one of Rainer Maria Rilke's *Letters to a Young Poet*, Fondane sent me an inscribed copy of *La Conscience malheureuse*, which had been published and advising just me, so caringly and kindly, that no one should approach the experience of real despair with that sort of romanticism which is so common among adolescents nor with the dilettante attitude of someone enjoying powerful

---

* Editor's note: I found a copy of Fondane's reply in one of D.G.'s Notebooks in the British Library. It has since been published in the *Bulletin de la Société d'Etudes Benjamin Fondane, BSEBF*, No. 3 (Printemps 1995, Jerusalem), pp. 2-4.

emotional experiences, but only when one is spiritually armed to struggle, like the devil to retain a good reason for living.

11 rue de la Bûcherie
Paris Ve
11.VIII.37

Dear Sir,

Last week I decided to go to stay in France for some time and your letter and your book arrived on the eve of my departure which is why I have hardly had time until now to write and thank you. I am very grateful to you for having sent me *La Conscience malheureuse* which was a pleasure I had in any case intended to give myself as soon as possible.

So far I have only read parts of it and I will write more when I have really read and thought about it. I was very moved by your letter, and I have a number of things to say to you. Although I do not in any way wish to discount the debt which I owe you for having helped me to formulate and 'clarify' the way I see things: still I believe that I would in any case sooner or later have reached this point by myself – I mean that your ideas may well be those I myself was seeking and had not just stumbled upon by chance. I also believe that it is impossible to have reached such a point of view without a struggle, without agonizing over it and without having made one's thought an integral part of one's whole life. As you say, how can it possibly be a mere question of the right kind of sensibility? Sensibility is something far too weak to stand up to the demands of despair.

Soon after writing to you I began a notebook of *pensées* under the title *Blind Man's Buff** which I would much like to show you sometime. You see I, no more than you, hold that despair (or rather the negation of despair) is an end in itself. A phrase which I found in Chestov expresses my ambition 'Creation *Ex nihilo*'. 'In the destructive element immerse', said Conrad, that is what one must do before being able to create, obviously. But most people who would agree with this, do not understand how *absolute*, how extreme this really is. One can strip oneself and yet not be naked.

I now hold the opinion that there is no creative work which is not, for its creator, the result of the need to find some protection against the powers of destruction, a shield against affliction. A work of art should

---

Editor's note: See section 6, pp. 457-9 for the only surviving extract.

grow like one's skin in response to the hostility of nature. To believe this is the same as believing in *the cry* which arises from us in spite of ourselves is it not?

What you call 'hope' I would call 'courage'. Courage to continue walking along the path no matter how difficult, in the face of contradiction and absurdity, courage to admit that one is afraid. But when one says hope one asks oneself hope in what? . . . and I can find no answer. Or I see this one possibility, that one day before I die I shall be able, in a moment of almost superhuman concentration, a moment of the integration of all my vital powers, to make a long-awaited *leap* and in so doing reach understanding and illumination which will make the long search and struggle undertaken blindly, worthwhile. I have in mind the principle of dis-continuity and also the idea of non-temporality (please forgive me for expressing myself so badly and with such confusion).

Once again my dear Sir I thank you for your most sympathetic reply. Believe me your sincere friend.

David Gascoyne

The first time I met Fondane in person was I think towards the end of the summer of 1937. 'Come and see me, if ever you find yourself in Paris again' he had written to me. I can no longer remember how I knew the address of the place where he used to spend some weeks in the summer on holiday, but as soon as I arrived in France that year, I went to see him in a little town (La Varenne Saint-Hilaire) south of Paris not more than three-quarters of an hour by train from the Gare de Lyon. After drinking tea together almost in the English fashion, though I don't think he had laid on this sort of refreshment especially in my honour, he took me for a boat trip on the little lake in front of the house where he had rented accommodation. He was an enthusiastic oarsman. He talked to me about philosophical questions in his own ardent way, which others have described far better than I could ever hope to do, while smoking his pipe which I came to think of as being an inseparable part of him. The following autumn and winter, it was always to number 6 rue Rollin that I went to meet him, usually at 10 o'clock in the evening. Not always once a week to be sure, but as often as he could find a free evening to receive me. Today I know very well that these meetings were for me a piece of good fortune and a great privilege and that it would be impossible to exaggerate how much I profited, and not merely intellectually, from them.

In an old building, next door to the one in which Pascal died, one reached his little flat at the top of some stone stairs, to be greeted at the door by the philosopher-poet, smiling as usual, but at the same time obviously serious and to my eyes somewhat mysterious. He led me in semi-darkness to his own sitting room, which was also his work-room whose decor was remarkable for the magnificent illuminated aquarium let in to one of the walls.

He then began the little ceremony of making Turkish coffee. After that we settled down to talk until midnight and sometimes much later. As a matter of fact, most of the time I listened to him talking about all sorts of things, a bit of politics, the latest news which became more and more sinister, and finally always on philosophy. To be sure we also talked a bit about poetry, but I had the impression that he was somewhat reserved when talking on this subject especially when talking about his own work; for myself I must admit that at this time I had just begun to see Pierre Jean Jouve, who did me the honour of discussing specifically poetic problems. In any case what I wanted to hear from Fondane was him talking about his ideas, existential philosophy, real thought . . .

When I read the special number of the review *Non Lieu* devoted to Benjamin Fondane I was very touched to see that E. M. Cioran could remember me and the fact that I had told him how I had met Fondane in the snow in the Boulevard St Michel on the very day, or was it the day after, the death of Chestov which he announced to me in just three words, without any expression. He gave me the impression of being deeply shocked by the loss of his great friend and master, an image of Fondane, which, as M. Cioran relates, actually haunted me for many months to come. And I can now say, much longer than that, for it was the last time in my life that I saw the writer who for such a short while was a friend for whom I had quickly acquired an enormous feeling of admiration and gratitude. In conclusion I would like to correct what M. Cioran wrote about me when he spoke of 'a tragic fate' which befell me 'in other circumstances'. I have passed through periods of complete sterility, many disappointments and nervous crises, but they are nothing which can possibly be compared to the experiences of the victims of the Nazis, above all to the experiences of a man as clear-sighted and sensitive as Benjamin Fondane.

THE MOST ASTONISHING BOOK IN THE ENGLISH LANGUAGE

During and for some time after World War II, I became an obsessed collector of a highly heterogeneous variety of second-hand books: Victoriana/curiosa, illustrated English and French children's books of the nineteenth century, Proto-scifi of the last 150 years, Utopias, every kind of Occultism: Paracelsus, Swedenborg and Boehme, magic, alchemy and Rosicrucianism – and alongside all these, every less well-known English poet from Skelton to the Nineties, diaries, journals and letters of all periods, and the works of Henry James. As a C3 civilian, touring the country as an actor with the Coventry Rep. for ENSA in the early and mid-1940s provided me with unrivalled opportunities for bibliomania: billeted each week in a different provincial town, North, South, East and West, with in every one of these towns at least one second-hand bookshop to be explored and scoured. Tunbridge Wells, for instance, abounded at that period in a fascinating profusion of such shops. And prices in the book-dealing trade in those days have never been so minimal since. When the War was over, living in NW London, I continued my frenzied hunt almost daily: a short Tube ride to Tottenham Court Road or Leicester Square brought me to Charing Cross Road and environs, in particular to Cecil Court, where today on the site of Watkins Occult Bookshop a shop bearing the founder's name still exists, though the revamped interior is unrecognizable to an old frequenter. I was able recently to impress the efficient young man in charge of one side of the store by telling him I could remember talking long ago to the old patriarchally bearded Mr Watkins about his memories of Madame H. P. Blavatsky.

It was in this shop, soon after it had come under the managership of old Mr Watkins' son, that one Friday afternoon I came across, by stooping down to inspect a dark lower shelf of miscellanea, a large heavy tome that preliminary inspection at once revealed as an item of unusual and peculiar curiosity. On the dark-blue cover and broad spine were stamped

---

An abbreviated version of this essay appeared in *Brought to Book: The Balance of Book and Life*, ed. Ian Breakwell and Paul Hammond (Penguin Books, 1994), pp. 75-9. The original typescript is dated 18.IX.92, and runs to fourteen A4 pages, single spaced. This is the 'second version'. The 'first version' of five A4 pages is dated (?1960).

in faded gold: *OAHSPE: A New Bible*, with a logo design of a circle containing what appears to be a maple leaf transfixed by a large Plus sign (+) rather than a cross. The title page, after the title just quoted, is full from top to bottom with subtitles in smaller typeface of varying sizes, too long to quote in full:

> The Words of Jehovih / and his / Angel Ambassadors. / A Sacred History / of the Dominions of the Higher and Lower Heavens of the Earth / for the past / Twenty-Four Thousand Years, / Being from the Submersion of the Continent of Pan in the Pacific Ocean, commonly called the Flood / or Deluge / to the Kosmon Era. Also a Brief History of the Preceding / Fifty-five Thousand Years, / Together with . . .

followed by two further paragraphs in larger characters, ending with:

> Formed / in Words / in the Thirty-Third Year / of the Kosmon Era.

Watkins' bookshop fifty years ago was not very well lit, nor was it spacious enough to allow one to examine large spread-out volumes closely. Opening *OAHSPE* at random, as I have just done today, I might have managed hastily to read such a passage as this:

> 8. The end of dawn is near at hand: I will give a feast, a very great feast. Go ye and survey the ground from Croashivi to the Lakes of Oochi-loo, in etherea, and for the length thereof make ye a width in the form of Fete;[1] and the road of the Fete shall be sufficient for the passage of twelve avalanzas abreast; and the depth of Fete shall be as from the surface of the earth unto Chinvat. Within twelve sios of Abarom, and of the height of the circuit of Bilothowitchieun shall ye carry the border flames; and the flames shall be of double currents, going and coming, that the food of the feast may be . . .

At this point, the page (no. 345) is divided in half, the lower being devoted to Chapter XV of 'The First Book of God', printed concurrently with Chapter XI of the 'Book of Cpenta-Armij, daughter of Jehovih'. The sample quoted is obviously far more exotic, and subtly more sinister than the Brontës' Gondal saga, which is straightforward and homely in comparison. I had time to glance at some of the later of the book's 891 pages and to catch sight of one or two of the 94 black and white plates illustrating them. These are a curious mixture of the pseudo-

---

[1] '*Fete* or *Fate*, signifying beyond me there is no appeal', Index to *OAHSPE*.

primitive and the would-be scientific. Plate 89, for example, purporting to represent a 'Sectional View of Golgotha Temple, 11,000 years before Kosmon', reminded me for a moment of the formalized frottage forests of Max Ernst, but on close examination one finds that the dark columns, some seven inches high, divided by narrow white bands, are made up of thousands of tiny close-packed crudely drawn skulls. Space does not permit further description of these numerous disturbing designs: they are definitely curioser and curioser.

It did not take me long to decide to purchase this very peculiar rarity, though it cost about all I had in my wallet that day, long before credit cards were thought of, and I took it home with me to Teddington, there to spend a weekend examining my astonishing find at leisure. (The adjective applied to *OAHSPE* in the title I have given the present article, which is a quotation of the first sentence of the Preface to the Eleventh American edition of the book, is by no means hyperbolical. The edition of *OAHSPE* at present in my possession is not the one that I bought originally, because after less than a week I took it back to Cecil Court and asked Mr Watkins Jr to take it back in exchange for something less astonishing, as I couldn't stand having it in my house at the time, and I believe I actually said: 'This book stinks'. The violence of my reaction was certainly not aroused particularly by the speciously unorthodox and in places specifically anti-christian doctrine the new Bible set out to propagate – Nietzsche's *The Anti-Christ* is accurately described in the Penguin edition's blurb as 'vivid and forceful' – or the way it peremptorily condemns the believers of all other creeds than that of the Essenes of Kosmon ('A Fraternity of Faithists') not just to oblivion but to hell; I was revolted above all by its unmitigated gigantism: it contains thirty-five 'Books', each on an average of thirty pages, divided into many chapters, and every one of these books of revelation swarms with excessive enumerations. Every entity apart from Jehovih and Kosmon appears to be multitudinously plural. Here is a specimen sentence from the end of the 9th verse of the IVth chapter of the 'Book of Aph, Son of Jehovih':

> Here standeth a hundred million come from Laygas; a hundred million from Inopta; two hundred million from Karduk; a hundred million from Buchk; two hundred million from Nin; two hundred and fifty million from Luth'wig; a hundred million from Pied; two hundred million from Raig; fifty million from Naivis; two hundred million from Dak'dak, and two hundred and fifty million from Od.

This delirious abandon to multiplication and endless nomenclatural glossolalia appears to me essentially symptomatic of a diagnosticable form of mental or psychic disorder. Such catalogues yield not an iota of the kind of pleasure that can be derived from encounters with the preposterous whenever some element of literary merit or ingenuity is involved, as in, for instance, the writings of Jean-Pierre Brisset or Raymond Roussel.

In spite of the immediate revulsion bordering on indignation that *OAHSPE* provoked in me, it was not long after I had persuaded Mr Watkins, (who assured me that the book, though rather odd, was of perfectly respectable provenance), to take it back with reluctance and exchange it for something less perturbing, that I began to regret having parted with it so hastily. Soon it had begun to haunt me.

★   ★   ★

During the immediately post-war period I found myself involved in attempting, with much difficulty and in unpropitious lodgings, to give expression to my teeming thoughts concerning the critical and problematic mid-century state of mankind and the world (although already aware of the unsatisfactory and misleading nature of all such abstractions) in a book to which I gave the title (inspired by a tentative familiarity with Jung's writings on alchemy) *The Sun at Midnight: Prolegomena to a Philosophy of Dialectical Materialism in the Service of Theocratic Revolution.* The philosophical basis for this project was to have been a synthesis of post-Marxist, post-Kierkegaardian theory, supported by a metaphysical basis that I amateurishly dubbed 'Logontology', persevering in the attempt to get an outline of all this written, despite an uneasy awareness of being far too uneducated to be able to work it all out professionally. I only refer to all this because the small, catholic and disparate reading I had undertaken in preparation for this would-be magnum opus had filled my mind with a confused medley of information regarding numerous fringe philosophies and religio-social theories and sects: Swedenborg, Louis-Claude de Saint-Martin, Ballanche, Fourier, Mrs Atwood, H. P. Blavatsky, the writers of *The Golden Dawn*, Yeats's *A Vision*, C. G. Jung's *Seven Sermons to the Dead*, et al, not forgetting all that I had already read about the post-Dadaist, proto-Surrealist so-called 'Period of Sleeping-Fits', during which materialist-minded poets employed the methods of practising mediums to contact 'the other side', thought of by them as the Unconscious mind. In view of all this, and considering that at the back of my mind there was always a vague fixed idea of Palingenesia, the coming of the Millennium, the Revolution that would at last reunify the nations and the split human psyche at the same time, it was only natural that from time to time I should remember having read in *OAHSPE*, during my brief ownership of the book, that (and these are the actual words, though at the time I could not have remembered them exactly):

In some form, directly or implied the Kingdom of Heaven, the Millennium, the Fifth Monarchy, the Theocratic Commune, the Social Commonwealth or whatever you wish to call it, is an essential feature of every bible in existence.

It would, I think now, be truer to say that I thought of *OAHSPE* ('pronounced O as in clock, AH as in father and SPE as in speak') not just from time to time but increasingly often. I had from the first been intrigued and puzzled by the existence since 1882 of a sect or cult made up of people calling themselves Essenes or Kosmon, or Faithists, and that they understood Kosmon to be 'a heavenly kingdom over North Guatama', and that Guatama signified for them America, also 'the meeting of nations and the dawn of Kosmon', and that they supposed the Kosmon Era to be 'when the inhabitation of the earth shall be completed'. I began to wonder who these people could be, how many of them there were, where would one be likely to find them, where and how often did they congregate, and, if they held ceremonies or services, what these would be like. Such questions are bound to lead to speculative fantasizing of a more or less arbitrary kind. My curiosity regarding them led me to ask everyone I knew who had any interest in 'the esoteric' whether they had ever heard of *OAHSPE* or Kosmon: almost invariably the answer was negative. One had to conclude that a group of people had for about seventy years been numerous and affluent enough to produce twelve American and four English editions of an enormous, well produced, illustrated book as big as a city telephone directory, while remaining so discreet about their creed and its very existence that only a handful of invisible cranks appeared to have heard of them; while if ever they had been investigated by a serious specialist in minority or fringe religions or cults, this putative researcher had been signally inefficacious in propagating his findings.

During my first stay in Paris after the end of the War, I was introduced by a friend with Quai d'Orsay connections to a number of people in diplomatic circles with literary or artistic interests. One evening during a small drinks party at the apartment of an attaché at the Greek embassy, a chance turn in the conversation stimulated me to start describing the special oddity of a cult that I'd come across called Kosmon; whereupon an elegant young Greek I'd never met before told me in fluent English: 'Oh yes, I know what you mean. My nanny was one. I remember her talking about it quite a lot when I was little.' This occurred years after I'd returned *OAHSPE* to Watkins' bookshop, and years before an American bookdealer in Oregon who had come to know of my continued interest in it kindly sent me the copy in my possession today. I was quite reassured to find that I had not imagined the whole thing, since at least one Englishwoman in Greece in the 1930s had actually been a practising Faithist.

It must have been at just about this time that one of my favourite Hitchcock films was released, called *The Man Who Knew Too Much*, which begins with Doris Day singing *Que sera sera* in Tunis, and ends with Ann Todd being discovered to be mixed up with a distinctly sinister group holding bogus services in a sort of Methodist hall in, probably, Bayswater. I came out of the cinema thinking: now that's exactly the sort of locale I've always imagined Kosmon initiates congregating in.

For some years I continued to speculate intermittently about the possible existence of an underground organization concerned with an aberrant fake book of revelations purporting to expound the secrets of the visible and invisible universes and their cosmogonies. A time came when my mental state began to deteriorate to such an extent that eventually I underwent a series of what are known as nervous breakdowns. Preoccupation with Kosmon and *OAHSPE* began to weave itself into the web of delusions and obsessions in which my inner life had become enmeshed. I still have a distinct recollection of an incident characteristic of the way I thought about Kosmon's imaginary devotees in those days (though I still cannot with complete certainty refer to the cult's *non-existent* devotees: it is just possible that a few linger on in California, or even New York, where *OAHSPE* first came into existence 120 years ago). After a night when I had been engaged in some now totally forgotten though I suspect disreputable activity, I found myself on the deserted platform of Bond Street Underground station awaiting the first Tube train of the day. A haggard middle-aged woman dressed in the crumpled remains of what must once have been a couturier's costume was straggling on a bench, getting up now and again to slouch to the edge of the platform and back. I observed on one of her cheeks a black streak that might have been made by a stick of anthracite and left there deliberately. I thought to myself immediately: that's how they recognize one another, it's a secret sign indicating that they belong to – I probably did not actually think of Kosmon by name, but that's what I felt. For a time, whenever I saw someone whose face had not obviously been cleaned that day, I believed I had recognized another member of a queer clandestine society. There is in fact no evidence whatever that the Essenes of Kosmon, (who are given two addresses on *OAHSPE*'s title-page, one a box number in Montrose, Colorado, and the other 2208 W. Eleventh Street, Los Angeles), constituted a secret society. The fact that the Preface to the First Edition of *OAHSPE* is dated 1882, and that this date corresponds to the emergence in the South of a sinister misuse of the letter K, as in the K K Klan, may possibly be blamed on the Zeitgeist of the day, but should not be supposed to indicate any racist tendency on the part of Kosmon, supposedly originating in a preoccupation with the origin and nature of the Cosmos. The Preface of 1882 claims that *Oahspe* 'is not a destroyer of old systems or religions. It reveals a new one, adapted to this age, wherein all men can be as brethren'. The Order of Freemasons, of course, has always made similar proclamations, and no longer tries to keep up any pretence of secrecy. These are rational and detached observations, however, of a kind I had become incapable of by the time the balance of my mind had become disturbed enough to be certifiable. During the ten years I spent mainly in France before the first of the breakdowns I have mentioned I no longer thought very often about Kosmon; I knew of no French phenomenon that could be considered connected with it, though the land of Reason has always been riddled with obscure cults. L. Ron Hubbard and Scientology were beginning to make the headlines, though, and were probably featured in *Paris Match* or *L'Express*.

A few years after having been sent back to England as a result of my first serious breakdown, I began to be obsessed with a combination of conspiratorial and parousial notions, in which both Kosmon and Scientology played a large part. The disorder I was suffering from when admitted to a large psychiatric establishment near Epsom was accompanied by a number of vehement convictions. I believed myself to be a vessel containing momentous insights that it was my bounden duty to impart. The world, society, civilization, was in imminent danger and everyone had to be alerted if it was to be saved. Though normally as politically and socially aware and responsible a person as the next man, the danger I envisaged in my illuminated state had nothing to do with nuclear holocausts or neo-nazi coups d'état. I believed intensely that there was a worldwide conspiracy going on, the intent of which was to rob us of our essential humanity and acquire domination of our minds and souls. Scientology was allied with the adepts of Kosmon at the heart of this conspiracy. Before being carried off by the police to the environs of Epsom under Section whatever the empowering order is called, I made an appointment with Mr Watkins and someone I believed to be his collaborator in the world of occult propaganda and, much to their bewilderment I now imagine, delivered them with a most serious warning, amounting to an ultimatum. When I had settled down in the place appointed for me in the Reception Ward of the hospital to which I had been taken, I realized that I was surrounded by people who would be specially susceptible to my message, and were in fact eagerly awaiting it without yet being fully aware of how much they needed it. This period of my life undeniably had its unpleasant side, and I emerged from it with my quite decent clothing in such a terrible state that before I was finally discharged, a male nurse had to accompany me to the local branch of Burton's to acquire a readymade replacement suit.

I have tried to give some account of my experiences of this time in a monologue entitled *Self-Discharged** that was broadcast by Radio 3 some years ago, and subsequently published in Satish Kumar's periodical *Resurgence*. A young publisher in Bordeaux is about to bring out a French translation of this account.[1] It was not possible to recount all the significant things that occurred to me during my temporary derangement in the time-limit of a half-hour programme, so no mention is made in this monologue of the nasty moment I went through when I discovered that the monosyllabically uncommunicative old man who had just been allotted the bed next to mine was actually a longstanding Kosmon initiate and official, and even had a copy of *OAHSPE* in a tin box that had to be kept under his bed, as there was not enough room for it in his locker and a proper safe place for it had not yet been found. I spent a whole night trying to get out of bed when everyone in the ward was asleep and my new neighbour was snoring, in order to appropriate the precious but deadly box and somehow dispose of it, but just at the moment when I thought I had secured my quarry, a prowling night nurse caught sight of my attempted action, and I soon found myself being forcibly sedated.

Towards the end of my enforced sojourn in a psychiatric institution, I found myself able, after a decade of hopeless unproductivity, once more to write. This is supposed to be an account of a book, not of my psychosomatic or writing problems; but there is a link. While still in hospital I began composing a series of aphoristic paragraphs in which I attempted to fix the more vivid insights that had come to me while I was 'out of my mind'. My friend Alan Clodd, of the Enitharmon Press, came out from London sometimes to visit me during my detention. He read some of these pages, before they'd been typed; apparently not finding them incomprehensibly delirious, he encouraged me to write more. Eventually I passed on to him some fifty pages of what my be described as 'inspired writing'; and within less than a year, Alan Clodd had published a small, beautifully printed and produced volume of fifty-five pages with a title-page that reads: *The Sun at Midnight: Notes on the Story of Civilization Seen as the History of the Great Experimental Work of the Supreme Scientist.* — *Aphorisms (Not yet in proper numbered sequence — As from the week-end in Amsterdam, May 2-4, 5 1969*. At the foot of the page my name, followed by Enitharmon Press / London / 1970. In the centre of the page is a

---

* Editor's note: See pp. 215-27, Section 3.

[1] Published as *Quitus* in *Exploration*, traduction et préface de Michèle Duclos (Bordeaux: Editions Dufourg-Tandrup, 1992), pp. 41-68.

reproduction of a drawing of 'the Hermetic androgyne' from a sixteenth-century manuscript; and at the end of the book is another drawing, from a different alchemical manuscript, representing 'Nature as woman and tree'. Both these designs were reproduced from a book that I had with me most of the time I was in hospital and seriously read in more lucid moments, Titus Burckhardt's *Alchemy*, published in 1967 by Stuart & Watkins (the same Watkins as the owner/manager of the bookshop in Cecil Court). *The Sun at Midnight* contained two poems, not deliberately related to its main theme, and my only remaining copy is one of a limited de luxe edition of 350 copies. By the time I'd fully recovered comparative sanity, I found the book somewhat embarrassing and could no longer identify myself with many of the maxims and often cryptic pronouncements contained in it. Aphorism no. 4, dated 10.V.69, is straightforward enough, and makes quite good sense today:

> For the bringing to pass of the final wonders of the Great Work it is necessary that the word *Community* should become more familiar in the world than the word Communism. *Everyone* is sick of the isms. Great News (for Sunday newspaper readers) . . .

Though I still regard Alchemy, in the way it has been interpreted by Jung, as providing a system of symbols invaluable for the understanding of developmental and metamorphic processes, I no longer refer to or use it continually as I did at one time.

The real reason for my referring to my odd and now very rare little book is that Aphorism no. 8 reads:

> Whatever has become of Kosmon and Oaspeh? Can they really exist? This is the most baffling mystery of occultism I have ever by chance stumbled on. The most authentically inauthentic pseudo-religion of desperate insanity.

Within a few years of publishing the book containing this query and categorical judgement, I began corresponding with an American book-dealer specializing in twentieth-century English poetry. Charles Seluzicki was at that time sending out his catalogues, some of which featured items of my own published work, from Baltimore; after the Three Mile Island disaster, he fled across America to get as far away from the vicinity as possible, and ended by setting up his business in Portland, Oregon, where that State was soon after disturbed by a spectacular volcanic eruption. He had read *The Sun at Midnight* and was offering it for sale at what seemed to me a spectacular sum of dollars. Within a short while he was browsing one day at Portland's second-hand book market and came across a copy of *OAHSPE* there. He recognized it at once, despite the misspelling in my eccentric collection of aphorisms, due to my not having seen it for about thirty years, and generously posted it across the Atlantic to me.

* * *

I believe that the *OAHSPE* that I originally found in Watkins' shop in Cecil Court must have been a third English edition copy, dated 1926. I have no recollection of its having contained a photographic frontispiece representing Dr John Ballou Newbrough, the author, or should one say agent or recorder, of the New Bible . . . formed in words in the thirty-third year of the Kosmon Era. If it had, I am sure that I should not soon have forgotten his very sane, calm and mildly brooding countenance, which might easily be taken for that of a typical mid-nineteenth century philanthropist. I have already quoted some sentences from the Preface to the twelfth American edition of 1951, which Charles Seluzicki sent me, and could well conclude this article simply by quoting further from the rest of its two and a half large pages. As I mentioned at the outset, it begins by stating that *OAHSPE* is the most astonishing book in the English language. I have to admit now that it remains for me one of the most astonishing documents of its kind that I have ever come across. In comparison, the book of Mormon, divided into twenty-five books of varying length, allegedly engraved on plates of gold discovered by Joseph Smith in 1827, written in the style of the Authorized Version of the Bible, is perfectly respectable and conventional. In a Penguin study called *Sacred Books of the World*, the editor, Dr A. C. Bouquet, commenting on the concluding Epistle of Moroni, 'a good deal of it in the style of such an early Christian sermon as the sub-apostolic Second Epistle of Clement of Rome', adds that it 'is painfully easy to invent material of this sort', and that 'the art of composing pseudepigrapha is by no means extinct, even among Christians of the nineteenth century.

Pseudepigrapha is no doubt a most fitting term to apply to the thirty-six Books making up the main part of *OAHSPE*'s overwhelming bulk. It is difficult, however, to believe that their composition can have been 'painfully easy'. The amount of invention of mythical entities, as manifold though more arbitrary than the strangely named beings peopling the Prophetic Books of William Blake, together with the numerous references to light, heat, electricity and their causes, the time-cycles far more enormous and complex than anything Vico divined, the evident familiarity with such concepts as relativity, the curvature of space, lens effect on the atmosphere of planets and other concerns of astrophysics, are sufficient in themselves to strain average credulity to the utmost. Strangest perhaps of all is the method employed in the composition of *Oahspe* revealed by the anonymous author of the Preface to the 1951 edition. We are first told that Dr John B. Newbrough was a graduate in both medicine and dentistry, gifted with exceptional powers of extrasensory perception, whose hobby for many years was psychic research. (It should be remembered that what soon became the international Spiritualist movement had first erupted in mid-nineteenth century America). 'After several years playing around with various mediums the good doctor became disgusted with the vacuity of the things they told him', disgusted also with the low grade of intelligence displayed by supposed out-of-the-body intelligences.

> The years between 1871 and 1881 were spent in spiritual purification during which time he became aware of supernatural guidance. Instructed to purchase a typewriter, which had just been invented, he did so. Upon sitting at the instrument an hour before dawn he discovered that his hands typed without his conscious control. In fact he was not aware that his hands typed unless he read what was being printed. He was told that he was to write a book – he must not read what he was writing until it was completed. At the end of the year when the manuscript was completed he was instructed to read and publish the book titled OAHSPE, a New Bible.

A few more extracts from the Preface already quoted will indicate the approved way to read the book, a way I have never attempted to follow. A long book would be necessary to present even an adequate preliminary analysis of this enormous anomalous text. Since receiving the copy I am now referring to, I have never done more than open it from time to time, examine passages here and there with fascinated but equally repelled attention, form a resolve to write something about it one day, and then put it back on the shelf wondering many things at once, among them the question of what sort of readership one might most appropriately address in an attempt to convey its most characteristic features. The would-be student of *OAHSPE* is told by its Preface:

> The reading of OAHSPE is an undertaking of the most assiduous care. It is not a book for the casual, superficial reader but for the earnest, persistent seeker of light.
> With humble but firm assurance, the following is offered as a correct method of study:
> BEGIN AT THE FIRST PAGE and READ CHAPTER BY CHAPTER. The three books titled Cosmogony and Prophecy,

Saphah and Bon's Book of Praise may be omitted at the first reading and reserved for later assimilation.

Do not skip around in OAHSPE in an effort to secure a 'general idea' of the contents. When this is attempted, a state of confusion results which is detrimental to a true understanding of the contents.

Without pretending to have attained anything like a 'true understanding' of the book's contents, I can nevertheless say that a reader who got no further than page three might appreciate something of the context of the New Bible's gestation — during the aftermath of the American Civil War, a time of increasing dissemination and acceptance of Darwinism and the popularization of 'Science' — and at the same time acquire a totally misleading impression of the tenor of most of the remaining 890 pages. After an opening section of one and a half pages of 26 verses called simply OAHSPE comes a two and a half page chapter entitled 'The Voice of Man'. Here are verses 33 to 37:

> They preach and pray in sufficient truth; but not one of these people practiseth peace, love and virtue, in any degree commensurate with their understanding. These religions have not saved from sin any nation or city on the whole earth.
> In vain have I searched for a plan of redemption; a plan that would make the earth a paradise, and the life of man a glory unto Thee, and a joy unto himself. But alas, the two extremes, riches and poverty, have made the prospect of a millennium a thing of mockery.
> For one man that is rich there are a thousand poor, and their interests are in an interminable conflict with one another. Labor crieth out in pain; but capital striketh him with a heartless blow.
> Nation is against nation; king against king; consumer against producer; yea, man against man in all things upon earth.
> Because the state is rotten, the politician feedeth thereon; because society is rotten, the lawyer and court have riches and sumptuous feasts; because the flesh of my people is rotten, the physician findeth a harvest of comfort.

Is it possible that these words were automatically typed a hundred and ten years ago? Can the young Dr Newbrough have studied the works of Pierre-Joseph Proudhon? Had he ever heard of Karl Marx? The last phrase is a cogent prophecy of a time when psychiatric counselling and therapy constitute one of the USA's most lucrative growth industries.

Here is the final sentence of the already quoted Preface:

On a hundred fields of eager research science is making, or about to make discoveries that proclaim OAHSPE as the ultimate textbook of Perfected Science.

The Essene Faithists believed that the year 1 of the Kosmon Era had been 1848, long known as 'the year of revolutions'. The kind of scientific developments that most preoccupied them (or Dr Newbrough or his control) have by now reached a scale as colossal as the innumerable infinities and time-scales that are strained after in page after page of *OAHSPE*. The strangest, and in a way most contemporary part of the book is that which concerns Cosmogony and Prophecy. It refers constantly to nebulae and what it calls vortexya. The word *orachnebuahgalah* is used to denote a vast unit of time that can be conveniently charted in periods of faith, arbitration, worship, learning, change, war and peace, repeated ad nauseam. It is indeed nausea that overcomes one more often than boredom when perusing these repetitive, swarming, nonsensical, grandiose compendia.

The whole nineteenth century was full, in the English-speaking countries of basically Protestant persuasion, of interpretations by theologians and cranks of the Book of Revelations, or Apocalypse. A minor surprising feature of *OAHSPE* is how little it relies on images and symbolism made universally familiar by the conclusion of the Christian Bible. The book which purports to replace this now redundant work, as well as the Koran, the Vedas and the teachings of the Buddha, has a Glossary of Strange Words, and a page of Hints to the Reader. The latter are chiefly designed to inform the reader about the Beast with four heads which possessed the earth till the Kosmon Era came along,

> As for Example: *Looeamong* was the false God who founded, by inspiration, the great sect called *Christians*. He is first mentioned in Book of Eskra, chap. xii; and his career is continued in the Books of Eskra and Es, until he is finally cast into hell, which corresponds in date to the time the pope established himself as viceregent on earth, and very properly because his God was *non est*.

The end of the Book of Discipline, with which *OAHSPE* tediously concludes on p. 844, is followed by forty pages of Index. The most significant thing to be learnt from an examination of the Oahspean Glossary and Index is that they are haunted by the ghost of Swedenborg. The prominence of references to Zarathustra is perhaps one of the most surprising things from the historical point of view, considering that Friedrich Nietzsche's immensely influential version of the Sayings of this legendary prophet did not come to be written until 1883. Anyone inclined to believe that there must be something to be taken seriously in C. G. Jung's notion of Synchronicity will surely feel that it is given support by odd coincidences such as this. Zarathustra is at the head of the List of Portraits, which follows the List of (80) Plates illustrating *OAHSPE*, after the Glossary. A small-type note tells the reader that Zarathustra

> erroneously called Zoroastra, [was] a Persian lawgiver who lived in the cycle of Fragapatti, eight thousand nine hundred years ago, the farthest back of all historical characters. Both Buddhist and Christian religions are said to be made up chiefly from the history and miracles of Zarathustra [. . . .] Zarathustra was of enormous size, and of neither sex, being an i-e-su.

The Index informs one that I-e-su (or Y-e-shuah) signifies without evil. There are in all fourteen portraits listed in two prefatory pages, said to be reproduced from the original paintings in the Kosmon Church; but a note at the end announces that 'Portraits were omitted from all editions later than 1891, due to loss of the original electro plates,' though 'Owners of OAHSPE desiring the portraits and an OAHSPEAN DICTIONARY may receive them free of charge from the Essenes of Kosmon', at their Los Angeles address. It is disappointing to anyone with an interest in Surrealism that these Portraits must surely have disappeared by now. If they are by the same artist as the one responsible for the illustrations interspersed in the text of *OAHSPE* they would probably be considered oddly primitive. On page 369, at the end of The First Book of God, there are plates representing two heads, Took-Shein and Che-Guh, described as Flat-heads, King and Queen. They strongly suggest Red Indian origin. Accounts of seances during the first half-century of the history of Spiritualism abound with Red Indian controls, founts of loquacious ersatz 'wisdom'. The name Algonquin occurs several times in the texts, transliterated as O-pah-E-go-quin: 'Forty mighty nations shalt thou found, and every nation shall be an independent nation . . .' 'And they planted the country over with corn-fields, and dwelt in peace.' This at least is reassuring.

During the course of writing this article, a new theory about the origin and composition of *OAHSPE* has suggested itself to me. I have been rereading Henri Michaux's account of his controlled drug-taking experiments, *Misérable miracle – La mescaline* (1972). In it there occurs the phrase, repeated in italics in the margin:

> *La métaphysique, saisie par la mécanique.*

I could never have thought of a better description of the impression created by the endless mass-production of portentously bizarre scriptures that *OAHSPE* represents. I looked back again to the preface: Dr John B. Newbrough, a graduate in both medicine and (hold on) dentistry. Before long the association this awoke came back to me clearly. William James, both in his *Varieties of Religious Experience: A Study in Human Nature* of 1902, and in a collection of essays published ten years later, refers to Benjamin Paul Blood's *Anaesthetic Revelation*, a pamphlet printed privately at Amsterdam (NY) in 1874. 'I forget how it fell into my hands, but it fascinated me so "weirdly" that I am conscious of its having been one of the stepping-stones of my thinking ever since.' Paul Blood was neither a doctor of medicine nor a dentist, but his first experience of being anaesthetized by ether or what was often called laughing-gas must surely have occurred during a visit to a dentist. Space does not permit any summary of Blood's stimulating philosophical thoughts, but it is relevant to quote him as saying 'in coming out of the anaesthetic exhilaration . . . we want to tell something; but the effort instantly proves that something will stay back and do the telling –' '– somewhat that any man should always perceive at his best, if his head were only level, but which in our ordinary thinking has grown into a thousand creeds and theories dignified as religion and philosophy.'

It appears to me fairly plausible to speculate that Dr Newbrough, whether or not he ever came across Paul Blood's rare privately printed pamphlet – himself, while still practising or studying dentistry, discovered the thrilling property of the principal anaesthetic of the day, and before long found that it enabled him to produce endless pages of exhilaratingly rhapsodic automatic writing, or rather typing, transported into an invisible realm where the secrets of the myriad universes in all their plurality were invoked by simple, no doubt oft-repeated inhalations of inspiring fumes. The prophetesses of old did no more, after all, when seated by their tripods. The good Dr Newbrough: his mind was furnished with considerable amounts of religio-historico-philosophical lore, but unfortunately his imagination had little in common with that of true poets. At least I do not think he can be accused of doing what he did in order to make a fortune, or of being a forerunner of Hubbard's Scientology or the highly profitable brainwashing of the Reverend Moon's followers.

HÖLDERLIN'S MADNESS

1

During certain epochs of history, separated from one another, as a rule, by long stretches of time, there is to be observed the phenomenon of a sudden upsurge of lyricism and of man's unconscious thought (which are indivisible). The mechanism of such outbreaks is as yet obscure; yet we can say, with reasonable certainty, that they accompany periods of change in the direction of society, periods of revolution. Thus, during the Renaissance, we see not only the birth of the incomparable richness of Italian painting, but also, a little later, the concerted appearance of all the Elizabethan dramatists and poets, a sudden astonishing flowering of passion and the word. During the time of the French Revolution, the industrial revolution and the appearance of the victorious bourgeoisie on the scene of history, we see the formation in Germany of the great Romantic movement, and in England, a lesser reflection, of the Lakeland school of poets and their successors. (While today, perhaps, we see the appearance of the Surrealist movement in France; and in England . . .)

It is of the German Romantics that I wish to speak. Let those who mistrust the idea of poetry manifesting itself in concerted historical outbreaks, for whom the poet's voice is unique and isolated, who, when they think of early nineteenth-century Germany, think only of Goethe and Heine – let these sceptics, shall I say, study in all its detail the wonderful period of *Sturm und Drang*. Mind linking spark with mind, thought and aspiration seeking to express themselves through many mouths at once, a simultaneous rallying to the summons of historical necessity – how else are we to explain this long procession, or rather this choir, of poets and philosophers, all contemporaries: Schelling, Fichte, Jean-Paul, Ludwig Tiecke, Hoffman, Achim and Bettina von Arnim, Clemens Brentano, Eichendorf and Mörike, Kleist, Chamisso, La Motte-Fouqué, Georg Büchner, Ritter, Novalis and Hölderlin?

They are poets and philosophers of nostalgia and the night. A disturbed night, whose paths lead far among forgotten things, mysterious dreams and madness. And yet a night that precedes the dawn, and is full

---

Introduction to *Hölderlin's Madness* (J. M. Dent & Sons Ltd., 1938), pp. 1-14.

of longing for the sun. These poets look forward out of their night: and Hölderlin in his madness wrote always of sunlight and dazzling air, and the islands of the Mediterranean noon.

In Hölderlin, in fact, we find the whole adventure of the Romantics epitomized in its profoundest sense: he carried within himself the germ of the development and the resolution of its contradiction. He was one of the most thorough-going of Romantics, because he went mad, and madness is the logical development of Romanticism; and he went beyond Romanticism, because his poetry is stronger than despair, and reaches into the future and the light.

2

Hölderlin was born in Germany, at Lauffen-am-Neckar, in the year 1770. His mother was then twenty-two years old; his father, a pastor and schoolmaster, died two years later. At the end of another two years, his mother remarried, to a Councillor Gock, a burgomaster of Nurtingen, who also died not long afterwards.

Hölderlin had a sister two years younger than himself, and a stepbrother six years younger. During his childhood, he was brought up exclusively by women: his mother, his grandmother, and his aunt.

When he was seventeen, Hölderlin entered the college of Maulbronn. His mother wished him to become a pastor, like his father; but the ministry never appealed to him, and he only agreed to enter this career against his will. In 1788, he arrived at the seminary of Tübingen to study theology, and here he formed friendships with more than one philosopher of his time, and particularly with Hegel. He met Schelling later.

He found his element in philosophy and poetry; theology meant little to him. He was constantly discontented at the seminary, and yet in 1793 he was admitted to the evangelical ministry by the Consistory of Stuttgart. At this time he wrote his first important poems, and his literary ambition began to grow.

A short time later he was appointed tutor to a difficult child, and the following year he travelled with his pupil to Iena and to Weimar, where he met Goethe and Herder. He had already begun *Hyperion*, his great Romantic novel, and he now decided that he wished to stay in Iena and to devote his life to poetry. He attended the famous course of lectures of the philosopher Fichte. Suddenly, he changed all his plans, and returned home to his mother.

By the end of 1795, Hölderlin had obtained another tutorial post, this time at Frankfurt, in the house of a merchant called Gontard. Susette

Gontard, the merchant's wife, was a young and beautiful woman, greatly admired in the town. She and Hölderlin fell passionately in love. He called her Diotima, after the heroine of his romance.

The year 1796 was perhaps the only entirely happy year in Hölderlin's life. He had finished *Hyperion*, he had made the first draft of his drama *Empedocles*, and had found his true poetic language. But the following year, difficulties arose in his relationship with Diotima, and finally, her husband having discovered their secret, there was a scene which ended in Hölderlin's leaving Frankfurt for good. This was one of the most serious events of Hölderlin's life.

He went to stay in Hamburg with a friend called Sinclair (or Saint-Clair), who was one of his most faithful intimates, and who afterwards recounted many of Hölderlin's *dicta* to Bettina von Arnim, and thus inspired her impressionable imagination with a desire to visit the demented poet.

From this time on, he had to meet with grave material difficulties. Parted from the woman he loved, without employment and without resources, he was forced, in 1800, to return once more to his family. He had lost much strength, both physical and intellectual, and his temperament had become dangerously unsteady. In the same year, he went to stay in Stuttgart, with another friend, called Landauer; and in 1801, he travelled to Switzerland, in the hope of obtaining a tutorial post as before: after an interview with him, his prospective employers changed their minds, and he was obliged to return once again to his mother's home. He wrote to Schiller to ask for help, but received no reply.

The first unmistakable signs of the approaching disaster began to show themselves. His style changed, his speech and manner became strangely inconsequent and abrupt. A chasm was beginning to form between him and the outer world.

At the end of 1801 he left home for Bordeaux, to undertake for the last time a tutorial engagement. Early the following Spring, he wrote his mother a clear and intelligible letter, but after that nothing is known of his actions until he appeared at his mother's house on 7 June in a state of obvious derangement. On 22 June, he received the news of Diotima's death. A period of hallucinations and of furious agitation ensued.

After a time, Hölderlin seemed to recover slightly, and was able to do a certain amount of work on poems and translations. In 1804, with the aid of Sinclair, he obtained the position of librarian to the Landgrave at Hamburg. Sinclair, with whom the poet stayed during this time, thought that he was well on the road to recovery, and that he only 'wore the mask of folly, from time to time, like Hamlet.'

But finally, in 1806, Hölderlin had to be sent into the asylum at

Tübingen. The outbreak was worse than before. A strait-jacket was necessary. When the crisis had abated to a certain extent, the patient was sent to lodge with a carpenter called Zimmer; and Hölderlin remained in the care of his guardian, at Tübingen, in a little room which looked out upon the river Neckar, for thirty-six years.

During these years, Hölderlin did not cease to write. For some time he was capable of writing only fragments, obscure and lacerated; but by the time his madness (which would today be called *dementia praecox*) had reached a certain stage, he began to write rhymed poems, in perfectly balanced form, expressive of great peace and wisdom.

Meanwhile, he was not forgotten by the outer world. Owing to the initiative of his step-brother, his poems were published, and their beauty and originality met with increasing recognition and esteem, particularly among the younger generation of Romantics. Many writers, and other people, began to come to visit the house of the carpenter Zimmer. Among them, in 1822, was a young man called Waiblinger, who related in his journal the following:

> It is now for six years that he has been walking up and down from morning till evening in his room, muttering to himself, without ever doing anything of any use. He often gets up at night, and walks about the house; he also goes out into the street occasionally. From time to time he goes out for walks with his guardian; or else he scribbles on any pieces of paper that he can get hold of, covering them with phrases which make no sense, but which seem to have a certain meaning here and there, and are infinitely strange. I examined a bundle of these pieces of paper; I found alcaic verses among them, perfectly rhymed but devoid of meaning. I asked whether I might keep one of these papers covered with his writing. When it is intelligible, he always speaks of suffering, Oedipus and Greece.

In 1830, the same young man wrote a detailed account of Hölderlin's madness, which contained the following passage concerning the poet's devotion to music:

> He still loves music. He has retained the technique of playing the piano, but his manner of playing is extremely strange. It sometimes happens that he remains seated at the piano for days on end. Then he pursues a single theme, almost infantile in its simplicity, and plays it to you hundreds of times until at last it becomes unbearable. Add to this the fact that he is sometimes seized by a sort of cramp, which forces him to run up and down the keyboard like lightning; and then the disagreeable scratching

of his overgrown fingernails . . . . When he has been playing for some time, and his soul has become softened, he suddenly closes his eyes and throws back his head. You would think him about to die or to vanish away altogether, but instead of that he begins to sing. Although I have heard him many times, I have never been able to discover in what language he sang, but he sang with heart-rending pathos, and it made one shudder to see and hear him. His song was characterized by sadness and melancholy.

During the course of a conversation with the writer Gustave Kühne, in 1836, Zimmer declared:

If he went mad, it was not because he hadn't enough mind, it was because he had too much. When the vessel is too full, and then one tries to seal it, it has to burst. And then when you gather up the pieces, you find that what was in it is spilt. All our savants study too much, they fill themselves with learning until another drop would make them overflow. And with that, they write the most impious things. In his case, it was his craze for out-and-out paganism that turned his mind. And all his thoughts stop at a certain point round which he turns and turns. It's like pigeons flying round the weathercock on the roof. They go round and round the whole time, until they drop from want of strength. Believe me, that's what sent him mad. All day long he has his books open on the table in front of him, and when he's alone, he reads passages aloud to himself from morning to night, declaiming like an actor and seeming as though he wanted to conquer the whole world.

Hölderlin died peacefully, of pulmonary congestion, in the year 1843.

3

The room where Hölderlin was shut up during all those thirty years, looked out upon a landscape of snow-capped mountain, dark forest and green valley, through which the Neckar flowed. In his madness, he transformed this earthly scene into the unearthly beauty and serenity of his last days.

In each of these poems, Hölderlin creates a world: a world of extraordinary transparency – clear air and dazzling light. Everything stands out in light and shade, in height and depth. In movement, and yet timeless. The images pass away, and yet Nature remains. Reading them, one thinks of the 'Songs of Innocence' of his near-contemporary, William

Blake, whom he so closely resembled. One thinks of the strange beauty that is revealed to us in brief flashes in the work of Beddoes. Reading the earlier poems, particularly *Patmos*, one thinks both of Coleridge (his *Kubla Khan*, and his life broken by the misery of drugs), and of Arthur Rimbaud, with his *Bâteau ivre* and his life of restless torment. (And of that other madman, Gérard de Nerval, the images of whose enchanted sonnets, with their archaic proper names – 'Le Prince d'Aquitaine à la tour aboli' – strongly recall the rare Hölderlin atmosphere.)

It is the parallel with Arthur Rimbaud, among all these poets, that strikes me most. The placing together of the names of Hölderlin and Rimbaud gives rise to a curious reflection.

Both these poets belonged to the tradition of the *seer*. That is to say that their *ars poetica* was an offspring of the Platonic doctrine of inspiration. They believed the poet to be capable of penetrating to a secret world and of receiving the dictation of a transcendental inner voice. 'Der Dichter eine Seher': 'Je dis qu'il faut être *voyant*, se faire *voyant*.'

For Hölderlin, as for almost all the Romantics of his period (and particularly Novalis), and for Rimbaud (as for Baudelaire of *Correspondances*), the writing of poetry was something far more than the act of composition; rather was it an activity by means of which it was possible to attain to hitherto unknown degrees of consciousness, a sort of rite, entailing the highest metaphysical implications and with a non-euclidean logic of its own.

What is it then, the secret world to which the poet penetrates, the world discovered by the poet-seer? 'The poet is he who sees,' wrote André Gide. 'And what does he see? – Paradise!' And in fact, this is so, if by Paradise we mean a state of autonomous existence unsubjected to necessity, a state of perfect freedom, without time or age, and if the non-rational imagination of the poet is distinguished precisely by its ignorance of Necessity's irrevocable laws and its defiance of the Aristotelian *ananke*.

But is not freedom 'the knowledge of necessity'? Yes, if we are speaking of human freedom, of the only freedom, that is to say, to which mortals can expect to attain here on earth. But the freedom towards which the poet aspires, the 'free' Freedom of Paradise, is, on the contrary, the non-knowledge of necessity, a state in which necessity does not exist. It is this aspiration that caused Novalis to proclaim: 'Life is a malady of the spirit', and Rimbaud to cry in his despair: 'La vraie vie est absente!'

During the course of his poetic development, Hölderlin passed first of all through the mysterious regions, the imaginary Mediterranean of his early *Antike Strophen*, then through the confusion and obscurity of the fragments belonging to the first period of his madness, into the sublime landscape of his last poems, which is, we can surely say, the landscape of Paradise, where 'the perfection has no plaint'.

Yet it must be remarked immediately that, in order to catch even so much as a glimpse of Paradise, the poet has to pay the price; for his undertaking is an attempt to transgress the laws of man's universe. The gates of Paradise are barred against us by the angel with the flaming sword; and the poet-seer, in attempting to escape that terrible interdiction is guilty of a promethean crime. Rimbaud, more than Hölderlin, was aware of this: 'Le poète est vraiment Voleur de Feu', as he wrote in his famous letter. If he had not become silent and renounced his work, he too would undoubtedly have gone mad. 'Je ne pouvais pas continuer,' he said later; 'et puis, c'était mal.'

Hölderlin, less conscious of the nature and consequences of his poetic undertaking, must nevertheless have known, in brief flashes of intuition, in what direction his path was leading him: witness the mysterious broken phrase that appears at the end of the poem called *Form and Spirit*, '– thou shalt go among the flames'. (One thinks of Rimbaud's season in Hell, and the broken incoherence of certain of his utterances, such as: 'Faim, soif, cris, danse, danse, danse, danse!') By the time he had reached the unearthly illumination of his last poems, Hölderlin's madness had become quite incurable. The carpenter Zimmer was perhaps wiser than one might think when he said: 'If he went mad it was not because he hadn't enough mind, but because he had too much.'

Out of all the turbulence of the epoch to which Hölderlin belongs, rises the giant Goethe, and with him, inevitably, Faust. The idea of knowledge accompanied by damnation is one of the basic ideas underlying the Romantic movement, and provides a key to the understanding of the whole period. The same idea occurs in even more poignant form than in *Faust* (– why did Goethe have to grant his hero a false redemption? –) in an unfinished story called 'Lenz', by Georg Büchner[1] whose scant but extraordinary work has been referred to as 'the end of Romanticism'. Here again we find a knowledge-thirsting poet fulfilling his destiny in madness (which is the equivalent to damnation). This faustian drama Hölderlin lived, and that is why he is, as I said before, a very epitome of Romanticism.

---

[1] Büchner was the author of *Wozzeck*, which furnished Alban Berg with the libretto of one of the most moving works of art of the twentieth century, an opera in which romantic music undergoes the transfiguration of a final agony.

Büchner's story 'Lenz' was founded on biographical material concerning the life of a real person, the poet Lenz who wrote 'Sturm und Drang' and thus supplied the period with a convenient catch-phrase.

Büchner, who died at the age of twenty-three, can be considered as being in some respects the prototype of both Rimbaud and the Dadaists.

Knowledge accompanied by damnation, the transcendental vision whose cost is madness. The Romantic movement, with which opened the capitalist epoch now drawing to its cataclysmic finale, seems like a voice proclaiming the historical command: 'Thou shalt go thus far, but no further!'

Will the future show the birth of a race who will have superseded this decree?

★ ★ ★

The poems which follow are not a translation of the selected poems of Hölderlin, but a free adaptation, introduced and linked together by entirely original poems. The whole constitutes what may perhaps be regarded as a *persona*.

The texts of the poetic fragments translated in the second part [of *Hölderlin's Madness*] are published in the edition of Hölderlin's works edited by Franz Zinkernagel (Leipzig: Insel-Verlag, 1926). I am much indebted in the preparation of the present text to the French translation of Pierre Jean Jouve: *Poèmes de la folie de Hölderlin* (Paris: J. O. Fourcade, 1930); and also the helpful criticism of Marianne Donhauser and of Carl Wilhelm Böhne.

POETS OF TOMORROW

David Gascoyne was born in 1916, and has already published several books, though it is some time since a volume of his poetry appeared. He says of the work printed here:

'This group of poems represents some of the various types of verse I have been trying to write during the last two or three years.

'The "Phantasmagoria", written primarily as a *divertissement*, is the first "Surrealist" poem I have produced since I decided, a few years ago, to abandon the "Surrealist" technique and general approach to poetry. It will probably be my last poem of this sort.

'I feel that poetry of the "magical" category, – product of sheer imagination, unrestricted by pure design and untempered by the wisdom of disillusionment, – may be more stimulating, more immediately satisfying to write; but in the long run is probably less rewarding, less consoling, than that resulting from conflict between the instinctive poetic impulse and the impersonal discipline, the unadorned sobriety of realistic "sense".'

Introductory note to a selection of his poems in *Poets of Tomorrow: Third Selection* (Hogarth Press, 1942), p. 25.

KENNETH PATCHEN

On the dust-jacket of *Cloth of the Tempest* is printed the following brief biographical summary:

> Born in Ohio in 1911, Patchen speaks for the generation whose destiny has been to grow up during one war and to go through another. He attended the Experimental College of the University of Wisconsin; was awarded a Guggenheim Fellowship in 1936; was one of three new poets to be added to Louis Untermeyer's revised Modern American Poetry; is married to Miriam Oikemus; and lives for the most part in New York.

The first collection of Kenneth Patchen's poems to be published was called *Before the Brave*. I have never had an opportunity of seeing this book, but I understand that the author does not regard it as representing anything but a preliminary and not mature stage of his development. It was followed in 1939 by *First Will & Testament*, 'like no book that has been published in these states,' as the anthologist Untermeyer called it. The unusually strong, indeed violent, if not exactly distinct, personality emanating from each of its 180 pages, made its appearance a memorable event in modern American letters.

In 1942 Patchen consolidated the achievement of his second book with the publication of *The Dark Kingdom*, of which the complete title, occupying the entire front page of the book, runs as follows:

> THE DARK KINGDOM stands above the waters as a sentinel warning man of dangers from his own kind. On its altars the deeds of blood are not offered; here are watchers whose eyes are fixed on the eternal undertakings of the spirit. What has been common and tarnished in these poor wombs, here partakes of immortality. In its windows are reflected the unreturning events of childhood. All who ask life, find a peace everlasting in its

---

'Introducing Kenneth Patchen', *Poetry Quarterly*, Vol. 8, No. 1 (Spring 1946), pp. 4–10. Also published in Kenneth Patchen, *Outlaw of the Lowest Planet*, poems selected and introduced by David Gascoyne (Grey Walls Press, 1946), pp. vii–xiv.

radiant halls. All who have opposed in secret, are here provided with green crowns. All who have been dragged through the cowled flame of this world, are here clothed in the bright garment of the tempest. Here all who sorrow and are weary under strange burdens – fearing death, are seen to enter the white throne room of God.

This book caused a *New York Times* critic to refer to Patchen as 'one of the poets whom historians will turn to for intelligence about the year 1942. He is the most impulsively romantic and imaginative of the younger writers.'

Since then, Patchen has published two further collections, the important *Cloth of the Tempest* in 1943, and a little earlier than this a small volume in the 'New Directions' *Poet of the Month* series, containing twenty-one poems and entitled *The Teeth of the Lion*, with the following corollary to the title:

> In white savage caps make a bloody pasturage where I am laid down break tear kill in a world of cheats defilers ratsinpinkwalls through the black camps where murder lifts the teaching but the girls by the lake and the green quick laughing kids in the schoolyard and the sad wise beautiful gentle clean strong good loving joys as I am made and you will know me.

On the dust-jacket of *Cloth of the Tempest* from which I have already quoted, after giving extracts from the entire American press referring to Patchen in the most laudatory terms, his publishers assert on the back flap: 'This record of critical praise and acknowledgement speaks for itself as strongly as Patchen speaks for America,' and conclude by referring to him finally as 'a modern of . . . tremendous importance'. Opening the book at random, a conservative reader, duly impressed by this evidence of the apparent acceptance by common critical consent of Patchen as an American poet of serious significance, may perhaps find himself bewildered, baffled, even outraged, to come upon the sort of thing of which 'Loves of the Tragic Owl', for instance, will serve as a fair example:

> Zeeeeen – Stillgrind twing flick. Bleeoook –
> Rattlesoft mouth –
> Lussssssssss lornhen –
>
> Tubitititit (bloody grass) ferngrim
> As an old man's brain –
> Sedghart ice-clothed in gray fur –

Turning the pages in search of further enlightenment, such a reader might well begin to suspect that someone's leg was being pulled somewhere on coming across pages on which crude grotesque drawings, scraps of cuttings from newspapers and encyclopædias are combined with provocative phrases printed mixed up with the rest in a dramatic layout (Patchen calls these divertissements 'makings'), or a childish outline drawing with the caption; 'Ragamuffin Playing With a Really Pretty Creature While His Poor Mother Roams Through the City Looking for Work.'

If this 'conservative' peruser happened to be one whose conservatism was simply the rationalization of his lack of intelligence or adventuresomeness or curiosity, as is occasionally the case with hypothetical readers flaunting this description, it would probably be simply a waste of his time and my own for me to attempt to mollify him with any sort of argument or explanation. But if, however, he should be a conservative whose mind were not quite closed to all reasonable persuasion, and always supposing that, as I believe, it is in fact possible, notwithstanding the apparently wilful irresponsibility of antics such as I have just indicated, to make out a case for recognizing Patchen as a writer deserving the serious attention of anyone interested in the authentic poetic utterance of our time, – and if it really were necessary to attempt some 'explanation' or 'justification' of the sometimes freakish results of Patchen's iconoclasm (to call it that), then the clearest way of doing so, it seems to me, would be by referring first to the odd phenomenon known as Dada, and then showing how Patchen's significance can perhaps best be seen in the light of that particular context.

To put it plainly: Kenneth Patchen is the lone one-man Dada of contemporary America.

The true significance, the unique historical importance of the non-movement (or anti-movement) known as Dada, born during and out of the First World War, has never as far as I know been adequately stated (that is, by any writer in English, at least; Georges Hugnet's comprehensive account published serially in *Cahiers d'Art* may be presumed to do it justice in French; it was, of course, in any case, pre-eminently a French phenomenon). Though this is hardly the place for me to start trying to make good this deficiency, the meaning of Dada might very briefly be outlined as follows:

At a moment of universal intellectual and moral degradation when the values on which Western civilization is supposed to be based were every day being spectacularly compromised by most of the official spokesmen of society, Dada was perhaps the sole visible sign indicating the existence of at least a tiny remnant among the living who were still determined not to participate in this general passive surrender of spiritual integrity, not to accept the terms of its betrayal. If this refusal expressed itself only indirectly, as from behind a mask, this was not on account of any prudent deference to civil authority, but because of the determining part that *irony* played in its expression. The mask assumed by Dada in face of the hypocritical official bluff of the *soi-disant* Christian world was that of a ferocious humour (UMOR as Jacques Vaché nicknamed it), the convulsive grimace of frantic absurdity. In a society organized solely for purposes of competitive commerce, the exploitation of subject races and the destruction (whenever necessary, and then with as thorough an efficiency as possible) of landscapes, armies, cities and even civil populations, yet in which that society's official representatives scarcely ever referred directly to the existence of these universally evident evils, though having the words *duty, self-sacrifice, heroism, the good of mankind, Christian civilization* and so on constantly on their lips, – in such a society, Dada's grimace implied, it is impossible to take anything seriously any more; all that is put forward as claiming reverence, respect or honour turns out to be hollow appearance concealing some ugly lie, so that none of the great abstractions by which we are supposed to order and justify our lives any longer make sense. What other honest and sincere expression can we give to our reaction to such a situation than a burst of furious, incoherent laughter? You have to laugh, since to weep is too embarrassing, and even sorrow is a 'noble' emotion that one has therefore had to learn to distrust at last. . . .

Most of those who actively participated in Dada were either writers or painters; which amounted to saying that nothing could be calculated to arouse their disgusted derision more effectively than literature and art. The *Mona Lisa*, for instance, was eminently suitable, they considered, for painting moustaches on; Rodin's *Le Penseur* made an excellent trade mark for a patent laxative; if a poem was to be expected of one, a page or two from the telephone directory would always serve. The Art of Letters, to a Dadaist, meant no more than a random item in a catalogue including poultry-farming, semantics, ludo, phrenology and colonic irrigation.

If, as Vaché wrote to André Breton in 1917, 'it's necessary to disgorge a little acid or old lyricism, let it be done abruptly, rapidly . . .' And: 'ART of course doesn't exist – so it's futile to go into a song and dance about it . . . So we neither like Art nor Artists (down to Apollinaire and HOW RIGHT TOGRATH IS TO ASSASSINATE THE POET).'

The review which eventually became the 'organ' of most of the Dadaists after the defeat of Dada, – that is to say, after they had realized that 'Dada could only continue by ceasing to exist', – had a title which seems plain and straightforward enough at first sight, but which actually was fraught with complex implication. It was called simply *Littérature*. For the contributors to this review, 'literature' was no more than a term of contemptuous ridicule; it was adopted as a label out of a sort of wry self-deprecation, rather as a collegiate 'mag' might style itself *The Tripe-Hound*, and in much the same spirit as that which led Erik Satie to label a really unexceptionally serious group of piano studies: *Dried-up Embryos*. This self-depreciation and defensive sarcasm was due to it being only as it were shamefacedly, as a result of an absurd, all-too-human feebleness of mind, that these writers wrote at all. The soundest justification of the habit that they could find was that of Knut Hamsun, quoted by André Breton: 'I write to pass the time'.

The close similarity between the Dadaist attitude to literature and the attitude of Kenneth Patchen is so obvious, I think, from the following passages, that I need but quote them to dispense with further commentary:

> And in particular ask me to tell you
> What I think of the present state of our American Letters
> As I think
> It stink –
> Together with the drippy jerks who commit it.
> 'The Impuissant Surrender to the Name & the
> Act & the Tensions of Ratheda'

> It is an absolute mistake to ladle out stress like a cook measuring off the ingredients for a cake. We've got a country full of cake-baking poets now, one just as good and just as bad as the next. – Poetry is writing. Maybe what I am talking about is not poetry (the stuff the critics are yammering about) . . . I am a writer and I shall write. The term 'poet' is a convenience of the middle-class. I declare myself a writer. I want room to move around. Spare me from the pawings-over of the cake-bakers.
> Preface to *The Hunted City*

> It is more than unusual to write about anything now. Hours of each day I pass in the work of perfecting a little racket which is designed to interest spinsters and schoolmarms of either sex. Tomorrow I have an appointment to visit a certain well-known poet whose work is done altogether under the influence of large checks from his mama who never quite went to bed with him. All his poems begin with x.
> 'I Never Had Any Desire So Strong'

Just as Dada expressed itself through a mask of absurdity the adoption of which was determined by the irony inherent in the Dadaist attitude, Kenneth Patchen, we find, has evolved in his more recent work a sort of *dramatic convention* for the expression of his attitude, which more or less amounts to a *persona*. The convention might tentatively be formulated somewhat like this: The poet, hypersensitive representative of humanity's loftiest ideals, is so appalled by the brutal realities of the contemporary scene that finally he has been driven literally out of his mind by the sheer horror of it all. And in his derangement, wandering bemusedly about the Bedlam of New York, from time to time he gives vent to poignantly incoherent fragmentary utterance . . . delirious . . . outpourings in which, among much that is strictly meaningless, there nevertheless shine forth now and then the cold hard gleams of a kind of truth which a merely sane writer would never have the face to articulate except in a very much more roundabout, watered-down way. For instance, in a poem rather significantly entitled 'None Stay the White Speech of His Wandering', after a couple of stanzas of unadulterated dementia, he suddenly hits out with:

> Death. Because when you are very naked
> You cannot clothe yourself with the partydress
> Of state or church or opinion or of being
> An article of merchandise on a country's
> Bloodlist. You will confine yourself to The Kingdom.

As another example, here is the end of a poem called 'The Temple of Diana':

> I am too angry to bother with this poem
> About the beauty of the world
> Who cares a damn about that now.

Or again, here is a small piece of truth about the life of Man as it is lived in America every day at this time:

> Rain dripping down from a rusty evespout
> Into the gray-fat cinders of the millyard . . .
> The dayshift goes on in four minutes.

The Kingdom to which the demented poet of Patchen's dramatic convention is said to confine himself is nothing more nor less than the domain of the solitary individual's irreducible integrity: the expression *son fort intérieur* describes it exactly. It is that unique corner of subjective chaos which has been colonized by his creative imagination, as Blake colonized Jerusalem, not as a sensitive dreamer's cosy hide-out against the hostility of the kingdom, forever inescapable after all, of mundane reality, but in very earnest as a guilt-determined *symptomatic reflection* counterbalancing our unpleasant 'real world' and standing as in a certain sense an indictment of it. Just as the enraged burlesque of Dada really constituted an indictment of the 'universal intellectual and moral degradation' that called it forth as a protest, at the time of the First World War. Time since then has lurched uncontrollably on, carrying all Dadaists well into their middle-age; André Breton, in 1942, was reproaching himself that he still had 'an eye for the sad recantations' of Louis Aragon, author in his youth of one of the most notorious of Dadaist poems (called *Suicide* and consisting simply of the letters of the alphabet), who had then recently been describing himself as 'looking very respectable indeed with all my decorations and my hair whitened by age,' and Breton a year or two later was himself to be found at least sufficiently respectable to be invited to deliver an official address to the Year's Leaving Class at Yale. The coming of the Second World War can hardly be said to have brought with it a very marked improvement on the intellectual and moral condition that I have described as being universal at the time of its predecessor. But if its coming found the first Dadaists settling down to middle-age, it could discover no alteration in the pure intransigence of the original Dada spirit, for that is something that cannot be tied down by dates. In the poetry, or whatever you like to call it, of Kenneth Patchen, it is to be found flaring as wantonly and gratuitously as ever.

A LITTLE ANTHOLOGY OF EXISTENTIAL THOUGHT

'*A valid philosophy arises only out of that revolutionary change in the way of contemplating human existence which is known today as existence-philosophy. That latter finds the material of its terminology in the domains which, as a knowledge of man, are simultaneously bounded and safeguarded by it. But it transcends them in its approximation towards being itself. Existence-philosophy is the philosophy of human existence which once more transcends man.*'

KARL JASPERS, *Man in the Modern World*
(trans. by E. & C. Paul, Routledge, 1933)

INTRODUCTORY NOTE

Existential philosophy, precise definition of which will necessarily remain controversial as in fact no such definition is usefully possible, is nothing new; and it is represented here not because it has recently become, in France — perhaps one should say, actually, in Paris — under the name of 'L'Existentialisme', a literary movement and an intellectual *mode printanière*; but because this movement, fashionable as it may be, is profoundly symptomatic of the historical moment in which we are living today. As a distinct tendency in the main tradition of European philosophic culture, it made its appearance about a quarter of a century ago in Germany, as the result of the spiritual crisis precipitated by the First Great War, and of the influence of Schelling, Kierkegaard, Nietzsche and Dilthey on those few philosophers who in Europe were best fitted by their tradition and training to appreciate the crucial historical significance of this crisis and the danger to our Civilization represented by the failure of European intellectuals to face responsibly the urgent necessity of seeking an answer to the many problems — not least of these the social one — to which it had given rise.

In France, it was by no means only with the advent of Jean-Paul Sartre on the literary scene that this tendency became a recognizable feature of the contemporary intellectual climate. Léon Chestov, Russian Jew exiled

---

Introductory notes to *A Little Anthology of Existential Thought* in *New Road* 4 (Grey Walls Press, 1946), pp. 176-8.

by the Revolution, the functionaries of which no doubt regarded his philosophy as representing the final stage of decadent bourgeois subjectivism, began in 1923 to publish a series of French translations of his works[1] which continued to appear until his death in 1938. The work of Jules de Gaultier, author of the remarkably original *Le Bovarysme*, who was one of the first in France to recognize Chestov's greatness, is not without unmistakable connections with existentialist thought, though these remain apparently still unremarked by the engrossed polemicists who have mingled their voices in contentious tumult recently. There was also, and indeed is still, that calmest of existentialists, M. Gabriel Marcel. Speaking with the professorial authority of a lecturer at the Sorbonne, M. Jean Wahl, heroic survivor of the Jewish concentration camp at Drancy, was, together with MM. Jules Corbin, Pierre Klossowski and Bernard Groethuysen, among the first to make known to the French philosophic public (an audience for which there was no equivalent at that time in England), the thought of such deeply significant German philosophers as Heidegger, Jaspers and Max Scheler. At the Sorbonne in 1937, on the occasion of the tercentenary of Descartes, Karl Jaspers first delivered his important lectures, *Descartes und die Philosophie*. In that year also Benjamin Fondane, poet of Romanian origin, already known as the author of one of the most distinguished metaphysical studies of Rimbaud, published a valuable contribution to the literature of existentialist criticism, *La Conscience malheureuse* (a title which refers to that feature of the Hegelian system which constitutes, from the existentialist point of view, its most fatal contradiction, thereby representing for active critical thought a possibility of liberation of the living (existential) spirit from the sterilizing bonds of abstract conceptualization).

The collection of extracts which follows purposely avoids conforming to an orthodox conception of what is meant by any strict definition of the term 'Existential'. The underlying and implicit principle discoverable in them all, in itself constitutes, for whoever may discern it, the essential criticism of that form of philosophical procrastination at present known under the name of 'Existentialism'.

The justification for the inclusion of Lichtenberg, for instance, is to be found in Schopenhauer's definition of him as 'an informal, empirical psychologist', and as such, a *philosopher* in contra-distinction to a *sophist* of the type which he names Herder as representing. Incidentally, it may be useful to remark that the distinction thus drawn between the true

---

[1] By Boris de Schloezer principally; among them *Les Révélations de la Mort, Potestas Clavium, Vox Clamantis in Deserto* and *Kierkegaard*.

philosopher who thinks for himself, and the sophist who thinks for himself, but has sufficient ratiocinative subtlety to be able to deceive himself and others into believing that he thinks for others (that is to say, as though he himself were not there at all), provides a particularly relevant illustration of the kind of distinction that today as never before should be drawn between the teaching of Christ and the teaching of Christianity. The passage from the Gospel according to St John has been included by way of indicating what are the essential pre-suppositions of all specifically Christian philosophic thought. The crisis in modern philosophy, of which the Existentialist movement is so acutely symptomatic, will perhaps find its resolution only when it is generally realized that the true Christian doctrine is in fact the embodiment of an absolutely practical philosophical attitude, and that it is this attitude which has been responsible for the vital continuity of the whole intellectual tradition of Occidental man.

BENJAMIN FONDANE

In *Rimbaud le voyou*,[1] which of all his prose works is perhaps the best known, Benjamin Fondane wrote: 'Rimbaud's poetry moves and overwhelms me; it seizes my very entrails.' It is precisely this that Fondane's poetry can achieve when he has finished discoursing[2] – done in the most fascinating manner – on the poet's need for reality. It takes hold at the centre of our being, it sends a shiver down the spine, it makes the nerves quiver. At bottom, I believe that it is a question of voice: some voices possess a special, unique tone, which affects us in the manner of certain notes which have the power to make glasses shatter because of the remarkable vibration of their sound waves.

I hope I won't be misunderstood if I confess that in the past, when I lived in Paris, I often found myself bewitched by the voices of popular singers: Piaf, certainly, but also Marianne Oswald, Brassens, Ferré, Catherine Sauvage . . . it is a matter of a spell, something inexplicable. In English we speak of 'a haunting refrain'. Benjamin Fondane often produces in me precisely that effect with his poems. To give an example, I immediately think of 'The Song of the Emigrant' which can be found in *Ulysse*.[3] Perhaps inevitably because of the similarity of the titles, this poem makes me think of Apollinaire's 'The Song of the Emigrant from Landor Road'; but the relationship, if there is one, is surely the mark of a kind of deep brotherhood. The two poems produce an enchantment capable, in certain circumstances, of taking you by the throat.

In an inscription in the second version of *Ulysse*, revised by Fondane during the final period of his life when he continued to live in Paris in a clandestinity which became more and more dangerous, these words by

---

[1] *Rimbaud the hooligan*, published 1933, the first essay written in France by Fondane. New edition 1979 by Editions Plasma (Michel Carassou).
[2] In his *Faux traité d'esthétique*, published 1937. New edition published by Editions Plasma.
[3] Published 1933.

Preface to Benjamin Fondane, *Le Mal des fantômes* (Paris: Editions Plasma, 1980), translated here by Roger Scott and Catherine McFarlane.

Saint-John Perse appear: 'It is time, o Poet, to destroy your name, your birth and your race.' This line is taken from 'Exile', a poem written, as far as I know, on Long Island, New York, after Saint-John Perse's arrival in America following the Occupation of France, and I don't know how Fondane came to be acquainted with this poem. But this late choice of quotation from Saint-John Perse is significant and revealing of more than a manner; the main reason and one which most stands out is that it expresses Fondane's state of mind at the moment when he began to work on this collection. It ought to be noted, too, that the word 'Exile' is that which translates the theme which had most haunted the poet Fondane ever since the need to express himself in poetic language had first seized him.

The other epigraph which Fondane chose for *Ulysse* is, curiously, in English: 'No retreat, no retreat/They must conquer or die/Who have no retreat'. Signed *Mr* Gay. Surely it can only refer to John Gay, author of the libretto of the famous *Beggar's Opera* which, through a quite bizarre transformation became the celebrated *Opéra de Quat'Sous* (*Dreigroschenoper*)[4] in the 1920s. It is difficult for me not to point out that there exists between Fondane and John Gay (the 'Mr' strikes me as an indication of the quasi-affectionate irony such as Dubliners often use when speaking of Swift as 'the Dean'), as well as between this particular poet and Bertolt Brecht, an affinity like that which I have suggested could exist between Fondane and Apollinaire. Guillaume Apollinaire, Bertolt Brecht and Benjamin Fondane are, at first sight, three completely different poets; but they have this in common: all three were more than ordinarily aware of fundamental movements of the spirit and of history and they shared an exceptional sense of humour – a capricious and pre-Surrealist humour in the case of Apollinaire, a cynical, bitter humour, reputed to be typical of Berliners as regards Brecht and, in the case of Fondane, a humour so distinctive it seems to me that it could perhaps be described as Romanian-Jewish, but for the fact that it was, more than anything, sardonic. Undoubtedly, this comic side does not show itself very often in Fondane's poetry, nor in any dazzling manner, but its existence can hardly be disputed.

It is not without interest either to point out that Fondane made quite frequent use of proper names, and this, too, could be considered a link with Apollinaire and Brecht. These names, whether of towns or countries, real, imaginary or mythological people, are all three well combined, in their different ways, to give them a very special resonance such that

---

[4] Kurt Weill's *The Threepenny Opera* (Hauptmann, Brecht), 1928.

we can no longer read them as they are named, without immediately experiencing some remanence or movement in the depths of the conscious mind, to hear like a subliminal appeal to a dormant emotion of nostalgic tonality. Change Mallarmé's famous 'I say a flower, etc . . .' to 'I say Croniamental, Marizibill, Cologne, London, Thomas de Quincey, rue Christine, Rosemonde, Julie, Tiresias'; or 'I say Jacob Apfelböck, Baal, Mackie Messer, Mahagonny, Maria Sanders, Puntila, Mother Courage'; or again 'I say Ulysses, Lusitania, Kiev, Warsaw, South America, Charlot, Marché-aux-Puces, Babylon, Jerusalem, l'Illysus, or even (?) Gog and Magog, Paris and Helen, Ca-ro-li-ne . . . , Clara, Chava, Suzy and Stephanie', – and what comes immediately into view? Some places, some people, some faces from dreams or from memory, mythical, undying, absent from this world of ours, like our 'true life', but such that in themselves, eternity has finally changed them.

The conjunction of these three poets, Apollinaire, Brecht and Fondane, is less fortuitous than it may seem at first sight again because of another factor: the song, in other words, the musicality or verbal music. It isn't here a question of this 'music above all else' on which Verlaine insisted, nor of a superficial attractiveness, but of a significant part of the whole talent of these three poets. There are series of words or phrases which can haunt us, as is the case with the 'haunting refrain' to which I have already alluded, something that carries us away and moves us to a degree which cannot be rationally explained. There are certain of Fondane's poems which almost demand to be set to music so that we can sing them. Would Benjamin Fondane have liked that? Unfortunately, I cannot confirm that. But what does seem to me indisputable is that Fondane possessed not only a wholly individual voice, but also an ear, assuming however that one could be distinguished from the other.

It remains an incontestable fact that music, as well as religion, can only be an opium, a distraction in the sense condemned by Pascal. But to reject it completely as if it only represents an equivalent of that kind of 'literature' which the Surrealists always affected to despise so much, seems to me the result of a misunderstanding as serious as it is frivolous. In order to have done with this question, I shall quote a sentence from the composer Ernst Křenek apropos 'the third Viennese School', because what he says seems to me to apply to Fondane's poetry and to the essence of what it is, with the constant theme of exile, one of its essential elements. Křenek, then, wrote somewhere: 'the language of the new music sounds first and foremost the Scriptural notes of cursing and of wailing; its colour is that of eschatological mourning.'

In the poem with which *Ulysse* begins, we read:

> The Earth was still there, she was firm,
> Yet I heard these future cracks,
> – I don't have to linger,
> – I don't have to trust him,
> – something will happen. Something, but what?

If these lines do not announce precisely the great eschatological problem, it is because I misunderstand what one usually wishes to indicate when using this term. This line appears at the end of *Ulysse*:

> Does God have his eyes open, during his own night?

Isn't one of the supreme eschatological questions there still? In 'The Poet and his Shade', one of the sections in *Titanic*, the second poem begins with these words:

> The storm is going to sweep away everything – let it come!

It has already been noted that in this collection of poems written shortly before the war which finished by consuming him, together with millions of other inhabitants of this shattered Earth which had become terrifying, Fondane, with a disconcerting accuracy, had foreseen this war which was on the point of breaking out. In truth, it was, rather, the prophetic expression of an awareness of an event – advent yet more decisive and mysterious than the war of 1939-45 with the Holocaust which accompanied it and the first nuclear explosions which ended it; that is, the present state of things in the world where spontaneously and popularly we have adopted the slogan *Apocalypse Now*. The poets, the true ones, know at the very core of their being that Something Else always remains hidden behind the chaos of the social and economic disintegration that surrounds us, and it is because he sensed that with such acuity that Benjamin Fondane's poetry retains such a vital presence.

If prompted to give my interpretation of the nature of this poetry, I would say finally that it is a poetry of cries, of suffering and of often despairing or ironically bitter songs, full of obsessions and fears. It is premonitory and prophetic poetry, of such evident clearsightedness that any commentary is superfluous. The landscape that it evokes is for the most part grey and misty, sordid and alienated, and one of the commonest images from the vegetable world is that of the stinging nettle. Indeed, the burning sensation that is left on the skin of anyone who has touched a nettle leaf strongly resembles the impression left by a large proportion of these poems, just as the smell of burning which accompanies the loud explosion of an electrical storm might be invoked to express the way in which they touch our sensibility. Sand and snow, ashes, rubbish and rubble, with all the most typical features of a world subject to cataclysm, some images refer to extremes, conspicuously geographical or climatic, but in actual fact metaphysical, these are the essential elements of an unmethodical descriptive catalogue that could be drawn up when attempting to present a summary, necessarily inadequate, of the subject matter of Fondane's poetry. If any potential reader insisted on demanding that an interpreter applies one of these facile labels to the poet Benjamin Fondane, I think that I would venture to describe him as Fondane the Gadfly, the spokesperson of the persecuted and of prisoners, the Seer, perhaps above all, Fondane the Rebel. It is clear from his last poems that he ended by accepting the role of poet-prophet in the ancient biblical sense: he warns mankind so that they might face the consequences of their flight in the face of the task to be accomplished, the responsibility to be met; he announces to mankind the superhuman anger that is going to be unleashed on all those who have committed the unforgivable. One of his poems published secretly under the pseudonym 'Isaac Lacquedem' in the review *Europe* is, unless I'm mistaken, a reprise of one of the most violent psalms in the Scriptures:

> Shining cities, you will fall
> in your turn, struck
> by fire, by the void,
> by the unforgiving.
> Your warriors will fall
> on all the steppes of the world
> ears of corn whose hail
> makes a delicious feast.
> Your daughters will prostitute themselves
> on the pedestals of your statues
> and your newborn babies will cry out
> for the milk of dead cows.

The epithet 'Rebel', perhaps transmuted at will into 'Revolting', would be similar to 'the Hooligan' that represented for him the Rimbaud who, with the exception of Baudelaire, was the poet whom he loved and who haunted him more than all the others; in his eyes the incarnation of the rebellion against habit, against the dictate of respectable and maternally tyrannical Reason, and against all that which is obligatory for the 'normal' adult male. In my opinion, Benjamin Fondane was neither a hooligan of any kind, not was he 'abnormal' in the sense generally understood. He did not spurn his responsibilities as a man: we know, for example, that he earned his living working like Brecht had to do for a while, in the cinema, and that he served in the French army at the beginning of the war. But his refusal to abandon the expression of what for Hegel was only 'simple subjectivity', and the aggressiveness of his temperament, drove him to conduct a relentless and continuous struggle against all forms of compromise and complacency, and certainly allow us to place him in the category of the 'rebels'.

It has often been pointed out that all poetry feeds on ambiguity and that poets delight in it (an observation that can be applied with particular aptness to English poetry since its beginnings). In 'No-Place', he admits frankly that he has been 'haunted' by puns (among other things), and since we know that puns represent one of the most fruitful kinds of poetic ambiguity and, according to Freud, constitute the very substance of language and of the workings of the unconscious and of dreams, I am not surprised to discover that in this series of twenty-two poems, entitled *Le Mal des fantômes*,[5] we immediately find ourselves right inside the realm of Ambiguity, which is certainly par excellence that of Ghosts. Already there is a question of ambiguity if we consider the word *le mal* in the title itself. At first sight that is understood easily enough, but is it a question of ghosts who are sick, who are ill, or is it rather the name of a malaise by which the poet feels himself afflicted; in other words, haunting fear and obsession? Furthermore, we can't ignore the fact that at the time during which these poems were conceived and written, Fondane worked on his study: *Baudelaire et l'expérience du gouffre*,[6] and so Baudelaire had to be one of the most important of the ghosts who haunted him during his hours of composition, and anyone who thinks of Baudelaire inevitably thinks of *Les Fleurs du mal*.[7]

Wishing to become a visionary, Rimbaud spoke of the need 'to make the soul monstrous'; while asserting that Fondane could not by any means be described as a 'hooligan', I have not denied that he was, all the same, like it or not, a 'hooligan' or, as I have expressed it, a seer, a prophet or, in the Greek tradition, a Cassandra and as such monstrous, rather a Tiresias without breasts, because his figure is thoroughly male. As a character in the mythology of modern poets, obviously he cannot escape from the family of the 'damned'; at bottom, that is tantamount to

---

[5] We have not attempted to provide an English equivalent for this title which is, in effect, untranslatable. A literal rendering would not suffice either as it would prove to be misleading. The problem lies in the nuances and shades of meaning of the French 'mal' which relates to notions of 'sickness' (as in *le mal de mer*) and something close to 'nostalgia' (as in *le mal de pays*).
[6] *Baudelaire and the Experience of the Void*, published posthumously in 1947.
[7] Baudelaire 1821-67: *The Flowers of Evil*, published 1857.

saying that he paid the price for his double gift of prophetic clairvoyance and Orphic speech, while accepting a wound and a curse. In Rimbaud, we are faced with the Alchemy of the Verb; in Baudelaire, it is the Alchemy of suffering that is the issue. Rimbaud abandoned his alchemical experiments following the *Saison en enfer*,[8] – and he could not continue, he explained shortly afterwards, 'and then it was bad'. It is hardly necessary to enumerate the relentless sufferings of Baudelaire: financial worries, disillusioning or cruel love affairs, scandals, syphilis, exile and madness. Chestov wrote in one of his first books that 'I am convinced that the best death is in all credibility that which is generally considered to be the worst: to die alone, in a foreign land, in a workhouse or, as the saying goes, like a dog under a hedge'. In the case of his friend and faithful interpreter, Benjamin Fondane, death in a gas-chamber at Birkenau could seem to be extremely in accord with that strange definition of the best way to pass away, but like the end of the difficult journey he had undertaken, it is indisputable that it bore the seal of fate.

In his *Tombeau de Baudelaire*, Pierre Jean Jouve[9] reminds us that 'the title *Les Fleurs du mal* is associated with the fruits of the Tree of Knowledge of Good and Evil. For some years the projected title had been '"Limbo". Limbo: ambiguous waiting-place on the margins of hell.' And as if these sentences of this other poet and passionate admirer of Baudelaire were not enough (it seems to me that their rapport with *Le Mal des fantômes* and its author is most obvious), I persist all the same in quoting as a final benchmark a passage drawn from the conclusion of Jouve's essay: 'Without malediction, [there is] no possible innovation. We need to pass through malediction in order to gain access to the secret kingdom of the image. A commonplace states that we must bring forth children in sorrow. As the kingdom into which the poet ventured was nameless, the poet had to seem like a monster.'

Nothing would dissuade me from the conviction that the two poets whom I had the opportunity of visiting often during the winter of 1938-9, were more alike than they themselves realized. Mention of the extraction of Evil from beauty, the experience of the darkness in mankind, above all the fruits of the Tree of Knowledge, represent a cohesion which provides such an obvious indication of Fondane's central preoccupations, that no reader even remotely familiar with his writings and

---

[8] *A Season in Hell*, published 1873.
[9] *Baudelaire's Tomb*, by Pierre Jean Jouve, 1887-1976. First published in 1942 by Editions de la Baconnière, Neuchâtel. Jouve was the editor of *Baudelaire, choix de textes: I. Poésies* (1943); *II. Critique* (1944), published by Le Cri de la France, L.U.F., Fribourg, with prefaces.

those of Chestov would require further comment. 'Limbo': is undoubtedly, the supreme No-place peculiar to ghosts, the forlorn, the exiled, the rootless and to undesirables.

Almost at the end of his life, Fondane made a very successful translation of William Blake's famous poem: 'O rose, thou art sick!' ('O rose, tu languis!'). Blake had been claimed by the Surrealists as one of their illustrious English precursors (to tell the truth, they would have suppressed his ineradicable mysticism, his familiarity with 'spirits' or ghosts of all shapes and forms). Blake has been called 'the man without a mask'. For Baudelaire, the mask was an important issue. Did Fondane wear one? *Who* was Fondane? He possessed a *persona*, yes, that of Ulysses, for example, probably the brother of the jew Leopold Bloom, the *Ulysses* of Joyce, great master of punning. Of his private life, if I may be permitted to speak of it it, I have retained the impression that his mask, to return to the word, was one of dignified reserve, which did not signify any compromise but rather the retention of a restless spiritual energy; at the same time, he expressed a particular joyfulness which could occasionally show itself in sardonic laughter. The philosopher presented an appearance of composure, the poet one of passion, nervous as well as infectious.

It seems that it was one of Fondane's last wishes that his collected poetry should bear the title *Le Mal des fantômes* in the eventuality, that has now been reached, of its definitive publication posthumously. There only remains enough space to point out that the sequence thus entitled is by far the most moving in all his work, heart-rending in its expression of distress and, I was going to say, of despair. But Fondane precisely in accordance with the ambition of the existentialist philosopher, had passed beyond despair, and there remained in him almost to the end a reserve of unshakeable courage; and for courage say love. It is not at all my intention to assume the role of a preacher or to try to utter some words of consolation, but nothing would prevent me from declaring that the inextinguishable spark of courageous love was not only the miracle of the concentration camps, it continues to embody the only thing capable of preventing us from putting an end to the entire human species.

Finally, I would end with a line from Dante's *Purgatorio*, which I could have incorporated just as well at the beginning of this preface:

    e il pensamento in sogno transmutai.

T. S. ELIOT

[...] In France, 1919 may perhaps be regarded by historians of the development of modern poetry as chiefly significant for being the year that saw the appearance in an early issue of a small publication called *Littérature*, founded by André Breton, Philippe Soupault and Louis Aragon, of the first of the texts that were to appear collected into a book the following year under the title of *Les Champs magnétiques*. These texts, the work of Breton and Soupault in collaboration, were the first known authentic examples of the kind of automatic writing that a few years later was to become known internationally as 'Surrealist'. In order to produce such texts, it is necessary for the writer to become temporarily entirely devoid of all personal concerns and preoccupations, – to escape in fact, not only from all emotion but from all ratiocination. I do not suggest, of course, that Eliot had he then been as aware as his friend or at least acquaintance, the one-time 'Imagist' F. S. Flint, of the latest developments in French poetry, – for *Les Champs magnétiques* though composed almost entirely in prose are undoubtedly poetic, both Breton and Soupault being (though at that time almost ashamedly) poets – would have approved or been enthusiastically appreciative of this phenomenon.

Eliot was certainly in his own way an experimenter and a pioneer, but he was an extremely cautious one. He was undoubtedly open to an awareness of the unpleasant underside of appearances, and with courageous unexpectedness admired Blake for being profound, innocent, honest and *terrifying* [my italics]; but his super-ego, or what he himself referred to as his Puritanical American upbringing, made him as disapproving as Matthew Arnold about whose criticism fifty years earlier concerning what he referred to as Anarchy he expressed considerable reserve. T. S. Eliot would, and no doubt did, look askance at the sort of discipline required to produce authentic specimens of the workings of the unconscious mind in the form of enigmatically irrational poetry and prose, tending to be full of psychoanalytic imagery. In the first of his

---

From the preface to Roberto Sanesi's Italian translation of *The Collected Poems of T. S. Eliot*, published as *T. S. Eliot – Poesie* (1983). These extracts have been transcribed by Roger Scott from D.G.'s 52pp handwritten text (the typescript sent to Sanesi and translated into Italian by him has been lost).

Four Quartets, written at the end of his poetic career, Eliot typically once more deplores 'undisciplined squads of emotion'. He could never have regarded Breton's conception of *L'Amour fou* with anything other than grave suspicion if not abhorrence. Yet in spite of this, I myself as a supposed specialist in Surrealism, have on several occasions been asked whether I regarded lines 366 to 386 in the concluding section of *The Waste Land* ('What the Thunder Said') as exemplifying the use by T. S. Eliot of a resort to unconsciously inspired imagery closely akin to that produced by the altogether different technique being employed at just the same time as *The Waste Land* was being written, by the group across the Channel who, two years after the English poem's publication, were to be officially united by the publication of Breton's first *Manifeste du Surréalisme*.

There is an undeniable degree of resemblance between the language and oneiric imagery of the passage of Eliot I have referred to, and certain passages produced by such writers as Breton, Soupault, Desnos and even Aragon, during the years 1920 to 1924, but if there is a connection, it can only be adequately explained by referring to an as yet unsatisfactorily formulated law of historical synchronicity, and the fact that no poet of integrity can avoid reflecting in one way or another the state of the world surrounding him at the time at which he is writing, however subjectively inclined and introspective he may possibly be usually considered.

It is a paradoxical observation to make, but André Breton, in his doctrinaire way, might well have been inclined to agree with Eliot's remark to the effect that 'the bad poet is usually unconscious where he ought to be conscious, and conscious where he ought to be unconscious'. I have just referred to André Breton as being apt to be doctrinaire, and his detractors did in fact come to call him the Pope of Surrealism. Towards the end of the decade which saw not only the publication of the (to the British intelligentsia) epoch-making *The Waste Land*, but also at least two impressive collections of critical essays, T. S. Eliot began to be regarded, at least by all his most intelligent younger readers, with that respectful deference which was constantly to increase until the award to him of both the Order of Merit and the Nobel Prize for Literature consecrated his by then unquestionable authority. I have been privileged to know both these equally but extremely differently remarkable men, certainly not well, as both were fundamentally difficult to make more than momentarily genuine human contact with, and as far as Eliot was concerned, I was never even one of his Faber poets, though I visited him on more than one occasion in his Russell Square publishing-house office.

I trust it will no longer be thought indecorous of me to observe that when I think of this markedly dissimilar pair, I can retrospectively detect in both of them an overriding concern with the principle of authority. If I were to explore the subject of a possible comparison to be made between T. S. Eliot, ultimately more or less a pillar of the Establishment, and André Breton, two years his junior and intransigently subversive to the end, it would take up the whole of the rest of this essay [. . .] but it would, I think, be fair to point out that Eliot as a young man aspired to the authority he achieved through an innate intelligence that was not so cerebral as Paul Valéry's (always respectfully referred to by him as M. Valéry) and a certain habit of superiority in which he received much encouragement he did not need. Breton could not live without a circle of younger people who hung on his word and opinions almost as to sacred writ; all the other Surrealists with any strength of personality of their own quarrelled with him. The fundamental reason for this concern with authority, which in Eliot's case partly took the form of his well-known declaration of allegiance ('classicist in literature, royalist in politics, and anglo-catholic in religion') was, I believe, that both men were far more acutely aware than the vast majority of their fellow men of the chaotically precarious nature of the human condition; of the risk to which the poet, whether he is aware of the fact or believes it to be the case or not, exposes himself, consequent upon stealing inspiration, if not Promethean poetic fire from Heaven. [. . .]

[. . .] Eliot the man, an enthusiastic reader and admirer of Dante, himself went through a period in his life that can be described without fear of exaggeration as a *Purgatorio*. T. S. Eliot was at one time considered by English and American readers to be the most outstanding modern example of an intellectual, difficult, élitist poet, a remote figure whose cold intelligence prevented him from sharing or being much interested in common human emotions. This misconception, which for a long while prevented the so-called common reader from approaching his poetry free of anti-intellectual prejudice, has fortunately long since been dispersed by a remarkably widespread recognition that there is to be found in a great deal of Eliot's poetry, not only much in the way of increased enjoyment to be derived from the beauty of his language and the scrupulous way it is used, but also an exceptionally valuable aid towards attaining a heightened sense of the drama of being an inhabitant of the twentieth century. Our time is surely one of which it may be said that the experience of spiritual emptiness and sterility, accompanied by a desire to recover something of the inner vitality and profundity of vision expressed in the greatest artistic achievements of the past, is increasingly universal. Because this is so, the poetry of Eliot is particularly meaningful to all who have felt, without perhaps being able to express this feeling in words, the sense of futility, fear of the future, bewilderment, and desire for the bedrock of genuine belief in life's purpose and value, that are inseparable from being truly alive in this present time. It is unlikely that Eliot would have been able to give expression to the most authentic existential questioning of what Heidegger calls *Dasein* had he not himself lived with special intensity that dark night of the soul which is the essential lot of contemporary mankind. This aspect of his role in modern literature is summed up in the single line of *The Waste Land* (which provided Evelyn Waugh with the title of a famous and symptomatically popular novel): 'I will show you fear in a handful of dust'.

ROLAND PENROSE

'Si ce sont les plumes qui font le plumage ce n'est pas la colle qui fait le collage.'

Max Ernst

'L'on souhaiterait qu'une image soutint les images.'

Paul Nougé

These two quotations, which I discovered as though by chance when riffling through the pages of Volume I of the *Œuvres complètes* of Paul Eluard in the Bibliothèque de la Pléiade edition, will admirably serve as initial illustrations of what it seems to me should be said by way of introducing this exhibition of recent works by Eluard's closest English friend, Roland Penrose. To begin with, although glue or paste clearly play but a negligible though necessary role in the creation of the pictures here on view, the feathers constituting what may be described as their outer plumage are just as clearly postcards. Max Ernst once also remarked: 'Il est quelque chose comme l'alchimie de l'image visuelle'. The transmutation process of which Penrose holds the secret is that by means of which the apparently banal commonplace material provided by picture postcards is transformed into the magic element of an enchanting new visual experience. Paul Nougé's desire for an image that would serve to support images is in this way satisfied by popular, stereotyped images that have become the support of the dominant image in each of Penrose's collage-pictures. Closely examined, for instance, the monument forming the central feature of Roland's homage to de Chirico, entitled with characteristic wry humour *The Fake Metaphysician*, turns out to be made up of a quantity of identical fractured photographs of guardsmen on horseback accompanying the Queen during a ceremony familiar to all tourists in London at the time of Her Majesty's official birthday. The discrepancy between the spectacle represented on the pieces of coloured card composing the units of the singular tower-like shape round which the scene centres and the enigmatic atmosphere which the whole combination

---

Introduction to *Roland Penrose, Recent Collages (A Commemorative Exhibition)*, Gardner Centre Gallery, University of Sussex (3-13 May 1984), pp. 8-12. First published in the catalogue *Roland Penrose – Collages Récents*, Galerie Henriette Gomès, Paris (1982).

engenders is similar to the incongruity producing an electric charge between the previously unrelated poles in the classic Surrealist image. Similarly, in the series resulting from a recent visit to Sri Lanka, during which the painter-poet acquired a stock of the postcards most ordinarily collected by travelling amateurs of the picturesque, the latter have been used in such a way that they have become auxiliary to the creation of such landscapes as have never before been apprehended by human perception.

In a lecture given in London in 1936 at the time of the International Surrealist Exhibition there, Paul Eluard said: 'Les peintres surréaliste, qui sont des poètes, pensent toujours à autre chose. L'insolite leur est familier, la préméditation inconnue'. Roland Penrose is indeed as much a poet as he is a painter, as he demonstrated in 1939 with *The Road is Wider than Long*, a text inspired by a journey through the Balkans, just as the aforementioned Sri Lanka series was inspired by a later trip, and described by Michel Rémy as a 'voyage polyphonique où les événements et les rencontres se déroulent simultanément à l'extérieur et à l'intérieur de l'auteur, des personages de hasard et du lecteur'.

That poetry represents a special, indeed essential category of thought is an idea that since the death of Heidegger, who gave increasing credence in his later writings to this conception, is at present beginning to appear after all to be a proposition worthy of serious consideration by all thinkers, however rational. We are beginning to realize that we ought to question what thinking itself is, and that the long prevalent tendency of rationalism to be dogmatically autonomous is adding to the dangerous confusion and conflict now afflicting all human affairs. We have patently forgotten that all thinking began by confronting an initial and ultimate Mystery, and no doubt the preponderant tendency is still to prefer to regard as mystification any attempt to urge the recognition that no amount of reductionism can ever wholly succeed in banishing Mystery from the legitimate domain of speculation.

This apparently misplaced digression into philosophy is intended to lead to the inference that Penrose's poetically artistic production does in fact have philosophic implications of the deepest and most actual kind. Once it is acknowledged that thinking is inseparable from representation, that representation depends on images, that images are inseparable from the faculty of imagination and therefore from memory, we are on the way to admitting that Surrealist images, particularly such as incorporate morsels of empirically evident instants of mundane reality, have perennial philosophical relevance.

We should not expect to find any particular predetermined meaning in pictures as those which Penrose presents to us; rather should we experience them by allowing them to happen to us. The Surrealist artist is the medium through whom what he allows to occur on his pictural surface comes into existence in order to question us and make us aware of the presence of Mystery, and the fact that all images continually conceal something Other while appearing to reveal what they represent.

One should not make the mistake of regarding such pictures as these merely as contributions to the aesthetic experimentation of any sort of avant-garde movement. The avant-garde as such has by now virtually disintegrated. Surrealism, however, remains part of a quest that had begun with the earliest cave-painters and leads to the realm of ageless aboriginal graffiti as well as of the visual records of those who at all periods have explored the more obscure corners of the microcosm.

It is of the essence of the image to make something be seen. On the other hand, copies and imitations are already degenerate types of the true image which, as appearance, makes the Invisible be seen and thus 'imagines' it, thereby making it enter into something which is extraneous to it. The image 'imagines' the Invisible, that is to say clothes it with a form.

Having begun with two quotations, I find it appropriate to end with another, this one from a lecture by Heidegger that discusses a phrase from a Hölderlin poem.[1] Its words make it seem warrantable seriously to designate Roland Penrose, without undue solemnity, Outfitter by Appointment to the Invisible.

I should like to conclude with a kind of little franglais rebus intended to sum up what strikes me as the foremost insight my friend and compatriot's pictural investigations can incite:

P	Peinture	Pictures
E	Elargit	Enlarge
N	Nôtre	Normal
R	Realité	Reality
O	Ou bien	Or else
S	Semble	Seem
E	Eventrée.	Eviscerated.

---

[1] From the lecture delivered in 1951 commenting on Hölderlin's use of the phrase '... dichterisch wohnt der Mensch ...' Collected in *Vorträge und Aufsätze*, 1954. Translated into French by André Préau and published by Gallimard in 1958 as *Essais et conférences*.

With reference to the philosophical comments contained in the above, I should like to acknowledge my indebtedness to, and recommend, Marcel Paquet's *Magritte, ou l'éclipse de l'être*, Editions de la Différence, 1982.

BENJAMIN PERET

Benjamin Péret was born in the neighbourhood of Nantes in 1899, and died in Paris sixty years later. At the age of sixteen, soon after the outbreak of the 1914-18 war, he ran away from home to join up, in order to escape from an 'odious' family rather than spurred by the least patriotic fervour, something so scathingly mocked in many of his most typical later poems. Demobilized in 1920, he discovered modern poetry by chance in a review left behind on a railway platform bench, and before long made his way to Paris to become a participant in the already declining Dada movement. In 1924-5, he was named as co-editor of the earliest issues of *La Révolution surréaliste*. Of all members of the Surrealist group, he remained ever the closest and most loyal supporter of André Breton, who in 1952 described him as his 'dearest and most longstanding companion-in-arms'.

Péret has been aptly designated by the term 'absolute anarchist'. But at the same time, as Octavio Paz (who knew him both before and after the War) has observed, Péret was, in a sense, a 'man of the past' if the present time is essentially nihilistic, as he could never be classified as a nihilist. In a text first published in 1959 and reprinted later by Eric Losfeld as a preface to one of the volumes of his edition of Péret's *Œuvres complètes*, Octavio Paz declared that

> this man . . . who believed in himself so little, who attached so small an importance to his poetic work – among the most original and most savage of our era – never lost trust in life. His despair and pessimism prevented him from forming illusions, but they destroyed in him neither convictions nor hope . . . Thanks to men like Péret, the night in this century is not absolute.

Benjamin Péret has repeatedly been described as one of the purest and most intransigent members of the Surrealist movement and his work is still regarded by many as disgracefully neglected. 'The group's anti-religious action, the permanent scandal it provoked, its poetic experimentation, all owe a great deal to this private man, whose work is finally to be

---

Introduction to Benjamin Péret, *Remove Your Hat & Other Works*, translated by David Gascoyne and Humphrey Jennings (Atlas Press, 1986), pp. i-xii.

seen as dominated by tenderness and humour,' an anonymous contributor to a Surrealist issue of the *Magazine littéraire* once observed; adding: 'His writing has the rare distinction of resulting from a constant refusal to *faire de la librairie* (entertain commercial motives).'[1] The tenor of this comment is echoed unanimously by all who knew and have written about Péret, from Philippe Soupault, to Philippe Audoin, Jean Schuster and Jean-Christophe Bailly.[2]

Prefacing the 1969 Gallimard/*Poésie* re-edition of *Le Grand Jeu* (1928), Robert Benayoun, another of Péret's younger friends, lays stress on his modest unpretentiousness and points out that he was never one to think of himself as 'the poet', or adopt the attitude of an inspired seer, a devotee of the muse or an ill-fated outlaw. 'His *I* was so magnificently *an other*', wrote Benayoun, 'that had he been addressed as: *Péret, poet*, he would no doubt have replied anti-militarily "unknown in the regiment".' This preface, written ten years after Péret's death, refers to *Le Grand Jeu* (that after forty years had become an almost unobtainable rarity) as one of Péret's major works, and goes on immediately to apologize for the use of such a qualification since, if the collection had to be qualified, its author would have preferred it to be referred to as one might to a pipe or a sea-urchin. Almost all his poems were dashed off at a sitting, never touched up or corrected, and promptly forgotten till a contribution to a review was required or the time came when his admirers began to feel a new collection of them was due.

During the post-Dada, pre-1924 period sometimes referred to in English as that 'of sleeping-fits', Péret, Desnos and Crevel (who had first introduced trance experiments to the group) were among those who most readily came out with spontaneous utterances from the unconscious. This especial gift for uninhibited spontaneity is the hallmark of all Péret's subsequent writing. From the first, also, his imagery and vocabulary are distinguished by their provisional everyday ordinariness and simplicity: braces, cabbage-stumps, beards, eggs, dogs, Popes and policemen, for instance, occur far more frequently than any paraphernalia of the rare and strange, both in his prose tales and in his poems, from the early *Au 125 Boulevard Saint-Germain* and *Le Passager du transatlantique* onwards. His constant use of current colloquialisms and adapted catch-phrases, particularly in his use of titles, can occasionally confront a translator with

---

[1] On reflection, a closer approximation of this expression might well be: write the kind of thing that Atlas Press would have no interest in publishing.
[2] J.-C. Bailly, *Au dela du langage. Une étude sur Benjamin Péret* (Eric Losfeld, 1971).

problems of the kind that Paul Brown and Peter Nijmeijer refer to in the Notes to their excellent bilingual Péret selection, *Four Years After the Dog* (Arc Publications, 1974).

When in 1936, after Roger Roughton's printer had inexplicably taken it upon himself to censor the first edition of the selection of translations that Humphrey Jennings and I had prepared for publication that summer, it was decided that we should alter the seemingly innocuous *A Bunch of Carrots* to something less provocative, we asked Péret to suggest some suitable alternative. He came up with a title of deceptive simplicity: *Chapeau!* It was then explained to us that this was an exclamation frequently to be heard during matinées in Parisian theatres during the *belle époque*, when ladies were apt to wear large and elaborate hats obstructing the view of the stage of those seated in the row behind them. Humphrey J. and I came up with *Remove Your Hat* as the closest rendering of Péret's emendation, three words instead of one yet no less peremptory than the original, unaccompanied by any SVP. At the same time I strongly suspected that Péret intended one to understand the implication, through the similarity and association between *chapeau* and *capote*, of what we reciprocally think of as a 'French letter', since the letters used by our printer were after all intended to make an English book. Such an interpretation may suggest the result of a more deliberate mental process than Péret was wont to resort to in such an instance; but if the association the altered title aroused in me was fortuitous, it is I hope one more example of the often felicitous results of what the Surrealists like to refer to as *l'hasard objectif*.

Péret's preoccupation with such figures of speech and with sayings of a proverbial nature was, to begin with, something he shared in particular with Paul Eluard, publisher in 1920 of the ephemeral series of mini-brochures known as *Proverbe*. Eluard's portrait of Péret published in a 1922 issue of *Littérature* may relevantly be cited here: *Qui est-ce, Benjamin Péret? Un homme ressemblant*. Three years later, he became Péret's collaborator in the compilation of a now pricelessly rare pamphlet: *152 proverbes mis au gout du jour*. Impossible to verify today which of the two was responsible for which proverb, but I'd be prepared to bet that among the contributions to this tandem opuscule the following three examples were Péret's: 'Beat your mother while she's young'. − 'He who sows fingernails reaps a torch'. − 'A corset in July is worth a horde of rats'.

For a special number of the Belgian review *Variétés* devoted to *Le Surréalisme en 1929*, Eluard wrote half-a-dozen pages of admirably combative presentation and defence of Péret's poetry, illustrated with numerous salient quotations, as in the following passage:

Truth is told very quickly, without reflecting, quite plainly, and for it sadness, fury, gravity and joy are only time-changes, won-over skies. For it mystery means only mysterious-indifferent elaboration. The path Mystery, evidence-paved. One doesn't explain since there's nothing to explain, because there's nothing but the truth:

> Mystery of man or reciprocally
> In order to explain what's needed
> Two men and three fish
> It's a mystery.

Eluard was also the author of the *prière d'insérer* leaflet (a type of text that even in France has now degenerated into what is known as a blurb) printed to accompany the publication in 1934 by the *Editions des Cahiers Libres* (and not, perhaps surprisingly but for now forgotten reasons, by José Corti's *Editions Surréalistes*) of *De derrière les fagots*. Brief as it is, this is perhaps the most just and striking tribute to Péret's early poetic production ever written. There is insufficient space here to quote it in its entirety: after reference to the extra-lucid images embodying this poetry, images clear as rock-crystal, as conspicuous as the *strident crying of red eggs*, follows the concluding sentence: 'It is my pride only to know men who love as I do this specifically subversive poetry, which has the colour of the future.'

This may be the place to point out something I shall not further allude to in these pages but which it would be important not to overlook if one were surveying Péret's life and output as a whole. In a compilation of Eluard's posthumously uncollected prose writings,[3] his eulogy of Péret (*Variétés*, 1929, quoted above) is closely followed by the brief preface he wrote in 1943 for a clandestinely published anthology, *L'Honneur des poètes*, of what was to become known as 'Resistance poetry'. Two years later Péret, while still in Brazil where for four years he had lived in exile, published *Le Déshonneur des poètes*, a pamphlet in which he denounced with characteristic virulence the very notion of poetry as an instrument of propaganda of any kind. After this, and the publication by Eluard in 1948 of his collection of *Poèmes politiques*, it is impossible to suppose that those two poets ever saw or spoke to each other again. In view of this, it is not altogether surprising that passing reference to the Surrealist group is to be found towards the end of the Manuels' vast and melancholy history of *Utopian Thought in the Western World* (1979).

★

---

[3] Paul Eluard, *Le Poète et son ombre – Proses 1920-1952* (Paris: Seghers, 1963, 1979).

All the poems that Humphrey Jennings and I translated between 1935 and '36, for publication by Roger Roughton in either his *Contemporary Poetry & Prose* or in the pamphlet with two titles brought out to coincide with the opening of the London International Surrealist Exhibition in the Summer preceding the outbreak of the Spanish Civil War, were drawn either from *De derrière les fagots*, which I think I must have brought back to England with me after visiting the Surrealists in Paris in '35 in order to collect material for my *Short Survey of Surrealism* first published later the same year, or from *Je ne mange pas de ce pain-là*. This latter collection first appeared in 1936, despite the fact that, as Eric Losfeld pointed out in the notes that appear at the end of Tome I of his 1969 edition of the *Œuvres complètes* of Péret, the twenty-eight poems it contains were for the most part composed (or, more exactly, improvised) between 1926 and '29, the two latest having appeared in the 5th number of *Le Surréalisme au service de la révolution* in 1933, and are therefore generally anterior to the poems making up *De derrière les fagots*. The collection is unified by the fact that without exception the poems it contains are *de circonstance*, many of them bearing titles that could have served to head the political columns of the newspapers of the period. Rereading the original series today, I find it difficult to reconcile its undisguised, rampagious tendentiousness – the very title is a contemptuous expression of disgust – with Péret's unqualified disavowal of the aims of anything like 'committed' poetry in his polemical pamphlet of 1945; but this is no place to enter into even the most cursory discussion of this particular issue.

Before recently rereading for the first time in too many years the two Péret pamphlets Roger Roughton published half a century ago, I was under the hazy impression that most of the few translations in them from *Je ne mange pas de ce pain-là* were by Humphrey Jennings; but in fact they were, it seems, fairly evenly shared between us. The title of the shortest of them marks it unmistakably as having been translated by me. 'Petite Chanson des mutilés' would be rendered by any competent translator of more than elementary experience as 'Little Song of the Disabled'. Curiously enough, both Jon Stallworthy, who enterprisingly included this item in his *Oxford Book of War Poetry* (in which it appears flanked by a 1915 Apollinaire 'Calligramme' translated by Oliver Bernard and Yeats's 'On Being Asked for a War Poem'), and Alastair Brotchie have expressed a preference for 'Maimed' in place of what I now take to be the accurate equivalent of the French word.

Looking through the 1986 proof of the poem translated as 'Unsettled' (the original, 'Variable', is the last in *De derrière les fagots*), I thought I had spotted an error which it would have been easy for a twenty-year-old with as yet scanty acquaintance with French *haute cuisine* to make. In lines 10 and 11 appears 'lobster . . . not yet quite cooked / in the American manner'. This must obviously, I thought, have been my makeshift version of *à l'armoricaine*, and ought to be left untranslated, in order to avoid appearing to patronize the sophisticated present-day reader by appending an explanatory footnote to 'in the Breton manner'. But the translation was, as it happens, by Humphrey Jennings, who was not only nine years my senior but had lived in France while I was still in secondary school. Turning to the French text of this poem, I find that line 11 does in fact read *à l'américaine*. Prior to the late 1940s, most English people were insufficiently aware of classic French menu items to have been able to appreciate the unexpected punlike variant that Péret came up with at this point in his poem. This may seem too trivial a detail to be discussed at such length. There is however another poem in the present collection, to which the English title 'To Pass the Time' has been given,[4] that contains a youthful inaccuracy on my part of a slightly more interesting nature. Before recent correction, line 12 of this piece read 'like a bottle of Leyde', displaying a no doubt deplorably deficient familiarity with both geography and the history of physics. An experienced translator would have immediately recognized that *une bouteille de Leyde* refers to what we know as a Leyden jar, defined in my dictionary as 'A glass bottle or jar coated inside and out with tinfoil used to accumulate electricity (invented at Leyden, city of Holland, in 1745)'. This is to me an interesting mistake on account of the fact that I should have been unlikely to make it at the more recent time when I was translating Breton/Soupault's *Les Champs magnétiques*. The first of these texts is called 'La glâce sans tain', and *tain* is precisely the tinfoil alluded to in the definition of a Leyden jar. Apart from that, there is a passage in one of Breton's writings in which he compares the formation of the trains of associated images in the un/subconscious mind revealed by automatic writing with the way that scraps of tissue paper will attach themselves to one another after having been in contact with a sheet of glass or an ebony rod magnetized by being rubbed with silk. The association of Surrealist experimentation with electro-magnetic phenomena seems to me a typical characteristic of the development of Surrealist thought, and because of this

---

[4] At the time of writing, the French original of this poem still mysteriously eludes me, as I am unable to locate it in either of the two volumes brought out by Eric Losfeld in 1969 and 1971 which contain all the poetry published by Péret between 1921 and 1959: the chief drawback of this otherwise invaluable edition is that it is devoid of all tables of contents.

I find it significant that the last line under discussion should have found its way into the Péret poem containing it. The translation of the title *Mi-figue mi-raisin* as 'Half-Fig Half-Grape' is an instance of choosing literalness rather than the possibly condescending anglicization of 'Neither Fish nor Fowl', which is in itself in any case a more boring expression apart from its clichéd familiarity; the literal version preserves the readymade Surrealist quality that must have appealed to Péret despite its being a commonplace in French. *De derrière les fagots* is another such vernacular expression, possibly now growing increasingly unfamiliar. It is a way of referring to something rather special reserved for an unusual occasion, family friends or an acquaintance one wishes to impress. Rare vintages, old liqueurs, a few last bottles of really good champagne, were kept *derrière les fagots* in the traditional household cellar. Péret's title is his flippant way of referring to uncollected poems that had been accumulating in folders or desk drawers until a publisher required a new book from him for his list.

*

In a series of interviews with Serge Fauchereau,[5] Philippe Soupault, when asked for his comments on Péret, replied:

> I knew Péret at the time of his arrival in Paris. He was shy and alarming. One never knew what he was thinking. He spoke little and seldom. He didn't display amusement (*ne ricanait pas*). Yet he would fly into a passion (and that's putting it mildly) whenever he caught sight of or encountered a priest. He became furious and insulted those he referred to as *ecclésiastiques*. What always surprised me was that he wrote poems that bore no resemblance to him. I learnt that Péret (it was he who told me) had written symbolist poems and undergone the influence of Mallarmé. It was a difficult admission. And yet, when I'd read Péret's first published poem, I decided to proclaim that this poet was one of the most authentic of all the Surrealists. And I think the future has proved that I was not mistaken.

On those occasions when I met Péret during the early summer of 1935, the impression I formed of him as a man was very much in keeping with the way Soupault describes him as having been fifteen years

---

[5] Philippe Soupault, *Vingt mille et un jours, entretiens avec Serge Fauchereau* (Belfond, 1980).

earlier. He was invariably to be seen in the evenings from 6 o'clock until dinnertime at the Surrealists' special tables, set end to end, at the *Café de la Place Blanche*, where he invariably sat at Breton's right hand. The daily discussion over, when Breton returned to his rue Fontaine apartment just round the corner, most of the rest of us would repair to a local bistro for the evening meal. Péret often accompanied us. At table he appeared to relax, and would generally end by becoming quite familiar and facetious. Yet one had the feeling that basically he was, as Soupault testifies, shy and reserved. With me he was mildly agreeable, never loquacious, and co-operative when I discussed with him the possibility of translating his poetry. I knew that, unlike many other members of the group who weren't painters, he earned his living with an everyday job (I learned later that this consisted of proof-reading for a left-wing publishing firm). He seemed to live alone and, unlike Breton and Eluard, somewhere on the Left Bank, probably near the Jardin des Plantes. One evening I shall never forget; instead of returning as I usually did after dinner by métro to my Left Bank hotel, I accompanied Péret on an auto bus. There were few other passengers, and we were standing on the rear platform. After a while, at a stop on the Avenue de l'Opéra, an unprepossessing young curé climbed on board. Having seen in a back number of *La Révolution surréaliste*, a photo captioned 'Our collaborator Benjamin Péret insulting a priest', I was hardly surprised to see my companion follow the soutane-clad ecclesiastic into the interior of the bus, where he forthwith spat on his victim before, having proffered some well-chosen execrations, returning to join me on the platform till the end of the journey. As far as I remember, I was not particularly shocked by the incident, though no doubt I suffered momentarily from the kind of embarrassment most of my compatriots would feel in such a situation; nor was there, to my recollection, anything like indignant remonstrance on the part of the bus-conductor. I couldn't help wondering what horrors of narrow-minded provincial Catholicism his upbringing must have inflicted on him to produce such long-lasting later revulsion. It struck me that on our side of the Channel, only an education at the hands of the Plymouth Brethren or particularly obnoxious Christian Brothers would ever be likely to produce a similar result. At any rate, Péret seemed not to bear me a grudge or regard me as either lily-livered or indoctrinated on account of my failure to participate in his conscientious demonstration, and we parted on congenial enough terms. I may have seen Péret again before leaving France later in 1935, but that is my last clear memory of him.

It is doubtful whether Péret was ever an at all fervent anglophile. At any rate, I do not think there can ever have been any question of his coming to England at the time of the International Surrealist Exhibition in London the following year. Not long after the exhibition had closed, the Spanish Civil War broke out, following the mutiny of Franco's troops in North Africa. Péret almost immediately set out for Spain to defend the Republican cause, but no doubt above all to combat the forces of extreme reaction nurtured by the worst sort of Catholic bigotry. Disillusioned by the dissensions he observed among representatives of the extreme anti-Stalinist left, he chose to enlist in the 'Durrutti Column' and took part in the battle for Teruel. After the ultimate collapse of the anti-Franco resistance, he managed to reach Barcelona and then France, only to find himself called up to join the French Army in 1939. Soon he was accused of attempting to set up a Trotskyist cell in his regiment, and in 1940 was sentenced to imprisonment in Rennes. Profiting from the confusion following the fall of France, he escaped to join the many other Surrealists then awaiting cross-Atlantic passages in Marseilles. While most of the others eventually made their way to the USA, Péret chose to set sail for Mexico. Here he wrote an account of his experience of imprisonment in Rennes that was published by Breton under the title *La parole est à Péret*; and later, the polemical pamphlet referred to earlier. He returned to Paris in 1948.

There has not been room in these pages for a more than rudimentary sketch of Péret's life and production, and it is to be deplored that to date there is so little in the way of biographical or critical Péret documentation to rely on. I understand this deficiency is being made good by a full-length biographical study due to appear before long in the States. Till then, one can only refer the determined reader to J. M. Goutier's *Benjamin Péret* of 1982, described in John Lyle's catalogue 'The Surrealist Movement' as: 'A dossier illustrated with photos, documents, texts by and about him by friends to show his relations with painting, politics, poetry and Mexico'. A bilingual selection from all Péret's books, translated by E. R. Jackson, is also available under the title *A Marvellous World* (1985) to those who can afford American imports. In 1984, Paul Brown produced in this country, under his 'Actual Size' imprint, his translation of *Le Travail anormal*, a sequence to be found in *Le Grand Jeu*, under the title *Irregular Work*; and the Field Translation Series publishes *From the Hidden Storehouse*, selected poetry translated by Keith Holloman (1981).

During the last ten years of his life, despite a steady decline of health due largely to unremitting penury, Péret appears to have continued to participate fully and fruitfully in the post-war Surrealist movement, remaining faithful to André Breton to the end. During this period he produced, as well as a precious handful of last poems, two notable anthologies, *Anthologie de l'amour sublime* (1956), and the posthumous

Anthologie des mythes, légendes et contes populaires de l'Amérique (1960). There remains one feature of Péret's life that it would not have been possible adequately to deal with here. But any future biography of Benjamin Péret will have to take account of what in all probability was the most singular and influential episode of his life: his relationship with, marriage to and separation from the Spanish painter Remedios Varo, whom he first met in Spain at the outset of the Civil War. They were married in 1937, and later she followed him to Paris, where she took part the following year in the last pre-war International Surrealist Exhibition. In 1942, she embarked with him to Mexico where, at the height of her power and success, she died of a sudden heart attack in 1963, four years after Péret's death, at the age of fifty. It seems to me inexplicable that so original a painter, one of the most gifted of all Surrealist women artists, should still remain unknown to all but a few on this side of the Atlantic. If the full story of her life with Péret were ever to be told* it would no doubt reveal as much that is still unknown about the poet, his character and the influence on him of this beautiful and altogether exceptional woman as it would about her and her work. In all probability, however, the full story of their relationship, and the part it played in Péret's later life, will ever remain in an area of shadowy speculation.

---

* Editor's note: Janet A. Kaplan's *Unexpected Journeys. The Art and Life of Remedios Varo* was published by Virago Press, London, and Abbeville Press, New York, in 1988.

NOVALIS AND THE NIGHT

I

The poet who was to become known by the name Novalis was born Georg Phillipp Friedrich von Hardenberg on a day in May 1772 when an eclipse of the sun took place, the eldest son and second of the eleven children of Heinrich Ulrich Erasmus Baron von Hardenberg and his second wife. The Baron was the proprietor of the salt-mines of Weissenfels, and a pious convert to the sect of the Moravian Brethren. The boy's delicate health in childhood led to a serious illness at the age of nine, after recovering from which he received a Gymnasium education. At the age of eighteen, he went on to study at the University of Jena, where he attended Schiller's lectures on poetry and a course on the philosophy of Kant, and was befriended by Friedrich Schlegel. He then went on to study law and jurisprudence at the University of Wittenburg, where he graduated in the summer of 1794, proceeding to serve a term of apprenticeship at Tennstedt with the magistrate Just who became his friend and later his first biographer. Following this Novalis spent two years as a functionary in his father's saltmining company at Weissenfels. At the end of 1797, he went to Freiberg, where he attended the courses of the celebrated mineralogist Gottlob Werner and studied the natural sciences, physics, chemistry and mathematics; he also became acquainted with animal magnetism, or galvanism, as practised by Johann Wilhelm Ritter. At Whitsun 1799, he returned to Weissenfels to occupy an official post in the management of the mines there.

The first meeting of the young von Hardenberg with Sophie von Kühn took place at her family's manor of Grüningen in November 1794, when she was still only thirteen. They were secretly betrothed in the spring of the following year. That summer, Novalis briefly encountered Fichte and Hölderlin at Jena. In November, Sophie, now his official fiancée, first succumbed to the fatal illness which, despite an operation at the hospital of Jena in the summer of 1796, was to lead to her painful death at her home in Grüningen in March the following year. Two

---

Introduction to Novalis, *Hymns to the Night*, translated by Jeremy Reed (Petersfield: Enitharmon Press, 1989), pp. 7-18.

months after Sophie's death, Novalis experienced, while mourning at her graveside, a vision that was to have a determining effect on the work by which he is best known. He did not survive his beloved for long, but died of consumption in March 1801.

To this bare outline of the outer facts of Novalis' life may suitably be adjoined the following summary by the philosopher Wilhelm Dilthey of its inner meaning:

> Novalis shows all things to us in his distinctive light. To pronounce his name is enough to make the world about us appear as it did to him – like a valley at rest in the calm of evening, disclosing itself to the traveller returning down the mountainside in the last rays of the sun: all around, the motionless warmth of the air; in the still blue sky, the blurred silver effulgence of the moon; the mountains encircle us, but with an intimacy in no way oppressive; it never occurs to us that on the other side are roads leading to towns and tumultuous regions. Everything contributes to this impression: Novalis' way of thinking, his destiny, the conditions in which he lived. He was so far from the noise of current affairs, withdrawn from life's pressing contact. On the threshold of maturity it befell him to experience those happy days at Jena when the romantic dream of the universe was blossoming, where Friedrich and Wilhelm Schlegel, Tieck and Schelling were conceiving the dream of a new poetry and a new philosophy. To what happened then, he imparts in some way the quality and the depth of his soul; before reaching his thirtieth year he dies. Over his memory floats a gleam of poetry, which extends to the words of all his friends whenever they evoke it.
>
> (From *Der Erlebnis und die Dichtung*, 1905)

II

Hymns to the Night is, with the exception of two brief texts on religious themes, the only complete work to have been published by Novalis during his lifetime. Of his other writings, all that remains of his initiatory romance, the *Disciples at Saïs*, are two preliminary chapters, while *Heinrich von Ofterdingen* consists of no more than a first part, which contains a few poems, and some sketches and notes for the remainder. The fifteen 'Canticles', or *Geistliche Lieder*, that he completed after the *Hymns*, were first published posthumously, as were the nine series of Fragments, or *Pensées*, written between 1795 and 1800, a selection of which is known by the apposite title of *Pollen*.

Novalis' most devoted French translator, Armel Guerne, has referred to 'toutes les facettes de cet unique diamant noir que sont les *Hymnes à la Nuit*', a phrase which serves usefully to remind us that the six *Hymnen* which make up Novalis' capital work should essentially be read as an ensemble of interdependent parts. If I have translated only the first two of them, that is because my German is so rudimentary that I do not feel competent to transpose the more strictly scanned and rhyming sections of Novalis' text into anything like an English equivalent. The result of translating these passages without taking their rhythm and rhyme into account would have been indistinguishable from the prose which precedes them. The kind of interdependence that careful reading of the *Hymns* reveals is paralleled by a similar interconnection between the keywords distinguishing each of them. The nimbus of meaning emanated by each of these words intermingles with those attached to the others in Novalis' individual vocabulary, simultaneously enhancing both an initial impression of nebulous otherworldliness and an increased comprehension of their inner sense when grasped in conjunction with one another. The resultant semantic density of Novalis' texts is aptly suggested by Guerne's choice of a faceted diamond as a metaphor characterizing the *Hymns*.

III

The *Hymnen an die Nacht* were composed at some time between 1797, the year of Sophie's death, and 1800, in the January of which year Novalis wrote to Friedrich Schlegel offering the work for publication in his friend's review, the *Athenaeum*. In a letter to Ludwig Tieck written two months later, Novalis remarked that he hoped Schlegel would excise the word *Hymnen* from the title; nevertheless the sequence first published later in 1800 in Schlegel's review retains its original name.

It is known that not long after Sophie's death Novalis happened to read Edward Young's *Night Thoughts*. Any resemblance between that work and the *Hymns* however, is purely superficial; whereas Young's first title is 'The Complaint', Novalis' poem is remarkable in its achievement of a serene transcendence of bereavement and mourning through the resolution of grief into rapture rather than resignation.

The title of Schubert's lied, *Nacht und Träume* (D827), composed some two decades after the first flowering of Romanticism, epitomizes the twin themes most dominant in the work of nearly all the most outstanding German poets of Novalis' generation and their successors. But the Night of Novalis' *Hymns* differs significantly in many respects from that of his contemporaries. Among these, Jean-Paul (Richter) produced a prophetic text (in a series wherein he recorded his dreams) that anticipates by more than half a century the questions and proclamations of Nietzsche's 'madman' in *Le Gai Savoir* (III, 125: 1882), demanding whether there could ever be an end to the nights succeeding God's assassination by mankind. In Jean-Paul's dream of the dead Christ, he 'gazed into the abyss, crying "Father, where art thou?",' but heard 'nothing but the storm that rages uncontrollably for ever', and saw 'the rainbow of all beings shining across the abyss *without being created by any sun!*'

The epoch heralded by the enthronement instigated by Robespierre of the goddess of Reason on the altar of Notre-Dame when the French Revolution was at its height had its philosophic basis formulated at the same moment by Hegel, whose purely abstract Absolute Spirit results in reality from the death of the living personal God of Abraham, Isaac and Jacob. It was in Martin Buber's analysis of this epoch, which he entitled 'Eclipse of God', that I first came across the words of Hölderlin that I used as an epigraph for my own *Night Thoughts*. 'Aber weh! es wandelt in Nacht, es wohnt, wie in Orkus, / Ohne Göttliches unser Geschlecht . . .' (But alas! our generation walks in night, dwells as in Hades, without the Divine . . .)

It will not be as out of place as might first appear to bring in at this point a passing reference to the best-known work of the 'minor' Victorian poet James Thomson, whose *The City of Dreadful Night* first appeared in 1874. Thomson first wrote pseudonymously under the initials B.V., standing respectively for Bysshe (Shelley) and Vanolis (Novalis).

The Night that inspired Novalis, however, cannot properly be qualified as dreadful; neither should it be confused with 'the dark night of the soul'. If night has a terrible aspect, when regarded as representing the Stygian darkness consequent on 'the death of God', it will ever continue also to exemplify the inexhaustible maternal power of recuperative latency, from which a new light may emerge to make life and death cease to appear contradictory. In the very first of the *Hymnen*, Night is already identified with *der Mutter liebe Jugend geigt*, after whose visitation Light, praised previously as the innermost essence of life, whose presence alone can reveal the kingdoms of this world in their miraculous splendour, appears comparatively jejune; while the infinite eyes that Night opens within us appear more divine than all the sparkling stars of heaven. It is plain that for Novalis, as for all the Romantics, access had become available as never before to the inner realm we now refer to as the Unconscious, the domain Goethe revealed as bring that of the Mothers, preternaturally ancient yet for ever young, being unbounded by Time or Place.

IV

Reference was made in the second of these notes to two types of interdependence that become apparent when one pays attention to the distinctive structure of the *Hymnen*. There are two further inter-relationships to be observed if more than a superficial appreciation is to result from reading them. The first is their intimate connection with Novalis' suffering, at the age of twenty-five, the loss of the adolescent Sophie von Kühn he was longing to marry. The other concerns the relation between the *Hymnen* and the *Fragmente* Novalis was accumulating both before and during the comparatively brief period when the *Hymnen* were being composed.

Little appears to be known of Novalis' encounter with Hölderlin in 1795 at Jena, beyond the fact that they did in fact meet there in the early summer. It was at the end of this year that Hölderlin first became tutor in the home of the Frankfurt banker Gontard, whose wife Susette became before long the poet's adored Diotima. By the autumn of 1797, Hölderlin had left the Gontard household in disgrace, his passionate affair with Diotima continuing thereafter only in secret and with frustrating difficulty. By that time, Sophie von Kühn was already dead. When Hölderlin first heard, in 1802, that Diotima had died, his mental balance was already gravely impaired; the news from Frankfurt led to worse disturbance, which led in turn four years later to confinement, followed by thirty-six years of sequestration. The differences between the two poets far outweigh any similarities they may be thought to share. Among these, even their tragic bereavements are entirely dissimilar. While Diotima's beauty was that of a mature housewife and mother, Sœfchen, however charmingly precocious, was still an inexperienced virgin. In a Fragment of 1798, Novalis refers to the *schöne Geheimnis* of the young girl, rendering her inexpressibly seductive, as being the presentiment of maternity, the hint of a future world sleeping in her in order to blossom later. The entries in his Journal written at the time of Sœfchen's death and during the period of mourning that followed it, may convey to some present-day readers a certain impression of morbidity, but they provide no evidence that the writer's sanity could ever have been in question.

In the daily Journal kept by Novalis after Sophie's death, between April and July 1797, the entry for 13 May is of particular interest, as it is to be found transcribed directly, in lyric form, in the Third Hymn: 'In the evening I went to see Sophie. Moments of overwhelming enthusiasm. With one breath I dispersed the tomb like a heap of dust – centuries seemed no more than instants – her presence became evident to me – I had the feeling she was on the point of appearing.' For the rest, the entries reveal the underlying conviction to be found associated with Novalis' virtual identification of Sophie with religion, in the special sense the word came to have for him. 'She is dead – consequently I shall die – the world is empty', he wrote in June. 'With her, the entire world is dead for me. I belong to the earth no more'. In a note written at about this time, Novalis declared: 'What I feel for Sœfchen is religion, not love. All absolute love, independent of the heart and founded on faith, is religion.' This faith of Novalis, as expressed in the concluding Hymns, conceives Night above all as the nuptial night wherein *animus* (the poet) and *anima* (the beloved) are at last reunited in an eternal embrace.

V

Underlying almost all that Novalis ever wrote, whether lyrical or speculative, from the *Lehrlinge zu Sais* onwards, two predominant themes are discernible: the 'doctrine of correspondences', and the process of initiation. 'Towards the interior leads the mysterious road. Within us, or nowhere, lies eternity with all its worlds, the past and the future.' This inner world, or microcosm, is inherent in and inseparable from the macrocosm of the physical universe; and each reflects the other. With this conception is concomitant the doctrine of correspondences as expressed by, for instance, Cornelius Agrippa when he wrote in his *Occult Philosophy*[1] that 'there is no member in man that hath not correspondence with some sign, star, intelligence, divine name, sometimes in God himself, the Archetype'. Novalis' observation that 'the human is a source of analogies for the universe' reveals his outlook as being fundamentally at one with that of such predecessors as Agrippa, Paracelsus, and no doubt above all Boehme. In a fragment to be found in his 'Encyclopedic project' of 1798-9, Novalis noted, under the rubric *Magic (Mystic Philology)*, that 'sympathy of the sign with the signified was one of the fundamental ideas of the Kaballah'. Similarly, under the heading *Grammar*, he observed that 'Man is not alone in speaking: the universe also speaks – everything speaks. – Unending languages. The doctrine of signatures'. And in declaring that 'the greatest good resides in the imagination', Novalis, knowingly or not, was echoing Paracelsus, according to whom 'Imagination is Creative Power . . . Imagination takes precedence over all. Resolute imagination can accomplish all things.'[2]

---

[1] English edition 1650.
[2] *Interpretatio alia Totius Astronomiae*, 1659.

The numerous and diverse fragments scattered like pollen by Novalis during the brief course of his creative life show him to have been gifted above all with intuitive power of a prodigious order. The three more substantial works culminating in the *Hymns to the Night* show the development of this intuitive follower of the Hermetic path to have been essentially that of an initiate. It is clear that the author of the *Hymns* is a neophyte who has undergone an experience leading him through confrontation with the reality of death, when his beloved is taken from him as Euridice was taken from Orpheus, to a new understanding and evaluation of this reality, identifying death with restorative Night. In the words of Mircea Eliade, referring to the mythic darkness corresponding to the cosmic Night, to the chaos before creation: 'we are dealing here with a double symbolism: that of death, namely the conclusion of a temporal existence, and consequently with the end of time, and the symbolism of return to the germinal mode of being, which precedes all forms and every temporal existence.' Eliade further points out that initiatory death is a recommencement, never an end, and that it is the condition *sine qua non* of a transition to another mode of being, a trial indispensable to regeneration, the beginning of a new life. It is surely significant that Ludwig Tieck should have ended his eulogy of Novalis by declaring him comparable 'among the moderns', only with 'the sublime Dante'. Just as Dante's *Vita Nuova* proceeded from his loss and vision of Beatrice, so the death and transfiguration celebrated in the *Hymns to the Night* are inseparable from Novalis' betrothal to Sophie. As the *Hymns* move towards their climax, the figure that was Sophie seems to emerge implicitly from their etherial, all-coalescing flux as at once Isis, the immortal Virgin symbolizing the purity of Nature before the Fall, and Sophia, the wisdom concomitant with illumination.

There is a tradition according to which the spiritual history of humanity is the supreme initiation, by means of which the Saviour of the World redeems mankind from separation from our true Self, the Godhead. The two concluding *Hymns to the Night* evoke an account of the withdrawal of the gods of the ancient world, following the disappearance of primordial Faith and Imagination, into the Night of slumbering latency. The birth of a new age is eventually heralded by the birth of the 'only Son of the first Virgin Mother'. Novalis then narrates the Gospel story in his own glimmeringly colourful language. A Singer, 'born under the sky of ancient Greece', arrives in Palestine to salute the miraculous Child, while declaring Death to be the path of eternal Life: *Du bist der Tod und machst uns erst gesund*. There follows a rhapsodic transcription of the passion, resurrection and ascension of Christ (whose name is never more than implied). The remains of the old world are left behind in the open tomb, while the inexhaustible chalice of a future golden age is proffered from on high. Long centuries pass, death ceases to be fearful, the new creation lives in ever-renewed splendour; and the penultimate Hymn ends in seven strophes of rejoicing, beginning with the words:

> Raised is the stone –
> Mankind is resurrected –

The final Hymn, *Sehnsucht nach dem Tode*, makes more explicit the conviction expressed in the fifth, that Death is the passage to eternal life, that Night restores to us all that day has taken away, and that night is preferable to day as death to life. The supposition that the poet's personal experience has its equivalent not only in the experience of each man in particular but also in that of humanity in general, endorsed by the work's concluding strophes, bears out the interpretation of it that would maintain it to be a record of initiation into a *Vita Nuova*. It would be false to regard Novalis as turning to the Night out of despair. He was like the wise Nicodemus of Henry Vaughan who

> saw such light
> As made him know his God by night

and knew there to be in God 'a deep but dazzling darkness'. He in fact found in the everyday, natural world a subject of endless wonder and fascination, as all the Fragments arising from his absorption in scientific studies testify. Through the death of Sophie which overtook him in the midst of them he came to experience the profound inseparability of love and faith. The *Hymns* are an expression of spontaneous faith without parallel in the contemporary world: faith rare as a grain of wheat preserved in some prehistoric sarcophagus, yet still manifestly capable of germination.

ELIZABETH SMART

In undertaking to write an introduction to the poetry of Elizabeth Smart, I took it for granted that readers of this *Collected Poems* would be familiar with *By Grand Central Station I Sat Down and Wept*. Truly a once-read-never-forgotten book, it was first issued in 1945 by Tambimuttu of Editions Poetry London. I hope, too, readers will be familiar with its less generally appreciated, less intense and dazzling, but more mature sequel of 1978, *The Assumption of Rogues & Rascals*. Both were republished in 1991 by Paladin simultaneously with the first English edition of Elizabeth's early journals, *Necessary Secrets*.

There are poets whose work can be appreciated by readers who know little or nothing about their lives. I cannot regard Elizabeth Smart as belonging to this category. Her first published work was recognizably autobiographical, and obviously written by someone whose lived experience and relation with language were those of a born poet. Those of us who were lucky enough to meet Elizabeth not long after her arrival in England in the middle of the Second World War were quite unaware of the fact that she had been writing all her previous life.

The early years of my acquaintance with Elizabeth soon became a lasting friendship, which I came to value increasingly the longer I knew her. Over the years I seldom heard her refer to her 'life before George Barker'; never, I think, to her lifelong ambition to become a writer of the kind she most admired; or to her implicit belief in poetry as the most serious form of writing.

Looking back, my most vivid memory is of a beautiful young woman who reminded me of a far more intelligent kind of Veronica Lake – an evanescent screen star whose appeal was at that time at its zenith. With reference to Elizabeth's poem in which she remembers me reading Baudelaire to her while she sat on the stairs during an air-raid with her babies in her arms, I can now see that I did so without proper realization of the fact that she too had been already familiar with *Les Fleurs du mal* in the original for about ten years. The scene as I remember it took place in the basement of A. P. Herbert's house in Hammersmith Terrace. He had put it at the disposal of Elizabeth and George, probably at the

---

Introduction to *The Collected Poems of Elizabeth Smart* (Paladin, 1992), pp. 9-17.

instigation of Julian Trevelyan, installed in nearby Durham Wharf. I'd forgotten the fire-bombs that night: south-west London saw a lot of them in those days. Soon after this incident, Elizabeth moved with her children to the safety of the country – Moreton-in-the-Marsh in Gloucestershire.

If I attempt to unravel such details here, it is because I find the patchwork weaving together of such remembered facts typical of the narrative method evolved in both her prose works and poems. During the years when Elizabeth lived at Tilty in Essex and later at Westbourne Terrace in Paddington, she was working hard and virtually without any interruption at copy-writing and journalism in order not only to support herself and her four children but also to have them well educated. In a series of notes first published in *Autobiographies* (edited by Christina Burridge, William Hoffer/Tanks, Vancouver B.C., 1987), she summed up this time in her life as follows:

> Love. Children. Earning a living. Friends. Drinking. Pushed too far to do much. Silent years. Desperate from hating. Desperate anxieties. So many levels. On one, it's a thin deep line straight to the point. On others up and down to deal with distractions.

And in a long, painful piece written in November 1976, Elizabeth discussed with herself the agony and boredom of struggling unavailingly to get something satisfactory written. I extract from it these two brief paragraphs:

> Painful dribbles, slow, so slow, pile up into a tiny heap, a tiny load of valuable old rubbish. My pile, a poor thing but mine own.
>
> Even $8\frac{1}{2}$ pages of rubbishy scribbling eases the pressure on my trapped explosive energies.

The year after these words were written, Jay Landesman's Polytantric Press brought out the collection of thirty-nine poems entitled *A Bonus*, described by Jill Neville in her introduction as 'distillations of experience which only someone who has suffered all but forgotten nothing could invoke'.

In the first poem, wryly entitled 'There's Nobody Here But Us Chickens', we are given lists of names which indicate the level of durability towards which Elizabeth constantly aspired: Auden, Byron, Blake, Thomas Traherne, Donne, Eliot, Dylan Thomas, Giacometti, and Braque. And this couplet occurs just before the end of this fifty-three line poem:

> (Sorry, Empson and Barker and good Sir John:
> I know you're there, but too young and flighty to lean upon.)

From her poems themselves, regarded as it is now possible to do as a whole, it is difficult to say on which poets of the past or present, if any, she thought of herself as most inclined to lean. Her voice, even in the early poems she produced before her arrival in England, is recognizably idiosyncratic and her own. Even the discovery in the late 1930s of the poetry of George Barker seems to have had no easily discernible influence on her style or use of language, except perhaps in such a poem as 'Song: The Singing Summer Streets'. The writer with whom to my mind Elizabeth Smart had the most striking affinity, though it seems most unlikely she was ever influenced by her, is Anna Wickham (1884-1947). While their lives and backgrounds were wholly dissimilar, their fervent independence and uncompromising honesty and sincerity make them appear kindred spirits. It is not surprising that the themes they most often tackled were basically the same: sexual union and disunion, partnership, motherhood, dissatisfaction, and the constant struggle to fulfil their intrinsic gifts. The first stanza of Anna Wickham's poem 'Self Analysis', first published in 1915, demonstrates the affiliation that can be seen to link two women poets of different generations:

> The tumult of my fretted mind
> Gives me expression of a kind;
> But it is faulty, harsh, not plain –
> My work has the incompetence of pain.

The common denominator apparent in this declaration and in certain poems of Elizabeth's, such as 'A Terrible Whiteness' and 'Rhyme Is Wrong', is certainly not incompetence, though the pain is evidently shared.

In his introduction to Anna Wickham's writings (Virago, 1984), R. D. Smith observed: 'From time to time Anna has a quirky, cheeky, wry truthfulness that recalls Stevie Smith.' This reminds me of a stanza in a poem in the present collection called 'The Muse: His & Hers':

> Stevie, the Emilys,
> Mrs Woolf
> By-passed the womb
> And kept the Self.

The poem is one of a group of eleven (*Eleven Poems*, Owen Kirton, Bracknell, 1982). Several of them confront the dilemma of a woman writer in her late sixties attempting to find articulation in verse of the obsessions she has had to postpone writing about when younger because her creative energy had had to be expended on domestic cares. Its main argument is that childless women writers are able to be far more freely prolific than exhausted mothers. I have quoted from it because it takes me back, through association, to the summer of 1957, when Elizabeth allowed me to stay several weeks in her flat in Westbourne Terrace in Paddington.

We spent a memorable day in the company of Stevie Smith, at the invitation of the painter Patrick Swift and his wife Oonagh, who occupied a studio-flat somewhere in the country not far to the north of London. After the meal, we all went out into the fields to hunt for mushrooms: a fairy ring, boleti, button mushrooms, and even the rare and startling *Phallus impudicus* hiding under a bush. Later, after a visit to Michael Andrews painting in a nearby studio, we ate the mushrooms for supper. Some tasted revolting, but none made us ill. Elizabeth and I accompanied Stevie Smith in the train back to Palmers Green, where we walked up the hill to the house she had lived in for sixty years. She had been amusing, sometimes caustic, but always agreeable. The fact that Elizabeth was at the time shackled to *Queen* and *House & Garden* provided a bond of sympathy between her and Stevie, who had spent so many earlier years of her life working for Newnes. As we left her door, I might have reflected that her loneliness was also her luck, as it allowed her to devote most of her time to producing her poetry.

During my stay, Elizabeth and I talked incessantly, both cold sober and after a few (and quite often many) drinks. We made almost daily excursions into Soho, usually visiting Muriel Belcher's Colony Room Club, where I would spend the afternoon waiting for her to return from the office where she made decisions or produced or deposited her copy. At this resort, one usually saw Dan Farson, Jeffrey Bernard, John Deakin, David Archer, or caught occasional glimpses of Francis Bacon. Though Elizabeth could seem the personification of candour, I now realize to what an extent this appearance was deceptive. A preoccupation with her mother seems to have haunted her until the end of her life, though it was not something she was ever likely to talk about. It was part of a nucleus of preoccupations that can be seen to have had a determining influence on all her later writings. It surprises me, too, that she so seldom discussed music with me, though she must have known it was something I particularly loved. I had no idea that when she was nineteen she had studied in London to become a concert pianist. I would never have imagined, for instance, her playing Scarlatti, which she had once done very well. Then there was the Surrealist couple, Wolfgang and Alice Paalen, who sent me their periodical *Dyn* from Mexico throughout the War, and the rogue painter Varda, all of whom I had met before 1937 through my friend Roland Penrose, but whom I never guessed Elizabeth had once known even better than I. And it was not until recently that I became aware of the role in bringing Elizabeth and George Barker together that had been played by Lawrence Durrell, whom I began to know well in the late 1930s.

A final incident that I recall with pleasure was a dinner-party at Mary Hutchinson's flat in Hyde Park Square. The other guests that evening included T. S. Eliot and his wife Valerie, to whom then he had not long been married. Mary Hutchinson had just agreed to finance David Wright's *X* magazine and had organized a fund in aid of David Archer. She had been close to the Bloomsbury circle and had known Eliot since her youth. Elizabeth had a sincere if characteristically uneffusive veneration of Eliot (as did George Barker, whose publisher and mentor Eliot had been for many years). This opportunity of meeting him in private in the happy golden autumn of his life was a privilege we both appreciated. Eliot was mellower and more benign than I had known him during previous brief encounters: in a word, he was typically uncondescendingly gracious.

It was Stephen Spender who, well over fifty years ago, first drew my attention to the distinction to be drawn between Eros and Agape. Almost all Elizabeth's poetry is inspired by one or the other, often by her own peculiar combination of both. An unusually alert libido and experience of physical and emotional passion are predominantly the source of many of her most characteristic early utterances. In later years this gradually became modulated into the expression of maternal love, love and affection for friends, and, from her childhood on but particularly at the end of her life, the love of 'nature', that is to say (she had no love of abstractions) love of flowers and plants, insects and birds. Her capacity for friendship and loyalty was perhaps the outstanding feature of her character. Compare the vulnerable, unhesitatingly generous sincerity evident in the poems dedicated to such characters as Jeffrey Bernard and Jeremy Reed.

To anyone aware of the circumstances of the death of her youngest child, Rose, the poem with which she commemorated this tragedy must be the most harrowing in this collection. It meant a lot to her to have been able to write it. Only great emotional courage and determination could have enabled her to find any words at all to express the grief which this event caused her.

In January 1934, Elizabeth was already writing in her journal about her 'will to work, and vows, and plans for writing, in a vivid conglomeration.

Writing and eagerness to begin at once . . . It comes down over me with an awful swoop . . . the desire to accomplish something written . . . and remorse at beginning twenty and having done nothing.' What is extraordinary is to find her still writing in early 1979:

> I find myself repeating things I said 40 years ago, coming upon them huffing and puffing laboriously, again, again, finding them – but they were never lost.
>
> If I could only show – *explain*; what? The good, the glory, the splendour, the greatness, the beauty, the beneficence.
>
> ('Diary of a Blockage', *In The Meantime*,
Deneau, Ottawa, 1984)

What was extraordinary about Elizabeth was the insatiable intensity of her spirit, which nevertheless made her so stimulating and such fun to be with; and her lifelong unyielding will to put this spirit's trials and adventures into words. We are still discovering how extraordinary it is that she so often succeeded.

3

MEMOIRS AND OBITUARIES

SELF DISCHARGED

So it must be some time since you guessed what became of me? Well, I never tried to make a secret of it, and guessed someone I knew would be bound to find out sooner or later. Having been certifiably insane is not exactly something one wants to have broadcast: on the other hand I'm not in the least embarrassed by it.

Am I cured? Well, it seems like it. I honestly don't believe I shall ever have to suffer from quite that sort of trouble again. It was like a dark tunnel, though the strange thing is that it seemed uncannily bright, so that I'm now able to remember almost everything in detail. The place, the people, the constant incidents. A good deal of unpleasantness, of course, yet at the time, I was in a state of what might be called manic euphoria. I find this hard to explain looking back.

One particular sequence of events often comes back to me. It entailed three quite different fellow inmates, and what became of them probably affected me more deeply than anything else in the asylum, though it wasn't till after I was discharged that I began to think of them as linked. Perhaps it would make things clearer if I were to start by explaining just how I came to be put away in the first place.

You say you saw a brief reference in the Press to the fracas I caused at the Palace. The mental disturbance leading up to this could be described as resulting from an advanced form of chiliasm. This took the form of an overwhelming conviction that the end of the world as we know it was at hand.

Not only that, I believed it my mission to impart my privileged intimation to the Royal Family, whom I imagined to have a special role to play in some gloriously Utopian future. All this was further complicated by an obsession with the menace of Scientology, which I thought was conspiring to take over the world in order to examine it in the manner of Mengelesque vivisectionists.

When I arrived early one morning at the gates of the Palace to communicate to the Monarch my inspired sense of the world's spiritual situation, I immediately found myself in conflict with earthly powers in the person of a young guardsman. After a short and undignified tussle I was interrogated by a surprisingly polite security officer. It was explained to me that while certain unavoidable investigations were being conducted I would have to wait in a convenient adjoining cell. Here I was affected after a while by an onset of claustrophobia accompanied by disconcertingly technicolour visual hallucinations centred round the peep-hole set in the steel door. In this small circular space I could clearly discern the distinctive yet unfamiliar features of a youth who appeared to be engaged in heated discussion with a woman I thought I had met the day before. I could hear mingled voices but what they were saying remained unintelligible. While I was still absorbed in these unprecedented phenomena, the door was unlocked and in came the security-officer, accompanied this time by two reassuringly plain-clothed individuals, who announced that they'd come to take me for a drive to a place they were sure I'd like to visit. Never doubting that this must be somehow connected with my supernatural assignment, I went out with them into the yard, climbed into their van and was driven away.

Our destination remained a complete mystery to me, though I was convinced it would turn out to be somewhere quite remarkable where a further crucial phase of my destiny awaited me. Finally the van slowed down as we approached an imposing mansion with a flight of steps leading up to a portico surmounted by a clock-tower. The van went round to the glass-paned side-door of one of the wings, which was opened by a man in a white coat from the belt of which hung a varied bunch of keys. He then led me round a corner into what I eventually came to know as the 'reception-ward'. As we passed down the long room, on the walls of which I was pleased to recognize reproductions from Corot and Constable, I became aware of the presence of a crowd of curiously assorted individuals, young and old, and the notion flashed into my mind that this was a place full of unfortunates awaiting the spiritual succour it was my peculiar privilege to afford them. Then I suddenly perceived the face of a youth lying curled up in untidy day-clothes on a bed half-way down the ward. I recognized that this was a face I had seen earlier in the day in the vision vouchsafed me in my solitary cell. As I moved momentarily towards him, the boy looked up in apparent acknowledgement with a smile of angelic sweetness that slowly transformed his usually blank expression. Seeing this my supervisor impatiently hurried me off to a nearby office, where a long process of interrogation, form-filling and other routine formalities awaited me. I could not then have known that the youth I thought I had recognized was to become one of the three exceptional cases I told you I was going to related to you.

It must have been more than a week before I managed to attain anything like a proper grasp of the reality of my situation. Since numbers of indisputably sane people find reality a debatable concept, you can imagine my predicament. To begin with my sense of time seemed to stretch in and out like a concertina. Institutions such as the one in which I found myself are scheduled to run according to strict timetables. To individualists like myself this can be irksomely hard to get used to; but when you're in a state of inner turmoil it does provide some sort of handrail to cling to. Before long my outer demeanour may have appeared acceptably calm and controlled, but I was still assailed by the wildest fantasies and misconceptions. Many of these developed out of my observation of my fellow-inmates. But besides the other patients there were all the members of the nursing-staff to be adjusted to, as well as the doctors and psychiatrists. There were dedicated and sympathetic nurses, others were unmistakably of the scoutmaster type, while a notable minority seemed to have mistaken the nursing vocation for that of the gaoler. The hospital's psychiatric director was both keenly perceptive and compassionate, but the opportunity of speaking to him was all too rare, as he never had more than a minute or two to spare for each patient.

But to return to the patients, and in particular the youth who'd attracted my notice on the day I arrived. It did not take me long to discover that he was regarded as the most seriously disturbed of all my fellow detainees. Though from his appearance one might have thought him still in his teens, he was, in fact, about twenty-five. Most of the time he looked harmless, serene but not stupid. He paid scant attention to anyone, but occasionally we would exchange smiles. He was dressed by a nurse before breakfast, after which he would lie down and curl up in a corner. Two or three times a week he was visited by his parents, a quiet couple in whose presence he became slightly more animated, though he would consume the biscuits and Mars bars they brought him only perfunctorily and scarcely responded to their efforts to engage him in conversation. Nevertheless he seemed at least momentarily to regard his mother with something like normal affection. When the time came for the callers to leave, he would follow them to the door with his eyes, then relapse at once into listlessness.

Every day when it was fine, the occupants of our ward were taken outdoors by a nurse to be conducted in an untidy, chattering and frequently quarrelsome group on a tour of the extensive grounds. Though I hated being herded in this way, I found it a relief to escape for a while from the confines of our common room, in which the only available distractions consisted of a snooker-table, tattered reading-matter and a black and white television set. After returning from a few of these excursions, I began to notice that the youth had invariably been left behind, huddled in his usual corner. One afternoon, we discovered that the television set, which at certain times of day attracted a numerous and argumentative audience, had been reduced during our absence to an irreparable wreck. The inoffensive-looking youngster was nowhere to be seen. He was in fact spending the first of twenty-four hours in a padded cell.

It must have been just after this incident that the doctors' monthly assessment of our case-histories took place. As a result of this, you could find yourself promoted, recommended to stay where you were, or demoted to a more strictly run ward. By the end of my first month, my outward behaviour had somehow convinced the authorities that my condition had improved sufficiently to warrant my being told: 'We've decided to move you over to Hartwell House tomorrow. You'll find quite a different set-up over there, it's really comfortable and you'll be much more free. If you settle down sensibly, there's no reason why you shouldn't enjoy it and make more progress.' In comparison with the packed and often chaotic reception-ward, my new surroundings seemed almost more like a hotel than a hospital: they included a lounge with deep armchairs and colour TV. In the entrance hall was a telephone that could be used by residents at any time without permission. What surprised me was that we were at liberty to visit a local pub between six and eight every evening. On the other hand, daily attendance at the Occupational Therapy Centre was obligatory. This was something I resented at first, though after a while I found I could amuse myself in my own way without too much interference from the burly, good-natured Central European in charge of proceedings there. His domain was a hall fitted out like a classroom, with a platform, piano, blackboard and rows of desks, and appointed with a kitchenette allowing tea, coffee and biscuits to be dispensed between sessions of word-games, gouache painting and bingo.

I had by now come to terms with the fact that we were all classified insane, but though most of the time I managed to retain an inexplicable vestigial lucidity I was powerless to control my teeming obsessions. None of the patients with whom I became friendly were unmistakably mad, nor were they all male, though of course the ward dormitories were segregated. One of the new friends to whom I began to be most attached at that time was a radiantly blonde Cockney girl called Gloria, whom I privately nicknamed Aurelia. She would listen to my often delirious outpourings with rapt attention which no doubt partly accounted for her attraction to me. Before long she developed the habit of presenting me every day with a flower which she had plucked uninhibitedly from one of the beds in the grounds. Gloria did not attend the Occupational Therapy Centre as regularly as she was supposed to, but when she did appear she was apt to provoke wolf-whistles. I became proud of what I believed to be my special relationship with this glamorous popular favourite. Not long after our first meeting she fell in love with an ex-inmate of Broadmoor, who had once killed a workmate but had by now recovered sufficient equanimity to be transferred to Hartwell House.

Most of the temporary friends I frequented during this period were drinking companions at the pub I referred to earlier. It was known to the locals as The Inmates Arms. During the hour or so we spent there I would contrive to quaff as many barley wines as time permitted. Gloria was addicted to a concoction known as a Snowball but would consume anything that could be topped with a glacé cherry, her companion from Broadmoor had a liking for rum nag, a geophysicist's gloomy son and his girl friend preferred shandies. Only one member of our group resolutely refused anything stronger than fruit juice or Canada Dry. This was a congenial character familiarly known as Mac, who was in fact of Scots descent, though her accent did not at once reveal the fact. Apparently in her late thirties, she wore her hair short and her clothes unobtrusively, displaying in her conversation a warmth tempered by wry wit. She made no secret of the fact that she was a member of Alcoholics Anonymous, and if teased on the subject was inclined to extol the virtues of the organization. Another thing about her that became evident before long was that she had an emotional preference for her own sex, a fact she neither paraded nor attempted to conceal. Only the most inveterate labeller would have been likely to describe her as a 'dyke', and the reassuring homeliness of her manner was the reverse of freakish.

It was at the time of those evening sorties to the pub that I found that I now had not only a few friends but also at least one significant enemy. This was someone I had noticed on being moved to Hartwell House, and then observed to be always at the centre of the other group to frequent the Inmates Arms, at the far end of the lounge. I took an instant dislike to him, certainly not because he was undisguisedly homosexual or because he did or said anything deliberately to provoke my antagonism, but because his arrogant demeanour and occasionally overheard snide remarks revealed him as belonging to the sleek, hard and spiteful type of individual most aptly designated by his own cronies as a perfect bitch. He must have sensed my antipathy, as he soon made a point of ignoring my very existence. I began to refer to him mentally as 'the Rodent'. When I discovered that he was kept by a wealthy, much older Harley Street specialist, who sent his chauffeur-driven Bentley to fetch his paramour away once a week, I was neither particularly shocked nor surprised. My observations involved, I must admit, a certain malign fascination.

About this time word reached the doctor who was assessing my case of my attempts to initiate my fellow patients into the secret of the impending spiritual revolution that alone could avert world catastrophe. However, the incident that precipitated my relegation to a stricter environment entailed a head-on confrontation with the Rodent. This took place in the Hartwell House entrance-hall, in which, as I think I told you, there was a telephone installed. I was sitting in a basket-chair reading a newspaper after lunch, when I was approached by an inoffensive elderly inadequate I knew only by sight. He was in a state of evident distress and wondered whether I might be able to help him. He needed to contact someone about a matter of some urgency concerning his wife, but was too inexperienced a phone-user to know how to dial the number. I offered to do it for him. I've never much cared for payphones, and now it seemed that the old man and I might not have enough small change between us to feed the box with the requisite coins. When I found myself having difficulty with the area code number, the whole operation began to seem frustratingly protracted. I became so absorbed in it that I failed to notice we were no longer alone.

The Rodent must have been hanging about behind us for some while before startling me with a sudden outburst of exasperated abuse. 'How much longer do I have to be kept waiting? Do you think the bloody phone belongs to you? I've got a really important call to make at once!' – 'But so has Mr Oates!' I protested. 'Can't you see that he's worried and that I'm doing my best to help him?' – 'To hell with the old fool,' squalled the Rodent, 'I've got to use that phone *now*!' A sudden convulsion of rage possessed me as I swung round. He must have felt menaced by my movement: in a flash he was hacking at my ankles with a pointed shoe, and in stumbling to the tile-paved floor I received a thrust in the ribs from his left elbow as he lurched forward to snatch the receiver from me. While trying to rise dazed from the ground, I felt my glasses slide off the bridge of my nose. Before I'd had time to recover them, my adversary had directed a vehement stamp to them with his heel, and I could hear the bakelite frame rattle as it splintered on the terracotta.

★

His final words to me before he proceeded to make his all-important phone-call had been, 'Smug officious bastard'. As a result of having had my glasses damaged during what was to be my last encounter with the Rodent I had to go about in a myopic blur for many weeks to come.

Soon after the occurrence, the time for the monthly review of patients' cases came round. The psychiatrist monitoring my progress told me that it had been highly irresponsible of me to risk provoking so notoriously susceptible a character as X – referring of course to the Rodent. It was clearly implied that any inconvenience I might suffer in being temporarily deprived of clear vision was entirely my own fault, and the whole incident all too typical of the deterioration in my development under the Hartwell House regime. He concluded that he had no other choice than to relegate me once more to the reception-ward.

A long, indeterminate period of despondency, loss of morale and renewed proneness to obsessive delusion ensued from this change in my status. A perilous hair-thin crack was running across the earth's surface that Summer and had just reached the spot on which the hospital stood, causing it every so often to tremble alarmingly. A flying-saucer landed one night on the playing-field in the grounds, leaving scorched traces of its landing-tripod clearly visible; a few newly admitted patients were recognizably Martian Fifth Columnists. A friendly East-Ender now established in the ward, who was always trying to persuade me to play cards with him, was surely correct in claiming to be Al Capone's illegitimate son by his secret British mistress, and was probably as dangerous a criminal as his father. The revelation I had in a dream at that time that a heap of gravel at the edge of one of the paths used for our walks was in fact a hoard of highly medicinal edible gold led to a disappointingly insalubrious experience. The leak in my mind that was intermittently causing my thoughts to be intercepted by others meant that I was increasingly in telepathic communication with those about me, rather as though I had my own private high-frequency radio band.

Among the few inmates I still recognized on returning to the reception ward was the boy who had attracted my special attention on my first arrival there. He seemed more aloof and apathetic than ever. By now I had come to think of him as Larry, as in Larry the Lamb, in keeping with my habit of conferring special names on my fellow inmates.

One day, I noticed that two nurses were having more trouble than usual in persuading Larry to take his place at one of the tables. Just as I was passing this wordless altercation on my way to my own seat, Larry's face was startlingly transformed from any resemblance to a lamb to the look of a ferocious leopard cub. A momentary influx of abnormal energy enabled him to break away from the constraint of his attendants and to lunge in my direction with clenched fists. The force of the blow that flung me to the ground took my breath away for a moment. When I uttered a cry it was more in startled amazement than in pain, though blood had begun to pour profusely from the broken skin above one of my eyes. Shock and impaired vision prevented me from witnessing the removal of the finally overcome Larry from the ward, and I was in fact never to glimpse him again.

When I started to tell you about my experience of going out of my mind, I decided to do so by way of concentrating on the parallel stories of three fellow internees in particular. Before long you'll see what it was they had in common that impressed me. As you'll no doubt have realized, getting oneself discharged from hospital is a far more involved process for mental patients than for the sick but sane. There's the question of orders and sections to be considered, waiting for some mysterious superior specialist to decide whether it's safe enough to let you go without risking your being brought back in a van within a week. The cut Larry inflicted on my forehead soon healed, but after he'd been taken from the ward where he'd been kept so long, my subsequent hold on reality became progressively more precarious.

*

Looking back on it now, the ensuing phase of my derangement seems to have been the most insidious. An insistent inner voice began to protest that I was being held captive under false pretences. Among all those about me, I alone was in my right mind. The psychiatric staff had been enjoined to sabotage my millenarian mission. I developed an urgent conviction that it had become my duty to discharge myself. After weeks of mounting desperation I decided to escape.

Providing myself with sufficient cash, evading the charge-nurse's attention, getting through the gate undetected, then finding my way to the station, turned out to require less cunning than determination. By lunch-time I was in London. My mind was now leaking more continuously than I had ever known it to before. On the bus from Victoria to Chelsea I established telepathic communication with more than half the passengers on the top deck. I alighted in the King's Road, and entered a pub at which I had once been a regular customer. I believed that the whole clientele knew who I was, though not where I had come from, and were assembled there to await some momentous message from me. My failure to impart my tidings intelligibly resulted in my finding myself confined once more in a cell, this time in Chelsea police-station. By the end of the afternoon I was ushered out to a waiting vehicle to be driven back whence I came. There was no mystery for me this time about my destination. The reception awaiting me at the asylum was unsurprisingly frosty. I was perfunctorily provided with a minimum of food and told to get my things together at once in order to be moved to the ward on the floor above. I was briskly awoken next morning to face life in what seemed like a tough reformatory.

My new companions ranged in condition and age from the keen-witted truculence of a juvenile delinquent constantly proclaiming his blameless normality to the virtual imbecility of an old fellow who'd become the charge-nurse's chief whipping-boy. All of us were referred to by the despotic superintendent and his assistant as 'lads'. Alleviations of our spartan routine were eagerly awaited and few. Among them was an occasional evening visit to a large room in a distant part of the building known as 'The Club' where a loudspeaker dispensed pop-music and a vending-machine soft drinks, while patients of both sexes danced together desultorily, sat around chatting or played table-tennis. And twice a week we had to attend classes in what was described as 'musical therapy', consisting usually of raucous community singing interspersed with soothing violin solos from the directress.

During this grim period amongst the intractable, I had one memorable encounter with the doctor specially assigned to inspect us. 'I felt you might be interested to know,' he informed me offhandedly, 'that the patient you had trouble with when you were still at Hartwell is now dead. When out for the afternoon recently, he managed somehow to get hold of a revolver and shoot himself. So you need no longer concern yourself with further worry from that quarter.' I did not tell him that I had hardly been worrying about the animosity of the Rodent whose existence I had already forgotten.

Since my original admission, my scant but comparatively decent clothing had undergone a process of constant deterioration. By this time I was reduced to going about looking like a tramp, with half my buttons missing and my trousers held up by a tattered necktie. This contributed to the sense of humiliation that it seemed to be the purpose of the ward's regime to instill. One morning when we were being marched off to musical therapy, the sky was already unusually dark; during the class rain began drumming so hard upon the glass roof of the hall that the sounds we were supposed to be making beneath became almost drowned by it. At the end of the class we assembled in the porch to be led back to lunch. The downpour showed no sign of abating. The nurse in charge decided to urge us to run as fast as possible through the torrent back to the main building. By the time we'd reached the upstairs ward we were breathless and wet, and in my case drenched quite to the skin.

A day or two after the cloudburst, I was engaged at the end of the afternoon in washing paint from my hands in the toilet at the back of the O.T. room when I was suddenly seized by an acute pain in the left side of my chest. I managed to stagger back to my desk, one hand on my heart, the other groping for support from benches. The bearlike therapist, who had lately grown impatient with my vagaries, was engaged in delivering a concluding pep talk and refused to be distracted. By the time we had reached the ward, however, I collapsed convincingly enough to persuade even our martinet of a charge-nurse that there was something genuinely the matter with me, whereupon I was sent forthwith to bed without my tea.

The following morning, my state was such that the doctor was summoned. Having interrogated me as curtly as ever, and heard me suggest that I might have had some sort of heart attack since every breath still made my left side ache, he observed that I obviously knew nothing whatever about the heart and demanded more precise details. His irascibility confused me and my answers faltered until he exclaimed impatiently: 'There's absolutely nothing the matter with your heart! All you've got is pleurisy. Why didn't you tell the charge-nurse sooner? Now we'll have to move you to the sick-ward.'

My sickness turned out to have been in a sense my salvation. A few heavy doses of antibiotic and three days of somnolent semi-consciousness resulted in my waking up one morning not only much improved physically, but mentally far more lucid than I had been for months. My new surroundings seemed a haven of peace, inhabited only by the quietly ill or the geriatrically bed-ridden. The staff were all humanely good-natured in comparison with the attendants I had left behind upstairs.

My convalescence now progressed at a surprising rate. Within a week I was up and about, and after ten days sufficiently mobile to be able to visit the hospital shop when I felt like it. I began to make renewed use of the library, and managed to get through a number of novels I might otherwise never have read, such as *Daniel Deronda* and *Goldfinger*.

In conversation one day with one of the nurses, I enquired whether he knew what had become of the youth I'd once thought of as Larry the Lamb. It was then I learnt for the first time that he had put an end to all possibility of either recovery or indefinite detention. Not long after my consignment to what I now thought of as the department of correction, Larry had broken into the cleaning cupboard. From its shelves he had unerringly selected a container of the most corrosive abstergent to be stored there and then swallowed the entire remaining fluid. Hasty resort to a stomach pump was of little avail. Irreparable harm had already been done to Larry's oesophagus and internal organs. After days of lingering agony, he died like a dumb animal, without apparently recognizing the devoted parents who had been summoned to his bedside.

★

In a psychiatric hospital, aggro and brawls provide dramas of daily occurrence. During my stay in one I became involved in many squabbles, but only twice experienced violent attack. Subsequently to discover that both my assailants had within a short space of time succeeded in killing themselves was a further unexpected shock. No matter how often I told myself that these two deaths were purely coincidental, and that I could not bear the least responsibility for them, I continued to entertain a superstitious sense of guilt. Their self-destruction left a bitter aftertaste that lingers with me still.

The doctor in charge of the sick-ward turned out to be more sympathetically discerning that any official I had so far had to deal with. It was not long before he divulged that he could foresee my discharge in the not too distant future. The nurse who'd known me from the time of my arrival noticed the wretched condition my clothes had been reduced to, and arranged to take me to an outfitter in the nearby local town to acquire a cheap new suit. The discovery that I had more money left in deposit with the bursar than I had imagined, and that I was not yet penniless, came as a further relief.

*

When I became aware that a group of the fitter patients were in the habit of leaving the sick-ward after the last meal of the day, I presumed they must have been allowed to visit the pub. I asked the doctor whether he had any objection to my joining them. He decided that he hadn't, as long as I got back by seven-thirty. 'It'll do you good to exercise your legs. But don't try getting drunk to celebrate your recovery, or you'll find yourself strictly confined to barracks again . . .'

Dusk was falling as I later left the grounds and made my way down the once familiar lane to the Inmates Arms. The saloon was almost empty, apart from a couple of fellow convalescents conversing quietly in a corner. I bought a cider and sat down to smoke a cigarette. As I sat relishing the everyday banality of this refuge from the routine of the wards, the sound of a familiar voice drew my glance towards the bar. It was the ever-beguiling Gloria, accompanied by her betrothed from Broadmoor.

In a moment she caught sight of me and hurried over to greet me like a long lost friend. 'Wherever did you come from, darling? I thought you'd been discharged ages ago! Did you get yourself sent back?'

I did not attempt to tell them the full story of my setbacks and misfortunes, but explained that I was recovering from pleurisy and expecting to be sent home in a week or two. 'I'm actually being discharged tomorrow,' announced Gloria, 'and so is Norman. They should've let me go at the end of August, of course. There was nothing really the matter with me. All they could say was that I used to get over-excited. Hyper-what's-it. When that great ape Ali tried to expose himself to me and got caught by a nurse, they made such a fuss, you'd have thought I'd been raped! As though I was interested! Thank God I've got Norman. You knew that we're getting married soon, didn't you? I just can't wait! He would've been out by now, only he made them let him stay on, just to keep me company like. I've always said he's as sane as any of the doctors, except where I'm concerned . . .'

I was delighted to see Gloria-Aurelia once more after so long, and said how lucky it was that I'd run into them on what was to be her last evening. She made me promise to keep in touch. 'Let's celebrate! What are you drinking? Cider? You must be joking! What you need is some of the hard stuff. I want another gin. Come on, they're not going to breathalyse you!'

I ended up by accepting a vodka and tonic, and said I wondered what Mac would say. Gloria's face unexpectedly fell. After a pause, she said: 'Of course, being out of circulation like lately, you wouldn't have heard. She was discharged just after the last time we met. Never could understand why she was here at all really, just knew she'd been terribly depressed to begin with. That girl she shared a flat with who went off and left her so as to live with a feller – wouldn't mind betting he was a queer too! – she must have been a rotten little cow. That was how the drink problem had started getting the worse of her, till this social worker managed to get her onto the everlasting water-wagon, so she thought. So there she was with only an empty flat to go back to, and naturally it wasn't long before she was back on the bottle, only worse than ever this time. She must have been still on drugs as well, as she ended up dead of an overdose. They couldn't find any close friends or family, so I suppose Social Security or something had to see to her cremation – she'd left a note saying that was what she wanted. Poor old Mac, I think it was bloody brave of her. Nothing to live for but the drink in the end, and she'd always hated that really. Always good company, though, wasn't she, when she wasn't in one of her moods, and generous too. Sorry to have to tell you about her death on our last night, I knew that you'd liked her, and she often told me how much she enjoyed talking to you . . .'

By the time Gloria had finished her sobering report, I had lost the spirit of celebration, and the next time I glanced at my watch it warned me that the moment had come to take a last farewell of one of the most comforting of my erstwhile companions and the man she was about to marry. It was dark by the time I got back to the ward, and before long I was in bed, trying my best to avoid the chill thought of Mac's lonely end in the world outside.

No doubt you'll be relieved to hear that there's now little left for me to tell you about my time in the asylum world.

What I want to end by saying is that I do not regret for a moment having been out of my mind. It seems to me now that in fact I went far deeper *into* it than I'd ever been before, and that having been able to return as sane as I am now, I can think of what happened to Larry, the Rodent and Mac in a way that helps me to understand the true cost of sanity better. If I've told you as much about those three characters as about myself, that's no doubt above all because they all chose to discharge themselves – from life. 'The whole world is our hospital,' says Eliot, and I'm still here only because I've learnt to live with it. I'm still stuck with the fact that I was savagely struck by two of the others before they killed themselves, while Mac ended by finding herself in an isolation ward she couldn't stand. Larry strikes me as having taken one brief look round at everyday life and found it so foreign and repellent that, though he couldn't explain why, he simply knew that he wanted no part of it. As to the Rodent, it's not hard to imagine the kind of causes that turned him into a bitter, twisted and destructive creature. The life he found himself having to lead disgusted him, till finally a paroxysm of self-disgust drove him to put an end to it. Mac's death was probably far more of a waste than theirs – to begin with she had far more ability to inspire as well as feel affection, and so was a real person, which the other two somehow hadn't been able to become. I find myself faced with the conclusion that it's as pointless to wonder why certain individuals find themselves dealt a completely unlucky hand of cards as it is to enquire why countless others, young and old, smokers or not, become victims of terminal cancer.

Since returning to my senses, I've tried not to spend too much time looking back to the period I've just been evoking to you. Whenever I do, I invariably end by wondering why three of my fellow patients took the way out they did, while I was able to recover a measure of disillusioned lucidity. Thousands of mental patients must end up by killing themselves every year, while I just happen not to have a suicidal nature. Then for some reason I find myself remembering a phrase I once copied down from something by Sir Thomas Browne: 'Life is a pure flame, and we live by an invisible sun within us. A small fire sufficeth for life . . .' And if I'm not in too gloomy a mood, I try to persuade myself that in even the most deranged mind a faint spark may be struggling to become a fire sufficient to live by. The idea of a limbo of latency to which such sparks could return may be a delusion, but I cannot believe it to be a dangerous one to entertain.

DAVID WRIGHT

Rule: When writing about another writer, especially if you feel him/her to be close to you in any way, avoid starting off with the word 'I'. Very well. David Wright, to my great pleasure, in early February last year ('78), sent me a most touchingly inscribed copy of *To the Gods the Shades*, accompanied by a typically kind, over-deferent letter, starting: 'It must be many years since we met – fifteen?' and a little further on: 'You were the first real poet that I ever met – perhaps you remember the time, Oxford around 1942, when you were living there (in Wellington Square wasn't it) and I came to know you through Audrey Beecham and Honor Frost. I must have showed you my rubbish then; this is what came of it.'

I remember those Oxford days quite clearly (I hasten to add that I myself was never an undergraduate at any university), and I particularly remember what he calls his 'rubbish', and I am definite about recalling my immediate intuitive impression that I had made the acquaintance of someone who was a born poet. Other memories of Oxford at that time are also vivid with me, but to recount them would entail a certain amount of purely personal revelation and this is not a fragment of my autobiography. I remember meeting David Wright at a somewhat later date, when he had already begun to publish poetry and to attract the attention of the discerning, I think at a time when he had just married Pippa, and they were living in a flat in Bloomsbury (Lamb Terrace).

C. H. Sisson has enquired about knowing David 'at Oxford, in Soho or in Cornwall'. During his Cornwall period, I must have been living in France most of the time, but I do not recall his actually living in Soho, though there were undoubtedly numerous *sorties* into that area just then, also undoubtedly of a bibulous as much as of a gregarious nature. I have known few poets (English or otherwise) who were not pretty 'good' in the sense of 'heavy' (so many words nowadays have acquired ambiguous meanings or sound pompous or prissy) drinkers, but David Wright was always, as I remember it, a very moderate one. My memories of these occasions are, naturally enough, somewhat blurred; but I do remember being struck by the remarkable way in which David coped with the

'David Wright: A Few Words of Reminiscence and Appreciation', *P.N. Review* 14, Vol. 6, No. 6 (1980), pp. 37-9.

communication problem. His ability to lip-read was (must still be) astounding; though I am ashamed to confess that, in spite of my claim to have been an actor, I was often reduced at crucial moments to having to write down on a scrap of paper some key-word, name or phrase, in the midst of an animated discussion. Also, I was amazed by his apparent knowledgeableness about *music* (condescending of me, perhaps; but all the same, for someone totally deaf since the age of seven!). Pippa is, I believe, musical, and had no doubt encouraged him; but what I thought extraordinary was David's ability to *hear* through his fingers, by placing his hand on the wood of a piano while it was being played, and appreciating the sound by means of the vibrations transmitted through his finger-tips. Apart from this, 'Monologue of a Deaf Man', of course, expresses most poignantly all the poet's feelings on this subject. And I should add that it has frequently been remarked that David Wright has an unusually sound grasp of prosody and a gift of cadence.

I have always been aware that David is endowed with a special appreciation of the value of friendship and of human relationships in general. Indeed, my immediate intention on being asked to write this piece was to start: I feel unusually guilty about David Wright, because as far as I can recollect, I never wrote to thank him for his last letter and gift to me. *To the Gods the Shades* is dotted with the names of friends of his, some of them dead, many of them dear to me also: George Barker, John Heath-Stubbs, Ralph and Julian Abercrombie, Jankel Adler, David Archer, Colquhoun and MacBryde, Dannie Abse and Patrick and Oonagh Swift. The latter couple were great friends of mine for an unfortunately too brief period; Patrick Swift illustrated David's Portuguese travel books, and is now, I believe, permanently settled in Portugal, hence my having lost touch with him, as with so many other people, alas, during a long period of growing depression and spiritual death; but he painted David's portrait, mine likewise, and those of many other congenial contemporaries; and I am sure that David and Pippa, Paddy, Oonagh and myself must on at least one occasion have partaken of many a jar together, though I cannot now remember exactly where or when. Elizabeth Smart was also a great friend of the Swifts, and surely also of David, and there was, I imagine, at least one meeting of all six of us. Obviously, it must have been at about the time that David founded and edited the periodical *X*. This was warmly supported and, I think, partly 'backed' by a very dear friend of mine, Mary Hutchinson, who was a fairly close neighbour of Elizabeth Smart's, north of Hyde Park, and I remember a dinner-party at Mrs St John Hutchinson's flat at which Elizabeth Smart, Paddy Swift, myself and almost certainly David and Pippa were present. It is alarming to find one's memory, of certain periods, at the least, beginning to fail with regard to friends with whom one has such sympathy as I have always had with David Wright, who incidentally published a prose-piece of mine entitled 'Remembering the Dead' in an early issue of the unfortunately short-lived *X* (I hesitate to call it a prose-poem: George Barker has poured such scorn on the whole concept of prose-poetry and insisted that it cannot be written in English!).

I now come to the final occasion of which I have a clear recollection of meeting David. This was at Godalming, near the village of Elstead, where my parents were then living and with whom I was staying during a visit to them from France. I had been over for the day to see George Barker at his cottage outside a village near Haslemere, not far away, just over the hill from his brother Kit's; and somehow or other, on our return, at the end of the afternoon, there occurred, by chance I should think, a fairly large but all too brief reunion of friends, of whom George, David and myself were perhaps the only poets but which seemed to consist of an unexpectedly numerous group of mutual pals. This took place in a Godalming pub, so it must have been between six and seven, for I remember David had to tear himself away from us to catch a train back to London for some evening engagement. My memory of him at this encounter is unusually vivid: his in some way somehow bear-like noises expressive of hilarity, frequent with him, and which always, I hardly know why, reminded me of Billie Bunter – this is meant to be understood only in the most affectionate sense: Bunter is of course a clown, which I cannot imagine anyone supposing David to be, but exclamations like *'Garooh!'* are close equivalents of David's ejaculations of mirth – so it was certainly a happy pub gathering at which I last saw David Wright, and though I greatly regret having outwardly lost touch with him since then, I am glad that it was in such an atmosphere that we last said goodbye, as since then I have gone through periods of depression and inability to communicate, about which it would be unsuitable further to expatiate here.

I was about to go on to a brief appreciation of the poetry of David Wright, and to say that my preference is for his poems of people and place, when a reference to the latter and a reminder that several of them are about places in Italy jogged my memory into another clear picture, a brief chance encounter with David and Pippa in 1950. This was in Venice. They unfortunately had to leave next day and I had only just arrived. I regret that David was not inspired to write a Venetian poem, but had the impression at the time that somehow he found the city disappointing, while I had fallen in love with it at first sight. However, as usual, I digress.

I have already written more than I had thought possible in the short time at my disposal, and I will wind up by making a few more appreciative remarks about poems that particularly appeal to me. As well as the already mentioned 'Monologue of a Deaf Man' (*'Et lui comprit trop bien, n'ayant pas entendu'* – Corbière), there is the equally early and very characteristic 'A Funeral Oration', ending: 'died believing in God' (shared common ground, I hope). 'A Thanksgiving' is marvellous, and comforting even to those who do not feel they have grounds for rejoicing. In 'A Fish out of Water', the second poem, 'Poetry Reading' is drily extremely funny and, alas, too true. 'On the Margin' is an admirable poem of, one hopes, premature summing-up, and expresses so much of what I myself should have liked to say about 'life and art'. And to mention just one other poem, about a person (I have already stated my admiration for his poems of places and people): 'E. P. at Westminster', which in its condensed brevity seems to me a model statement about an undeniably fine poet and, in spite of everything, great man, but about whom nearly all poets of my, I should say our, age have extremely complex feelings (at any rate, I know mine are where Pound is concerned).

David Wright ended his letter to me which I began by quoting from by telling me the address he said he had been forced to move to by the continuation of the A66 mini-motorway. I have some engagements 'up north' in the autumn, and it would indeed be a great delight if my wife, who adores meeting the poets I have been lucky enough to have known, and I, were able to find the time to visit him and Pippa. Meanwhile if this should appear before another meeting should be possible, happy birthday, David, – reaching sixty is not all that terrible after all, I have found. And before long I will write you, at last, a long, rambling letter.

ANTONIA WHITE

Within a year of my first enthusiastic reading of *Frost in May*, I was fortunate enough to find myself personally acquainted with its author, Antonia White. Our first meeting was in the Autumn of 1936. The original mutual friend who introduced us to one another could conceivably have been Cyril Connolly, who when I was young kindly enabled me to meet a number of distinguished writers, nearly all novelists, and had shared with Antonia a concern for the welfare of the erudite but manic-depressive Logan Pearsall-Smith (American-born author of the once reputed *Trivia*, in case the name should ring no bell for younger readers). But there's not much doubt in my mind that our first meeting came about through the agency of Emily Holmes Coleman, the American author who died some years ago and had when I first met her already published what I think may be described as a largely autobiographical novel, *The Shutter of Snow* (now for many years out of print but fortunately and deservedly about to be rescued from oblivion by Virago Press).

Emily H. Coleman's novel deals with the experience of living through a period of what was then most often referred to baldly as lunacy; and if the description was indeed as I have suggested founded on fact, it must have been indicative of one of the most obvious reasons for the unusually strong bond of sympathetic understanding which existed between these two writers for many years. Antonia White had herself been through a very similar experience, and wrote a marvellous account of what it is like to go out of one's mind and find oneself in the shadowy, frightening world of hospitalized schizophrenic alienation, in the still little-known *novella* called *The House of Clouds* (which must, I think, have made its first appearance in *Life and Letters*, edited by Desmond MacCarthy, whose assistant Antonia had been for a while).

It is not yet possible to say whether Antonia White left any testamentary request, as did the late W. H. Auden (in vain), that her biography should not be written after her death. It seems to me unlikely that she would have done so; her fundamental modesty was such that it might

---

'Antonia White: A Personal Appreciation', *The Literary Review* 21 (July-August 1980), pp. 12-13.

even have made the idea that one day someone should want to write her life story seem surprising or unlikely to her. It would be quite impossible for anyone to give in an article as brief as this anything like an adequate idea of the richness and the sometimes dramatic vicissitudes of her life – the variety of jobs by means of which she felt she must earn her living, never trusting her ability to support herself by means of creative writing alone in more than the inevitably squalid poverty her honesty told her she was too fastidious to be able to endure, despite her unquestionable courage and determination – or perhaps most importantly of all, the number of her friendships; the exceptional intensity of her inner life, and the breadth of her cultural interests and knowledge.

My own contribution to such a biography would be no more than a small one, nor do I see myself as having played more than a minor and all too brief role in Antonia White's life, crucially important though the role she played in mine now seems to me to have been. The first entry in the Journal that I kept during the year 1936/37 (which Enitharmon Press are to bring out later this year) is dated October 22nd, 1936, and ends with a review of new acquaintances I felt were likely to help my life take a new direction after the inevitable feeling of let-down that had followed my involvement in that summer's Surrealist Exhibition excitements. I quote: 'Antonia White, Emily's friend, whom I met for the first time last week, and from whom I received an invitation this morning, also interests me very much: an extraordinarily lively intelligence and at the same time completely feminine: I look forward to knowing her better, but have a feeling that we shall not meet very often.' At this point I inserted some time later a bracketed exclamation mark, for the inaccuracy of this preliminary intuition regarding our future relations was indeed to prove striking. The next entry, only three days later, starts: 'Never to know what is waiting for one round the corner – it is too much. How could I have guessed that what happened on Wednesday was going to happen? It is true that I knew that I was going to have to change, but not at the cost of so much stress, of so grotesque an occurrence as that which has just taken place. . . .'

What had happened was not exactly qualifiable as *grotesque*: my use of that word is indicative simply of my own feeling of inadequacy and immaturity, my astonishment at finding that I could be regarded as worthy of serious attention as partner in a possibly intimate relationship with a woman about fifteen years older than myself.

Shortly after our first real meeting Antonia wrote to me: 'I want nothing but that you should feel free with me and that I should feel free with you'; 'An infinite number of relationships are possible between us and the only one that has any value (if by a happy chance we find it) is the one which gives us the most increase of life and freedom. You have already given me some increase of life — I hope I may have something for you but we cannot tell yet'; 'We have met at a time when we are both in a transitional stage — the next year is probably a critical one for both of us.'

A brief interpolation ought perhaps to be made here, explaining that Antonia White was at that time in the midst of undergoing a lengthy and expensive course of psychoanalytic treatment.

The next entry I'd like to quote from my Journal was written on the eve of my departure for Barcelona, where for a month or two I was to work for the Catalonian Propaganda Ministry. I spent the night before leaving England at Antonia's flat, as she seemed unduly upset by the thought of our being separated just as we were really beginning to get to know one another, and I did not want her to feel that my political concern demanded that I should sacrifice a precarious but precious personal relationship to it. My account of what ensued reads as follows:

> Next morning, a protracted and uncomfortable parting. We were both carrying attaché cases as we left the flat. We had coffee in a place in the Fulham Road, and Antonia said it was as though we were in a railway station already. She insisted on giving me 10 shillings as a parting present for 'my birthday' — to buy books with in Paris. She had a bus to catch, and just as it drove up to the edge of the pavement where we were standing, she slipped the note into the pocket of my raincoat. It fell through onto the pavement without my noticing it. She jumped onto the bus; we waved; it drove away. I walked on towards World's End. When I felt in my pocket for the note, it had gone: I walked back to the bus stop, but it had already vanished. I saw an old man fingering what looked like a 10-shilling note, but could not bring myself to ask him whether he had just picked it up. This seems to me to present a perfect example of Freudian 'objective chance' ('The Psychopathology of Everyday Life'), and reveals to me the disillusioning truth about my relationship with Antonia far more clearly than any conscientious self-examination could ever have done.

It would be useless to deny that Antonia and I had our occasional squabbles or clashes: she undoubtedly had much provocation. 'The only trouble with you,' she wrote to me once,

> is that you are too lady-like: you make us all feel coarse. James was lady-like too, and it made him fall into the trap he most feared — vulgarity. It stops him from being a first-class artist. He

made the mistake of selecting *beforehand*; one must accept everything and select *afterwards*. In the end, James' books are eunuchs: they produce no new *life*. What you can learn from him is a superb *method*. He confuses *chastity* and *castration* [. . .] I believe for once I quarrel with the New Testament. I think it is better to be damned *whole* than saved with only one eye.

I did not take this lying down and, while realizing that her asperity was principally due to her having just gone through an unusually difficult patch in her analysis, made a quite sharp rejoinder to the effect that if there was one thing I refused to accept responsibility for it was for making anyone feel *coarse*; and I went on to defend Henry James to some extent, though not actually reminding Antonia that it was she herself who, because of her enthusiasm for his novels, particularly her favourite, *The Ambassadors*, had first persuaded me to tackle reading him. In fact I am as grateful to her for introducing me to James as I am for having communicated to me her love of Jane Welsh Carlyle and her brilliantly fascinating letters. A novel we both particularly enjoyed and discussed was Alain-Fournier's *Le Grand Meaulnes*, and we shared also an enthusiasm for the novels of the French-writing American Julien Green, with whom Antonia later entered into correspondence and eventually friendship after meeting him, to my envy, in Paris.

Mention of Paris brings me to what will have to be a final reminiscence, and a happy one, concerning a long weekend Antonia spent in Paris, where I had been living for nearly two years, at the end of January 1939. During the autumn and winter that followed Munich, I had myself embarked on an too brief course of psychoanalysis with a greatly gifted woman analyst who summed up my principal problem with regard to women and work (if you can call writing poetry work) in the words of the French saying: '*La Mariée est trop belle*'; which may perhaps partly explain the sort of problem Antonia had to cope with in her relationship with me. Be that as it may.

For some time already I had been frequenting the group surrounding Henry Miller at the Villa Seurat, and had become a friend of Lawrence and Nancy Durrell. I had had no difficulty in persuading Miller and Durrell to recognize in *The House of Clouds* an exceptionally interesting human document and a beautiful piece of writing. When Antonia came to Paris, a supper-party was arranged at Miller's studio-apartment, and I believed she enjoyed the occasion very much; though it might possibly not have passed off quite so well had Henry Miller's friend and aegeria Anaïs Nin been present, as their very different life-styles and equally strong personalities would probably have mixed like the proverbial oil and vinegar. The result of this tiny incident in the history of Anglo-American cultural relations was that *The House of Clouds* was subsequently reprinted, with Antonia's pleased and mildly surprised consent, in one of the last issues of the now extremely rare and oddly-entitled periodical which Miller and his friend and admirer Lawrence Durrell had the running of for a while, *The Booster*.

Alas, during the War, the correspondence between Antonia and myself, which had at the outset been fairly copious, dwindled into non-existence, and there ensued long periods when I saw her only briefly and intermittently. But I did start writing to her again a little while after returning to live in England in 1964. Happily, I have been able to preserve a few last letters from her, but there is now no space left to quote anything more and I must simply conclude by saying that Antonia, during the final decades of her life, because of her increasing hearing difficulties and a certain determined self-sufficiency always characteristic of her, gave one more and more the impression of having become a recluse, still struggling bravely to write every day but, having had a life so full of what the terrible cliché calls 'meaningful human relationships', seeming to be mostly content with the company of the cats of which she had always been particularly fond, feeling perhaps a certain sympathy with the Whitman who thought he could turn and live with animals. . . . And in fact, Antonia's eldest daughter told me that at her mother's funeral a mysterious black cat appeared just under the altar and later at the graveside. I'm sure that this little feline tribute would have delighted Antonia, who was not given to superstition, just as it might have amused the Colette whom she translated so incomparably.

As for human tributes, I am personally convinced that it is true that all those who have given unstintingly of themselves, in their loves and friendships as in their writing or other creative activity, reap a deserved harvest of affectionate remembrance, and that this will most certainly prove to be the case as far as that fine novelist, psychologist and unique human being who was Antonia White is concerned.

TAMBIMUTTU

Tambimuttu died in a London hospital on 22 June as a result of cardiac arrest, having suffered a fall at his Bloomsbury HQ a few days previously. Known to anyone with the least claim to his acquaintance as Tambi, his full name was Meary James Thurairajah Tambimuttu, and he was born in 1915 in Sri Lanka, then Ceylon. Having already published three youthful collections of verse, he arrived in England in 1938 to set about organizing with singleminded enthusiasm the publication of *Poetry (London)*, with which his name became indissolubly associated. The second word of this title was in fact added only after the first two numbers had appeared. The first, which came out in the Spring of 1939 in the wake of a prospectus distributed at the end of the previous year, contained work by a score of contributors, including Walter de la Mare, Herbert Read, Stephen Spender, Louis MacNeice, Lawrence Durrell, Dylan Thomas, George Barker, Philip O'Connor and Nicholas Moore. Hector Whistler's original cover-design was of a calligraphically decorative nature, centering round an enigmatically baroque motif, which those who had set eyes on Tambi during his earliest London days recognized as a formalized representation of the Literary Editor, with the long, convoluted black coiffure characteristic of his Jaffna Tamil origins. The General Editor named on the cover of the first number was Anthony Dickins, the first of a series of faithful assistants.

The *Sunday Times* for the week following Tambi's death printed a brief notice by Lawrence Durrell, who first encountered Tambi before I was able to do so myself. 'My very first meeting with him,' wrote Durrell, 'was at a rendez-vous off Tottenham Court Road, where he had rented a room in a cheap boarding-house, and lay in bed late of a morning, going over his plans to bring poetry to the public at large . . . Of course,' he added, 'there were later and more affluent times and more up-to-date offices.' The most notable of these during Tambi's early years as an editorial impresario were those allocated to him by the newly reorganized firm of Nicholson and Watson in their Manchester Square building, off Marylebone High Street. Here for some time he held perpetual court, a great variety of literary characters of that period passing in and out every day. The Hog in the Pound pub in nearby Oxford Street was then also

---

'Tambimuttu (1915-1983)', *P.N. Review* 34, Vol. 10, No. 2 (1983), pp. 7-8.

much frequented by Tambi's friends, staff and contributors. Despite the boisterous camaraderie which one remembers from Tambi's headquarters in those days, a great deal of dedicated work went on there during the years 1943-6.

When the funds and impulse that had produced the initial series of six issues of *Poetry (London)* were exhausted, Tambi devoted himself to publishing, under Nicholson and Watson's financial aegis, his PL Editions books, which Alan Smith's meticulous *Antiquarian Book Monthly Review* checklist of 1979 reveals as having run to over sixty items, by writers as diverse as Kathleen Raine and Henry Miller, Charles Williams and Vladimir Nabokov, Anne Ridler, W. S. Graham and David Wright, Lawrence Durrell, Jacques Maritain and Conrad Aiken, to name some of the best known. And Tambi induced the collaboration in his ventures of such artists as Henry Moore, Barbara Hepworth, Graham Sutherland, Lucian Freud and others including, more recently, John Piper, and the presentation by Sven Berlin of the Cornish 'primitive' Alfred Wallis, by S. W. Hayter of the influential refugee Jankel Adler.

Of course, Tambimuttu was instrumental in introducing to English readers many notable Indian writers of our time; and at the end of his life he was closely involved, as President of the Indian Arts Council in the UK, with projects of Anglo-Indian cultural exchange. He was also, from his earliest days here, willing to propagate modern European literature of the highest quality, publishing in his magazine translations of poems by Jules Supervielle and Eluard, poetry and prose by Pierre Jean Jouve, and in book form the first collection of Michael Hamburger's Hölderlin translations and his versions of *Twenty Prose Poems* by Baudelaire. He was responsible for one of the earliest English monographs on Lorca; and for two anthologies, one by Pierre Seghers devoted to French wartime Resistance poetry, the other called *The Green Continent* and presenting work by leading Latin American writers. He was enthusiastic about literature from the United States and had plans to publish both Cummings and Pound. It should not be forgotten that he was the first to publish Elizabeth Smart's *By Grand Central Station I Sat Down and Wept*.

After the War, a new series of *PL* was launched. It continued intermittently until 1951. Then Tambi departed for New York. Here he persuaded Alexander Calder — as earlier he had persuaded Henry Moore — to produce his own version of the lyrebird emblem Tambi had adopted as his trademark, and the design adorned the cover of the first of four issues of *Poetry London-New York*. This is not the place to record the American vicissitudes of Tambimuttu; nor did I intend to write a potted biography. I will pass over the American experience and welcome him back to England in 1968. He set up the Lyrebird Press in London upon his return. Over ten years later the first of two issues of *Poetry London/ Apple Magazine* appeared. One of its most intriguing features was a group of poems revealing that Iris Murdoch is not simply a novelist and retired teacher of philosophy. The advertisement announcing this last of Tambi's editorial ventures quoted Dylan Thomas, who had once written to him: '. . . You've shown, in your introduction, how much you believe in the good of poetry and in the mischief of cliques, rackets, scandal schools, menagerie menages, amateur classes of initiate plagiarists'. This was followed by an even weightier pronouncement by T. S. Eliot: 'It is only in *Poetry (London)* that I can consistently expect to find new poets who matter.'

One must offset Eliot's benevolent comment (a number of Faber poets appeared in the pages of Tambi's magazine) with Geoffrey Grigson's assertion 'The axis which runs through *Poetry (London)* is that all poems are poems equally worth printing. The only axis is to have no axis, beyond that faith in muddle and contradiction which has made *Poetry (London)* the most foolish (if representative) periodical of its time.' The acerbity of this judgement is neither to be accounted for nor discounted by the fact that a number of poets who appeared in Grigson's *New Verse* which first appeared in 1933, went on to allow themselves to be printed in Tambi's magazine. Grigson's expressed attitude is an aspect of the strict integrity which has made him not only a respected critic, but a distinctive and respectable poet in his own right. His disapproval is no doubt fundamentally to be explained by Tambi's possibly starry-eyed flamboyantly-expressed belief that 'every man has poetry within him . . . no man is small enough to be neglected as a poet . . . each poet is a leaf, a significant leaf of Poetry, the multifoliate tree'. Though they would not have expressed it thus, two of the co-founders of Mass Observation, Charles Madge and Humphrey Jennings, undoubtedly at one time shared something like Tambi's belief. This belief was also very much a part of the original creed of the Surrealists, who never tired of quoting Lautréamont's dictum: 'La poésie doit être faite par tous, non par un.'

As I shall ever be indebted to Tambimuttu for publishing the first collection of my poems to be taken seriously by certain critics, it is not possible for me to express in conclusion a wholly unbiased or definitive opinion regarding him. He was warmly impulsive and loyal; he inspired loyalty and affection in a wide variety of not inconsiderable people; he could at times be exasperating but, as our wise mutual friend Robin Waterfield sometimes said of him, 'One has to take Tambi like the weather'. His worst fault may well be said to have been his generosity. The reproach that someone, especially a man of letters, is generous to a fault, is unfortunately one that is now in increasing decline.

GEOFFREY GRIGSON

1933 was one of the most auspicious years in my life. Harold Monro's widow, Alida, his help-mate at their Bloomsbury 'Poetry Bookshop', had persuaded Cobden-Sanderson, publishers of Monro's posthumous *Collected Poems* (prefaced by Eliot), to accept and bring out in the early autumn my first and only novel, a precocious effort called *Opening Day*. In July and September, A. R. Orage printed my first contributions to *The New English Weekly*, of which he was the following year to encourage me to become for a while the art critic. The advance royalties for the novel, which failed to bring me overnight celebrity but received kind notices from Harold Nicolson and Mary Butts, together with what remained of a small legacy, enabled me to make my first trip to Paris, where I spent my seventeenth birthday. Here I made many new acquaintanceships, in particular that of Cyril Connolly, who had found *Opening Day* promising and the cosmopolitanism of a teenager intriguing; and visited the studios of a number of artists, among them S. W. Hayter, Max Ernst and Jean Hélion. It is recollection of Hélion's brilliant conversation and of the austere abstractions he was producing at that time, as harmoniously architectured as the pictorial spaces of Poussin, that persuades me that I must by then have already met Geoffrey Grigson. His *New Verse* had made its first appearance that year, and the result of my first attempt to write a purely 'automatic' Surrealist poem had appeared in one of its earliest numbers. Grigson was then one of Hélion's principal British admirers, and I am convinced that it must have been he who had urged me to visit him when in Paris, and had even communicated to me the painter's address, which otherwise I do not know how I should have been able to find.

In referring to 1933 as having been an auspicious year for me, I was thinking above all of the good fortune that befell me then in having three notable editors display a favourable interest in my potential gift as a writer. It was an auspicious year for contemporary poets in that Geoffrey Grigson then provided them, in *New Verse*, with a platform that now seems peculiarly appropriate to the period. In *The Private Art: A Poetry Note-Book* (1982), Grigson (without doubt one of the best anthologists of the century) writes:

'Man of Principle', *Grigson at Eighty* (Cambridge: Rampant Lions Press, 1985), pp. 39-45.

I am not against anthologies, as long as they are not attempts to enforce a poor idea of poetry, as long as they discover, and as long as they are born of excitement and generosity.

These words are exactly applicable to the kind of periodical that *New Verse* represented at its inception. I have just spent over an hour in going through *The Private Art* again in a vain attempt, despite having got to know the book well by now, to discover the passage where Surrealist poetry is referred to in terms suggesting that its author has no objection to it as long as its picturesquely (not the word he uses) irrational imagery is the unfaked product of the unconscious. It was no doubt the spirit of discovery, alluded to in the above quotation, which kept *New Verse* so alive throughout the comparatively few years of its existence, and that prompted its editor to accept and print some of my earliest Surrealist-type poems (it was not until 1935 that I went back to Paris to collect the material for my *Short Survey of Surrealism*). Before becoming finally, as it seemed, disillusioned with the idea that I might turn out to be worthy of continued propagation, Grigson went on to publish other immature poems of mine, which I feel must have had some merit, since he accepted them, and also a few translations from Eluard, Arp and even Giacometti. My capacity as a translator was still in those days elementary, but Grigson found my version of Eluard's poem 'Au Présent' of 1936 (its title incorrectly translated as 'At Present') satisfactory enough to be reprinted in one of the volumes of *The Year's Poetry* edited by him. When reading *The Private Art*, I was reminded by Grigson's appreciative references to Marceline Desbordes-Valmore of the occasion of my first visit to Eluard's apartment in the rue Legendre, which ended by his reading to me a number of his favourite poems, among which was one by this woman, whose name at that time was completely unknown to me, but whose work was recently associated by Yves Bonnefoy with that of both Coleridge and Rimbaud.

The debt of gratitude I still feel I owe Geoffrey Grigson is not, however, due simply to the fact that through him I became installed as one of the younger Thirties poets he considered worthy of attention, or even that through him I met for the first time, on Sunday afternoons in his Keats Grove garden, many poets whose friendship I came eventually to treasure, such as Norman Cameron, Charles Madge, Kathleen Raine and Gavin Ewart, but to his allowing me to have tea with him about once a week for a while in a secluded café (strictly speaking 'tea-room') in a court off Fleet Street. Those were the days when Geoffrey, as I had by then begun to address him, was earning his living as literary editor of *The Morning Post*. These sessions, often lasting an hour or more, undoubtedly exerted a crucial formative influence on my development at that time, though it seems unlikely that it was Grigson's deliberate intention that they should do so. Geoffrey Grigson is more than ten years my senior, and by the mid-1930s had already developed his rigorous but never rigid, personal but universally applicable standards of taste, and he applied them with the kind of intransigence I came later to associate with André Breton and the Surrealist group dominated by him; though I hasten to add that Grigson never struck me as seeking to achieve dominion, but rather as particularly appreciative of the diversity of the gifts and inclinations of those he frequented or allowed to frequent him. I can't help regretting that I did not start writing a journal before October 1936: had I done so I should now perhaps be able to cull from it some verbatim details of those absorbing café conversations of fifty years ago. Their abiding significance for me now is, I believe, that they encouraged in me discernment and appreciation of excellence in the arts, as well as abhorrence of humbug and inauthenticity. Honesty compels me to admit that the liveliest recollection I retain of my meetings with Grigson when I was still in my teens is of how on each occasion he would spend some time airing his pet hate of the week. The *rouspéteur refoulé* in me considerably relished, if with certain circumspectly concealed reservations, the virtuosity and usually justifiable truculence of these diatribes. The principal reservation I harboured with regard to what Grigson imparted to me during our tête-à-têtes of that time related to the evident influence on his opinions of his unwavering admiration for the person and works of Wyndham Lewis.

In *The Private Art*, published two years ago, Geoffrey Grigson notes: 'Inside Eliot there was a capsule of the unpleasant'. Has it never occurred to him that in the eyes of many, by no means all of them outstanding 'ninnies', there was inside Wyndham Lewis a clumsily disguised letter-bomb of unmitigated offensiveness? At the time of our early meetings I had already, despite my youth, read a considerable amount of Wyndham Lewis's writings, and I had been understandably excited by the vigour and visually evocative prose of *Tarr* and *The Wild Body*. But the skilfully conducted polemic of *The Caliph's Design* seemed to me even then to be vitiated by an unworthy resentment aroused by the acclaim already accorded Picasso; and while fascinated by *The Childermass*, I was repelled by what appeared to be the ill-dissimulated jealousy of Joyce apparent in the concluding section of the first part of that unclassifiable work. Equally rebarbative to me was the paranoid loathing of certain supposedly eminent contemporary literary figures embodied in the interminable *The Apes of God*, avidly though I had read it at the time of its first appearance. Further discussion of my inability to share Grigson's veneration for this important but often ultra-equivocal British equivalent of a Marinetti would constitute an inappropriate digression here. I am aware that seriously to suggest that any but the most superficial comparison could be drawn between Marinetti and Wyndham Lewis would be to prove oneself a ninny indeed. The bombastic Italian publicist with a dubious streak of genius (too often a dubious term in itself) could never have become a masterly painter, for one thing. I am also aware of getting involved in a plethora of judgemental adjectives. An amusing way to end this divagation might be to add that my first sight of an original Wyndham Lewis painting, an unforgettably vivid one at that, occurred in the flat of a man commonly supposed to have been the model for one of the savagely ridiculed characters, all caricaturist's cutouts, who make up the cast of *The Apes of God*.

In the Introduction to the Penguin edition of his anthology of *Unrespectable Verse* (1971), Grigson writes: 'Luckily the true condition of most of us is mixed; is grey, rather than piebald.' Before reaching the age of thirty, I'd been lucky enough to have undergone and assimilated the influence of at least half a dozen individuals with minds of unusual distinction (to name whom might be considered ostentatious if not invidious), all of whom shared with Geoffrey Grigson the characteristic of being mixed, piebald, ambivalent or self-contradictory. Since grey is hardly an astringent colour, perhaps they were unlike 'most of us'. One of them, a French-writing Romanian-Jewish poet and philosopher/critic exterminated at Birkenau, was a single-minded claimant of the freedom to become consistent through self-contradiction. None of them would have been so creatively stimulating as they were to others had they been monochrome. But on reading *The Private Art* with exhilarated satisfaction, what struck me more than the number of apparently self-cancelling contradictions I believed I could detect in it, was how many times I felt wholly in accord with the thoughts and judgements expressed in it, and how many admirations and enthusiasms as well as dislikes and aversions, I found myself sharing with the author. Coleridge, Blake, Leopardi, Hölderlin, Novalis, Hugo, Baudelaire, Mallarmé, Hopkins, Whitman and Trakl: – all have been preoccupations of mine for many years and occupy prominent places in my private Pantheon. I do not make such a statement in the expectation of obtaining some sort of deflected kudos thereby, but because it proves at least to my own satisfaction that, as I claimed earlier, Geoffrey Grigson was indeed a formative influence on my development during an impressionable phase of my youth; and because I am lastingly grateful that this should have been the case.

As I write this, I am unable to suppress a gnawing misgiving as to Grigson's possible reaction to what amounts to a proclamation on my part of a kind of kinship with him. He might well, I realize, repudiate any affinity with what he may consider at present my outlook and the nature of my achievement to be. Ever since a deplorable serio-comic incident at least thirty years ago, involving what I've always believed to be a futile misunderstanding arising from a tactless enquiry on my part with regard to Samuel Palmer, the subject of Geoffrey's incomparable study which had then just appeared, my feeling has been that by inadvertent ineptitude I burnt the boats, so to speak, between him and myself. This situation saddens me; and it may not have been improved by my, as I thought, dutifully sending him a copy of my *Journal 1936-37* when it was published four years ago by Alan Clodd's Enitharmon Press. An entry in it written in March 1937 describes a visit to the house in Hampstead that Grigson had then just moved to from Keats Grove on an evening when I met Kenneth Allott and his wife there for the first time: I will not quote from it here, but it might well create an impression of callow brashness and worse. It is at least not typical of the mildly affable youth with lofty aspirations that I may then have appeared to many acquaintances to be.

Prolixity has once more carried me beyond stipulated length. Let me therefore hasten to end by quoting some words from *Tarry Flynn*, a novel by Patrick Kavanagh I finished reading this morning, that at once made me think of Geoffrey G.: 'Stones, clay, grass, the sunlight coming through the privet hedge. Why did he love such common things?' Not only his poems make it clear that Grigson, probably quite as much Cornish as Tarry's creator was Irish, is a man who notices such things and has long since found his own undemonstrative way of celebrating them. (Why, I'd like to know, has his wonderful book on an archetypically English barn been allowed to go out of print? Too uncommercial a venture?) He too now evidently loves France and things French as much as I do; but it is a particularly acute sense of Englishness that I value in him as much as anything else. To him, as to Humphrey Jennings, I owe the development of my own feeling for the Englishness of, for instance, the Wiltshire Downs, Cranborne Chase and the Isle of Purbeck; of Gilbert White, Stubbs and Bewick; of Hampstead Heath and the City; of Herbert, Blake and Tennyson. In other words he, as much as Humphrey, helped me rediscover my own real roots. In *The Private Art*, Grigson writes of comforting himself for the fact that most people read newspapers and not poems 'by thinking of the ripple caused by throwing a small stone into a large pond. On the shore of the pond the ripple is felt, without knowledge of the pebble, by whatever creatures may live there.' While avoiding the impertinence of proffering my estimate of the size of the stone Geoffrey Grigson's life and writings may represent, I am glad to have had an opportunity to record my appreciative response to the ripple aroused by them.

EDGAR MORIN

At the end of 1984, the *Editions du Seuil* reissued in their encyclopaedic pocket series *Points* (consisting of works by hundreds of authors, among whom are to be found, for instance, Ivan Illich, Konrad Lorenz, E. F. Schumacher, Teilhard de Chardin and Chögyam Trungpa) a work by Edgar Morin published three years previously by another firm: *Pour sortir du XXe siècle*

Edgar Morin, born in 1921, had already published a score of works in France, among the first of which was *L'An zero de l'Allemagne* of 1946. Having founded the Committee of Intellectuals against the War in Algeria, Edgar Morin has developed during the last two decades a multi-disciplined, personal body of thought – anthropological, biological and sociological – that has been acquiring of late an ever increasing recognition in this country. That his name is as yet less well-known here than those of many of his French intellectual contemporaries is no doubt largely due to the fact that his work resists simple classification. His only book to date to have appeared in English translation is *La Rumeur d'Orléans*, primarily a sociological study of incidents that took place in 1969 in a sober provincial city involving an outbreak of antisemitic hysteria that rapidly attained the dimension of myth.

Only two volumes of what is probably Morin's most ambitious project, *La Méthode*, have been published so far; they are to be followed by three more. The aim of his 'method' is clearly to demonstrate the basic unity of mankind by redefining what he considers to be the lost paradigm of human nature, regarded not only as that distinctive of *homo sapiens/ faber*, but more and more obviously also of *homo demens*. Dissatisfied with what has until now passed for anthropology, Morin is seeking to broaden the scope of the study of man by taking fuller account of the complexity of human phenomena, by recognizing the importance of still largely neglected ecological factors and of the need to integrate into an ever incomplete science an awareness of both existential and cybernetic insights. Any assessment of the present complexity of human affairs is obliged not only to be alert to the prevalence in them of the role played by disorder, accident and the indeterminate, but also to pay due attention

'Thoughts of Edgar Morin', *Resurgence* 113 (November/December 1985), pp. 14-16.

to the continued functioning of myth, magic and the irrational. Morin's search is directed above all to a way of thought capable of releasing us from the autocratic reductionism of a science that is aggravating rather than elucidating the crisis that threatens us with extinction.

THE MYTH OF OBJECTIVITY

Pour sortir du XXe siècle may be read as a summary of the most cogent findings in the domains explored by Morin's theoretical writings, and as an introduction to the work of one of the most independent and astute French thinkers of our time. It is a book offering no panaceas, indeed it is implicitly as distrustful of clearcut conclusions as of what its author terms 'the techno-bureaucratic myth of progress'. Rather it is a sustained exhortation against the acceptance of over-simplified solutions, and a relentless exposure of the perilous confusions inherent in the current strategies of language engaged either in information or persuasion regarding fundamental social concerns. Unable to reflect on the world in which we live or to cope with the innumerable problems by which it is convulsed without having constant resource to a certain number of prime words (*maître mots*), we ought, Morin warns us, to be constantly aware that all such words have become corrupted – 'degraded, obsessionalized, reiterated at random, pretending to indicate knowledge or explanation of everything'. The prototype of these seemingly indispensable words may well have been the Hegelian *Geist*. In the field of contemporary politics and social studies it has become evident that what they once purported to illumine they in fact camouflage.

Edgar Morin begins his book by narrating a personal anecdote illustrating the ineradicable fallibility of individual perception of objective events. Later he draws attention to the attempt by the empirical sciences to eliminate subjectivity by means of propagating what Theodore Roszak has denounced as the myth of total objectivity. Throughout his entire polemic he inveighs, tacitly or explicitly, against the prevalent tendency of partial systems, ideologies and theoretical explanations to assume autonomy and proclaim themselves all-sufficient.

It is reassuring today to find a thinker who is a director of France's National Centre for Scientific Research (CNRS), pre-eminently one would suppose an inheritor of the Cartesian tradition of insistence on clarity and distinctness, so ready to concede the illusory nature of the omnipotence of the Reason apotheosized by the Revolution with which the Enlightenment culminated, and stressing the importance of distinguishing between rationality and rationalization.

> Reason can evolve and can transform itself; it can, as Adorno and Horkheimer have said — and as far as I'm concerned proved — achieve autodestruction. Reason is not a quality, a virtue that *homo sapiens* inherited from nature at birth. Reason, or rather rationality, is the application to the data provided by experience of principles of coherence. A discourse prompted by the principle of disjunction/reduction can be totally rational when, in biology, for instance, it retains and formulates only the molecule or the gene, ignoring the individual, or life. But in other respects, such discourse is demented. A structural or althusserian discourse can arrive logically at the conclusion that man does not exist, that a myth, a phantom or an illusion of common sense is alluded to by the word; such a discourse, coherently developed from its own premisses, is absurd in the sense that, excluding the data and deprived of the concepts which would necessitate its envisioning man, it concludes that he is non-existent.

Considerations of this kind lead Morin to insist repeatedly on the urgency of developing the kind of reason that is *open* to dialogue and prepared to undertake constant self-criticism, as opposed to the type of rationalization classically defined by Freud as the self-justificatory mechanism of states of neurotic disorder.

BIODEGRADABILITY OF TRUTH

Pour sortir du XXe siècle is divided into three main sub-sections, as interrelated as the complex issues it discusses are interdependent. Adequately to summarize its contents within the scope of an article as brief as this would be impossible. Its distinctively French contribution to international debate is notable above all for the pertinence with which it draws attention to the most crucial questions facing all who are seriously concerned with the problem of human survival. In the opening section (*Savoir voir*), Morin declares that while we thought we'd been living in the century of the Revolutions of want which would get rid of want, we are in fact suffering the want of this century's revolutions (the word I have rendered as want is the more comprehensive *misère*). And he goes on to ask: 'Must we not critically re-examine, not the idea of revolution, but the prime (maître) word Revolution, Revolution-Salvation, Revolution-Solution?' The second part is entitled *Le jeu de la verité et de l'erreur* ('The interplay of truth and error' seems to me the closest approximation). In it not only is the problem of truth presented in relation to its relativity, but truth is shown to be subject to what Morin calls its 'biodegradability'. If every truth exists with given conditions and limits of existence, it can die outside the context of such limitations. 'Truths which are not biodegradable are illusory and counterfeit insofar as they pretend to transcend the mortal conditions of existence.' Morin sees the limiting conditions of truth as implying the anthropological limit/condition of a subject-believing-in-the-truth. 'Error precedes man, but with man truth comes into view. There can be truth only for a human subject.' Man shares error with animals, but introduces a new source of error on account of his need to resort to the abstraction of ideas in order to attain a grasp of the concrete; and ideas both bring about and prevent our communication with reality. Morin wishes to share his conviction 'that we are still in the depths of night concerning knowledge of the relations between our brain/mind, ideas, and the outer world. We are still in the prehistory of the mind.' 'Finally with *homo sapiens/demens* a new order of reality has made its appearance, an order able to participate in error and truth both at once, while being at the same time both on this side and beyond truth and error: *the myth.*'

A few pages later, Morin further clarifies his conception of myth by explaining that the question is not simply one of demystification, (revealing the lie in the utilization of myth), or of demythification (for not only do myths embody our 'truths', in other words our aspirations, but we are unable to live without myths), the question is one of treating myths in their innate complexity and working with/against them. Any way of seeing things that is unable to take the nature of myths seriously is clearly inadequate. And this consideration of myth leads Morin on to another formulation of one of his most constant themes: 'All reducing/simplifying thought can but impoverish, denature and mutilate the problem of truth and error.'

MEANING OF CRISIS

In the third main section of his book (*Où va le monde?*), Edgar Morin subjects the term 'crisis', which has in our time been so hard worked as to seem almost emptied of content, to rigorous examination. In the process he adopts as his own a phrase of Antonio Negri's: 'Crisis is not the opposite of development but its very form'. In Western societies, Morin maintains, the crisis of civilization, the crisis of values, of the family, of the State, or urban and rural lifestyles, are so many aspects of the from henceforward *crisique* (untranslatable neologism) being of our societies, which while most certainly threatened by this ubiquitous state of crisis, have at the same time come to live by it. He goes on to contrast the rampant and undisguised crises of the USA-dominated Western bloc with the suppressed, carefully camouflaged crisis of Soviet-controlled countries. *'We find ourselves paradoxically and simultaneously in a World-wide Stalinistic era and a world-wide Americanistic era.'* Morin's bleakest final conclusion is that we are *in the planetary iron age*. The world in which we live is at the same time in crisis, in evolution, in regression and in revolution. Instead of selecting one of these four aspects and eliminating the others, we ought to realize that we are living them all at once. Fully to recognize the complexity and confusion of the planetary iron age is a vital prerequisite for emerging into a more confident certainty with regard to the century ahead.

> It is not absolutely certain, it is only probable, that our civilization is moving towards autodestruction, and if there is autodestruction, the role of politics, of science, of technology, of ideology will be of capital importance, whereas politics, science, technology, ideology, if there were increased awareness of the situation, could save us from disaster and transform the conditions of the problem.

The message of *Pour sortir du XXe siècle* is not an optimistic one. But its pessimism is the reverse of nihilistic. Morin believes that we are in mortal peril. But he tells us that this peril ought not to be thought to be represented by the atom bomb alone, which in itself involves only uranium or hydrogen. The most insidious peril is in the synergistic conjunction of all-powerful States, of techniques of manipulation, of subjection and wholesale destruction, allied to frenzied myths. The peril with which we are faced lies in the confluence of forces of political, technological, biological and informational enslavement, and the concurrent unleashing of demographic, economic and ecological forces.

Edgar Morin finally encourages the belief that all can still change in the convulsions which are either the throes of an eventual end of the world or of the eventual birth of a world. He encourages us to rethink, more radically and urgently than ever before, the greatly degraded, polluted and brutalized concept of revolution. It is not a final struggle we have to face, he would have us believe, but a new initial struggle. What has to be envisioned is a new birth, which would be inseparably linked to the birth of our still inexistent and only potential humanity. We should try not to accomplish the promises of evolution, but to revolutionize evolution itself. It is change that has to be changed. Here is surely a vital reformulation of what readers of this review have come to understand by *Resurgence*.

S. W. HAYTER

All those to whom he imparted his greatly varied range of etching and engraving techniques, came before long to regard Bill Hayter as a faithful friend, such was the exceptional warmth of his personality, his humour, tolerance and informality, counterbalancing the strictures of his professionalism.

Among the best-known of his early pupils were the Surrealists Max Ernst, Miró and Tanguy. He was closest to André Masson in the gestural virtuosity of his alternately fluid and jagged line. Expressive of the impetuous dynamism animating his work as teacher, inventor and craftsman, the colour of his paintings grew ever more glowing towards the end of his life, as though in defiance of the increasingly depressing shadows of recent decades.

I first met him in 1933 during my first visit to Paris. Julian Trevelyan was then the most notable English painter among his already numerous pupils. Our meeting occurred near his Montparnasse atelier, at a rue Daguerre address later inhabited by the distinguished Cork poet John Montague, who now possesses possibly the finest collection of Hayter engravings in Ireland.

It was Hayter who first took me to meet André Breton, the father of Surrealism, at the foot of Montmartre in 1935. His contemporary, Roland Penrose, was at that time another close friend, and the following year he became an important liaison officer on the committee headed by Penrose which organized the International Surrealist Exhibition which startled and enlivened London in the summer of 1936.

Two of Hayter's foils and eleven etchings were among some 400 exhibits to be seen on the New Burlington Gallery's walls. After the outbreak of the Civil War in Spain, he collaborated with Paul Eluard in producing *Solidarité*, an anthology sold in aid of the Republicans, to which he, like Picasso and others, contributed an etching. In 1938 he produced a series of engravings for Eluard's *Proie Facile*, now to be found reproduced in the NRF edition of *Oeuvres complètes*.

In the 1950s Hayter returned once more to Paris, setting up his atelier this time near the Observatoire, and continuing to teach new generations

Obituary in *The Independent* (7 May 1988).

of artists, when not travelling abroad to attend ever more frequent retrospectives of his work.

In 1934, as the brash teenage art critic of A. R. Orage's *New English Weekly*, I concluded a review of a Leicester Gallery exhibition* by remarking that Hayter's engravings 'give pleasure through the sheer perfection of their finish and rich variety of surface alone, whatever their merits as design may be. The union of technical and formal content is most successful in *Figure Caught in a Net*, an extremely fine piece of work and a most tempting bargain for the perspicacious collector.'

Fifty years later, I did not have great difficulty in persuading him to illustrate a recent poem of mine, which a bookdealer/publisher in Portland, Oregon, wanted to bring out as a broadsheet. When it later appeared in a limited edition of 170 copies, it displayed alongside the poem a vigorous, complex figure of Hephaestus and his net made with a single Nue line against a yellow background.

When the last time I was in Paris I went to visit him as usual, Bill Hayter had just returned from a game of tennis, which he still played regularly, though by then turned eighty. I am told that the night before he died he went out to dine with friends, no doubt as ever the most endearing and exuberant of guests. It was difficult to think of him as an old master, but the master of twentieth-century engraving he has undoubtedly been for the past fifty years.

---

* Editor's note: 'Some Recent Art Exhibitions' (1 March 1934).

JULIAN TREVELYAN

Julian Trevelyan belonged to the distinguished family associated for over a century with Darwin, Huxley and their descendants.

After happy years of education at Bedales, he went on to Cambridge, there to join the prodigious generation of the late 1920s and early 1930s which included Jacob Bronowski, William Empson, Humphrey Jennings, Charles Madge, Kathleen Raine, George Reavey and Michael Redgrave, with many of whom he maintained friendly relations throughout their lives. Indeed he had a gift for friendship surpassed only by his gift for painting.

While in Cambridge, he became a member of the group known as Experiments, and contributed to its magazine in 1930 a text devoted to dreams, in which he declared, 'To dream is to create' – the first indication of his later affiliation with Surrealism. His decision to become a painter led him to Paris, where from 1931 to 1934 he studied at Stanley William Hayter's Atelier 17, a workshop in Montparnasse devoted to engraving and associated techniques.

In 1933 it was my good fortune at the age of seventeen, to be introduced to Trevelyan and his teacher. Julian in his turn introduced me to Vieira da Silva, his neighbour at the Villa Brune, near the Jardin des Plantes. Da Silva was one of the most remarkable woman painters of the mid-twentieth century (her portrait of René Char was reproduced in *The Independent* to accompany the obituary of the poet, 24 February 1988), and Julian later became her fervent advocate in England.

His own work at this time, exhibited for instance at the *Salon des Surindépendants*, continued to be experimental in many directions, incorporating such materials as matchwood and cork into his canvases. The line he developed in drawings and etchings, web-like and suggestive of the nervous system, also belongs to this period, as does his admiration for Hayter's friend, Alexander Calder, who had not yet invented mobiles, but fascinated all who saw it with his circus wrought of wire.

In 1936 Trevelyan was one of the twenty British artists represented in the International Surrealist Exhibition, which caused a sensation that summer at the New Burlington Galleries. The following year he was one

---

Obituary in *The Independent* (14 July 1988).

of the principal instigators of the Exhibition of Surrealist Objects at the new London Gallery, which he opened at midnight disguised as a blind explorer.

After the outbreak of war in 1939, he became involved in camouflage work, like several other painters of his generation, such as Roland Penrose, unfit for active military service. Julian referred to these researches as 'visual warfare'. When the job took him to the Middle East and he was asked by local authorities to fill in an official form, coming to the question 'What is your religion?' he wrote 'Surrealism'.

Soon after the return of peace, Durham Wharf, Julian Trevelyan's studio directly overlooking the Thames at Chiswick, became the scene of a series of memorable boatrace-day parties at which, one year or another, it seemed that half the artistic and literary population of London, with many friends of other kinds, were happily gathered together.

After the break-up of his marriage to the potter Ursula Darwin in the late 1940s, Trevelyan accompanied the painter Mary Fedden and a party of her friends on a prolonged painting tour of Sicily which had two fortunate results. One was that the colours and shapes of the Sicilian mountainsides and rooftops inspired a number of remarkable canvases in which a landscape style new in Trevelyan's work is evident. The other was his eventual marriage to his principal travelling companion of that time, which brought him forty years of fruitful happiness.

From this time on, although he never lost his enthusiasm for the dreamlike and the fantastic, or the use in his pictures of unconventional material such as flotsam and jetsam recovered from the Thames, he became increasingly well-known for landscapes of both home and abroad, as well as straightforward subjects celebrating everyday life, the freshness and individuality of vision of which brought him wide popularity. There came a time when VIPs arriving at Heathrow were able to catch a glimpse of a Trevelyan adorning the lounge reserved for them.

He had been a Royal Academician for some years, and an exhibition of his work at a Henley-on-Thames gallery, which opened in mid-April this year, was a sell-out. The day before his death he was busy working in the studio of a neighbouring friend. Like his friend and one-time teacher, Bill Hayter, his passing involved neither sickness nor pain.

I last saw him at a lunch party on 26 June, at which Kathleen Raine, among his close friends since their days at Cambridge, was also present. We agreed that we had not seen him looking so fit and serene for many a year. It will take a long time for his death to sink in.

SALVADOR DALI

The names of two of the most celebrated and popular figures in the history of modern art are linked by a singular coincidence. Vincent van Gogh and Salvador Dalí both inherited the first name of a pre-deceased elder brother, a peculiarity that may be considered a determining factor in their respective developments. Though wholly dissimilar as painters, both are associated with insanity, van Gogh through struggling with and succumbing to it, Dalí through successfully exploiting his simulation of paranoia in particular, proclaiming that the only difference between himself and a madman was that he was not mad.

The incidents of Dalí's pampered Catalan childhood, spent in Figueres, where in 1904 he was born the son of the town notary, and of the summer holidays spent at Cadaqués on the north coast of Barcelona, provided him with the obsessive imagery and haunting rocky seaside landscape settings to be found in all the paintings which first made him famous during the pre-war decade of 1929-39. The rotting corpse of a donkey on a beach, the head of a hydrocephalic child, shells, ants, grasshoppers and cypresses, were all lodged ineradicably in his memory during his most formative years.

In 1921, following the trauma of his doting mother's sudden death, Dalí left Figueres to study at the principal academy of Fine Arts in Madrid, where he occupied a room in the capital's undergraduate *Residencia*. Here, during the next two years, having distinguished himself as much by his intellectual brilliance as by his eccentricities and dandified appearance, he was befriended by two of the most distinguished of his contemporaries, Federico García Lorca and Luis Buñuel. In 1926, Lorca was to compose his 'Ode to Salvador Dalí'; and Buñuel was to collaborate with Dalí in 1929 in producing the first Surrealist film, *Un Chien andalou*.

Dalí's exceptional gifts as a painter had already been recognized by both Picasso and Miró before he arrived in Paris in 1929. André Breton, the Surrealists' maestro, introduced his exhibition of that year by hailing his art as 'the most hallucinatory known until now'. It was also in 1929 that Dalí first encountered Gala, Russian wife of the poet Paul Eluard,

---

Obituary in *The Independent* (24 January 1989).

the woman – destined to exercise a paramount influence over his subsequent life – whom he married after the Eluards' divorce in 1932. Gala's likeness now became a predominant part of the repertoire of Dalí's pictorial obsessions, such as *The Angelus* of Millet, William Tell, Lenin, a Hitlerian nursemaid and Mae West. In his life she played the role of midwife, monitress and muse.

Having early assimilated the ideology of Freudian psychoanalysis, Dalí went on to elaborate under the influence of Jacques Lacan, the 'paranoiac-critical method' which led him to fill his most characteristic works with double and often multiple images, scrambled metaphors and visual puns. 'My whole ambition in the pictorial domain is to materialize images of concrete irrationality with the most imperialist fury of precision,' wrote Dalí in 1935 in *The Conquest of the Irrational*, an essay accompanying a series of reproductions in a booklet brought out that year by the New York dealer Julien Levy, on the occasion of Dalí's third American exhibition.

The frontispiece consists of a colour-plate of *Gala and the Angelus of Millet*, which portrays Gala in her prime, wearing an embroidered jacket, seated on a wheelbarrow, with hands folded in her lap, her head silhouetted against a framed reproduction of Millet's *Angelus*: the male figure in which Dalí interpreted as concealing an erection with his hat, while facing a female like a praying mantis, both staring fixedly at the faeces at their feet. This small painting is impeccably executed in a style evincing admiration for Vermeer and Meissonier.

Among the other plates in this publication is one reproducing a poster, headed 'Salvador Dalí The Surrealist Mystery of New York in 1935', which perfunctorily presents an assortment of Dalinian imagery: a flabby watch, the bowed head of 'the Great Masturbator' surmounted by an inkwell and fastened with safety pins, soiled night-wear, edibles, ants, a tiny father and son in the distance – in a manner suggestive of the announcement of a freak-show booth at a circus. Dalí's *Conquest of the Irrational* was about to become synonymous with the conquest of the international art-market and the media by the most assiduously exhibitionist showman of the century.

Before finally leaving France in 1940 to take refuge for many years in the United States, Dalí had already succeeded in attracting a group of distinguished and lucrative patrons, among them the Prince de Faucingny-Lucinges, the Visconte de Noailles and, in England, the extravagant Edward James. In America, his prestige patented from the start by the approval of Alfred Barr of the Museum of Modern Art, he immediately secured the favour of a clientele of even wealthier collectors, such as Caresse Crosby, Helena Rubinstein and Huntington Hartford.

There can today be hardly any notable city in America that does not possess in its local museum at least one work by Dalí, if not always of notable quality. After the defeat of France, many members of the Surrealist group also found themselves in America, headed by André Breton, who in 1934 had already hauled Dalí over the coals on account of his enthusiasm for Hitler, in whom he could only see a spectacular exponent of delirium. Breton, finding that the American public of the 1940s regarded Surrealism as almost entirely synonymous with Dalí's pictorial contribution to the movement, coined an anagrammatic epithet expressive of his scornful disapprobation, Avida Dollars.

With the tireless support and incitement of Gala, for whom opulence was the most indisputable appanage of genius, Dalí had before long accumulated the foundation of a fortune to be surpassed at one time only by that of Picasso. Fully aware of the Freudian unconscious's identification of money with excrement, he would have regarded being filthy rich as a necessary component of the Dalinian identity.

There can be no doubt that Dalí willingly collaborated with commercialism in compromising his gift by a repetitive exploitation of the more luridly sensational products of his imagination. Few serious critics would now maintain that the quality of Dalí's later output ever again reached the level it achieved prior to 1939. *The Spectre of Sex Appeal* of 1935, and *Soft Construction with Boiled Beans: Premonition of Civil War* of 1936, may be regarded as two of the most powerful icons expressive of the *Zeitgeist* of their epoch, and are probably as close in spirit as anything produced by a modern Spanish painter to Goya's late (black) works, his *Saturn Devouring his Children* in particular.

At the other extreme, vast works of 1959 and 1960 such as *The Discovery of America by Christopher Columbus* and *The Ecumenical Council* impress one above all as epitomizing, with consummately slick technical proficiency, a sprawling pictorial rhetoric of an emptiness one might, formerly, have believed Dalí incapable of attaining.

When a respected art critic and broadcaster declared to me recently that, as a practising Catholic, he regarded Dalí as the greatest religious painter of our time, he was probably thinking particularly of the *Christ of St John of the Cross*, acquired by the Glasgow Art Gallery in 1952. The painter himself once declared to an interviewer, in one of his not unprecedented moments of straightforward candour, that although a painter of religious subjects he did not regard himself as possessed of religious faith. If his representation of the vision described by the Spanish saint is capable of impressing many viewers as an inoffensive yet potent image, that is no doubt due to the fact that the painter restrained himself in this case from adding any unexpected details to an austere visualization.

To many other people, the depiction of Gala as the Virgin Mary, even in *The Madonna of Port Lligat* 1949 (a picture approved of by the Pope), cannot but appear somewhat ludicrous if they are aware of the model's most publicized propensities. If the latter painting succeeds, it is as an example of high-class kitsch; to judge from reproductions of it, the specious and unredeemed kitsch of the *Sacrament of the Last Supper* to be seen in the Washington National Gallery can hardly fail to repel any genuinely religious person.

It must nevertheless be allowed that Dalí succeeded in preserving throughout the ten years he spent in America and at least two subsequent decades based at Port Lligat near Figueres, an apparently inexhaustible inventiveness, despite inevitable fluctuations in the quality of his facture. He managed to introduce the element of the random associated with *tachisme* into otherwise rigorously controlled compositions. He extended his personal bestiary to include blazing giraffes, stalk-legged elephants and camels, rhinoceroses, geodesic snails and a pet ocelot.

His later works incorporate numerous allusions to both quantum and nuclear physics. To his hallucinogenic period, *circa* 1970, corresponds a renewal of virtuosity in style and use of colour. But even more astonishing than his capacity for invention was the creative energy that enabled him to participate not only in incessant media events and 'happenings', but to make a vast number of contributions to the realms of fashion design and jewellery, film (work for the Marx Brothers, Hitchcock and others), ballet and opera sets and costumes (*Bacchanale* at the Met, *Salome* at Covent Garden), interior design and cookery, but above all book illustration.

Though never surpassing the incomparable plates he designed in the 1930s to illustrate Lautréamont's *Les Chants de Maldoror*, Dalí provided innumerable drawings and engravings to accompany luxury editions of *Macbeth*, Montaigne, Dante, the Bible, Ronsard, Apollinaire, Mao Tsetung, and André Malraux. Late in his career, this department of his production led him into becoming involved with the complications of forgery, fraud and litigation, no doubt still to be sorted out.

It should not be forgotten that Dalí may also be considered a remarkable writer. *The Secret Life of Salvador Dalí* is perhaps the most fascinating and amusing autobiography ever produced by a painter. His polemical writings on modern art, backed by a lifelong familiarity with the works of great and less well-known artists of every period and school, display an aggressive and often pungent wit. His analysis of *The Tragic Myth of Millet's 'Angelus'* elucidates in baroque terminology the complex thoughts behind some of his most significant productions.

Professor Rafael Nadal, once the contemporary and friend of Lorca and Dalí at the Madrid Students' *Residencia*, has assured me that one cannot pretend properly to understand Dalí unless one has some grasp of the peculiarly Catalan notion of the buffoon, a figure rooted in local folk mythology, whose function is satirically to deflate anything commonly accorded respect, by paradoxically inflating it, by means of histrionic exaggeration. 'Even when one is playing games,' Dalí is reported to have remarked, 'there is a shred of more or less bitter truth.' It must always have been difficult to be quite sure that Dalí was not being serious when sending up even himself, or not sending up what he appeared to take seriously.

In 1935, Dalí employed me on Eluard's recommendation, to translate the twenty-five-page essay *La Conquête de l'irrationel*.* Every day for about a week I sat at a table in his rue Gauget studio wrestling with this task, with the aid of occasional explanations from the author or, more often, from Gala, whose French was much easier to understand. The room was full of objects, paintings and an easel was behind my back, but a long, narrow mirror at my feet enabled to observe whatever went on in it.

Dalí in those days had not yet fully developed his magisterial later persona, though his moustache was already impressive, and at lunch the maid would regularly be sent out to find a replacement for the baguette of bread, which was never sufficiently long.

During the week I was there he had matters of business which kept him away from home, but whenever he had time to spare he would resume work on his current canvas. I was thus privileged to witness something of the outwardly calm frenzy with which he attacked the work in hand. Sometimes screwing a magnifying lens in one eye, sometimes using a brush with only three hairs, he became transformed into an intensely absorbed extension of his hand, completely oblivious of my presence or of any other distraction whatever. The passion that possessed him then must have been at the core of the incredible energy that kept him going throughout all the years of his subsequent fame, when his public life was a continual circus, and his flabbergasting turnout never diminished.

Such was the energy that must have been at the root of the resilience that kept him alive after the tragedy of Gala, finally estranged in her separate tower, and helped him survive so long the disastrous fire at the castle at Púbol in August 1984.

---

* Editor's note: 'Conquest of the Irrational', translated by Gascoyne, published 20 July 1935 by Julien Levy (New York).

EILEEN AGAR

It can have surprised few who knew the painter Eileen Agar to learn that she came from an unusually cosmopolitan background.

Her father was a prominent member of the British business community that dominated Buenos Aires society at the end of the last century. His firm manufactured agricultural machinery, in particular the windmills on which Argentinian irrigation once depended; his American wife was heiress to a biscuit-making concern. Their three daughters soon came to be known as *Tres Cosas Buenas* after a brand of biscuit particularly popular at the time. Eileen and her sisters shared a happy childhood in comfortable circumstances which included frequent ocean crossings to visit family and friends in England.

By the time Eileen was sent with one of her sisters to her first school at Canford Cliffs in Dorset, the Agar family had begun to spend most of its time on this side of the Atlantic, with a London house in Belgrave Square and a manse for autumns in Scotland in which to pursue a social round of entertaining, tennis, golf and bridge. At Heathfield, near Ascot, Eileen's second school, her art teacher, the RA Lucy Kemp-Welch, a favourite painter of farm-horses and ponies in the Edwardian era, recognized her as specially gifted and told her she should always have something to do with Art. After 1914, the Agar girls attended a third school, Tudor Hall, in Kent, and before the end of the war Eileen Agar was attending a finishing school to perfect her French and take lessons in the use of oil paints at the Byam Shaw School of Art in Kensington. Before going on to study under Tonks at the Slade, she went for a while to classes at Leon Underwood's studio, Brook Green, where she became friendly with Gertrude Hermes, Blair Hughes-Stanton, D. H. Lawrence's step-daughter Barbara Weekley and an American who was later to introduce her to Joseph Bard, the most important man in her life.

Eileen Agar last saw Argentina when she went back to celebrate her twenty-first birthday with a grand party at Buenos Aires' Hurlingham Club. She returned to study part-time at the Slade, and make the acquaintance of such fellow students as Oliver Messel, Cecil Beaton and Rex Whistler. Their less well-known contemporary Robin Bartlett, however, provided Agar with more satisfying companionship, and while

---

Obituary in *The Independent* (19 November 1991).

on holiday with him and her family on the Isle of Wight he became her lover. Her determination to go and live with him provoked a row with her conventional socialite mother, as a result of which she left home for good.

After leaving the Slade in 1924, and having travelled with Bartlett in France and Spain for a while, the following year Agar agreed to marry him. Neither of her parents attended the Chelsea wedding, and shortly after it her father died of cancer, leaving her £1,000 a year. Financial independence did not, however, allay her growing disillusionment with her marriage, which was virtually over within a year. Not until meeting Joseph Bard in 1926 did Agar realize that she had never been in love before.

At the time of their auspicious first encounter, Joseph Bard was embroiled in a foundering marriage with Dorothy Thompson, a forceful American journalist who later became the wife of Sinclair Lewis. He was a good-looking, charming Hungarian writer, conversant with every aspect of European culture. The moment of his settling into a ménage with Agar in Fitzroy Square in 1927 coincided with her discovery of her true individual vein as a painter. Bard exerted no direct influence on her artistic development but her creativity was continually stimulated by her relationship with him. There can be no doubt that the two most important factors in Agar's life were Joseph Bard and, later, Surrealism.

During their early years together, Agar and Bard often went abroad, living at times in Italy, at others in Paris, the South of France and the Basque country. At Rapallo they were befriended by Ezra Pound, and through him met Yeats, Osbert Sitwell, Adrian Stokes and other visitors to the region in a Paris gallery. André Breton introduced Agar to Paul Eluard: none of them could have had any idea that one day she would be among the exhibitors in an important international exhibition of Surrealism in London. In Menton before the end of the decade, Alec Waugh and his younger brother Evelyn began to take an interest in Agar and her companion.

When Bard began to be published in England, he decided to settle permanently in this country. By 1930, he and Agar had moved into flats in the same building in Bramham Gardens, Earl's Court. From about this time, Agar's friends included Julian Trevelyan, Paul Nash and Henry Moore, who in 1933 persuaded her to exhibit with the London Group. Her painting had by now become almost entirely two-dimensional, the representational element reduced to fluent outlines suggestive of figures and natural objects. A summer spent at Swanage with Paul Nash drawing inspiration from rock-forms and driftwood had stimulated her to create poetic objects. Her studio-apartment at Bramham Gardens, centred round a remarkably elaborate clock designed by her architect friend Rodney Thomas, became a sort of grotto-bower, full of cunningly juxtaposed objects, and adorned with fishing-net and rope. It was here that early in 1936 Roland Penrose and Herbert Read came to select three of her paintings and five objects to be shown at the International Surrealist Exhibition that opened at the New Burlington Galleries in June of that year. A chapter-heading in Agar's *A Look at My Life* asks 'Am I a Surrealist?', indicating that she did not apply for association with the movement, but was spontaneously adopted by it.

The first item listed in the New Burlington Galleries' catalogue was Agar's *Quadriga*, inspired by a photograph of a horse's head on the Parthenon, according to the artist, who explained: 'One horse's head became four ghost heads, agitated, beating rhythmic cabalistic convoluted signs expressing movement and anxiety, each square a different mood. Were they the four horses of the Apocalypse?' This work, in effect a powerful mid-twentieth century mandala (symbol of the universe), now belongs to the Tate Gallery's permanent collection.

Another Agar work to be found in the same collection is the head known as *Angel of Anarchy*, originally featured in the London Gallery's 1937 Exhibition of Surrealist Objects and Poems and reproduced on the cover of its catalogue, but subsequently lost: in 1940 Agar recreated a more flamboyant second version featuring embroidered fabrics, feathers, fur and a head-dress of beads and shells reminiscent of African fetish objects, and added a blindfold to symbolize what she then saw as the uncertain future of mankind.

The entry devoted to her in the official *Dictionnaire Général du Surréalisme et de ses environs* adjudges that rather than in Agar's more decorative paintings it is in her collages and objects that 'un esprit surréaliste à l'accent ludique' is most happily to be found embodied. The playful element most obviously apparent in her best-known work is nevertheless counterbalanced by the underlying sense of malaise that produced her apocalyptic horses and blindfold anarchic head. In 1949, Agar's Hanover Gallery show was reviewed by Geoffrey Grigson, one of the most exigent and shrewd appreciators of modern British art, who wrote: 'The paintings attack, they do not wait for an introduction, neither are they mean, timid or indecisive.'

At the beginning of the war, Agar and Bard got married. In 1975 they moved from Bramham Gardens to West House, Melbury Road, on the south side of Holland Park. Though Bard never produced anything as significant as the study of *The Mind of Europe* he had planned in his youth, in later life he became a familiar figure at meetings of PEN International and the RSL. After his death, Agar wrote: 'Joseph was the warmth of my life for nearly 50 years . . . I would never have chosen a different husband.'

Bard was a gregarious, talkative and usually high-spirited companion. Despite his love of England, he was nevertheless an exile at heart, who never ceased to mourn the passing of the kind of culture epitomized by Freud, Leo Frobenius, Karl Kraus and Oskar Kokoschka. He was able to camouflage his melancholy side with the aid of Agar's unfailing vivacity and readiness to share his widely-ranging interests. She specially appreciated his occasional propensity for the sardonic. At the end of her life, she wrote: 'For true sociability, being agreeable is not enough. Joseph was a master of true sociability.'

Agar also wrote; 'Musing about my life in the late 1980s, I wonder at my own energy. I see myself hailing innumerable taxis and being driven to Soho or the East End, to galleries or dinner parties.' In 1988, friends of all ages, old and new, found her dominating with apparently unabated energy the private view of her work at the now unfortunately liquidated Birch and Conran Gallery in Dean Street, Soho. The liveliness of the canvases surrounding her was enhanced by her use of the acrylic paints she had begun to favour in 1965. On this occasion she presented me with a copy of her autobiography, then just out, *A Look at Myself*, in which I was charmed to discover an account of Dylan Thomas and myself dropping in uninvited on a party at Bramham Gardens as long ago as 1934. In the photo on the cover of the book Agar is shown looking out with typical curiosity through a magnifying glass at her interlocutor/reader, wearing a black dress printed with random white numerals. I still have a vivid memory of her in 1937 with Joseph at a dinner party, which also included Stephen Potter and the Farjeons, in a Chelsea apartment overlooking the Thames, at which Agar was wearing a dress distinguished by having *AMOUR* printed all over it.

Some time ago Eileen Agar discovered that despite initial nervousness and lack of enthusiasm she rather enjoyed making an occasional appearance on television. Already in 1948 she appeared on the small screen wearing a *Ceremonial Hat for Eating Bouillabaisse*, while in the mid-1980s she charmed the audience at one of Jonathan Ross's chat shows. It is much to be hoped that the BBC will show a repeat of the *Omnibus* documentary devoted to her career.

PL EDITIONS AND GRAHAM SUTHERLAND

Before the end of the 1939-45 war Geoffrey Grigson had inaugurated with *The Poet's Eye* a series of anthologies with unifying themes illustrated by contemporary artists; and after the war, Faber's *Ariel* series of pamphlets containing a single poem appropriately illustrated continued to appear. Tambimuttu, however, probably deserves to be credited with having been the first editor since Harold Monro of the Poetry Bookshop to promote collaboration between poets and artists. In 1943 he was responsible for the publication of collections by Kathleen Raine, Nicholas Moore and myself, illustrated by Barbara Hepworth, Lucian Freud and Graham Sutherland respectively.

When, after accepting my *Poems 1937-1942* for publication by PL Editions (Nicholson and Watson), Tambi asked me if there were any particular modern artist I should like to have the book illustrated by, I immediately thought of Graham Sutherland. Not only had I seen the two paintings he had contributed to the International Surrealist Exhibition of 1936, I had more recently had several times occasion to look at *Entrance to a Lane*,* a work of his that had been acquired early in the war by my friend Peter Watson, then installed in an apartment in Kensington which contained part of his collection. I asked Peter with some diffidence whether he thought Sutherland might find my poetry of sufficient interest to make him consent to illustrating it. Peter then sent a typescript of my poems to Sutherland at the White House in Trottiscliffe, Kent, which long continued to be his English address. Before long we learnt that he would indeed be willing to provide a certain number of illustrations for my book.

During the months that Graham Sutherland spent preparing his designs at intervals between his regular output of paintings, I went down to Trottiscliffe to meet him and his wife Kathy. They were reassuringly kind and understanding, and we made friends at once. I found Graham a quiet man, both warm and reserved, obviously possessed of a faith which found an affinity with something expressed in my poetry, though

---

Tambimuttu: Bridge Between Two Worlds, ed. Jane Williams (Peter Owen, 1989), pp. 112-18.

* Editor's note: *Entrance to a Lane* (1939) and D.G.'s poem of the same name appeared on facing pages of the Tate Gallery anthology, *With a Poet's Eye*, in 1986.

he seemed unwilling to discuss this explicitly. In fact, I think the kind of understanding we came to regarding the nature of the illustrations must have been essentially non-verbal.

In the end, eight designs by Sutherland were used for the book which Tambi first published in his PL Editions series in 1943. The front cover shows four peaks transpierced by a stylus or pen against a fiery background; while the back cover design represents three large moths against a lunar circle, evidently inspired by one of the five poems 'From the French of Pierre Jean Jouve' contained in the second section, a version of Jouve's 'Les papillons' (from *Matière céleste*, 1936). It is unlikely that Graham was familiar with the original French text, and I did not explain to him that I had taken a certain liberty in entitling my translation 'The Moths': though moths may sometimes be referred to as *papillons de nuit*, the proper term for them is *phalènes*. But because it is widely supposed that moths have a strong sexual connotation for the unconscious, especially in the female mind, and the imagery and content of the poem are of so unmistakably sexual a nature, I felt that moths were more likely to be the subject of the poem rather than butterflies, traditionally associated with Psyche and the discarnate soul. The third design is for the title-page, which is handwritten in black on three white insets against a soot-black ground. My name is written in what appears to be a tidied-up version of my actual signature, though without the Greek Ɛ I picked up in youth from an admired schoolmaster. My handwriting had by that time become unnaturally florid, under the influence an increasing use of Benzedrine was beginning to exert over me. Whether the Sutherlands ever suspected that I was daily using an amphetamine, still at that time a perfectly legal and easily obtainable substance, I never knew, but it would not surprise me to learn that they did surmise something of the kind.

The remaining five designs correspond to the five main groups into which the collection is divided. The first comprises the sequence of eight poems entitled *Miserere*, and Sutherland wrote this word across a blank space at the foot of an otherwise black, red and whitish composition suggestive of an imaginary landscape as it might have appeared at the moment of the rending of the veil of the temple, over which floats a celestial orb with a sorrowful eye and streaming three trails reminiscent of those of the comet in the Bayeux tapestry, which may have been inspired by the 'stricken sun' incapable of regeneration referred to in 'Tenebrae', with which the sequence opens, or the 'netherworld's/Dead sun' in 'Ex Nihilo'. It is forty-five years since I saw the originals of Graham's illustrations, but from my copy of the 1948 reprint of the book it is clear that coloured chalk as well as gouache and inks were used in their execution. The title illustration of the second section, designated *Metaphysical* (a term I had at one time thought of changing to *Metapsychological*), is to me the most mysterious of the set. It obviously represents a being, and just as obviously one of a supernatural order. There is nothing about it to suggest a phantom. It has no wings and so is unlikely to belong to the host of angels, though in a poem entitled 'The Descent' belonging to that part of the book there is an allusion to 'that Angel's eye'. On the right side of the page the figure's arm is swathed in broad, cape-like drapery, the white tinge of which merges into descending folds of grey, balanced on the left by a small greyish cone that looks as though it might be a cuff. But the most cryptic thing about it is that its head has no face or features, but resembles a visor without perforations for the eyes, surmounted by what at first sight appear to be four plumes. The breast or chest below the head tapers to an impossibly slender waist. If one knows that Graham Sutherland was a Roman Catholic, prolonged contemplation leads to the irresistible conclusion that the image might have derived from the Sacred Heart of popular pietist iconography, for the plumes could well be transmuted flames, appearing against a pink-tinged sky. I have always found this quasi-Surrealist apparition deeply impressive, and at least in its inscrutability appropriate to the subliminal depths the poems it precedes were intended to invoke.

The third and central section of the collection is occupied by a five-part poem originally written in English soon after the death of Alban Berg in 1935, then entirely rewritten in French during the summer of 1939, after my return earlier that year from Paris, where I had been living since 1937. Three of the subtitles of *Strophes élégiaques à la mémoire d'Alban Berg* are borrowed from movements of the composer's *Lyric Suite* for String Quartet; and two lines in the third part, 'Intermezzo', are borrowed from a poem in Baudelaire's *Le Vin* sequence, set by Berg in Stefan George's translation as an aria with orchestral accompaniment. Sutherland's illustration portrays, in the lowest third of the page, a shrouded reclining figure, 'watchful in the grave of time. . . .' Above him are placed two apparently fractured stones, the one on the left inscribed with the word ELEGIAC. Above them float a number of curved black and grey forms that cannot be specifically identified but are clearly related to the horned or thorny configurations which form a recurring part of Sutherland's pictorial repertory from 1937/8 until the end of his life.

A striking amalgamation of horns and thorns with an amorphous human figure with arm raised as in quest furnishes the motif of the sub-title page headed 'Personal'. This image prefigures Sutherland's exploration of emblems and the emblematic undertaken immediately after he had completed illustrating my poems. It may be understood as a visual metaphor representing the labyrinthine path of one both on the horns of a dilemma and preoccupied with a thorn in the flesh. If thorns are a theme anticipating numerous future works, the standing forms of the twin monoliths which are the subject of the plate illustrating the concluding section, *Time and Place*, are to be found in various forms in a great many later works, and also look back to certain early records of neolithic monuments. These seemingly rock-hewn forms each taper to a narrow base; their wider tops are pierced by crescent-shaped holes through which are to be seen, like eyes, to the left the moon in its last quarter, to the right the sun, shown once more in a 'stricken' aspect. Between them, lower down, appears a curious small form that can scarcely be described even as anthropomorphic, though it seems to have twisted arms and legs. The poems of this last section reflect civilian experience of the early years of the war. A certain affinity may be discerned in the last of Sutherland's illustrations to *Poems 1937-1942* with some of the wartime paintings of Paul Nash: the chalky quality of a dead moon, the desolation of Nash's dead sea of crashed planes.

In the collection of the Graham and Kathleen Sutherland Foundation at Picton Castle, Dyfed, there are a number of illustrations to *Poems 1937-1942* that were not used in the book as it was eventually published. Three of them are reproduced (in black and white) in Roberto Sanesi's 1979 study, *Graham Sutherland*,[1] all described as illustrations to 'Poems' by David Gascoyne, 1942, and as being 17 x 13 cm in dimension; but one of these is mistakenly identified, as it contains a number of words quoted from a seventeenth-century metaphysical text I am unable exactly to identify, and the other two are evidently abandoned *ébauches*. One of these has 'Metaphysical II' written on the top right-hand corner, though it has no resemblance to the enigmatic supernatural figure referred to earlier, but appears to be a faceless standing form culminating in an enormous mouth uttering what may be flames being breathed out towards a dim winged creature. The other bears simply the date 1942 and consists of a black lower band surmounted by a disorganized mineralogical landscape of unfinished, contrastingly dark and light shapes, above which appear a faint indication of a disc and what may be a preliminary version of a moth.

In the previous paragraph I alluded to Sutherland's period of interest in emblems and the emblematic. At this period of my life I had become an avid collector of a variety of types of second-hand books. In the small shop of a refugee art-book dealer in Cecil Court next to Watkins, I one day

---

[1] Centro d'Arte/Zarathustra (Italy), 45 pp. Italian text with English translation, 199 illustrations, 22 colour plates.

came across and immediately acquired a number of remarkable plates from a dismembered seventeenth-century emblem book, probably Dutch. This led me on to form a small collection of examples of the genre, in which poems are printed facing often quite elaborate emblematic designs, sometimes by curiously gifted graphic artists. The best-known English poet to have had his poems, loosely to be characterized as 'devotional', illustrated in this way is Francis Quarles. At the time immediately after the publication of my *Poems*, the idea of illustrated anthologies began to appeal to certain publishers, despite wartime printing difficulties. I succeeded in compiling an anthology to be called *Emblems and Allegories*, and the work of Quarles was naturally prominent among the numerous poets I drew on for examples in my assembly. Originally I think my idea was principally to demonstrate that – though there was never in England a school of symbolist poetry as significant as that of late nineteenth-century France, or that could accurately be described as such – one could show how symbolism of the emblematic and allegorical type had played a considerable role in the development of English poetry. On one of my visits to Trottiscliffe, I took the typescript of this anthology and a copy of Quarles's Emblems with me to show to Graham. He at once became keenly interested in the field, and before long produced a number of illustrations, particularly of Quarles, not many of which I actually saw at the time. Some of them have occasionally been published in catalogues and reviews, particularly in one issue of Tambi's *Poetry (London)* magazine.*

During the period when I got to know Graham and Kathy Sutherland, being unfit for military service I managed to obtain employment as a professional actor, adopting the pseudonym David Emery after my mother's maiden stage-family name, and for a year toured the country with the Coventry Repertory Company, playing in farce for ENSA. One week we found ourselves quartered in Tunbridge Wells. While there we had a day or two off for some reason, and while roaming the town I came across a fishmonger's offering a large, rare and delicious fish, probably rainbow trout, at what seemed a bargain price, and impulsively bought it. At a loss to know what to do with the delicacy, but knowing that Trottiscliffe was within easy distance and that Kathy Sutherland was a most excellent cook, I rang up Graham and announced that I should be arriving at the White House before long with a surprise. On reaching the Sutherlands', however, I found that my piscine present was not welcomed with the degree of enthusiasm that I had imagined the era of strict rationing might have induced. Kathy Sutherland was a very organized

---

* Editor's note: Vol. 2, No. 9.

housekeeper who did not, I think, care to have her schedule unexpectedly altered. Both she and Graham were otherwise, however, as kindly welcoming as usual, and I think enjoyed the fish as much as I did in the end. The incident was no doubt mainly the result of my having become by that time largely dependent on Methedrine, one of whose effects on me was to stimulate the indulgence of unpredictable whims. Soon after the war I had a brief meeting with the Sutherlands in a Knightsbridge flat, during which Kathy, recalling this episode, confirmed my impression that, though tolerant of eccentricity, she did not really care for it beyond the point at which it becomes downright abnormality.

The last occasion of meeting the Sutherlands that I clearly remember took place in 1950 in Venice. I spent a couple of months there that summer, having received a generous travelling grant from the writer known as Bryher, daughter of a shipping magnate millionaire. At the end of my stay I found myself the guest for a week of Peggy Guggenheim, with whom I had a friend or two in common, at her Canal Grande truncated palazzo. During my stay there, Graham and Kathy Sutherland were visiting one of his dealers in a pleasant, less palatial apartment on the opposite side of the Canal, and Peggy asked me to accompany her when she was invited there one evening to dinner. Though our host may have wondered how I had managed to inveigle my way into high café society, the Sutherlands betrayed to me no sign of such speculation, albeit I was then still inclined to be paranoid on account of the after-effects of abusing amphetamines (which by now had fortunately become much more difficult to obtain). Graham's picture dealer, by the way, came later to a sadly unfortunate end.

From the mid-1950s till the mid-1960s I became increasingly incapable of producing a single satisfactory line of poetry; even postcards to my family required considerable effort, let alone letters even to close friends. I was extremely fortunate at this time to become the house guest at Aix-en-Provence and in Paris of a painter, widow of a painter, to pay tribute to whom this would be an inappropriate place. During these years I was still suffering from the after-effects on the central nervous system of prolonged dependence on amphetamines, and continuing to use a mild compound known as Maxiton, then still freely available in French pharmacies. But even more than this I was suffering from guilt at not having written enough to justify my thinking of myself to be specially gifted, and from a badly damaged self-esteem. Though my hostess had a Peugeot and enjoyed driving about Provence with me, and though I am sure the Sutherlands would have enjoyed meeting her as well as been welcoming to me had I ever suggested that we should drive over to see them at their Riviera studio and home, it never seriously occurred to me to make any effort to bring this about. I regret this all the more now that I know that Graham's regard for my poetry cannot have evaporated, as I thought it must have done, over the years, since proof to the contrary is provided by the fact that he continued to produce designs in illustration of them, such as the 'Inferno' with the text in his own hand, reproduced on a folding sheet in *Poetry London/Apple Magazine*, Vol. I, No. 1 (Autumn 1979). By that date I was beginning to recover from the last of the three serious mental breakdowns that had resulted from the long, apparently hopeless period of my non-productivity; but even then my reaction to this extraordinarily fascinating pictorial comment (dated 1978) on the experience of inner emptiness, so widespread nowadays, seems to me today to have been incredibly numb. Now that Jane Williams has brought to light still further proof, with the design found among the many papers and manuscripts Tambimuttu left behind when he died, which appears to have been intended to illustrate such a poem of mine as 'Mountains'* (belonging to the *Metaphysical* section of my *Poems 1937-1942*), I intensely regret that neither Graham nor Tambi are here any longer to receive from me some living sign of my gratitude for their continued faith in me and my work, now that I have fully recovered a normal degree of self-confidence.

---

* Editor's note: Reproduced in illustration on p. 76 of *Tambimuttu: Bridge Between Two Worlds*.

LAWRENCE DURRELL

When Cyril Connolly, Henry Miller and Lawrence Durrell were first published in Paris by the Obelisk Press in the mid-1930s, Connolly told Miller that I was a young English Surrealist. Miller then sent me a proof copy of 'Open Letter to Surrealists Everywhere'; and when in the late summer of 1937, having settled into a Paris garret, I went to see Miller in his Villa Seurat atelier, he at once introduced me to the 25-year-old Durrell, just back from Corfu and the most ardent admirer of Miller, whom he had not yet known long.

Within a month, Durrell had allowed me to read a typed copy of *The Black Book* completed in Greece earlier that year. The letter I subsequently wrote to him appears as an entry in the journal I was keeping at that time (published in 1978 with a generous introduction by Durrell himself). In it I tried to tell him how much 'the simple fact of having read your wonderful objectivization of the universal spiritual squalor and disintegration of the inhabitants of the British Isles' had helped me to realize that it was exactly from what in his book he termed the English Death that I was then struggling to free myself. From that time I tended to identify myself more and more with what Durrell had expressed in a few sentences on the last page of his first serious book:

> To be or not to be. It is in your capacity as Judas that you have chosen for me. The question has been decided. Art must no longer exist to depict man, but to invoke God. It is on the face of this chaos that I brood.

Yet, since another of the voices in *The Black Book* declares flippantly, 'Metaphysics is the refuge of the actor,' a point of view perfectly in accord with that of erstwhile logical positivists, I might well be justly accused of perverting Durrell's central preoccupation in his youth by using the previous quotation to present him as a God-seeker, ripe for some sort of conversion. Any reader of his later novels will know that nothing could be further from the most obvious truth about their author. It can nevertheless be maintained that, though his was probably one of the most sophisticated intelligences of his generation, he was from the

---

Obituary in *The Independent* (10 November 1990).

start concerned above all with the spiritual condition of nihilistically-inclined twentieth-century man.

When *Justine* first appeared in 1957, a few weeks after we had exchanged visits in Provence, he sent me a dedicated copy. I went on, as did innumerable fascinated readers in many languages, to absorb the whole of *The Alexandria Quartet*, generally considered his greatest and most satisfying achievement. In it he was at last able to embody his rich cosmopolitan experience, his insights into the psychology of sex, pain and death, and his mordant wit, and from then on to earn a comfortable living free of financial care. Never a hedonist of the kind he sometimes lovingly depicted, he never allowed fame and success to affect his spontaneously generous and questing disposition.

Among his friends and all who knew him, Larry Durrell's loyalty and generosity must long have been legendary. I have space to cite only one personal instance of his kindness. During the first winter of our acquaintance, I had so little money that I began to depend on almost daily midday meals with him and his first wife, Nancy, at their Parc Montsouris flat, and was thus saved from falling a prey to serious under-nourishment. These occasions were almost always accompanied by endless conversation as we had found we shared many other than literary interests, but above all, the ambition to become European rather than 'parochial' writers. In those days, too, we were seeing a number of mutual friends as well as Henry Miller and, eventually, Anaïs Nin, to both of whom Larry had become particularly close. (Larry and I began at this time to appear in Anaïs's already mythical diary, he much more favourably and for longer than I; but that is another story.)

Before 1939, Durrell would often tell me that I could have no idea of how wonderful life could be until I had known the Mediterranean, and would even invite me to stay at his family's Corfu home, though in those days I could never have afforded the fare. After that, on account of his postings in Egypt, Buenos Aires, Belgrade and Cyprus, we might have lost touch with one another completely; yet whenever chance brought us together again, though briefly, he would at once renew the warmth of our friendship as though we had last seen each other only a week ago.

Though no doubt it is as a novelist and travel writer that Lawrence Durrell will be best remembered, I have always thought of him as first of all a poet, and know that his paramount ambition was to be considered a good one. As to his not being usually regarded as such by most of his readers, I have heard him declare: 'If Eliot and George Seferis can recognize and appreciate the quality of my poetry, that is enough for me.' Recent criticism has tended to be dismissive of such a work as *The Black Book*, to which *The Oxford Companion to English Literature*, for instance, refers as 'a mildly pornographic fantasia, peopled by prostitutes and failed artists', thus ignoring the exceptional vitality, virtuosity and zest of its language – in other words the first sound of his real voice, as he himself later described it.

This 'angry young man' of the Thirties was in fact a born poet. It is startling now to realize that Durrell's *Collected Poems* were first published by Faber as long ago as 1960 and the completely revised edition already thirteen years ago. Though without doubt his best poetry was written before he was forty, I hope there will be at least a small posthumous collection to add to the main corpus. Though he liked to deny it, he continued to write poems occasionally in private notebooks, probably to the end. He was resigned to his poetic voice's having been ousted by that of his abundant prose, of which the most recent example is *Caesar's Vast Ghost*, but he must nevertheless have regretted it. Of his light verse, at least 'The Ballad of the Good Lord Nelson' must be destined to certain immortality. Yet there are many beautiful poems inspired by Greece, love and children, that should find a place in any decent future anthology. One uncollected poem of which I have a typescript is entitled 'Omega Grey', a significant title in view of the footnote explaining it: 'Omega Grey is a naval paint used as a camouflage; it is the deepest shade before absolute black.' It is dedicated to 'H.M.', and it would be surprising if these initials did not stand for Henry Miller. Absolute black is suggestive of the dominant tonality of the later *Avignon Quintet*, in which contemporary Albigensian Manicheans, convinced that the world is completely in the power of 'Monsieur', the evil Demiurge, secretly assist one another to commit suicide and thus escape further bondage to him.

In 1984, Durrell was on a rare visit to the French capital from Sommières, his long-time last residence, nearer to Nîmes than to Avignon and not in the supposedly decadent orbit of the latter city. I had just arrived in Paris with my wife at the end of a tour of five university cities, and was delighted to succeed in fixing a rendezvous with my old friend at the Coupole. We found at that favourite resort of far-off times, not only Larry, whom my wife had been longing to meet, but Miller's ancient friend Fred Perlès with his Scottish wife. For a moment it seemed not impossible that Miller, Anaïs and other contributors to their little mag *The Booster* might come breezing in. Larry told my wife: 'If that old bugger your husband won't write a poem to you, then I'll do it myself.' And this despite his then being strictly on the wagon for a while because of his already declining health. (Such abstinence could not have lasted for long. Durrell's capacity for holding his liquor was prodigious. He seemed able to put away quarts of wine and spirits without ever becoming offensive or quite out of control.)

When I was lucky enough at the end of November 1989 to pay a last weekend visit to him and his devoted final companion Françoise at Sommières we found him quietly serene, as comic and amiable as ever, happy among a large group of local friends gathered for a Sunday lunch that went on till after dark. He had found that drinking white wine from dawn till dinner combined with the practice of Zen meditation and mild indoor exercise could keep him happy and the growing shades at bay. 'If you but knew,' cried Mephisto in his own version of the legend, *An Irish Faustus*, 'the loneliness, the spleen, the boredom.' 'Come here and take my hand, poor fellow bondsman,' Faust replies. The play these lines come from was first published in 1973. Between then and the end of his life, thanks greatly to Françoise, the shade of his Mephisto was laid to rest.

GEORGE BARKER

GEORGE BARKER AT SEVENTY

Towards the end of a poem that George Barker wrote as a 'nosegay' for my sixty-fifth birthday [1981] occurs the line: 'and now, I think, you know that all thought is illusion'. If I properly understand these words, I believe they are true. When Robert Fraser wrote asking me to contribute to this Barker supplement of *P.N. Review*, he suggested that I discuss the significance I feel Barker's presence has had for my own work and for my generation; later in his letter he referred to a derogatory remark I once made, in my 'intimate' *Journal* for 1938, to an essay by Barker that had just appeared in *The Criterion* and to his then recent collection *Calamiterror*. I can disclaim as much incompetence as inclination to assess George Barker's poetry from an academically literary point of view. What I once thought of *Calamiterror* has no longer even marginal relevance. I was then only twenty-one and predictably brash, reacting, I hope without jealousy, to what at that time struck me as George's tendency towards a type of poetic rhetoric that ran counter to, or provided a substitute for, the kind of thought that – as he rightly wrote in that 'nosegay' – I now realize to be in a sense an illusion.

I can truthfully say that never, since the appearance of *Thirty Preliminary Poems* in 1933, have I been consciously influenced in my own writing by Barker's poetry, though I have constantly felt that, though what I was trying to write myself was of a somewhat different order, we were both fundamentally companions on the same journey.

What is my generation? Approximately that of those born between 1914 and 1924. More than half of the members of that generation whom I once knew are now dead. One of the things I most envy about George is the way he succeeded in commemorating, in words that will undoubtedly endure, a significant number of our mutual friends, about whom I too would willingly have written had I been able, feeling as I do that the Elegy represents one of the most permanently valuable types of poetry

---

Obituaries in *The Independent* (29 October 1991) and *The Tablet* (1 November 1991), and *George Barker at Seventy* in *P.N. Review* 31, Vol. 9, No. 5 (1983), pp. 59-60, collected in *The Fire of Vision*, ed. and intro. Roger Scott (privately printed for Alan Clodd, 1996).

that can be perpetrated. I am grateful to George for having written so generously and vividly about various figures worthy of remembrance and of posterity, such as David Archer, the Scots painters Colquhoun and MacBryde, their mentor Jankel Adler, Michael Roberts, Randall Swingler, Eliot, MacNeice, Tom Blackburn and, of course, Dylan ('the one undoubting Thomas'). I can claim to have met George's mother, the inspirer of one of his most popular poems, and to have known at one time or another many members of his unusually large family. But to return for a moment to the page in *Paris Journal* referred to by Robert Fraser: how I wish that he had remembered a quotation earlier in the same entry from a letter from our close friend the late Antonia White, 'Barker sends his love'.

In Joseph Chiari's *T. S. Eliot: A Memoir* (Enitharmon) I came across this sentence: 'To write about a friend or about myself is as alien to me as it was to Eliot, who shared Pascal's view that *le moi est haïssable* . . .' This remark makes me feel almost ashamed of my urge to note down a few incidents typical of my relationship with George Barker. Our first meetings in Holborn's war-destroyed Parton Street, for example; visiting Hampton Court with him on the eve of his departure just before the War to take up a teaching post in Japan; his patience with my occasionally dropping in on him, Elizabeth Smart and their first babies, often late at night, soon after he had returned during the War from America and was living in a flat in Hammersmith Terrace; a day spent with him in Surrey, near Elstead where my parents lived in retirement for a while, where he owned a cottage in the middle of a field overlooked by a hill surmounted by the house in which Tennyson spent his last days; his coming over to Aix-en-Provence during the time I was living in a friend's house there, and in the evening sharing with him the experience of a marvellous performance of *Don Giovanni* at the Aix Festival; making the fatal mistake in his company, late one evening at a tabac-restaurant on the Quai Voltaire in Paris, of washing down oysters with brandy; the remarkably pleasant experience of staying briefly with him during the hottest days of one of the finest summers since the War in his suitably noble and ramshackle home in Norfolk; the delight of finding him to be the only other British guest to have arrived at the riotous first International Poetry Festival of Rome . . . But I have neither time nor space to evoke the electric and hilarious nature of our conversation, disputes and gossip, and George's inexhaustible flow of verbal felicities and apocryphal anecdotes.

Glancing again through the pages of *Homage to George Barker* published ten years ago, I was interested to find two conflicting views of *The True Confession of George Barker*. Discussing George's bent towards what he legitimately categorizes as 'occasional poetry', Karl Miller observed that 'while *The True Confession* must be regarded as occasional . . . it's not a good example'. C. H. Sisson, on the other hand, had this to say: 'It is to the permanent shame of the publishers of the *Collected Poems 1930-1955* that they would not admit to that volume *The True Confession of George Barker* "which Mr Barker wished to include", as a footnote to the table of contents explains. It was to date and probably remains his best poem.' At the end of the same paragraph, Sisson significantly relates that on first meeting the poet, he realized that he 'was in the presence of a profound humorist'. I personally have never considered the so-called *True Confession* to be anything like Barker's best poem prior to or since 1955; in fact, I positively dislike it. The reasons which prevent me from finding it admirable have nothing in common with those apparently prurient ones which motivated disapproval in certain quarters. I dislike it not simply on the possibly inappropriate ethical ground that I do not consider it to be a 'true' *Confession*. I fail to appreciate it because, amusing though it may be as a diversion, it could lead some readers to form a false notion of Barker the man. I seriously consider it to amount to gross self-misrepresentation. Though I do not know whether the incidents narrated in it are accurately recorded, I can point out that these are editorially selected and presented, moreover, with 'morose delectation'. I believe the subject of the *Confession* is a much more admirably respectable character than the 'autobiographer' wishes us to credit him with being, even if genuine candour may not in this instance be one of the qualities that make him so. At the same time, I suspect that he may be reprehensible in ways quite other than those vaunted in too many of its stanzas. George's being the 'profound humorist' Charles Sisson observed him to be, and his aptitude to resort to the kind of Mask referred to in an essay by Patrick Swift, may be thought to go some way to explaining away what I most object to in this poem.

In *Homage to George Barker*, the essay which in my opinion displays the most percipient understanding of Barker is that by Patrick Swift. Swift links Barker unequivocally with European rather than insular tradition; St Augustine and Kierkegaard, for instance, are referred to, as are Baudelaire and Pierre Jean Jouve. Swift did not, as he might well have done, refer to another Christian apologist, Pascal, to whom – on account of the latter's leaning to Jansenism – Pierre Jean Jouve was (as Jean Starobinski suggested) probably closer than most orthodoxly Catholic French poets. Like Barker, Jouve was in any case *non-pratiquant*. But I have no desire to add here a redundant gloss on a comprehensive essay that is indispensable to any reader determined to get to the roots of Barker's poetry at its best. Barker has undoubtedly shared many of the sternest convictions of T. S. Eliot, once his mentor and the poet about whom he has written with as sympathetic an understanding as anyone of our generation. In the *True Confession*, George seemed to be out to demonstrate with gusto that for him the self was indeed hateful.

I agree with Paddy Swift that it is necessary to recognize the fundamentally Catholic outlook in Barker's most significant work. George will always appear to me as an almost archetypal Lapsed Catholic. If he suffers complexes, then one of them must surely be involved with the kind of guilt that is commonly associated with being such a one. This also means, I think, that he is intimately familiar with what was once known as the Agenbite of Inwit. The Irishness inherited from his mother is another factor that ought not to be ignored. Added to this, I should guess him to have been at least intermittently haunted by an unusually repellent vision of the Beast with Two Backs. But I only refer to these afflictions, if such indeed they be, in order the more to stress the triumphant assurance of his septuagenarian emergence.

I have never forgotten something George wrote to me in a letter of July 1939: 'Unfortunately I have to add that one is what the literati term a *powet*. This is so bloody embarrassing and inconvenient.' He has put up with this kind of embarrassment courageously and with cunning. It is probably not wholly unconnected with his suggestion to me that 'all thought is illusion'. To be thought too seriously thoughtful is a serious embarrassment to most Englishmen. Taken in isolation, that particular phrase seems to convey the result of some sort of variety of Zen Buddhist meditation, while clearly recognizing the illusory nature of the conclusions reached by pure and unaided ratiocination.

I recognize and salute in George Barker a poet whose work has never ceased to develop, who has been almost uninterruptedly prolific, whose themes have been basic and perennial, and who has remained faithful to his exceptional gift, enriching our language and literature to an extent that remains to be estimated. It would be a simple pleasure to enumerate those of his poems I most admire, or to compile a miniature anthology of my favourite lines; but such is the unified diversity of Barker's published poetry that every reader could do as much and in each case produce a different result. I would rather end by paying homage to the unique combination to be found in his work of a plangent music reminiscent of Dowland's with a remarkable range of imagery, concise *concetti* and fierce *fioretti*, resplendent, ominous, or both at once, forged out of an intense personal experience of our particularly 'hard times'. If one believes that this century has represented one unprecedentedly critical occasion, then Karl Miller was right when ten years ago he drew attention to the apparent predominance of 'the occasional' in Barker's work.

To illustrate this I go back to the most memorable of George's pre-1939 poems, 'Elegy on Spain', and adduce the following stanzas ('Dedication to the photograph of a child killed in an air raid on Barcelona') which remain as applicable to the pictures of massacred innocents in Beirut that have been inflicted on us of late as they were to victims of the Spanish tragedy in the 1930s:

> O ecstatic is this head of five-year joy –
> Captured in its butterfly rapture on a paper:
> And not the rupture of the right eye may
> Make any less this prettier than a picture.
> O now, my minor moon, dead as meat
> Slapped on a negative plate, I hold
> The crime of the bloody time in my hand.
>
> Light, light with that lunar death our fate;
> Make more dazzling with your agony's gold
> The death that lays us all in the sand.
> Gaze with that gutted eye on our endeavour
> To be the human brute, not the brute human:
> And if I wear your gaze upon me ever,
> I'll wear the robe of blood that love illumines.

There are many current definitions of poetry's purpose; but if one happens to believe that it is to bear witness to the inescapable nature of man's present predicament, while at the same time transfiguring the testimony by giving it utterance that can encourage such endurance as that defined by Barker in the second of these stanzas, then his poetry may be regarded as a vindication of the type of poetic enterprise that too often today tends to be regarded as portentously 'apocalyptic'. What it offers us, in fact, is authentic 'News of the World'.

OBITUARY IN *THE INDEPENDENT* (29 October 1991)

On 10 November 1990 *The Independent* published an obituary written by me on learning of the death of Lawrence Durrell. The night before last John Fairfax telephoned me to tell me that his uncle George Barker had just died. Two of the poets of my generation I most admired and to whom I felt closest have died within a year of each other.

On George's sixtieth birthday, Martin Brian & O'Keeffe published *Homage to George Barker* containing contributions from twenty poet and critic friends, some of them now dead. One of these, Paul Potts, a great frequenter, like George, of Soho/Fitzrovia in its heyday, described Dylan Thomas, George Barker and myself as the three major poets of his generation.

I have never much cared for majors, but concede that at one time it was a general tendency to link our three names together. After all we three had the same publisher, David Archer of the small Holborn-based Parton Press. George, who memorialized in elegy many of our mutual friends, dedicated more than one of his poems to David Archer, as he wrote poems to and about Eliot before and after his death.

In the 1973 *Homage* there are four pages by Karl Miller. He recalls having once quoted a comment, published in *Scrutiny*, in 1934, to the effect that George Barker's 'malady is an ingrowing soul; his virtue is that he has diagnosed it. His prescription is excess; he will rage himself out . . .' To have raged for more than sixty subsequent years, both in and out of print, is a remarkable record.

To diagnose George as an Excessive and student and veteran of catastrophe appears to me still remarkably apposite. George's constantly generous and encouraging attitude to the young, to tyro poets and students of his works, is illustrated by the anecdote with which Karl Miller concludes: 'A student was pouring out a bottle of beer for him, none too well. "Tilt it, boy. Tilt it," said George. "Tilt everything in life." ' The phrase 'dear boy' was addressed by George to friends and acquaintances, not indiscriminately, throughout his life. The words must surely bring back the sound of his voice to whoever had heard him use them.

My own memories of George are many and various: staying with him and his first wife Jessica in the mid-1930s in a cottage at Plush, near Piddletrenthide, in Dorset; a week before he had been visited there by Lady Ottoline Morrell, tipped off by Alida Monro as a young new lion for her then-declining coterie; saying goodbye to George at Hampton Court before his departure in 1939 to teach in Japan; George and Elizabeth Smart soon after their return from New York during the war; George in a small dwelling in the middle of a field near Petworth; George staying on the Riviera and coming over to Aix-en-Provence to accompany me to an open-air performance of Mozart's *Don Giovanni*; meeting George unexpectedly at the riotous first international Poetry Festival of Rome, actually at Ostia; reading with him, William Empson, W. S. Graham and others at the Queen Elizabeth Hall under the direction of Harold Pinter, who greatly admired him; and many other readings and festivals.

In 1983 Michael Schmidt's *P.N. Review* produced a special number in celebration of George at seventy, which included contributions by Michael Hamburger, Sebastian Barker, George MacBeth, David Wright and John Heath-Stubbs among others, including myself, at greater length than ten years previously, when all I could produce was an old poem. Referring to the occasions I have just evoked again, I wrote of being unable adequately 'to evoke the electric and hilarious nature of our conversation, disputes and gossip, and George's inexhaustible flow of verbal felicities and apocryphal anecdotes'. I ended by paying homage to 'the unique combination to be found in his work of a plangent music reminiscent of Dowland's with a remarkable range of imagery, concise *concetti* and fierce *fioretti*, resplendent, ominous, or both at once, forged out of an intense personal experience of our particularly "hard times".'

A year ago I was invited by the British Council in Madrid to take part in the ceremonial unveiling at the Residencia de Estudiantes of a plaque commemorating the death in the Spanish Civil War of six British poets and writers who went out to defend democracy against Franco. Having written no Spanish civil war poetry myself I had great satisfaction in reading the opening and concluding stanzas of George Barker's 'Elegy on Spain', perhaps the most memorable of all his pre-1939 poems.

OBITUARY IN *THE TABLET* (1 November 1991)

When I first met George Barker in 1933, I was unaware that he had already published a year previously in *The Twentieth Century* review an essay entitled 'Poetry and Contemporary Inertia' which began by observing 'By the phrase contemporary inertia I designate the condition which society today is lying in, an inability to originate a decisive movement into the future'. Barker was then nineteen. The somewhat older *New Signatures* triumvirate of Auden, Spender and Day Lewis were just emerging to express in their different ways a similar dissatisfaction with contemporary inertia. Barker's early essay went on to declare that 'the poet is a poet because he is aware that in him the community is identified and articulate. Thus poetry will cease to be vitiated by the liabilities of the individual, and will be simply elucidated by his personal disinterested obsession with words'. This declaration of sixty years ago still stands up today as evidence that Barker from the beginning embodied a poetic position as seriously responsible as that of any of his contemporaries or for that matter of most of the best known younger poets of today. What he referred to as the vitiating 'liabilities of the individual' have given rise in his case to much over-attention to his unusually eventful private life; but as long ago as 1937 Stephen Spender in an issue of *Left Review* perceived that he was not 'as absorbed in the private crisis of his own personality' as was frequently alleged.

Earlier this week, I wrote for the *Independent* in immediate reaction to the news of George Barker's death last Sunday a few personal reminiscences of our long friendship, and hurriedly referred to two compilations of tributes from his numerous friends and admirers published to honour both his 60th and his 70th birthdays, the latter marked by a special number of *P.N. Review* in 1983. Two articles, the first by the Irish painter Patrick Swift in the volume of *Homage to George Barker on his 60th birthday* produced in a limited edition in 1973 (with Swift's portrait of George as frontispiece), the second by Martin Jarrett-Kerr, C.R., in the *P.N. Review* of ten years later, go straight to what is to me also, though raised as a Protestant, the fundamental point to be made about Barker's work as a whole, in both poetry and prose, and that is that he is above all a religious poet, irreversibly influenced by a strict Catholic upbringing. The *Daily Telegraph*'s obituary on Tuesday laid stress on George's belief that 'the only subjects for poetry are death and sex', and referred to a rebellious strain of Roman Catholicism that may have led post-war critics to find his work lacking in social relevance. Any critic obtuse enough to maintain that his pre-war poetry lacked 'social relevance' could easily be confounded. In this century's last decade, when it is difficult to find among the intelligentsia any representative figure holding profound and genuine religious beliefs of any kind, let alone an understanding acceptance of the doctrine of original sin, the full weight of Barker's contribution to twentieth-century English literature cannot yet be expected to receive proper recognition. In his 1983 article for *P.N. Review*'s Barker number, entitled 'Priapus at Prayer' (*The Theological Inside of George Barker*), Martin Jarrett-Kerr maintains that 'Most of Barker's poems are prayers. Even (or especially) the blasphemous ones'. He also quotes what he describes as a squib of George's: 'All theological speculations aggrandise a God who, like a film star, can forgive everything save not being talked about', and comments: 'I'd like to see that pinned up in the Divinity Schools'. More importantly, this cleric observes: 'Barker may have been polyphiloprogenitive, but he deeply cares for his family and his children'. George came from a large, loving Catholic family, and gradually produced an even larger and quite as affectionate one of his own. He also produced two collections of poetry for children and an 'Alphabetical Zoo' which evince a deep love and understanding of children in general and are comparable to the best of de la Mare in the genre.

But as a study of Barker 'as a Catholic Christian, or as a romantic driven from the wilderness of his original position that is Catholic and

Christian', I personally find Patrick Swift's 'Prolegomenon to George Barker' in the 1973 festschrift by far the most literate and penetrating ever to have been devoted to the subject, and regret having no space left to quote from it further.

In the tribute to Barker at seventy that I contributed to *P.N. Review* eight years ago, there is a paragraph that begins: 'I have never forgotten something George wrote to me in a letter of July 1939: "Unfortunately I have to add that one is what the literati term a *power*. This is so bloody embarrassing and inconvenient." ' This was to me a pretty bloody embarrassing misprint. What George had written was a jokey misspelling of the term *poet*, with a 'w' in the middle. Long years after, I see that eventually George may be seen to have been indeed a power, like one of Shelley's legislators. A hundred years ago this month, the greatest rebel in modern literary history, Arthur Rimbaud, died in misery with an amputated leg in a Marseilles hospital, and was reported by his pious sister to have undergone a final reconversion to Catholicism. He had detested the literati of his time and eventually the calling of poet so much that in his early twenties he turned his back on poetry for ever and wanted never to have it talked about again. Fortunately for us, George endured the embarrassing inconvenience of fulfilling the gift he was born with for the rest of his life, and even got married a second time (to Elspeth Langlands, long-time companion and mother of many of his children) in a beautiful ceremony in the Catholic church of Sheringham on the coast near his Norfolk home. With white hair and a beard, once dashing and turbulent George was at last venerable and happy, and that must be how all who were there will most want to remember him.

4

REVIEWS

SOME RECENT ART EXHIBITIONS

At the Mayor Gallery there is now being shown a most interesting exhibition of paintings by modern Continental masters, most of them, I believe, from the collection of exiled Alfred Flechtheim, of Berlin. The list of artists represented is extensive. It contains Picasso, Braque, Juan Gris, Matisse, Derain, Léger, Lurçat, Masson, Chagall, de Chirico, Klee and Max Ernst. Most of the tendencies in present-day painting are to be found in the work of these artists. There are unfortunately no canvases by Marcoussis, Kandinsky, Dalí or Tchelitchew in the exhibition, but of course there is not enough room for every artist of note in the not very large Mayor Gallery.

In every collection of this kind Picasso seems to overshadow all the other artists about him. The secret of this virtuoso is ever a mystery: master of a score of styles, never since he started painting has he ceased to experiment, to change, chameleon-like, as soon as he has perfected one technique or manner. Dozens of Paris's petits-maîtres would never have existed without Picasso's ever-fertile invention to inspire them; they must find it difficult to keep up with him. Among the Picassos shown at this exhibition there are three extremely fine pictures which strikingly testify to the diversity of this artist's genius. There is a magnificent early Cubist period portrait, *La femme aux poires*, which is, like the *Dame jouant de la mandoline*, of which Wyndham Lewis writes in *The Caliph's Design*, 'a powerful and inventive variation on Cézanne'. *Harlequin*, a large, bright canvas that instantly demands attention, is closer to objective reality, in the manner of the portraits painted just after the War. The third, *Baigneuse*, is an example of the later Picasso, that is, the style of three-dimensional abstraction with which he made us familiar about 1929. This last it is not so easy to be enthusiastic about: I am inclined to believe that Picasso's search for aesthetic truth in this direction must be fruitless, even though he may bring all the resources of his perfect technique to bear upon his problem. But it is a problem that no living artist but Picasso is likely to solve.

Braque is the perfect colourist; he has achieved a super-refinement of colour; his sensibility has been cultivated to its furthest extreme. And

---

The New English Weekly (15 March 1934).

what else is there in his painting? After a time one is forced to the conclusion that Braque's mastery of colour and his technical brilliance cover the emptiness and the sterility that so many contemporary painters must arrive at sooner or later if they have not the indefinable quality of, say, a Picasso. Gris undoubtedly had this quality; it made him the most satisfying of all the Cubists. I do not believe that Derain possesses it; so often his painting is nothing more than a hollow display of virtuosity. Sometimes one feels the same thing about Matisse. Matisse, however, is represented by, among other, more formal pictures, one of his *fauve* landscapes, full of a wild vitality that reminds one of van Gogh.

HENRY MILLER

There are remarkably few writers at any time of whom it can be said that they write from the very bottom of their epoch and of themselves. Because they are so rare, we should greet their appearance with all the greater an enthusiasm; yet only too often they are met with a conspiracy of silence. This has so far been the case with Henry Miller, whose *Tropic of Cancer* (1934), and *Black Spring*, published last June, have received scarcely half a dozen mentions in the English press. No doubt this is partly due to the fact that these books have had to be published in Paris, by the Obelisk Press (which brought out a Continental edition of James Hanley's *Boy*, after that work had been so shamefully banned in England). Those who have had an opportunity of reading them are all the more responsible, therefore, for seeing that their importance is justly recognized.

Henry Miller is probably a little tired of being compared with Fernand Céline; yet it is only by referring the reader to the *Voyage au bout de la nuit* that one can indicate the particular quality of his writing. He has the same unbounded pessimism, the same catastrophic vision of a world stifling in disease and filth. He has not, however, the same acid and relentless bitterness as Céline, and is not in the least inhuman. And much as I admire the French writer, I believe that Miller's experience is a wider one. It is more generous, more varied, and more intensely lyrical. His lyricism is perhaps his most remarkable characteristic:

> One looks down from the Brooklyn Bridge on a spot of foam or a little lake of gasoline or a broken splinter or an empty scow; the world goes by upside down with pain and light devouring the innards, the sides of flesh bursting, the spears pressing in against the cartilage, the very armature of the body floating off into nothingness. Passes through you crazy words from the ancient world, signs and portents, the writing on the wall, the chinks of the saloon door, the card-players with their clay pipes, the gaunt trees against the tin-factory, the black hands stained even in death.
>
> It's staggeringly beautiful at this hour when everyone seems to be going his own private way. Love and murder, they're still a

Comment, Vol. 11, No. 39 (19 September 1936), pp. 88-9.

few hours apart. Love and murder, I feel it coming with the dusk: new babies coming out of the womb, soft pink flesh to get tangled up in barbed wire and scream all night long and rot like dead bone a thousand miles from nowhere. Crazy virgins with ice-cold jazz in their veins egging men on to erect new buildings and men with dog collars around their necks wading through the muck up to the eyes so that the czar of electricity will rule the waves; . . . a brand new world is coming out of the egg and no matter how fast I write the old world doesn't die fast enough. I hear the new machine-guns and the millions of bones splintered at once; I see dogs running mad and pigeons dropping with letters tied to their ankles.

Passages such as these are not occasional highlights; they merge into their context and form an integral part of Miller's style. There is expressed in them, as in all his pages, the violent poetry of an epic view of the present age.

Neither *Tropic of Cancer* nor *Black Spring* altogether escapes from the accusation of formlessness. The first is an endless odyssey like Céline's; the second, apparently, scattered incidents from a huge autobiography. Their formlessness seems a part of their very nature, and is excused by the intense sincerity of the cry which goes up from them. Both books are born, as their author insists, 'out of the street', the products of a life spent at the heart of the modern world, in Paris and New York, in constant contact with its horror and its misery. Politer literature fades away into futility in comparison. Miller's writing is of the kind which makes ninety-nine per cent of contemporary novels seem entirely superfluous.

'Un écrivain américain nous est né,' Blaise Cendrars wrote when *Tropic of Cancer* first appeared. Henry Miller is one of those Americans who made the great trek to Paris during the 1920s, in search of something. Unlike most of them, he has stayed there, for in finding Paris he has found himself. 'I am a man of the old world,' he says, 'a seed that was transplanted by the wind, a seed which failed to blossom in the mushroom oasis of America . . . The climate for my body and soul is here where there is quickness and corruption.' Like Dostoievsky, his spiritual adventure has driven him down into the world of whores and dreamers, failures and drunkards, in search of that ultimate bright purity which glitters through the murk. So that at last he gets beyond despair, and achieves a kind of gay and triumphant stoicism. Is it so difficult to realize that without hope of any kind one can be desperately, exultantly confident that anything can happen?

Miller's chief weakness is perhaps his complete indifference to politics, to anything resembling an objective view of society. He realizes that society is falling to pieces, he refuses to believe that there is any hope at all for the future. 'What are we waiting for?' asks one of his characters. 'For the next Ice Age! It's coming to-morrow morning. You'll go to the window and everything'll be frozen tight. No more problems, no more history, no more nothing. Settled.' In the end we must admit that irresponsible fatalism of this kind is born of ignorance of historical cause and effect and of blindness to social and economic reality. We can console ourselves, however, by reflecting that he would probably never have been able to give us his unique record of the Last Days of World Capitalism if he had attempted to make it conform to any Weltanschauung other than his own.

F. T. PRINCE

This book will have been in my possession for at least a year by the time this notice appears. Ever since 1938, when Fabers brought out his distinguished first collection, I have been glad to count myself among F. T. Prince's many admirers. When his second book, *Soldiers Bathing*, came out after the War, I was scandalized that so remarkably gifted a poet should have been able to find no other publisher than The Fortune Press to present it, in a format unworthy both of the author and of the poems it contained, so deceptively slender and poorly produced, indeed, that I have unfortunately been unable to preserve it and cannot now tell how many shorter poems from it have been discarded in this most valuable and one can only hope not final book, for which Peter Jay and Anthony Rudolf are to be congratulated and thanked.

Fabers atoned for their failure to be responsible for *Soldiers Bathing* by bringing out *The Doors of Stone* in 1963; but at that time I was in France and on the verge of the first of a series of mental breakdowns, which meant that I never bought the book and have only recently discovered that its contents are as remarkable as any previous work and show a continued development and broadening range. The more recent *Drypoints of the Hasidim* and *Afterword on Rupert Brooke* I happily received on publication and found the first especially moving and attractive, possibly because of my own attachment to what I know of the Hasidim and that great man, Martin Buber. The unexpected poem about Rupert Brooke also struck me as exceptional in its perceptive insight and made me begin to reconsider my no doubt unfair conventional opinion of this unfulfilled 'minor Georgian', obscured for us, it would now appear, by a bogus posthumous glory.

The only review of the *Collected Poems* that I can now remember having seen was that by Neil Powell in No. 14 of *P.N. Review*, and I remember that it struck me as an all too typical example of the treatment now accorded to poets over sixty who have never been classifiable as clearly representative of a definite tendency in modern English poetry. To begin with, the article was headed by the one word: 'Professorial'. The fact that F. T. Prince until recently earned his living honourably but

---

'F. T. Prince: a belated tribute', review of F. T. Prince, *Collected Poems* (Anvil Press Poetry/The Menard Press, 1979), *Pennine Platform* 2 (1980), pp. 9-12.

not actually with wholehearted enthusiasm as a professor of literature surely does not warrant this faintly damning label. That he is undoubtedly an extremely well-read, possibly erudite man, does not make his poetry 'bookish' or cerebral, any more than the fact that it contains a certain number of references to subjects and writers who may be supposed to be unfamiliar to the probably non-existent 'average' reader necessarily makes it difficult or obscure. If it were obligatory to associate F. T. Prince with a particular persona, I for one would certainly not lumber him with that of an academic. He is an unusually private person who writes poetry that is neither private nor hermetic. Apparently he is inclined to be addicted to self-deprecation, and his own preferred image of himself seems to be that of a scrivener, 'bent over at the task/Of truth-telling'.

Though having no wish to dwell on one particular article that happened to seem to me a little less than fair, I must say that for the same critic to call the volume under discussion 'A slightly disappointing book' and then proceed to point out that 'Soldiers Bathing' is Prince's most anthologized poem (the kind of fact that no poet who gets a single poem hung round his neck cared to be reminded of), while on the very next page he enthuses about the *Collected Poems* of Kingsley Amis (whom may the Junior Establishment preserve!) finding the best thing about certain poems in it to be their still pristine 'freshness and crispness', does constitute the sort of thing that causes me to heave a huge sigh of resignation. Neil Powell states that he was a schoolboy in 1962, while I must confess that I left school in 1933, so obviously there's no escaping the dread inevitability of the generation-gap, something so much chattered about that I'd come to think of it as probably much of a myth.

I have accused a younger critic of being less than fair without intending to cast any slur on his critical integrity; and I am bound to admit that he has the advantage over me of clearly possessing a greater degree of that detachment which is practically synonymous with the objectivity I have always striven for when writing occasional pieces of criticism. With regard to the poetry that is my subject here, I might as well also admit that such an objectivity is exceptionally difficult for me to achieve. Mr Prince, a notable 'loner' among the poets of his generation, may not be particularly pleased to learn that a poet of my own somewhat younger one should find it so easy to identify sympathetically with a great many of the ambitions and recurring preoccupations expressed in his work as I do. Were it not for the fact that F. T. Prince's work in many ways epitomizes the sort of poetry that seems to me to be worth devoting the best part of one's life to attempting to write, I should not have been wanting to produce some sort of appreciative recognition of his *Collected Poems* ever since the book appeared last year, however. There is hardly a single poem in it that is not notable, always for its sheer felicity of verbal cadence, frequently for a memorable, quite personal peculiarity of phrasing, its fresh clarity of vision, its restrained yet poignant expression of emotion. The technique is as elegantly accomplished as that of any poet now writing. What I find particularly noticeable is Prince's equally skilled ability to handle long, comparatively loose lines and, perhaps more characteristically, to resort to the use of a terse brevity of expression, as in the concluding lines of an early poem I have always found particularly appealing, 'For Thieves and Beggars':

> . . . seeking
> A naked word we find
> A dead man lying on his back
> Under a sooty tree. He went in want.

Nothing could give me greater satisfaction than to discuss at length the many other poems that have given me special pleasure and that I know I shall always be able to read again with undiminished relish, but as space is limited I shall have to be content to mention only a few of the numerous items that make this book so varied a depository of riches. Mention must be made (ignoring the justly acclaimed anthology piece) of 'Apollo and the Sybil' (in which a certain affinity, not apparent elsewhere, with another fine and at present insufficiently appreciated poet, the late Vernon Watkins, is to be detected); as also of the splendid 'The Old Age of Michelangelo'. Among the poems first published in *The Gates of Stone* there are a few short lyrical pieces that remind one of the lyrical tradition best typified by certain poets of the last century, to cite any one of which could be misleadingly specific, but that manage at the same time to suggest the kind of lapidary quality one might associate with the stone of this section's title without ever appearing laboured, which would be a contradiction of their lyricism. If I say that it is hardly possible to prevent Browning coming to mind after one has read the outstanding sequence comprising 'Gregory Nanzianzen', 'Campanella' and 'Strafford', I do not mean to imply that Prince's style ever even momentarily suggests that of the Victorian pioneering master of the form; similarly, when I say that the unusually beautiful stanzas forming the sequence called 'Strambotti' at once make me think of some of Dante Gabriel Rossetti's translations from the Italian, I am not forgetful of the fact that the form F. T. Prince has used is supposedly of Venetian origin, while Rossetti's versions, so much admired by the young Pound, are almost always based on Florentine models, but intend to indicate that the evocation of a special Italian 'period' tone is similarly successful.

If I am bound to say that the last poem in the book, a hitherto unpublished piece concerning the novelist Sterne, leaves one with the feeling that it contains a plethora of apparently direct quotations from the *Journal to Eliza*, nothing on the other hand that might be said in praise of 'Memoirs of Oxford' could adequately convey how moving and valuable a record this is of a poet's dedicated quest for his own true identity, for meaning and for excellence. The whole of *Collected Poems* is evidence of the eminent degree to which F. T. Prince has succeeded in achieving this triple aim. He is surely to be numbered among those twentieth-century poets who will be valued eventually for having written his work from an experience of the kind that leads through trial and suffering, and maybe what the worldly regard as failure, to something far greater and more rare than knowledge in the Aristotelian sense, which is of course spiritual wisdom.

DENIS ROCHE

To review this book is to face a challenge, a risk and a temptation. To embark on such an undertaking with confidence one would to begin with have to be something of an authority on structuralism, which I most certainly am not. One ought to be impersonal, yet I have introduced the first personal pronoun already, just as one should be sufficiently objective to be able at least to give some impression of freedom from all partiality, and yet I have on the whole in the past found the whole structuralist tendency, and the work of the writers generally associated with the review *Tel Quel*, somewhat off-putting.

I cannot resist first observing, with reference to structuralism, that like all the modern movements that have become familiar talking-points for the international intelligentsia, the figures originally considered to be representative of it, or of the ideas of the *Tel Quel* group of writers somehow associated with it, have by this time, with maturity, all become quite distinct individuals, each with his own personal preoccupations and characteristics; which is, of course, exactly what happened in the case of one of its most exciting and creative predecessors, the Surrealist movement, quite differently oriented though it was and still remains.

All questions of ideology aside (and here I allude specifically to the ideas of Lévi-Strauss and Jacques Lacan), it seems reasonable to suppose that if in about fifty years' time the writings of Barthes, Derrida, Butor, Michel Deguy or Denis Roche continue to be read, it will in all probability be purely on account of their particular personal achievements and not as exponents of the theoretical aims that literary historians will doubtless long persist in ascribing to them as the common denominator enabling them usefully to be lumped together.

Of all his colleagues and close contemporaries, Roche is perhaps the writer most difficult to categorize. *Dépôts de savoir et de technique* would appear the be at least his fourteenth publication, and it has made its début in the series '*Fiction & Cie*', originally instituted by Roche and one or two of his fellow spirits. He has written 'novels', 'essays', 'poems' and works which are a hybrid of poetry and prose, but no doubt it is as the

---

'Sweeping the world's surface', review of Denis Roche, *Dépôts de savoir et de technique* (Paris: Seuil, 1980), *Times Literary Supplement* (3 October 1980), p. 1088.

author of what the *Tel Quel* group invariably refer to as *texts* that he would prefer to be considered.

The whole of the rest of this article could be devoted to a completely non-committal but none the less incomplete enumeration of the amazingly varied and heterogeneous references and quotations concerning autobiographical, literary, photographic, artistic, musical, archaeological, erotic and miscellaneous material to be found in this collection of 'dépôts'. The preface, which is entitled 'L'escalier de Copàn' for some reason not at first sight obvious, though admittedly preceded by a photograph of a Mayan staircase, consists of twelve pages which manage to make fairly clear what the author intends the term *dépôt* to signify, the immediately apparent, only minimally ambiguous, sense of 'deposit/depository' being hardly adequate to convey the complex scope and constructional method Roche has evolved for the ensuing nineteen 'texts'; though after writing the second of these, he tells us, he decided that he no longer wished to have the kind of thing he was beginning to produce described even as 'textes'.

But it will not take anyone long, after even a cursory reading of the *dépôts* themselves, to realize that they can in fact most baldly be described as examples of a new type of literary 'collage', or of the 'cut-up' method we have come to associate with William Burroughs (itself a variant of a procedure inaugurated by the Dadaists): Roche prefaces 'Dépôt No. 7', entitled 'Vacalli', with this quotation from Burroughs: 'And his blank, periscope eyes swept the world's surface'.

Similarly, Gertrude Stein's constant repetition of simple phrases appears to have been adopted by Roche and elevated to the dignity of what he somewhere describes as the verbal equivalent of the leitmotif.

The range of the *savoir* deposited for exhibition in this book is astonishing: the 110 notes and commentaries appended to the final *dépôt*, 'Je vous dois la vérité en littérature et je vous la dirais', alone contains quotes from or references to, among dozens of other sources, an entry in Michelet's Journal concerning Rubens and Hélène Froment, John Rechy's *The Sexual Outlaw*, the Ned Kelly gang, Robbe-Grillet's beginnings as a painter, a photograph of Vivien Leigh and Clark Gable reproduced in *Cahiers du Cinéma*, problems concerning Italian dialect expressions, Egyptian archaeological discovery, classic Japanese literature, Blake, the contemporary poet Jacques Roubaud, Pasolini, Les Krims, Kafka, Joyce, Joris Ivens, Wedekind/Berg's *Lulu* text as translated by Jouve, Conrad's *Heart of Darkness*, Wittgenstein, Jacques Lacan, Stockhausen, *et j'en passe*.

Inserted in the *dépôts* are also to be found a considerable number of autobiographical details, so that the reader not knowing much about

Denis Roche as a person is easily able to gather that he is a man of many parts, that, as well as having a great interest in architecture, he shares with his wife (?) Françoise a passion for photography, that they have a wide circle of friends by no means restricted to the *Tel Quel* group, most of these friends apparently as devoted to the art of photography, *le cinéma* and candour as Roche himself, the quality of candour in his own case exemplified by frequent references not only to what we would call candid camera-shots but to what would appear to be an intense but nowadays no doubt perfectly normal interest in every imaginable sexual permutation. An insatiable curiosity is obviously one of the principal mainsprings of the highly complex registering apparatus known as Denis Roche who, despite all his presumed attempts at distanciation, phenomenological bracketing, specimen quotation 'mounting' for preservation, technological terminology and apparently blank gazing through 'periscope eyes' at the contemporary cultural scene, remains recognizably an entirely human being, and in fact one who is first and foremost a poet.

In this particular guise, it seems typical of him that his first collection of poems should be entitled *Récits complets*, though it consists of pieces that for the most part could not possibly be categorized as narratives or even 'reports' (a word used by the late Humphrey Jennings to describe some of his Surrealist period literary quotation collages). This *recueil*, published in 1963, contains one poem entitled 'Liberty-grappe', written the previous year, which is already indicative of several of Roche's enduring distinctive tendencies: the bilingual title; the idea of word/association cluster inherent in the use of the word *grappe*, now one of the terms frequently used by exponents of semiotics; the casual introduction of a certain Miss Simpson who, though she in no way seems to justify the poem's classification as a *récit* (*complet* or otherwise: surely an intentional ambiguity is present here), may be thought to anticipate the Miss Elanize whose *Idées centésimales* provide the title of the collection with which the writer was to follow up that first one two years later; and the use of three phrases in quotation-marks.

The title of Roche's next book of poems, which appeared in 1968, was *Eros Energumène*, conveniently suggesting both a special preoccupation already alluded to, and another of this author's propensities, which is what I believe Francis Ponge has called 'la rage d'expression'. And, as I have started to list his specifically poetic productions I will conclude by mentioning *Le Mécrit* of 1972, the title of which constitutes as far as I can make out a Joycean-type coinage and leads me irresistibly to regard Roche's writing activities as a continuation of the series of *attentats* on the habitual use of language already considered by the earliest Surrealists in about 1918 to have been inaugurated by Lautréamont some half-century before them.

Roche was born in 1937 at about the time I was beginning to become a disaffected member of the British branch of the Surrealist movement (I am at present engaged in an attempt to salvage the essentials of the positive contribution of Breton and his associates to this century's cultural/philosophical achievement from its history till now). Surrealism was, and for a surprising number of old and young faithfuls remains, above all, an *adventure*; and it is the adventurous aspect of Roche's undertaking that most attracts me. His dogged determination to go on trying to find fresh and if possible startling ways of writing is undeniably admirable, even if to one who was once a typical 1930s left-winger and has never entirely foresworn his commitment of that time there does seem to be a certain element of fiddling while Rome burns entailed in the activities of the *Tel Quel* nucleus. Having just said that Roche appears to desire, like his Surrealist predecessors, to startle *if possible*, I'd like to draw attention to the present quasi-impossibility of 'making it new'. Roche in his *Dépôts de savoir et de technique* is clearly shoring up his fragments against not just his ruin but those of industrialism and what's left of our civilization. But a novelty harbingered by and inseparable from demolition (or 'destructuralization') is by now a hoary concept.

To hark back for a last time to my own youth: one of the little books I then discovered and often read with enthusiasm was Marcel Schwob's *Livre de Monelle* of 1894, in which one can come across such utterances as '. . . Et pour imaginer un nouvel art, il faut briser l'art ancien. Et ainsi l'art nouveau semble une sorte d'iconoclastie. Car toute construction est faite de débris, et rien n'est nouveau en ce monde que les formes. Mais il faut détruire les formes.'

Today, all aspirants to any form of significant expression can but be aware that artistic experimentation and/or linguistic exploration and recodification cannot help us much, existentially speaking, still less hope to achieve authentic novelty. Roche may call the texts in his collection *dépôts*, sometimes even *antéfixes* (sculptural ornaments, usually of terracotta, to be found decorating the edges of roofs and thought to be of Etruscan origin, according to Roche), the fact remains that Eugene Jolas would undoubtedly have hailed them excitedly as just the right sort of material to include in his international Paris-based avant-garde review of the first post-war era, *transition*.

Nevertheless, anyone interested in the current state of letters abroad will probably find these concoctions as absorbingly stimulating as they are undoubtedly ingenious, and that they display abundant signs of professionalism and dedication; and there I would leave the matter, were it not that I cannot quite suppress the suspicion that Denis Roche is a typical inheritor of 'the sad privilege of a new sophistication', as George

Steiner defined it in a recent article on an account of the 1939-45 holocaust (of which the ghastly details were common knowledge by the time the generation born shortly before the war had reached adolescence). I cannot help wondering whether a cheerful absorption in photography, extending the frontiers of poetic structuralism, gallantry, friendship and technological gadgetry, is not an indication of a certain degree of that callous condition of satedness which endangers the humanity of all of us, whatever our age or condition. But Denis Roche is possessed of a feeling for beauty sufficiently strong to make it difficult to continue to maintain a posture of ironic objectivity in the face of the sanguinary shambles threatening to overtake us. By all means play it cool, man, in other words, but do not fool yourself into regarding all emotional expressions of desperation as hilarious.

MARCEL JOUHANDEAU

The first collection of any consequence of my poetry was illustrated by Graham Sutherland, and contained a section devoted to Personal Poems, headed by a couple of aphoristic paragraphs from Marcel Jouhandeau's early *M. Godeau Intime*. They ended with this question, which at the time seemed very relevant to my youthful self-dramatizing self: ' "N'est-ce pas l'Enfer: cette solitude continuelle de la vie?" '. Earlier, as a fitting epigraph to the Journal that I kept in Paris during the year or two I spent there before the war, I had affixed this phrase from Jouhandeau's *Algèbre des valeurs morales*: 'Etablis-toi-véhémentement dans la sublimité de ton regard . . .'; though I now like to think I used this quote with a certain wry irony. In a journal entry for 1 March 1940, I found that I wrote: 'And much though I appreciate and admire M.J.'s writings, particularly the *Algèbre*, I can't help feeling there's a certain flaw somewhere, something that I don't quite trust: perhaps it is a too overbalancing proportion of "the aesthetic" in his attitude. In any case, compared with a figure such as Kierkegaard, he is but a minor author, no matter how remarkable a one, despite his own enormous self-esteem.'

When the war was over, I found that the one or two later Jouhandeau works I was able to look into confirmed this feeling about there being some sort of flaw in him, though I believe I would no longer then have ascribed this as due above all to an overpreponderance of 'aestheticism', despite the fact that by that time I was pretty well 'into' Kierkegaard and must therefore have been aware of the Danish philosopher's well-known 'three stages', and the severe distinction to be drawn between the 'merely' aesthetic and the truly religious. Jouhandeau is to my mind one of the best twentieth-century writers of French *qua* prose stylist, as most readers of this posthumously published *Journal* will surely agree, even if reluctantly; but it is difficult not to be irritated at times by the obtrusion of a certain sort of preciosity into a few of his early works, such as the otherwise undoubtedly fascinating *Opales*. And there was something I didn't care for at all about his post-war *Don Juan*.

'Misguided tour', review of Marcel Jouhandeau, *Journal sous l'Occupation suivi de La Courbe de nos angoisses* (Paris: Gallimard, 1980), *Times Literary Supplement* (5 December 1980), pp. 1375-6.

Marcel Jouhandeau was born in 1888, the son of a butcher in a small country town near Limoges, the Guéret which under the name of 'Chaminadour' he has probably immortalized in some of his best novels, short stories, barely fictionalized memoirs and chronicles. Though for many years a dedicated *professeur* at a school in Paris run by priests (necessarily for the most part of a broad-minded persuasion), Jouhandeau was able to produce an astonishing amount of written and published work belonging to a variety of categories, including at least four plays. Perhaps of all his books the series which most appealed to the general public, as it will in all likelihood continue to do, is that devoted to exceptionally candid and, it is fairly safe to guess, generally truthful (even if occasionally 'touched up' or playfully exaggerated) accounts of his married life with the ineffable Elise, of which the best known are *M. Godeau Marié, Elise* and the nine volumes of *Scènes de la vie conjugale*.

Journal sous l'Occupation covers the period 1939-45. The note on the back cover gently understates the cause of the most serious of the *angoisses* described at the end of the book by referring to Jouhandeau as not having great political discernment. His intense preoccupation with an inner life, of a quite genuinely religious though dubiously orthodox Catholic nature, his untiring devotion to his work as a schoolmaster and to his pupils, and the harassments of being married to an ex-cabaret dancer turned Xanthippe, left him little time to pay much attention to such unpleasant political facts as the burning of the books in Germany, the activities of the notorious police-chief Chiappe or the existence of the Cagoulards, to cite but a few items of the kind that were disturbing the majority of French writers during the 1930s. There is no factual justification for saying that Jouhandeau was pro-Franco, but if he was, it would have been on account of such deludedly idealist notions as those that misled Roy Campbell, for instance. His anti-Communism was not that of the most reactionary bourgeoisie in the West but rather that of a self-made intellectual of peasant stock, whose piety told him to accept without much question what the clergy he frequented advised him with regard to this subject.

In April 1941, Jouhandeau, wishing to visit the Creuse region in order to attend to some business affairs connected with a few small properties he owned there, applied for the visa that would enable him to cross over the frontier into the so-called 'free zone'. A lady of his acquaintance, wishing to help him obtain this necessary visa, invited him to a reception at which she promised she would introduce him to a German functionary she happened to know who could easily be persuaded into arranging for Jouhandeau to be given it at once. The lady, who appears to have been no more than one of the by then well-established author's many admirers, did in fact introduce him to a certain Lieutenant H, who agreed fully to comply with any request Jouhandeau might have to make of him.

Four months passed before the benevolent Nazi (a term seldom employed in these memoirs) officer summoned the writer, who had begun to give up all hope of receiving any aid from that quarter, to come and see him. The interview had not lasted long before it became clear that Lieutenant H's interest in Jouhandeau was connected only with luring him into visiting Germany, not with helping him to make a short, quick trip into his native countryside and back. Jouhandeau vigorously declined the offer of a cultural excursion to the land of Goethe and Beethoven, declaring himself to be neither a journalist nor a political writer; he added that in any case he was not free to accept, the date proposed for his tour of Germany being precisely that of the first day of term at the establishment which employed him. No problem, he was told, M. Abel Bonnard (a notorious collaborationist) will take care of all that and provide a replacement for you while you're away. Jouhandeau protested that M. Bonnard had nothing whatever to do with the kind of teaching (*enseignement libre*) he was involved in. Where M. Abel Bonnard is powerless, the helpful lieutenant at once replied, Mgr Baudrillat can always be counted on, and we'll contact him on your behalf immediately. The trap had been impeccably prepared.

Jouhandeau went home worried, and the next day confided in the head of his school, a much-respected Canon, his misgivings about this German jaunt now planned for him. He was told that after thirty faithful years of teaching he could hardly render the school a greater service than by accepting the Nazi's offer (care must no doubt have again been taken to avoid denominating the cultivated officer's affiliations with strict accuracy), in order that by so doing he might help to bring about the repatriation of the Canon's second-in-command, whose absence was felt to be increasingly detrimental to the school. So Jouhandeau suppressed his personal feelings of repugnance and prepared to embark on the kind of visit which at about that time many other prominent figures, notably from the very different but no less prestigious world of show-business (such as Maurice Chevalier and Danielle Darrieux) had been inveigled into making.

On 3 October 1941, he noted down what the friend he trusted more than anyone else in the world had said to him: 'Tu peux seul te permettre de faire ce voyage, sans que je t'en veuille'. He concludes the first brief entry in his *carnet de voyage* by stating that he has always loathed cowardice; but adds that nothing in his inmost self disposed him to be complaisant towards *l'occupant*. Two days later, in the company of someone scarcely known to him who had been substituted for the friend he had been assured would be making the tour with him, he finds himself in Bonn, and after being obliged to appreciate the splendours of the Rathaus and gather a few hasty impressions of Beethoven's house, he ends by wondering: 'Pour qui et pour quoi suis-je ici? Parce que depuis que j'ai su lire, comprendre et sentir, j'ai aimé l'Allemagne, ses philosophes, ses musiciens et pensé que rien ne serait plus utile à l'humanité que notre entente avec elle. En 1940, j'ai observé de très près ce qui s'est passé et il est indéniable, à moins d'être de mauvaise foi qu'après leur victoire les allemands auraient pu nous traiter plus mal.'

Jouhandeau had a romantic idea of Germany, and there were then, and possibly always will be, many like him in most non-Germanic countries. His view that Germans by and large are as decent as any other Europeans is not disgraceful, and certainly never sufficed to qualify him as a traitor to the essential values of the French ideal of civilization. As his nocturnal meditation in Bonn testifies: 'En Allemagne, je me sens français plus que nulle part ailleurs'. But his attempt to set his conscience at rest for having allowed himself to undertake his journey will not satisfy the intransigently unforgiving, who never much cared for Jouhandeau's persona anyway; but for the record he declares that during his whole life he had never written more than one specifically political article (the two or three others that followed it didn't count in his own eyes, he adds).

At the end of this passage, however, he touches on the spot where he was probably most vulnerable, that is, the Jewish question. If one were to see in his visit to Nazi Germany a result of his reflections on this particular question, one would be grossly deceiving oneself, he asserts. Whatever Jouhandeau's reflections on the theme of anti-semitism may have been, they can scarcely have been as irrational as those of Léon Bloy, for instance, himself a Jewish convert to Catholicism or in any way analogous to the rabid obscenities of Céline (now rehabilitated to the extent of being raised to the status of a twentieth-century classic). As Jouhandeau saw it, all he was trying to do during the autumn of 1941 was to prove that a Frenchman is not necessarily a Germanophobe, even in the then prevailing circumstances. 'Bien plus, je souhaiterais faire de mon corps un pont fraternel entre l'Allemagne et nous,' are the concluding words of his apologia. There is surely a touch of involuntary pathos about the typically ambiguous silliness of these words.

This compromising excursion, which later was to contribute much to the *ennuis* and *angoisses* he had to endure, took the observant Jouhandeau from Bonn via Mainz to Frankfurt, where he inspected Goethe's carefully-preserved house with emotion; then on to Heidelberg, where his guide informed him that in his opinion the apparently ubiquitous militarization of the nation was a merely temporary affair and that a renewed preoccupation with *Geist* was imminent; from thence to Fribourg, where an encounter with a citizen looking like a wild boar ended with the stranger's enquiring of Jouhandeau whether he was going out hunting, followed by the confession that he personally had a horror of hunting and could never understand why anyone should expect him to go off to harm a hind whose dying gaze would be like that of a girl in her early teens. Lindau, then Munich led him to Salzburg, where many unforgettable days of his youth had been spent, and where he has this reflection, which is relevant to the whole subject of Jouhandeau the writer: 'La poésie est un monde à part dans lequel on vit en marge du monde. Comment faire partie de quoi que ce soit, quand on me ressemble? d'un groupe, d'un parti, d'une nation? Je m'y révèle abstrait, pour ne pas dire distrait ou absent. . . .'

In Vienna, Jouhandeau was rather taken aback by the Oberbürgermeister's declaration that any sort of fanatic is nearer the truth than those who are neither hot nor cold. In Baden, he notes: 'Il y a deux êtres en moi: celui que tout le monde voit qui porte mon nom. L'autre caché, mystique, dont le nom est secret, connu de Dieu seul.' In Berlin itself, where having had a hint of what would eventually nearly happen to himself by overhearing a journalist telling a member of his party, apparently a distinguished Scandinavian poet, that he'd pay dearly for his trip one day, he was finally ushered into the sanctum of Joseph Goebbels. That Goebbels was short and limped (because of his club-foot) everyone must have been already well aware: Jouhandeau also noted that in physical appearance, only his head mattered. He fixed his gaze on his interlocutor like a snake, in order to sum up the other's powers of resistance. After trotting out the well-known spiel about the approaching German victory over Bolshevism being followed by a Europe in which each nation would keep its own distinctive features and identity, he went on to declare that he had no wish for the British Empire to come to an end, as Germany could hardly expect to gain anything from inheriting it. Finally, he went so far as to admit that the defeat of the Third Reich was a possibility, adding that the dynamism of his country was such that were that to occur it would sooner or later recover its power.

In Weimar finally, in a room which had once been Bach's, he is moved as he rereads the first letter he has received from Elise since leaving France and which leads him to reflect: 'Ne vous aime-t-elle que seule? Sans vous? Ne m'aime-t-elle que sans moi? Sublime, elle l'est toujours dans le fond d'elle-même; de trop près, cela vous échappe.' Indeed, as might have been hoped for by Jouhandeau's fans, the *Journal* contains a great many anecdotal additions to the portrait of the by now legendary

Elise, a figure no novelist could possibly have imagined. In 1942, for instance, her characteristic sense of economy leads her to decide that the house which, as she was constantly reminding Marcel, was her own property, should in future be heated by a system she had just discovered whereby all that was necessary to keep them warm and lit could be provided by converting into fuel the entire waste-products of the household, including the human. On Easter Day 1943, Elise makes up her mind to go for once to Mass, though quite prepared to admit herself to be a pagan at heart. 'What shall I take with me?' she asks her husband, finding a conventional missal inappropriate. 'The life of Milarepa?' he suggests; but she finally decides on Rimbaud's *Les Illuminations*. In July of the same year, Jouhandeau notes that during the preceding twelve months he has been obliged to borrow 150,000 francs in order to satisfy the architectural whims of Elise (his *Elise Architecte* is entirely devoted to her passion for designing and supervising extensions to her house).

It is hardly necessary to describe Elise as eccentric. The first thing she would as a rule tell you, if you had the privilege of being presented to her, was that she had been the original 'Belle Excentrique' for whom Erik Satie had specially composed his well-known little dance-piece. In June 1943, at a dinner-party given by Florence Gould and Marie-Louise Bousquet, Jouhandeau was introduced by Ernst Jünger, (whose admirers always declare he was never really a Nazi) and was informed by that highly cultured and well-read man that nothing about the author of *Chroniques maritales* or their other principal character, Elise, had been to his taste. The outcome of this meeting was that when the party broke up, Jünger and a Swedish Count decided to accompany Jouhandeau back to his home. When they arrived, at 2 a.m., it was to find Elise up and waiting for Marcel with an anxiety she was immediately able to mask by beginning to knit with absorption. Soon a typical domestic scene developed, of an unintentionally farcical nature, during which the full proportions of Elise's almost epically monstrous egocentricity were duly revealed. Before making his departure, Jünger took Jouhandeau aside and told him that now he could properly appreciate the *Chroniques maritales*, and he finally took his leave with the words: 'Comme a dit le comte, Elise est un monument et naturellement les monuments intéressent l'histoire.'

This would seem to be the last word on the subject of Elise; but it must be added that she was capable at times of showing great tenderness and loyalty to her husband. Three terse remarks demonstrate the side of her that one cannot but admire: 'Rien n'existe, rien ne mérite d'exister, excepté le caractère', 'Je préfère les époques terribles à celles ou l'homme se contente d'être un ruminant.' '– Mourir pour mes idées, je ne m'en plaindrais pas. J'ai horreur du neutre, comme la langue française.'

Jouhandeau himself had an undisguised antipathy towards 'les Britanniques' (though he had had a certain number of English friends, such as Raymond Mortimer). He believed our dominant characteristic was what he called our *morgue*, not too easy a word to translate but which my favourite dictionary renders as haughtiness, arrogance, self-sufficiency and conceit. At the same time he felt that the English are *Messieurs* (gentlemen, presumably) and will remain so, no matter what they do, even in their victims' opinion. 'Ils auraient bien tort de se gêner, de ne pas employer les balles dumdum, de n'avoir pas brûlé Jeanne d'Arc, de n'avoir pas fait mourir de langueur Napoléon, puisque rien ne peut les déshonorer.'

What with opinions of the kind just quoted on Jouhandeau's part, and the inflexibly strong if eccentric character of Elise, it is not to be wondered at that the closing section of the book should be called *La courbe de nos angoisses*. The utter indifference of Elise to the attitude of others led her on one occasion to tell a woman beside her in the street who asked, while they were watching a procession of goose-stepping Nazis go by, whether she didn't think such a performance typical of barbarians, that she had nothing to say to her about barbarism but that her experience as a ballet-dancer had taught her to recognize a difficult exercise when she saw one and that self-control through discipline couldn't be called barbaric; she concluded the exchange with the remark: 'Try and goose-step yourself, Madame, and you'll soon end up on your backside.'

Toughness alone will have seen the couple through the trials that lay ahead. Jouhandeau was always so essentially honest, however wrongheaded he may have been, that he would never have claimed to be anything but a weak character, even exaggerating his 'abjectness' as though in imitation of all those saints who were convinced they were the wickedest sinners on earth. The real crisis, when it came, brought out the best in both of them, and they have some enjoyable tragi-comic adventures in the household of an extremely equivocal lady who offered to shelter them at a time when anonymous letters and sinister telephone calls were daily warning them that retribution was imminent. The end of the book is both dramatic and revealing. Stress drives Jouhandeau to write some of the best of his brief, aphoristic paragraphs: 'Quelle que soient la religion, la nationalité, la race, la classe, les opinions de quelqu'un, quelles que soient ses fautes, ses faiblesses, ses erreurs, en lui la personne humaine a droit au respect et quiconque l'outrage, même criminel, manque à son devoir le plus essentiel envers la dignité de sa propre espèce, dignité que rien ni au Ciel ni sur la Terre ne saurait ni entamer ni effacer.'

ANGELOS SIKELIANOS

At the outset of this notice, may I say that I have no qualification whatever for reviewing a selection of translations of Sikelianos's work, presented in the present book with the original text, except that of having a keen interest in modern European literature, and in the relations between men, myth and poetry, which seem to be illustrated with unusual salience in this particular instance. Possessing not even the rudiments of Greek, I have had to rely for what small acquaintance I may have with modern Greek poetry – Cavafy, Seferis, Elytis, Ritsos – on translations, especially of course those of Philip Sherrard, to whose name Edmund Keeley's must at once be added, as he was Mr Sherrard's collaborator not only in the work of which the book here considered is the result, but also in the helpful and stimulating *Six Poets of Modern Greece*.

Right at the beginning of the succinct introduction we are told that Angelos Sikelianos, 1884-1951, was in some ways a traditional poet, more so than Cavafy, twenty years his senior, or Seferis, a few years younger than he was. Then we are informed that 'one' (the introduction presumably being the result, like the translations, of collaboration between Edmund Keeley and Philip Sherrard) is reminded by Sikelianos's early work of some of the 'nature' poetry of Dylan Thomas, because the intimate, dynamic relationship between the poet and his 'local habitation' is to be discerned in both poets. This is an interesting point to have made for the English reader and I certainly would not contest it, though I think it could be suggested that the affinity between Sikelianos and the Lithuanian-born French poet O. V. de L. Milosz is considerably greater. Both Milosz and Sikelianos might, it would seem, be said to have experienced at a crucial moment of their lives something like an initiatory spiritual illumination, which I doubt that Thomas would ever have claimed to have received, being to some extent inhibited by an inherent suspicion of pretentiousness and a dislike of all metaphysical speculation. The question of 'local habitation', incidentally, is one that may be found haunting all true European poets since at least the time of Schelling,

---

Review of Angelos Sikelianos, *Selected Poems*, translated and introduced by Edmund Keeley and Philip Sherrard (Princeton University Press, 1979. U.K. Allen & Unwin, 1980), *Temenos* 1 (1981), pp. 246-56.

referred to in the introductory notes as having been quoted approvingly by Sikelianos because he asserted that mythology contains all religious truth in it, that religion is not mythology but that all myths are true and constitute revelations of what *always exists*.

Before going on to a necessarily inadequate comment on the poems/translations themselves, I should like to add that such a book as Mircea Eliade's *Myths, Dreams and Mysteries* is a considerable aid towards a proper appreciation of Sikelianos's content, as it represents an invaluable *aide-mémoire* concerning the original world-wide belief in a primeval paradisiac state, the subsequent exile into a harsh and onerous reality, and the universal nostalgia for the prelapsarian condition not to be dismissed as it is wont to be by rigorous Freudians as a mere longing for the irresponsible safety of the mother's womb. Sikelianos's translators tell us of the special importance for this Greek poet of the role of poetry and the poet in the ancient tradition of his country, the conception of the poet as 'standing at the centre of his world as inspired prophet and seer, teacher and mystagogue'. I mentioned Mircea Eliade because he is one of the modern authoritative writers who have paid particular attention to the tradition to be found in various forms in almost all 'primitive' cultures of the poet as intermediary between mortal men and the realm of the divine and extra-temporal, climbing up a Tree or Ladder into domains inaccessible to the uninitiated, there to receive mysterious but vital revelations from some supreme supernatural source. The shaman in so many supposedly primitive societies seems always to have had to undergo a drastically painful initiation into the interrelated secrets of sexuality, death, and the sacredness of human ancestry and of Nature; and the shaman is the prototype of what has survived, it may now seem miraculously, in the tradition that re-emerged at approximately the beginning of the last century of the poet as seer, 'agent for bringing into close communion the mortal and the divine', as the introduction already quoted from defines him. Sikelianos's poet-seer persona 'often seems larger than life, almost a voice in nature that transcends humanity', the translator-authors add. This may account for Lawrence Durrell, whose knowledge of Greek poetry is undeniably intimate, even if his taste and preferences are understandably personal, having remarked to me that Sikelianos put him in mind of someone cast in the mould of a d'Annunzio. Though ignorant of Greek, the self-evident authenticity of the poet represented by the twenty-five poems that have been selected for translation in this book is that of a figure of an altogether different order of importance, though possibly I underestimate d'Annunzio, that to me dubiously flamboyant and equivocal sacred monster (in the stage sense) of twentieth-century literary mythology.

The specifically national tradition of Greece, ethnically considered, is best represented in this collection by the long poem 'The Village Wedding'. Space permits no more than five lines of quotation that may give some indication of the tone and angle:

> Breeze suddenly brushing
> the bridegroom's knee
> like a white veil.
>
> Creation of man from the beginning
> at the Word of God.

I hope it will not be inept or superfluous to comment here that the close connection between Greek and Russian Orthodox ceremonies and these two nations' unusually strong traditional sense of the innate holiness of sex and soil enable one to connect this particular poem with an earlier and perhaps more radical work, Stravinsky's powerful *Les Noces*, though I am well aware that such comparisons are risky.

'The Village Wedding' is free in form, a rhapsody rather than an epithalamium. There are several shorter poems in the collection of which the form is far stricter, such as sonnets, and the beautiful, apparently quite early 'The Mother of Dante', the regular and rhyming quatrains of which the translators have, I think wisely, refrained from attempting to reproduce in the English version they have arrived at. The late 'Hymn to Artemis Orthia' ('a goddess of the hunt, of the fertility of both human beings and beasts, and of childbirth', a note informs us) is an obviously deeply significant and emotionally resonant poem of some length. In it, what was perhaps the principal of the early Greek female initiatory rites – whether one considers the Maenads or Corybantes as having priority in this respect is a question which would divert what was supposed to be a brief article in the direction of a disquisition that would be finally irrelevant to poetry altogether – is evoked in vividly sensuous imagery and fiercely severe terms. For the last time, I must quote from Eliade on 'Women's Mysteries': 'It is not the natural phenomenon of giving birth that constitutes the mystery; it is the revelation of the feminine sacredness; that is, of the mystic unity between life, woman, nature and the divinity . . . The girl or the initiated woman emerges from the innermost depths of her being, and this consciousness – obscure though it may be – is experienced in symbols.' In this last sentence we have the justification for referring again here to Eliade, for such symbols are obviously the same as those used by the inspired poet such as Sikelianos, and come from the 'ancient springs' that Kathleen Raine has memorably defended.

'Daedalus', the poem which follows the 'Hymn' just discussed, is another piece that appears to have sprung from profound depths, much as its subject's son fell from a dangerous height; and it ends with the adjuration:

> climb always
> with slow even wings the heavens of our Thought,
> eternal Daedalus, Dawnstar of the Beyond.

If my memory does not betray me, I quite recently made the observation in something I wrote that there exists hardly any significant poem, by which I mean one worth studying and rereading any number of times, that is not susceptible to what until recently was as a rule referred to as hermeneutic analysis, though I understand that, in France and America at least, the more favoured current term is semiotics (which possibly is not to be confused with the kind of philosophical examination so remarkably exemplified by Heidegger's commentaries on the poetry of Hölderlin and a few of his successors). What made me mention this is that it strikes me as obvious that the poems of Sikelianos belong to the category I have just tried to indicate. For instance, simply the words from 'Dionysus Encradled', *'my Christ and my Dionysus'*, quoted for their particular significance for an understanding of the poet's mature ethos in the translators' introduction, could easily lead one to a study of considerable length, so vastly rich in implication and so contemporary in relevance is the conjunction of these two inexhaustibly meaningful Names. The introduction, to make a final reference to it, tells us that the present selection may suggest an imperfect image of the poet Sikelianos finally conceived himself to be, that is 'the sleepless artificer (. . .) with a lifelong commitment to the role of poet-prophet in the tradition of Pindar and Aeschylus or, in more recent times, of Hölderlin, Yeats and Saint-John Perse'. At least the first of these three names alone reinforces my conviction that Martin Heidegger (who died four years ago at the age of eighty-seven) would have found in Sikelianos, had he had time to read him, a modern source of exactly the sort of 'given' utterances that inspired some of the most stimulatingly cogent of his later writings; all the more so in that Sikelianos, like the German philosopher, was apparently haunted all his life by a vision of the freely intuitive clarity of the pre-Socratics, with their primal insights which it seems increasingly imperative that we should strive somehow to re-experience at present. Both poet and philosopher would surely have agreed that one of the most vital things to be recaptured and thought through in this way is the nexus of fertilizing truths that are to be discovered embedded in the two Greek words *phusis* and *poiesis*, only very elementarily to be translated as nature and poetry but in their full and subtly complex sense as fundamentally seminal terms as the previously mentioned mythological pair, Christus and Dionysus. But perhaps the poetry is in the mystery, and I am well aware that there are many who maintain that discursive glosses on poems such as those of a poet like Sikelianos at his most inspired risk losing something of the communicative force of the text commented on. But here I must once more check myself and try to come to some sort of satisfactory conclusion.

Although, as often tends to happen to me nowadays, I shall have to end without having been able to indicate half the things I thought should be said when I began writing this article, I am determined to work in a further reference to that outstanding French-language poet of Lithuanian origin, whom I have long admired but only rediscovered and read again recently, O. V. de L. Milosz. I understand that the second issue of *Temenos* is to contain a comprehensive study of this remarkable solitary genius so that fortunately I need say no more about him here except to point out that he was as obsessed by the notion of a lost paradise of pristine innocence, by our present sense of homelessness, and by the poet's initiatory capacity and/or function as any of the poets with whom Sikelianos may be compared. Whether or not Milosz will ultimately be considered to be as important a poet as Saint-John Perse is a fruitless and irrelevant question I shall not attempt to answer. What can be said is that the former, described by the supremely intelligent Valéry, without irony, as 'terribly pro-profound', underwent during the last month of 1914 something like a period of great illumination, the results of which are to be discerned in all his later writings; whereas so far as I am aware the Nobel Prize winner never made any claim to have had an exceptional experience of a mystical nature. These remarks are by way of preamble to a quotation from the *Epitre à Storge*, written by Milosz in the middle of the First World War:

> But we shall die, Storge, and we shall enter into that blessed state wherein ceaselessly dissatisfied multiplication, division and rhythm find the supreme absolute number and the immutable and perfect finale of every poem. It is the second love, it is the Elysium of Master Goethe, it is the Empyrium of the great Alighieri, the Adamandroni of the good Swedenborg, the Hesperides of the unfortunate Hölderlin. It is already here – but what does that word 'here', O Storge, exactly mean? – yes, and spread throughout universal matter, matter that is infinite and therefore deprived of movement and place. Happy indeed the spirit of affirmation that discovers, here and now, that sure and unique reality, that Isle of Patmos, land of beatitude, where the accomplishment of the mind's movement is the correspondence with the immobility of infinite matter.

'Only connect.' One possible connection that can be made with this brief extract from a text resulting from the revelation received by Milosz referred to previously is that with Teilhard de Chardin, whose strangely similar though quite differently formulated world-vision as expressed later in *Le Milieu Divin* began, it seems, to be intuited by him at the same time as the 'Epistle to Storge' was being written (I think I should add that I owe this pertinent observation to one of Milosz's commentators, Jacques Buge).

All in all, it seems to me justifiable to suppose that if one grants that poetry and prophecy can in the era now probably approaching its end still be found in the work of certain European poets to be on occasion more or less synonymous, then one will also be prepared to admit the strong possibility that what such poets are prophesying is one and the same mysterious Thing. This word is certainly not intended to suggest anything to do with the 'reification' of which we have already heard more than enough; it is in fact simply the translation of the expression of the term *la Chose*, used by a woman friend of mine, who writes poems in French of a mystic and meditative nature, in a brief fragment that I have no doubt anticipates this necessarily unspecifiable but undeniably imminent spiritual Event of decisive importance to humankind. Yeats has already been cited as one of those poets of our time with whom Sikelianos may be said to have an affinity. Yeats's best-known poem of an indubitably prophetic nature is 'The Second Coming'. In Sikelianos's 'Dionysus Encradled', Mother-Night, surely identifiable both with primordial chaos and with an all-pervading eschatological obscurity, is evoked, and after mention not of a leonine sphinxlike shape in the desert but of the Serpent of the Abyss, the poet asks himself:

> Is God, eternal God, being born again
> tonight as a young child?

The question has been asked as it will continue to be in so many different ways that it would be impossible to enumerate and distinguish them here. Yeats's 'rough beast' does not reassure us with an intimation of a return of anything that could possibly be described as the Divine in the sense understood by any kind of Christian believer. There are probably not many ways in which Yeats can be described as having had much in common with Stefan George, but one can at least point out that they can both be said to display the unmistakably national characteristics of their respective countries, which incidentally has caused both of them to be over-hastily labelled by some as having had fascist or Nazi leanings (a type of misunderstanding I haven't the time to refute or unravel), they both moved steadily forward from an initial *fin de siècle* symbolist-type 'dreaminess', to use an unsatisfactory word to indicate a tendency manifesting itself in a variety of ways throughout Europe round about the turn of the century, towards an increasingly lapidary style and a growing concern with the dimension of the invisible; above all both came in the end to adopt that stance of aristocratic aloofness which in its apparently coldhearted scorn of the plebeian can be mistaken for a disdain of the kind of values still recognized in 'free' countries as making us specifically human. This apparent digression is leading me to the observation that poetry of a prophetic nature, that directs our imagination towards the future as well as the eternal present which embraces it, is of an optimistic or pessimistic nature according to the fundamental make-up, faith or lack of it, of the poet sufficiently gifted to write it. This is, of course, an oversimplification, because, at least in my opinion, optimism and pessimism may be likened to the two lenses of a pair of spectacles necessary to the reflective individual in order to correct a universal astigmatism brought about by a civilization based on a fundamental dualism which, as Octavio Paz[1] observed recently, is tearing us asunder. But in order to make quite clear the point I wished to make about poets of the category to which Yeats and George may be considered to belong, while Sikelianos, it seems to me, ought not to be, I should like to insert here a quotation from Karl Jaspers' 'Tragedy is not Enough':

> Tragic knowledge invades and breaks through, but does not master reality – there is too much it leaves untouched, forgotten or unexplained. It lures us into an exalting world of grandeur; and thus, despite all clear-eyed honesty, it obscures the truth. – Tragedy becomes the privilege of the exalted few – all others must be content to be wiped out indifferently in disaster. Tragedy then becomes a characteristic not of man, but of a human aristocracy. As the code of privilege, this philosophy becomes arrogant and unloving; it gives us comfort by pandering to our self-esteem.

'Horseman, pass by' – and be content to be wiped out along with the unhappy multitudes, as the nub of this passage might be paraphrased. It is possible that I am doing Yeats a mischievous injustice in interpolating his famous last words in this particular context. All that Jaspers said in the short book just quoted from, first published here[2] in 1953, however,

---

[1] Octavio Paz, 'Poetry and History' in *Anthology of Mexican Poetry* (Thames and Hudson); reprinted by Penguin Books in *Octavio Paz: Selected Poems* (1979).
[2] By Gollancz.

appears to me to be still valid with reference to the state of the world, and the poet (prophetic or otherwise) in it, today. And to conclude this divagation, I should like to refer the reader wishing to read a comment informed by a combination of erudition and profound spiritual insight on the situation and significance of prophecy in the present century to the pages headed 'Prophecy, Apocalyptic, and the Historical Hour', to be found in a collection of texts by Martin Buber entitled *Pointing the Way*.[3]

To conclude, let me quote some of the last lines of the last poem in this collection of translations of poems by Sikelianos, entitled 'Agraphon' (meaning literally, a note tells us, 'unwritten thing', but now a term used to refer to a saying or tradition about Christ either not recorded in the Gospels or incapable of being traced to its original source), in order to illustrate the humility of the poet's final conception of his role and the piercing keenness of his vision of the actual world and whatever may lie before us. The kind of parable told in the poem concerns Christ's pointing out the beauty of the teeth in the skull of a dog's carcass the stench of which the disciples about Him had found offensive. I do not know whether or not this is one of the stories to be found related in the Oxyrhynchine fragments, but it is not entirely unfamiliar and may I suspect have had something to do with the inspiration of Baudelaire's poem 'Une Charogne'. After relating the brief, possibly apocryphal story related by the 'agraphon' of the title, the poet, referring to himself as 'the very least of men', pondering Jesus's words and standing before Him, prays that it may be granted him to see

> – something glittering suddenly
> deep inside me, above the putrefaction,
> beyond the world's decay, like the dog's teeth
> at which that sunset You gazed, Lord, in wonder:
> a great pledge, mirror of the Eternal, but also
> the harsh lightning-flash, the hope of Justice!

If it is permissible to descend for an envoi from the sublime to the trivially immediate and I hope not apparently facetious: Were I to hazard a little prophecy of my own with regard to the reception of this book by typical representatives of the current generation of critics in this country, I shouldn't hesitate to predict that their intrepidly disabused but parochial superficiality will prompt them to regard Sikelianos's seriousness and (dread term of disapprobation!) 'solemnity' with a mixture of undisguised

---

[3] Edited and translated by M. S. Friedman (New York: Harper Torchbooks, Harper & Row, 1957).

suspicion and distaste. To make one really ultimate connected quotation with regard to this state of affairs, George Steiner, in *The Death of Tragedy*, tells us (apropos of Ibsen, though I find the sentence not altogether inapposite to the Greek poet I have been discussing): 'Yet there remains a chance of miracle; in sharing mortal danger the dead may awaken'.

JEREMY REED

If I had never heard of Jeremy Reed before, I feel sure I should nevertheless have at once recognized in this book a distinctive new voice. But Jeremy Reed's work has appeared widely in magazines and from the small presses, and I have read several of his shorter previous little-press edition books already (including notably *Saints and Psychotics*, published by Alan Clodd of Enitharmon).

It is unfortunately impossible in a brief review to convey an adequate idea of the richness of imaginative range and the maturity of technical control manifested in this book, which Jeremy Reed himself, incidentally, considers to be in most ways his first. But to give some idea of the kind of subject-matter, one needs to begin by explaining the choice of this collection's title, for the benefit of such readers as might conceivably suppose Bleecker Street to be one of those innumerable locales that have had a 'blues number' named after them. In fact, the volume is prefaced by a couple of brief quotations, one from Webster, the first from Hart Crane (extracted from a poem called 'Possessions'):

> And I, entering, take up the stone
> As quiet as you can make a man . . .
> In Bleecker Street, still trenchant in a void.

Here we have an immediate clue to one of Jeremy Reed's most enduring obsessions, or rather one of the principal figures in the kind of personal mythology he has built up for himself and upon which his imaginative vision is most often to be found centred.

With Hart Crane, the homosexual boozer who wrote himself dry, to describe him in coarse journalistic terms, and who finally flung himself into the Atlantic on a return voyage from Florida to New York – an American *poète maudit* if ever there was one, and one of the few twentieth-century American poets who can reasonably be categorized as 'visionary' – is now inseparably linked the name of Samuel Greenburg, a sort of consumptive New York Chatterton if one thinks of him in terms of legend, but rather a Rimbaud who died in hospital (aged

---

'Gascoyne's Choice', review of Jeremy Reed, *Bleecker Street* (Manchester: Carcanet, 1980), *Poetry London/Apple Magazine* 2 (1982), pp. 72-3.

twenty-three) like the latter, rather than in an attic. If one takes his startling originality into account, the quality in his fragmentary manuscript remains qualified as 'unspeakably eerie' by Crane, who had no hesitation in adopting many images, phrases and turns of diction from the unknown dead boy and thus in a way immortalizing him without being aware of doing so. And it is astonishing to think that one of Jeremy Reed's earlier sequences, *The Isthmus of Samuel Greenburg*, though published in 1976, was actually written three years before that date, and already shows a singular originality and a distinct style very much his own.

The back-cover note to *Bleecker Street* says that Jeremy Reed has been called a 'latter day Jacobean', which, however misleading such labels may sometimes turn out to be, does seem to me in this instance to have considerable justification, not simply because he is 'much possessed by death', as who is not, but because of his obvious feeling of affinity with that still possibly underestimated but certainly extraordinary phenomenon, Thomas Beddoes, for some time referred to, if at all, as 'the last Jacobean'. It may not be altogether irrelevant to recall in this connection that at the time when I first began occasionally to encounter Dylan Thomas, I became aware that he had been possessed since his early 'teens with a passionate enthusiasm for Beddoes and that he and our mutual friend Norman Cameron had a long-term, never-to-be fulfilled ambition to reduce the vast and untidy *Death's Jest Book* to stageable proportions. I cannot refrain from observing, before leaving this aspect of Mr Reed's poetic character, that Djuna Barnes – to whom 'Toque', which I consider to be one of the most outstandingly remarkable items in this collection, is dedicated – is the author of that unique (and mutilated, were it but known) masterpiece *Nightwood*, the gorgeously baroque prose of which is resonant with Jacobean undertones and reverberations.

It might be said here that it is debatable whether the *expression* of emotion is in fact a function proper to specifically contemporary poetry, though as I've said before it is impossible to conceive of a born poet who was not gifted with unusual sensibility and hence liable to experience the basic human emotions with a perhaps heightened intensity, and also to be moved by certain things that the so-called normal man does not have the capacity or at any rate the inclination to notice or react to. But insofar as Jeremy Reed's poems convey an indication of the emotions felt in relation to the subject-matter, which the spokesmen of characteristically *modern* poetry have declared to be of secondary importance ('A poem should not mean but be' might be the ruling maxim of a large number of French and continental poets as well as of many Americans), then I do not think it misleading to describe them as predominantly bleak in feeling, sometimes suggesting a precarious balance on the verge of despair held back only by a furious desire to continue creating poetry of ever-increasing insight and formal control. The degree of development of the latter which he has already achieved is strikingly demonstrated in such a poem as 'Marlowe's Letter to Thomas Walsingham' in the present collection.

Finally, it should be remarked that in Jeremy Reed's poetry the provincial narrowness of outlook and awareness that made so much of the British poetic output of a decade or two ago appear so dull and limited in aim, when compared with what was being written elsewhere in the world, is conspicuously absent. By way of bringing this article to a conclusion, I should like to quote the second of the two stanzas which constitute the poem entitled 'Elegy-Europe', as the lines seem to illustrate so well the kind of qualities that this poet possesses:

> I show you my fingers; how they are bald
> with tracings over paper for the one
> poem that's concealed on the other side
> of language, not the Wall. We're dressed in white,
> but invisible to the underground.
> Your fatigue would demand a hotel but
> we're never sure of what is composite
> or who. Nor why the key-holes are stained red.

JULIEN GREEN

This is the eleventh volume to date of Julien Green's Journal, and its title is intended to suggest its predominant theme, which is that of travel and places. The countries visited by Green during the years recorded here include Britain, Greece, Turkey, Iran, Austria and Belgium. What seems astonishing in the passages detailing his impressions is the pristine spontaneity of the appreciation he accords to everything he encounters, whether anew, as when revisiting England, or for the first time, as was the case in Greece and Turkey. In his late seventies Green was able to perceive and relish with the delight of a young poet the beauties of parts of the world that many a thoughtful, sensitive man of that age might find irredeemably stereotyped by the eyes and utterances of innumerable previous sightseers.

For a reader familiar with the voluminous Journal of André Gide, often regarded as the classic example of a twentieth-century French man-of-letters' contribution to the genre (though some might consider Paul Léautaud's even vaster chronicle to have an equally valid claim), it is difficult to avoid the parallel that can be drawn between the personal notations of Green and those of Gide. It is consequently gratifying to find, on the fifth page of Green's latest volume, the following comment, occasioned by a brief glance through the recently-published correspondence between Gide and Henri Ghéon: 'Ce monde-là ne m'a jamais attiré, je veux dire tout ce qui gravitait autour de Gide. Lui-même, si passionant, attirait et propageait autour de lui des ondes d'ennui'. This can hardly come as a surprise to anyone who has struggled through countless pages by Gide monotonously registering tea with Martin du Gard, practising Chopin and arid exchanges with, say, Jean Schlumberger. It is, however, doubly interesting in this connection later to come across, in an entry dated January 1978, Green's account of an afternoon's conversation with a friend during which the latter talked to him at length, 'et d'une façon que je n'hésite pas à appeler sensationelle', about Gide's Journal, affirming that, despite official declarations to the contrary, large parts of it remain unpublished and that these abound with indiscretions; but,

---

'Good places and bad', review of Julien Green, *La Terre est si belle . . . 1976-1978* (Paris: Seuil, 1982), *Times Literary Supplement* (1 October 1982), p. 1072.

comments Green, 'de quel Journal cela n'est-il pas vrai?' Indiscretions, *oiseuses* or otherwise, can hardly be said to abound in any of Green's Journals. In this one, nevertheless, there is a significant example of that combination of frankness and reserve which may be thought most typical of him when writing of subjects usually qualified as 'intimate':

> Assombri toute la journée par une trop longue conversation sur la sexualité des deux genres et autres! Je ne supporte plus qu'on m'en parle parce que j'en ai trop souffert. C'est un lourd et sombre sujet. Je me rends compte aujourd'hui que, pour me dégager de toutes ces choses, il a fallu une sorte de miracle intérieur dont je n'ai pu que constater les effets sans jamais en saisir le détail.

The first entry of *La Terre est si belle*, headed May 21, 1976 – London, tells of listening that evening, in a garden near Carlyle's house, to the ravishing, distinctive song of a thrush that could be seen perched on the end of a black branch. The next day, Green refers to the small rose-brick house in Winchester to which Jane Austen retired to die, the stone slab above her remains in the Cathedral and the stained-glass window commemorating her, which causes him to remark: 'Avec quel amour l'Angleterre prend soin de ses écrivains, une fois morts!' Before returning to Paris early in June, he has seen and described Salisbury Cathedral and Stonehenge with admiration and fidelity.

Early in October of the same year he and his companion arrived in Athens, after a journey defined by him as 'le vieux rêve que je porte en moi depuis ma prime jeunesse'. The day after his disembarkation in Greece, he made the traditional clamber up to the Acropolis with the friend always referred to as Eric, reflecting afterwards: 'Pendant toute ma jeunesse, je pensais à la Grèce comme à une patrie et un peu de tout cela m'est revenu en voyant ces colonnes qui demeurent pour moi les plus belles du monde'. Two days later, while visiting Sounion and there again marvelling at the Hellenic ruins, Green made a discovery:

> Sur une des colonnes, ce malappris de Byron, comme tout le monde, voyons et touristes, a gravé son nom, car son aristocratie souffrait d'intermittences. Les signatures de son temps ne sont pas rares dans ce marbre profané, mais la signature du poète est très appliquée et plus profonde que les autres; on s'est donné beaucoup de mal pour être sûr que le temps n'efface pas le nom illustre. C'est la gloire, si l'on veut, et elle vaut ce que vaut la gloire: à peu près quatre sous.

There are not a few eminent writers from whose pens the conclusion of this paragraph might arouse a suspicion of perfunctory rhetoric, but such is Green's unvarying sincerity that any such reserve would in this case be ill-judged. It is exactly such sincerity that before long leads him to admit to a degree of disillusionment with the dream of Classic harmony and perfection he had once cherished so ardently: 'Qu'est-ce que j'attendais? Je ne sais pas, mais toutes ces ruines, si belles soient-elles, m'apparaissent comme les débris d'une magnifique vision fracassée. Le charme est rompu.' A few days later, having been to Epidaurus to experience the incomparable acoustics of its amphitheatre, in which a Greek actress, unemphatically reciting a monologue from the *Antigone*, caused Green to hear the word *thanatos* traversing the consecrated space like, he says, a black bird, he reached Mycenae, where he comes to the conclusion that 'Des deux Grèces, c'est la violente que je préfère'.

It would, however, be an error to infer from Green's preference for the dark side of Greek antiquity that he is in general predisposed most to appreciate in the world of appearances those aspects which might appear to correspond to the frequently sombre world of the imagination depicted in many of his best-known novels. From Greece, he travelled with his companion directly to Turkey, there to explore certain of the superimposed sites of Byzantium and Islam, starting with Istanbul. Green immediately fell under the spell of a type of culture and architecture wholly other than that of the country he had just left behind. Though fascinated by a certain grim vision revealed to him by Greece, he confesses that he fell unhesitatingly in love with Constantinople, and though aware that in 1976 it was, as it remains, impossible to rid oneself of an intuitive apprehension of the increasingly rapid decline of the world we are used to, he succumbed with pleasure to the outward peace and undisturbed beauty of the neighbourhood of the Bosphorus.

In November 1977, having just returned from a visit to Iran, and referring to his sister Anne, to whom he was particularly devoted and who has now sadly predeceased him, he writes that, while attempting to tell her something about the mosques of Isfahan, 'je devine à son regard soudain trop attentif qu'elle pense à autre chose. Elle a comme moi horreur des récits de voyage, surtout lorsqu'ils se fortifient d'un étalage de cartes postales, et je me tais.' Fortunately, the places recorded in his Journal never seem to have inspired in him a similar reticence. The twenty pages devoted to recording a tour of Wales and the North of England in May 1977 are uninterruptedly absorbing. It is diverting to learn, for instance, that Green, on arriving at Cardiff, found the sandwiches served him in the entrance-hall of his hotel there the best he had ever eaten. His Welsh tour, indeed, appears to have enchanted him in sundry ways. From Wales, he passed on to Chester where, he records, in the Cathedral, 'protestante pourtant, on me glisse un *leaflet*, une feuille sur la confession qui me surprend un peu. Elle est mot pour mot et presque toute entière catholique, absolution comprise': an intriguing sidelight on the workings of ecumenicism. Liverpool is designated a 'ville d'une laideur effarante', but in the nearby Lady Lever Art Gallery at Port Sunlight, which struck him as 'a sort of paradise', the chronicler found much to admire among the numerous Pre-Raphaelite works that are housed there. Having enjoyed York and Durham, on 15 May Green writes: 'Ce matin à Haworth. Il faut être du pays pour prononcer ce nom convenablement. En aboyant un peu on y parvient. C'est chez les Brontë que nous allons, visite fort important pour moi qui leur dois beaucoup.' Towards the end of this entry occurs a passage that well illustrates the affinity Green obviously feels with the Brontës. Behind their Rectory, he explains, stretch 'les "moors", les vastes landes ondulées qui sont le royaume du vent, coupées de vallons où le silence se réfugie comme un voleur. Ces hauteurs, appelées "wuthering" pour le désespoir des traducteurs, l'énorme voix tantôt sourde, long mugissement sinistre, tantôt éperdue, menaçante, les traverse comme une plainte venue d'un autre monde.'

La Terre est si belle . . . is much concerned with celebrating aspects of the objective world that still inspire both aesthetic and spiritual delight, and might well lead one to conclude that for Green, in spite of everything, the planet we inhabit remains a good place on which to spend our lives. An entry dated 9 February 1977, however, makes one of the first of many allusions to the writing, proof-correction and publication of the latest of his novels: 'Beaucoup travaillé à mon roman (*Le Mauvais Lieu*). La petite Louise est une mystique égarée dans un enfer, qui est le monde.' The following May, in Wales, he interrupts his chronicle of pleasant peregrinations to note that, because it is impossible for him to remain alone in a room without being impelled to attack paper with pen, he is continuing to work on this novel; and recalling what he had written fifty pages earlier, he comments: 'Cela m'assombrit parce que la vérité du roman est aussi intense que la vérité d'un cauchemar, et celui qui fait le cauchemar y croit. Me voilà loin du Pays de Galles, ce pays dont le nom souffle le vent des légendes.' Before the middle of July, he has finished correcting the proofs of *Le Mauvais Lieu*; and on 24 September, he records in the Journal: 'Mon roman a paru. Il est là, sur ma table, avec cette couverture qui reproduit une peinture de Munch: *Puberté*. Paraîtra-t-elle scandaleuse? Qu'appelle-t-on scandaleux de nos jours et comment s'y prendon pour scandaliser?'

Green's use of the word *mauvais* appears to be subtly personal: he clearly intends it to convey something rather different from the conventionally pejorative sense generally attached to it. In qualifying the air of

Manchester as *mauvais*, for example, he is implicitly suggesting something more sinister than what we mean by 'bad' in common parlance, a sense that cannot be distinguished from the *air mauvais* that repels and fascinates him at Mycenae. The *mauvais lieu* in Green's novel is specifically a house of assignation of a peculiarly squalid description, which at the same time typifies, as noted by the novelist while still writing the book, the actual world of modern man, *un enfer*. The story the novel tells is that of the inevitable destruction in such a world of an incarnation of incorruptible innocence, the adolescent Louise, who might well be seen as a spiritual sister of Little Eyolf. The fact that Green was simultaneously engaged in treating this chilling theme and experiencing the world about him with wholehearted delight may at first seem paradoxical. The apparent contradiction becomes more easily acceptable if one understands the term 'world' to represent a domain that is at once 'given' and 'projected'. The world presented through the eyes of Julien Green in this Journal is 'so beautiful' that he desires to embrace as much of it as possible with avidity; yet he makes it clear that he is nevertheless continually aware of its implacable hostility to what he most values in the human essence. As to the question regarding the nature of the power that ultimately rules 'the world', this is unequivocally answered by the entry with which the journal concludes. It tells how, on 2 August 1978, Green received a visit from a Jewish friend who had previously discussed his spiritual tribulations with him. This time he declared to his confidant: 'I suffer and I suffer because others suffer'. Yet he avowed that in the Cathedral of La Spezia he had realized that Christ was God. 'Dieu Enfant, dit il. – L'Enfant tient dans sa main le globe, dis-je alors. – Oui, c'est ainsi que je l'ai vu.'

VINCENT VAN GOGH

The salient feat achieved by Viviane Forrester in her new study of van Gogh is that of bringing out anew, and revealing in all its intricacy, the psychodrama hidden by the now commonly accepted stereotype of the artist. Half-way through her book she clearly indicates the degree of confusion confronting anyone attempting to elucidate her chosen subject:

> Personne, dans cette histoire, n'est simple. A travers les lettres, les témoignages si crus, si spontanés, apparaissent innombrables, des fluctuations au gré des émotions, des circonstances: chacun est aux prises avec ses fantasmes, ses désirs, ses haines refoulés. Tous sont contradictoires. Vivants. Et tous sont perçus par Vincent, lequel est perçu par eux, à travers les miroirs déformants des subjectivités troublées par l'inconscient, et compliquées du reflet, des interférences d'autres subjectivités.

The *dramatis personae* of the van Gogh saga can be reduced to a relatively small cast of essential characters; but a more than superficial understanding of it requires consideration of a number of relatives, friends and acquaintances to whom proper attention has seldom been paid by any one biographer or critic. Viviane Forrester may to some extent have been selective in appraising the relative importance of these more marginal roles, but she cannot be said to have neglected to name any individual who had the least significance in the story. It would seem that almost everyone he ever knew or met had some sort of significance for Vincent, on account of his inherent capacity for emotional involvement with those about him, and the respect accorded by him to everyone, perhaps in particular to the humblest. This unfailing generosity was accompanied by the shrewd perceptiveness peculiar to innocence, rarely deceived by deficient integrity and never impressed by the self-importance of routine respectability. Viviane Forrester frequently draws attention to the astonishingly lucid self-awareness that accompanied the savage, intermittent inner disturbances by which van Gogh was afflicted

---

'Distorting mirrors', review of Viviane Forrester, *Van Gogh ou l'enterrement dans les blés* (Paris: Seuil, 1983), *Times Literary Supplement* (9 December 1983), p. 1386.

during the concluding phase of his existence, an awareness no doubt correlative with that characteristic self-detachment which became increasingly indistinguishable from what is commonly diagnosed as dissociation of the personality.

Viviane Forrester's attitude to the question of what is still generally regarded as van Gogh's madness is unequivocal:

> A quoi bon faire état des innombrables diagnostics, un véritable catalogue de tous les effets 'folie' dont on affuble van Gogh? La 'maladie'? Il y avait Vincent, non dissocié. Il y a eu la pensée de Vincent, aux limites; son désir fracassé, son désir projeté. La maladie? Ce fut surtout la 'santé' des autres, leur prétendue santé; ce fut l'absence organisé d'identité des autres . . .

And she goes on to quote, not surprisingly, from Artaud's commentary on van Gogh, 'le Suicidé de la Societé'. This might suggest that her point of view has some affinity with the theories elaborated during recent decades by Foucault, Laing or Thomas Szasz; but having ostensibly little faith in any ideological system, she refers once, in passing, only to Freud.

What emerges as the *clou* of her analysis of van Gogh's psychological dilemma is the paramount importance she attaches to the fact that exactly a year to the day before his own birth his mother was delivered of a stillborn first child, later interred outside his father's parish church at Zundert under a stone inscribed with the name Vincent Wilhelm van Gogh. To argue, as this book does from the start, that Vincent I, as its author calls this amorphous being, haunted the conscience and the unconscious mind of his namesake and successor throughout his apparently disastrous career, may strike one at first as a hazardous undertaking; but the case is made so cogently that I, for one, have been persuaded that it does, in fact, end by shedding valuable new light on a destiny that can now be seen to have been, despite all odds, triumphantly creative.

Another innovatory feature of Viviane Forrester's treatment of her subject is the thorough-going exegesis it contains of a work by Dickens that attracted van Gogh so much that he read it repeatedly. This was the last and perhaps least well-known of the *Christmas Books* series, a story some 100 pages long, first published in 1853 under the title 'The Haunted Man'. It does indeed contain many remarkable symbolic analogies and parallels with some of the painter's most constant preoccupations, as well as evidence contributing support to the conjecture that he never succeeded in repressing all recollection of the Vincent who had preceded him and whose life he had usurped. Dickens's story begins and ends by quoting the words of an inscription engraved on a panel of the chamber that provides the tale's principal setting: 'Lord, keep my memory green!'

Viviane Forrester's comment on the end of van Gogh's life-cycle is as caustic as it is laconic:

> Arles? Vincent a trente-cinq ans. Saint-Rémy? Trente-six ans. Auvers? Il y meurt à trente-sept ans et quatre mois. Théo mourra à trente-quatre ans.
>
> C'est vite fait d'assassiner les gêneurs. Et de capter les biens qu'on leur a estorqué sous la torture. Et de nommer ces biens un héritage.

Purists may find her style somewhat *gênant*, insofar as it confronts them with an unusual profusion of italics and exclamations marks; others may take exception to her exceedingly personal approach. But that her book is packed with question-marks seems to me an indication of one of its principal virtues. It is calculated to rearouse any interest one may still preserve in a painter now popularized to an unprecedented degree, and to stimulate the asking of a number of fundamental questions, not only about the life and work of van Gogh, but regarding the pernicious functioning of the art-marketing system in modern society.

LAWRENCE FERLINGHETTI

Here is a prime example of a regrettably rare genre: an exercise in topical reportership by a poet of international repute. The tensions between the Reagan administration and the new Soviet leadership, the daily dramas of the Middle East, may at the moment be claiming most of our attention; but Central America continues meanwhile to simmer with an explosive unrest that cannot for long be ignored. This account of Ferlinghetti's brief sojourn in Nicaragua early in 1984 is a salutary and informative reminder of the state of affairs in a small but unusually representative Latin American state in which a form of necessarily 'revolutionary' socialism is struggling to emerge from the overthrow of one more repressive colonialist-controlled dictatorship.

The ostensible object of Ferlinghetti's visit sounds almost romantically ideal: 'to give the poet and Minister of Culture, Father Ernesto Cardenal, a seed from a flower at Boris Pasternak's grave which had been given to him by the Russian poet Andrei Voznesenski at a poetry reading against war at UNESCO in Paris'. He also went to deliver the first copies of City Lights' *Volcán*, an anthology of Central American poetry, and to see the Sandinist revolution for himself.

The poet-priest who is Nicaraguan Minister of Culture emerges from these pages as a vividly impressive character. His first appearance is as head of the welcome-party awaiting Ferlinghetti at the airport, 'wearing a black beret and a white *cotona*, or short-sleeved blouse and blue jeans'. He also wears an angelic smile and a white beard, is in his late fifties and was once a disciple of Thomas Merton's at his Kentucky Trappist monastery. The day after his arrival, Ferlinghetti has lunch with Ernesto Cardenal at the seaside. They drink rum together, and the American poet finds that without his beret, the Father has white hair almost to his shoulders. Ferlinghetti is reminded by Cardenal's use of the word *usura* during their conversation that Ezra Pound had been one of his poetic masters. Then journalists arrive to ply him with questions which he answers with tireless sweetness which causes his visitor to qualify him once more as 'angelic'.

Review of Lawrence Ferlinghetti, *Seven Days in Nicarague Libre* (San Francisco: City Lights, 1984), *Ambit* 102 (1985), pp. 51-4.

Temperance and fortitude, he insists (. . .) are the distinguishing characteristics of the Revolution and of the *junta* directing it. *Junta*, he points out, doesn't mean a military dictatorship; the dictionary simply says it's a 'group'.

Ernesto went on to say that the Sandinist model for the Revolution is neither the Cuban nor the Soviet, and that for himself as a priest the model is the kingdom of God. And with his vision of primitive Christianity, it was logical for him to add that in his view the Revolution would not have succeeded until there were no more masters and no more slaves. 'The Gospels,' he said, 'foresee a classless society. They foresee also *the withering away of the state"*.'

Cardenal is clearly one of those aberrant priests who have been causing Pope John Paul so many painfully sleepless nights. Opposite the passage just quoted, Chris Felver has a photograph of a radiant Father Cardenal, surrounded by rapturously smiling beach children. At the bottom of the facing page, Ferlinghetti adds the comment: 'Earlier this season, the ships and port of Corinto on this coast were set afire by *contras* financed by the CIA, that international terrorist group'.

Though undisguisedly of the Left, as the last quoted remark makes obvious Ferlinghetti is far from being a rabid propagandist. Asked: 'Why have you come?' by a couple of journalists soon after his arrival, he finds the question excellent, and explains that he sees his visit as 'a voyage of discovery, hoping to discover the Sandinistas are in the right, and that I might take some public stand in their favor, rather than the political silence maintained by many U.S. writers today. (Not exactly with that much-vaunted objectivity of North American journalists, I hope at least I have an open mind, but a mind not so open that the brains fall out.)'

★

Ferlinghetti's claim to be open-minded is fully justified by the entry chronicling the fourth day of his visit, when he paid a visit to *La Prensa*, the opposition newspaper, generally a pro-capitalist journal, to interview in his editorial office Pablo Antonio Cuedra, whom he describes as 'the very important poet and editor known for his opposition to the present regime, for both poetic and libertarian reasons'. Cuedra had taken part in an International PEN Club meeting the previous autumn in Venezuela, where he had declared:

> I am against the direction of the revolution taken by the Sandinistas. If I have stayed within the country and kept my position

> in *La Prensa* . . . it is exactly because I believe that the attitude of directing culture, censorship and the creation of a conscience in the service of an ideology . . . is fatal for a culture. That is why I am in a rather disagreeable struggle.

There is no room here to quote further from Cuedra's long defence of his position, but his final sentence is one likely to arouse sympathetic echoes in many European writers, and not only those of Right-wing allegiance: 'As soon as literature begins to be in the service of something it stops being literature and turns to propaganda'. One may disagree with this argument without necessarily feeling bound to denounce it as symptomatic of dishonest casuistry. The Nicaraguan Culture Minister, Father Cardenal, was later to send Ferlinghetti an official statement regarding censorship and the position of *La Prensa* in particular. It comes as no surprise to find *La Prensa* strictured in this statement for openly defending the enemy and condoning the actions of the CIA. Cardenal had, however, described Cuedra to the visiting American as 'a major poet' despite his hostility to the current regime. Ferlinghetti describes parting from Cuedra at the end of their interview 'amiably enough, I believe'; he continues, 'we understood each other, as poets. He wanted to talk poetry, not politics. We exchanged books of poetry. The inscription in his book read: "*Su lector y amigo* – Pablo Antonio Cuedra". – "Quite aware",' concludes Ferlinghetti, 'of the "totalitarian intolerance" often exercised by the Left as well as the right in the U.S., I shook his hand and wished him well as we parted. If the Sandinistas really believe, as they insisted, in a "democratic pluralism" in their government, I wished to be a part of it.'

During the evening following this meeting, Ferlinghetti went to meet the Minister of Agriculture, Jaime Wheelock, who seemed to him a very literate man, '– a young intellectual one might meet at Columbia University'. Wheelock told him he would rather talk to poets than politicians, and expressed more interest in what poets have to say than what he might hear from government functionaries. This cordial conversation, which included some discussion of the improved lot of farmworkers, ended with Wheelock, a lawyer credited with being one of the main theoreticians of the Revolution, posing for a photo by Chris Felver, which shows him looking calm, straightforward and handsome in his uniform against dark shrubbery. Only after their parting did it occur to Ferlinghetti that he had 'neglected to ask him the most pertinent question from the point of view of American labor. Why had the government suspended the workers' right to strike? Or perhaps I hadn't asked because I knew what the answer would be, and he knew I knew, so why go through the charade? At the present stage of socialist regimes in the world, the answer is always the same: expediency.'

*

The virtual climax to Ferlinghetti's Nicaraguan trip took place on the fifth of his seven days in that country. After visiting Father Cardenal in his Ministry of Culture office, a converted bathroom in a villa in a park that once belonged to Somoza, and then taking part in a reception given by one of Nicaragua's leading publishing firms, at which Sergio Ramurez, novelist, editor, *comandante* in the National Directorate and founder of the liberation's literary movement 'Ventana', was in evidence. Ferlinghetti finally found himself, having been invited to attend a meeting of the ASTC (Association of Sandinista Cultural Workers) at their arts centre, where about fifty people were assembled seated in a circle outdoors, called upon to make a speech. 'Suddenly I wish I had in my pocket a list of "the best minds of my generation" and of the greatest and most respected established writers in the USA who are publicly and actively supporting the Sandinista regime – but such a list is short. (How many of our most famous novelists, for instance, have bothered to take the two-and-a-half-hour flight from Miami and see for themselves what's going on here? . . .')

Faced with the artists and intelligentsia of Nicaragua, Ferlinghetti, overcome by sudden misgivings, launched into what he describes as 'a diatribe on nationalism in general', only to find that this was definitely not what they wanted to hear. When the floor was subsequently open to questions, it became apparent that what his audience specially wanted to hear about was writing and especially poetry in the USA today. Ferlinghetti then gave them his view that

> North American poetry right now seems to be in a deep sleep or, hopefully, in a state of gestation. Some writers are just too well fed, by government grants or university writing programmes. Some are not so well fed but lack the stimulus provided by war, rapid change in society, or revolution as in Nicaragua now. Poets are not especially honoured in our land, having for the most part abdicated any vatic or prophetic role – with some large exceptions. As such, poetry has been relegated to a most ephemeral place – position as 'filler' in most large publications, though published profusely by small presses throughout the land.
> *What it takes is inspiration, and hunger.*

*

This diagnosis of the present state of American poetry strikes me as remarkably similar in most respects to one that might well be applied to our own (British) poetry scene – 'with some large exceptions', I would like to add, though only about half a dozen names occur to me, and to divulge them would be wholly irrelevant to this article. One can only trust that by the turn of the century the best British poets of today will turn out to have been not only hungry but inspired. What I do know is that I have not read many recent English poems manifesting even a covert concern with Nicaragua, or with any other of the Latin American countries; and I confess that I do not myself at the moment feel impelled to make good this deficiency.

It seems hardly necessary to conclude by asserting that Ferlinghetti's travel journal displays him as an honourably conscientious witness and an engagingly readable reporter. Chris Felver's many photographs add an invaluable visual accompaniment to the text: one particular study in black and white commemorates the culminating moment of Ferlinghetti's presentation to Ernesto Cardenal of the seed from Pasternak's grave. The conclusion to which his observations led the San Francisco poet is that the Nicaraguan endeavour points to a future 'United States of Central America' as a real possibility. On the last night of his tour he encountered one of the most important men in the government: Daniel Ortega Saavedra, the Coordinator of the National Directorate, accompanied by the Minister of Foreign Affairs, Father Miguel d'Escoto Brockmann. During the course of this final conversation, Daniel Ortega 'pointed out that at the moment the total effect of President Reagan's policies was to *impede* Nicaragua's progress towards any free elections and towards any kind of democratic Nicaragua. He also added that they fully expected, as soon as Reagan was re-elected, he would send the invasion forces.'

Since that concluding meeting of Ferlinghetti with Nicaraguan government officials in February 1984, Reagan has been overwhelmingly re-elected, but has as yet prudently avoided further direct armed intervention in Central American countries whose policies he no doubt regards as posing a threat to the kind of democracy that ensures the freedom of competition and profit. On Ferlinghetti's penultimate page is printed a box containing a statement by Daniel Ortega defining the kind of democracy aimed at by the Sandinist regime. These are its two concluding sentences:

> For us democracy is truly to love one another; which is to say,
>   to bury self-centredness, greed, and the thirst for gold.
> That is to say, to bury the exploiter and to raise the exploited up
>   out of their graves.

It is as easy to be blasé about the naiveté of such utopian ideals as it is cynically to see in such words a prelude to expedient slaughter. But it is better to be grateful to be still living in a world in which the expression of such sentiments can be seen to demonstrate that it is still possible, despite the desperate forces of reaction, to believe in a more human form of society.

HUMPHREY JENNINGS

Having made a dozen or so 'documentary'-type films during the last war, some of them now acknowledged as unique masterpieces of their genre and revived as such on television, Humphrey Jennings died in 1950 at the age of forty-three. He had suffered an accident in Greece while engaged on what would in all probability have been in any case his last film. In New York the following year Ruthven Todd, under the imprint of 'The Weekend Press', issued a pamphlet of ten pages containing all Humphrey Jennings's mature poems. It had an introduction by Kathleen Raine, his friend since their days together in Cambridge in the late 1920s, when the influence of I. A. Richards had been at its height and William Empson, Jacob Bronowski and Charles Madge were among the most brilliant of their contemporaries. It was in collaboration with Charles Madge, his close friend and Blackheath neighbour, that in 1936 Jennings had inaugurated the Mass-Observation movement, later predominantly associated with the name of the anthropologist Tom Harrisson.

These facts and many others were recorded in a book by Anthony Hodgkinson and Roger Sheratsky published in the United States in 1982 by the New England University Press under the title *Humphrey Jennings – More than a Maker of Films*. In the seventh chapter of this study, under the heading 'Unfinished Projects', the authors explained that

> Jennings's plan, cherished throughout his adult life but never finally realised, was to use Milton's concept (of Pandaemonium as the capital of Hell) as the title of a collage-anthology of quotations from contemporary Englishmen of the 17th, 18th and 19th centuries. In his work, intended to be published as a four-volume paperback, indexed, cross-referenced, and profusely illustrated, Jennings planned to display and juxtapose ideas from those centuries, notably those commenting on the machine and its effects upon society.

'A poet's way of bringing order out of chaos', review of Humphrey Jennings, *Pandaemonium 1660-1886: The Coming of the Machine as Seen by Contemporary Observers*, ed. Mary-Lou Jennings and Charles Madge (André Deutsch, 1985), *The Tablet* (23 November 1985), pp. 1232-3.

The authors noted that *Pandaemonium*, like Benjamin's "greatest ambition", was never published nor completed during its composer's lifetime'. They went on: 'Jennings's papers still lie, untouched for years, in the vaults of a London bank. After Humphrey's tragic death, Jacob Bronowski tried to have the existing papers published, but found it difficult in those days to duplicate the handwritten passages. Even when Charles Madge and others had typescripts prepared for publishers, problems continued . . .'

Having been aware of and fascinated by Humphrey Jennings's project since the mid-1930s when I first came into contact with him, through Surrealism and then Mass-Observation, and having become more or less resigned to its becoming ultimately forgotten, it was for me a moment of special excitement when, at the end of the summer, an advance copy of *Pandaemonium* reached me. Jennings's elder daughter, Mary-Lou, explains at the end of her brief introduction how, as the result of a conversation ensuing from the Riverside Studios' 1982 retrospective exhibition of her father's paintings, drawings, photographs and films, she approached Charles Madge to ask him if he would complete his original work on the manuscript by helping her compose a final version, and how he then went through the whole of the original material yet once more, enabling Mary-Lou to decide with him on the final selection. Madge's equally brief preface explaining his 'Editorial Tasks and Method' makes clear how dauntingly complex an assignment confronted him when he came to edit the material accumulated by Jennings over a period of some thirty years three decades previously. It would be hard to overestimate the amount of diligence, skill and dedication that Charles Madge, and Mary-Lou Jennings in collaboration with him, have exerted in order to make possible the final publication of such an unprecedented compilation as *Pandaemonium* represents.

Humphrey Jennings was obviously extraordinarily well-read, not only in traditional English literature, major and minor, in all its variety, but also in the work of such social, religious and scientific thinkers as were contemporaries of, for instance, Milton, Gray, Blake and Dickens. He was equally familiar with the writings of most of the most original, controversial and vital thinkers of the first half of the twentieth century. I do not particularly remember discussing C. G. Jung with him, nor Jungian dissidence from the materialism of Freud, exclusively revered by orthodox members of the Surrealist movement, nor in particular the concept of the Collective Unconscious, arguably of fundamental relevance to the original ideas underlying the theory of Mass-Observation in its early stages; but it strikes me that his choice of the term 'animistic', which occurs several times in the notes accompanying the texts he selected, was an especially felicitous one. It avoids the kinds of misunderstanding that inevitably arise from the use of such words as 'religious', 'metaphysical', or 'transcendental', while unmistakably implying recognition and acceptance of *anima*, the soul.

It also ties in with the thought of Coleridge, one of whose notebooks is significantly entitled *Anima Poetae*, and who was for I. A. Richards, and many of those influenced by him, the most eloquent spokesman for the English Imagination, and hence for the image (also the keystone of Surrealist and most other modern French poetry and painting). Charles Madge knew and understood Humphrey Jennings's conception of the all-importance of the image better than anyone, and what he has to say on the subject in his preface is invaluable; though even more so is the 'Note on Images' that he wrote for the Jennings memorial pamphlet published by the Institute of Contemporary Art in 1951.

On the eve of its publication, *Pandaemonium* was discussed with Hermione Lee by Mary-Lou Jennings, Charles Madge and Lindsay Anderson on Channel 4's weekly book programme. The film director, conveying his assessment of the personality and achievement of Humphrey Jennings, about whom he has written with enthusiastic discernment, used the word 'nobility', and I believe that all those who knew Jennings would agree that this was indeed one of the most salient of the qualities distinguishing both his character, at once tough and endearing, and his vision.

Writing on some aspects of Jennings's work in 1954, Anderson said that 'he had a mind that delighted in simile and the unexpected relationship'. This special gift for seeing everything in terms of clusters of interlinked associations and essential characteristics found its supreme expression in the unclassifiable work that has now at last emerged phoenix-like from the vaults of a bank. It may not be of quite such grandiose proportions as it might have attained had its architect succeeded in completing it himself; but as it appears today it is, as he would have wished, of easy access to an incalculably varied audience.

It contains 372 extracts, the first 'The Building of Pandaemonium' from *Paradise Lost* and the last a passage from William Morris's *A Dream of John Ball* headed 'The Day of the Earth'. The extracts are arranged in chronological order, and divided into four parts, corresponding to what Jennings once noted as 'a possible pattern': '17th Cent. The Idea. 18th Cent. The Means. 19th Cent. The Man.' The fourth part, containing over a hundred passages written between 1851 and 1886, now bears the subtitle: 'Confusion'. Charles Madge has compiled an appendix, and there are a number of illustrations, including a 'Water-Insect or Gnat' from Robert Hooke's *Micrographia* of 1663, an engraving after John

Martin of an Iguanodon from *The Book of the Great Sea Dragons* of 1834, and Gustave Doré's fabulous vision of Ludgate Hill from the series which provided van Gogh with inspiration during his stay in London.

Pandaemonium should properly be read first from beginning to end, as a continuous documentary-montage-filmscript concerning the coming and immediate consequences of the Industrial Revolution. It is then possible to treat the book as what it also is, a fascinating anthology that can be dipped into at random according to the reader's individual inclination. Such a reader is likely to find at least some passages already familiar to him, but also to find these freshened and illumined by a deeper significance in the context Jennings has devised for them. And every reader will probably discover extracts from certain writers hitherto unfamiliar to him that will stimulate him to investigate their work further.

During the latter part of this century, it seems to be growing apparent that the vanguard of scientific thought has become increasingly conscious of the inseparability of the observer from what he observes; in other words, subjectivity can no longer be regarded as 'mere' reflection, but has to be recognized as an integral factor in the process of the most dispassionate recording of data or enunciation of formulae. Humphrey Jennings was a man who thought passionately; this by no means diminished his capacity to be objective. His implicit convictions and the bias influencing his choice of the parts making up the vision which is his legacy were unavoidably personal, despite a constantly self-critical attempt to achieve a balanced all-round view. In the introduction written up by Charles Madge from extensive notes left by Humphrey Jennings occurs a passage which makes clear his fundamental standpoint with regard to his material:

> *The Means of Vision* – a matter (sense impressions) transformed and reborn by Imagination: *turned into an image.*
> *The Means of Production* – matter is transformed by Labour.

Behind this can be detected an inherent sympathy with the tradition of guild socialism, so that quotations from and references to Robert Owen, Tom Paine, Cobbett and Engels are hardly surprising; but all these are counterbalanced by mention of Burke, Bentham, Darwin and Huxley. Of modern historians, passing reference is made only to G. M. Trevelyan. Though a good deal of light is thrown on the by now notorious Protestant work ethic, no mention is made of R. H. Tawney. If G. K. Chesterton had fitted into the time-span covered by *Pandaemonium*, it seems likely that his special brand of Catholic and English socialist idealism would have found some place in Jennings's patchwork.

As it is, the most considerable Catholic writer represented is Gerard Manley Hopkins, who apart from being essentially apolitical, probably leaned towards a guarded conservatism, with regard to the affairs of this world. What is interesting about the extract from his Journal for 1871 that appears in the concluding section of *Pandaemonium* is that it ideally combines the materialist and animistic currents of thought that are shown interacting on each other throughout the whole book. It is a scrupulous account of Hopkins's observation of the phenomenon of evaporation, as exemplified in clouds and 'for instance over our Lenten chocolate': in this case the eye of a scientist and the language of a poet combine for once in unforgettable fusion.

The conclusion to Jennings's own introductory notes on the purpose of his book may well serve to round off this review also:

> The relationship of production to vision and vision to production has been mankind's greatest problem.
>
> Unless we are prepared to claim special attributes for the poet – the attribute of vision – and unless we are prepared to admit the work of the artist (that is to say the function of 'imagination') as an essential part of the modern world, there is no real reason for our continuing to bother with any of the arts any more, or with any imaginary activity. No reasons except money, snobbery, propaganda or escapism. In this book however it is assumed that the poet's vision does exist, that the exercise of the imagination is as indispensable a function of man like work, eating, sleeping, loving.

An assertion so cardinal to the current state of the imaginative arts in society makes the survival of *Pandaemonium* seem nothing less than providential.

JOHN CORNFORD and CHRISTOPHER CAUDWELL

By the time this article appears, Dr Cunningham's invaluably extensive compilation will already have been out for a year. By the time it was published in 1986, the same author's *Penguin Book of Spanish Civil War Verse* was already six years old. The introductions to both these books might be said to be required reading for anyone wishing properly to appreciate the writings and personae of Caudwell and Cornford. Dr Cunningham's grasp of the complex political and literary background of the later 1930s against which these two figures, and their numerous fellow-combatants and contemporaries, must be seen, seems unsurpassable. His fluent presentation of the period's history is fascinatingly informative; his critical comments are notable for their trenchant acumen. *Spanish Front* contains two of Cornford's best-remembered poems and two of his letters to Margot Heinemann, as well as extracts from what the *News Chronicle* published as 'Last Letters of a Hero', that is to say of Christopher Caudwell, less well-known as Christopher St John Sprigge (his father's surname), whose last poems must have been written before July 1936. It also contains 380 pages of writing, mainly prose, by over a hundred authors, for the most part British, but also American, French, Spanish, Italian and German, some of them among the most distinguished representatives of twentieth-century literature. I could well have devoted an entire article to discussing this exemplary anthology but that is not my brief; and in any case it might be felt that it would be unsuitable for one to review a book in which is to be found even a minor – and to me now somewhat incongruous – contribution by the reviewer.

The simultaneous publication, by the consistently enterprising Carcanet Press, of work by Caudwell and Cornford ought not to create the misleading impression that there is much similarity between them other than that of their both having been convinced, well-grounded Marxists who lost their lives in the Spanish Republican cause. There is sufficient disparity between their ages (the elder born in 1907, Cornford

---

'Action urgent and its nature clear', review of *Spanish Front: Writers on the Civil War*, ed. Valentine Cunningham (OUP, 1986), Christopher Caudwell, *Collected Poems* (Manchester: Carcanet, 1987), and John Cornford, *Collected Writings* (Manchester: Carcanet, 1987), *Poetry Review*, Vol. 77, No. 3 (1987), pp. 26-9.

in 1915) to warrant describing them as having belonged to virtually different generations. There was a significant difference between their respective family and cultural backgrounds. It seems unlikely that they had ever heard of one another when they were killed.

Space permits only the most cursory summary of the salient biographical facts concerning Christopher Sprigge/Caudwell. By 1934 he had published a novel and some stories in the detective genre, numerous articles relating to aviation and a textbook on this specialist subject, as well as much routine news journalism. His parents had been Catholic converts, and such education as he received was infused by the tenets of that religion, which before long he abandoned. He left school at fifteen and escaped university, so that he may justifiably be classified as a polymath autodidact, and a most brilliantly endowed one at that.

Alan Young, editor of Caudwell's *Collected Poems 1924-1936*, tells us in his succinct Introduction that the firm of Aviation Publications Ltd., of which by 1933 (the worst year of the Depression) Sprigge/Caudwell had become director, finally went bankrupt, and that it has been suggested that this may have led him to question for the first time the nature of capitalist economics. Towards the end of the following year he undertook a thorough course of reading in the Marxist canon, i.e. the writings of Marx and Engels, Lenin, Stalin and other Russian dogmatists; and during the following years wrote the posthumously published essays that make up *Studies in a Dying Culture, Illusion and Reality* and three other collections that earned him an assured reputation as perhaps the most lucid and rigorous Communist critic and theorist of the pre-War period.

Only one or two poems of Caudwell's were published in reviews during his lifetime. The selection published as *Poems* by his confidential friend Paul Beard in 1939 cannot have reached a wide audience, and until now the main body of his work has remained unavailable. Though I read *Illusion and Reality* not long after its first appearance and remember having been impressed by it, Caudwell's poetry was something I knew nothing about before reading the present volume. It struck me immediately that this is in the main work deserving repeated readings, which I have not yet had time to give it. It is polished and technically accomplished in a traditional style, dense with allusions that may not always be familiar, and able soon to convince the reader that its author had achieved an unmistakably individual voice of his own.

Alan Young writes: 'Christopher had read fairly widely in poetry. There are echoes of Thomas Hardy, Robert Graves, Rupert Brooke and Wilfred Owen, for example, in his early poems, and of Shakespeare, Skelton, and other British poets'. Among these others, I would add at least Donne, Dryden and Swift. The modern poet with whom Caudwell seems to me to have the closest affinity is Edgell Rickword, though Alan Young, who edited the two volumes of Rickword's literary criticism published by Carcanet a few years ago, never refers to him as having any connection with Caudwell. It would seem in fact highly unlikely that Caudwell ever came across either Rickword's scarce first collection, *Behind the Eyes* (1921), or the more remarkable, long neglected *Invocations to Angels* that followed it seven years later. The fact that Rickword is superior as a poet to Caudwell (who might had he lived gone on to equal him), which seems to me obvious, is also beside the point. What matters is that it can undeniably be claimed that the two poets share a close similarity of diction, tersely Augustan, and a preoccupation with patently parallel themes, just as both were persuaded that Marxism provides the approach most proper to a twentieth-century writer. Writing of Edgell Rickword's *Collected Poems* in 1948, Roy Fuller remarked that Rickword's work was distinguished by what post-war poetry needed most badly: 'intellect, form, bitterness'. These are the features most characteristic of the Caudwell revealed in this edition of his poetic output.

Though restriction of space does not allow me to linger over discussion of those poems my subjective judgement considers to be the most notable in Caudwell's output, I cannot bring myself to leave the topic without drawing attention to at least three items. Bitterness is the distinctive flavour of most of the later (post-1934) poems in this collection, and in particular of the sequence entitled 'Twenty Sonnets of Wm. Smith'. Though acquaintance with the work of Rickword can almost certainly be ruled out as a possible influence on Caudwell's poetic development, this series inevitably prompts one to wonder how familiar he may have been with Meredith's *Modern Love*, forty-two sixteen-line poems that have all the concentration characteristic of the sonnet. While we are aware of the distress Meredith's unfortunate marriage brought him and the circumstances which must surely have inspired what are today his best-known poems, it is impossible to speculate, in the absence of all but the most meagre information concerning Christopher Sprigge's private life, on the extent to which personal experience gave rise to the sequence in question. Wm. Smith is more suggestive of Everyman or A. N. Other than of Hugh Selwyn Mauberley. But his reflections on the nature of modern love at least fifty years after the emergence of Meredith's sequence, though never achieving so memorably conclusive a line as: 'We are betrayed by what is false within', nevertheless constitute both a series of skilled variations in sonnet form and a commendable document concerning the sexual *mores* and attitudes typical of the pre-war middle-class intelligentsia, prone to a cynicism and sense of disgust that even a late Victorian could scarcely have experienced. The 'Kensington

Rime', written slightly earlier in the same period as the 'Sonnets', is a strangely original ballad that evokes mingled echoes both of the Ancient Mariner and of Auden's Miss Edith Gee. The concluding poem in the collection is the 35-page verse drama 'Orestes' (originally 'Orestes in Harley Street'), which Alan Young regards as 'Christopher Sprigge's finest single poetic achievement' and describes as 'both serious and funny, its ironic and playful surface barely holding down its depths of pain, bewilderment and grief'. While recognizing it as undoubtedly impressive, I personally find its 'farewell to the illusions of mythic psychology' a trifle too protracted, and Athene's concluding peroration disappointingly unauthoritative and flat, deliberately so though the author may have intended it to be.

Only 23 of the approximately 200 pages making up the *Collected Writings* of John Cornford are devoted to his poems, and of these, only three were written in and about Spain and the Civil War. The rest of the book consists of essays and articles, mainly polemical, and Cornford's letters, mostly to his mother Frances (poet and wife of distinguished Professor F. M. Cornford), a contemporary friend (Tristan Jones), and finally to his one true beloved, Margot Heinemann (he had already been briefly married to another young woman). This article being supposedly concerned above all with poetry in connection with the Spanish Civil War, it is with some regret that I feel myself obliged to pay less attention to the personality and social commitment of Cornford as revealed in his prose writings than to his potential reputation as a poet. It is sad but necessary to say that this reputation will probably continue to remain centred on a single poem, four originally untitled quatrains addressed to Margot Heinemann, whose name has now become permanently associated with it. It is a lyric of the most unaffected simplicity, that a responsive reader would find poignant even if unaware that its author died in battle at the age of twenty-one. In his Introduction to the *Penguin Book of Spanish Civil War Verse*, Valentine Cunningham refers to it as 'arguably the best English poem of the war'. He adds: 'It is of course a love poem; that it's written in a revolutionary war is merely incidental: there are no slogans, barely any politics at all, certainly little but the naming of Huesca to pin it to any particular time or place. As readers have, in fact, frequently observed, it could be the work of any soldier, to any woman, in any war, at any time'.

Of the two other poems written by Cornford in Spain during intervals in the fighting, the longest, 'Full Moon at Tierz: Before the Storming of Huesca', consisting of four groups of three stanzas, appears to be the result of an attempt to produce a poem capable of satisfying the hardest of Party-liners, containing couplets such as:

> We studied well how to begin this fight,
> Our Maurice Thorez held the light

and ending:

> Raise the red flag triumphantly
> For Communism and liberty.

The last of Cornford's three Spanish poems is 'A Letter from Aragon', first published in *Left Review* a month before his death in November 1936. It is a straightforward, free-form documentary piece, opening with the twice recurring line:

> This is a quiet sector of a quiet front.

It should at once be observed that neither of the poems last referred to shows any sign of living up to the remarkable promise evinced by the score or so written by him while at Stowe and Cambridge between 1932 and 1936. These must surely rank as examples of some of the most mature schoolboy/undergraduate poetry ever produced. Despite evident echoes of a close reading of Eliot and (according to a letter to his mother) Roy Campbell, as well as Graves and Auden, they represent something rather more than competent exercises in the mode most typical of early and mid-thirties poetry. In the overtly Marxist writing of his Cambridge period, it is clear that after leaving Stowe he moved steadily towards a severe rejection of what dialectical materialism often refers to as 'mere' subjectivity, expression of which soon became for him something the bourgeois poet collapsed or retreated into.

Both Valentine Cunningham and Jonathan Galassi (editor of Cornford's *Collected Writings*) are agreed in regarding it as impossible to guess how the convictions of those young Marxists who were killed in Spain would have developed had they survived the War and gone on fully to realize where adherence to Communist orthodoxy would have led them. Both Caudwell and Cornford had by the time of their deaths developed quite distinct personal 'subjectivities' which would inevitably have entailed, had they remained faithful to their innate poetic gifts, their coming into eventual conflict with the official Party line and the stereotyped literary mode expected of its followers. Had Cornford persisted in the feeling of 'contempt for all artists' he admits to in a late letter to his mother, he might well have ended by abandoning poetry as a means of self-expression altogether, although he went on to comment that this contempt might soon turn out to have been only a passing phase. In any event, he would doubtless have gone on to become the most 'legendary' of Spanish Civil War poets. I glimpsed him once or twice before his departure for Spain, in the tiny Parton Street (between Holborn and Bloomsbury) that since its obliteration by the Blitz has by now itself, with David Archer's Bookshop and Press, together with one of the bookish Left's frequent rendezvous spots, Meg's Café opposite, passed likewise into legend. With his notable dark good looks and quiet air of dedication and natural authority, he inspired a respect and even awe that I was by no means apt normally to feel at that age for someone only a year my senior.

Valentine Cunningham has taken pains to point out that the idea of the Spanish conflict being especially a poets' war has become an entirely fallacious myth. The writers and poets actually involved in the fighting represented only a very minor proportion of those under arms in the International and other Brigades, and those indisputably gifted poets who lost their lives in battle were less than a half-dozen in number. It should also be observed that the revolutionaries of those days can only mistakenly be regarded as romantics. Utopian though the ideals they fought for may have been, their politics were austerely reasoned and by their own standards pragmatically realistic. The Party faithful had to fight hard against any sentimentally humanitarian tendency to doubt the justice and necessity of the Moscow Trials and purges, the beginning of which coincided with the outbreak of Franco's rebellion against Spanish democracy. Communist discipline and voluntary self-abnegation paid scant concession to any inclination that could accurately have been labelled romantic. There was nothing histrionic about the gesture of solidarity with the workers and peasants of Spain made by so many intellectuals of all classes in so many countries when they hastened to become actively identified with the antifascist cause. Today I persist in regarding with deep mistrust any approach to poetry that perseveres in considering politics of all colours as something ultimately irrelevant to an authentic interest in the poetry of our own period or of either the immediate or the distant past. The three books reviewed above provide a timely antidote to any such approach if it is in fact significantly extant at the present time.

PIERRE JEAN JOUVE

When Pierre Jean Jouve died in 1976, at the age of ninety-one, he left behind him two distinct bodies of writing, the first of which he had come to regard as 'manqué' and unworthy of perpetuation. In 1925, as the result of a spiritual crisis, a radical change of direction and remarriage, he rejected *en bloc* as unsatisfactory some twenty items published during nearly twenty years. Three years later, in the 'post-face' to *Noces*, the first collection Jouve considered authentically representative, he declared: 'The poetic principle obliges the poet to disown his first work'.

The decisive factor determining the *vita nuova* Jouve was to undertake after the end of the First World War was his relationship with Blanche Reverchon, a friend of his wife nine years his senior who, when he first met her in Florence, and then in Salzburg, during the course of 1921, was already a practising doctor and psychiatrist. Their subsequent marriage in 1925 resulted in fifty years of fruitful companionship. Jouve's inner life, influenced by mystics such as Ruysbroeck, Teresa of Avila and John of the Cross, and to be found reflected in the poems of *Noces*, was soon to become, through association with his second wife, an inner life conceived as grounded in the Unconscious, site of the Eros/Thanatos conflict and of *la scène capitale*. In 1960, Jouve published a sequence called simply *Proses*, which contains the poem 'Trésor', the subject of which is unmistakable:

> Tu es trésor par l'intervention que tu as osé faire jadis pour transformer en moi cent choses de profondeur, et me conduire à moi-même. Tu es trésor par la présence constante et fidèle à tous les tourbillons, crises, malheurs passagers. . . .

The edition of his writings now published in celebration of the centenary of Jouve's birth is aptly entitled *Oeuvre*: its two volumes, one devoted to his poetry, the other to his prose, make their interdependence more apparent than it may have been before. Its most distinguishing feature, however, is that it unites for the first time between the same covers

---

'The ascetic sensualist', review of Pierre Jean Jouve, *Oeuvre* Tome I et Tome II (Paris: Mercure de France, 1988), *Times Literary Supplement* (6 May 1988), p. 505.

the works rejected by their author in the mid-1920s, and those issued between 1925 and the end of his life. In each case the early work occupies the second half of the volume. Much of it was published in slim and limited editions which, by the 1980s, had become extremely rare and difficult to obtain. In a brief note prefacing Tome I of the *Oeuvre*, Yves Bonnefoy discusses 'Le problème des premiers livres' and persuasively argues the case for making the suppressed work available to the increasing number of admirers and students of Jouve. He regards it as not unworthy of the greater author Jouve was later to become, and its republication as justifiable above all by its revelation of the developing mastery of prosody which distinguished Jouve's contribution to the poetry of his time.

The second half of the first volume of the present *Oeuvre* also contains 100 pages of 'Textes retranchés', that is to say of poems and stanzas from later, published collections that some compunction had led the poet subsequently to discard. Immediately after restoring these *disjecta membra*, the book turns back to reproduce in its entirety Jouve's first *plaquette, Artificiel*, all but two copies of which appear to have been destroyed soon after its appearance in 1909. Its first pages reveal at least three constants: epigraphical quotations from Mallarmé, whose influence was to become apparent again after 1945; a dedication to Debussy, indicating an unusually strong empathy with the art of music that remained Jouve's for life; and the presence in the first line of the initial poem of the word *chevelure*, destined to play a paramount role in the masterly novella of 1932, *Dans les années profondes*, and in many of the 'Hélène' poems associated with it.

The publishers claim the Édition du Centenaire to be both exemplary and definitive, 'car jamais on n'était allé aussi loin dans la divulgation de l'oeuvre "interdite" d'un des plus grands écrivains de ce siècle'. If Jouve is indeed one of the greatest French writers of the century, then a fundamental reason for this is without doubt the uncompromising ruthlessness of his quest for perfection, the severity of his self-criticism. Having once achieved an assured notion of what constituted his mature aims as a writer, he pursued them with undeviating consistency. No one who knew Jouve during the period between the 1930s and '60s would be likely to forget his reluctance to discuss in any detail the work referred to here as *interdite*. If this later attitude, as expressed with laconic lucidity in certain passages of his autobiographical *En Miroir* (1954), can be described by Bonnefoy as resulting from a 'tension un peu trop délibérément hautaine', it was none the less wholly typical, for better or worse, of the artistic persona that Jouve had by then patiently evolved. Though the *Oeuvre* presented here – both its contents and the order of them – apparently accords with wishes expressed by Jouve before he died, it seems sadly ironic that so intransigent an artistic conscience should have ended by endorsing an – in some ways – unsatisfactory compromise.

Adequately to sum up here the principal characteristics of Jouve's post-1925 output would be impossible. Among eleven collections, the second, *Sueur de sang* (1933) together with its two pre-war sequels, is perhaps most representative and distinctive. It is prefaced by the essay, 'L'Inconscient, spiritualité et catastrophe',★ which amounts to a manifesto announcing the kind of poetry that had emerged from a full awareness of the unconscious mind as conceived by Freud, and of its relation to both the basest and the most sublime levels of the human psyche. The opening couplet of *Sueur de sang* sheds light both on this underlying dualism, and on the fascinating pair of novels Jouve was engaged in writing at about the same time:

> Les crachats sur l'asphalte m'ont toujours fait penser
> A la face imprimée au voile des saintes femmes.

The novels *Hécate* (1928) and *Vagadu* (1930), eventually reappeared in one volume entitled *Histoire de Catherine Crachat*. The heroine is a star of the silent screen, Garbo-cum-Lilian Harvey, who in the first part is seen reduced to a state of spiritual checkmate and moral aridity, but is gradually liberated, restored and transformed through psychoanalysis in the second part. The authenticity of this astonishing double narrative must be recognizable to anyone who has had the least experience of psychoanalysis. The technical skill of its presentation had already been evident in its two immediate predecessors. Precocious passion for an older married man, an equally ardent but thwarted religious vocation, murder of the beloved, years of imprisonment followed by self-banishment after release and a serene ultimate acceptance: these are the ingredients of a novel, *Paulina 1880* (1925), that should by now be recognized as a classic. It is set in nineteenth-century Italy, and is clearly inspired by Jouve's two years' residence in the neighbourhood of Florence. *Le Monde désert*, which followed it two years later, is equally remarkable but less easily summarized. Set in Switzerland at the end of the First World War, it is concerned with the troubled relationships uniting three characters: the homosexual son of a pastor, a French poet and a mysteriously fascinating Russian woman named Baladine (like the actual Mme Klossowska Jouve had known personally, friend of Rilke and mother of Pierre Klossowski and the painter Balthus). This triangular situation leads to a suicide which does not resolve the tension it entails but leaves it open towards the future.

★ Editor's note: D.G.'s translation, *The Unconscious, Spirituality, Catastrophe* was published in 1988 (Child Okeford: Words Press).

Histoires sanglantes (1932) are described by Jean Starobinski in his introductory essay as a series of capriccios: tales of 'mystery and imagination' inspired by privileged familiarity with the catacombs opened by Freudian analysis, often subtly sardonic in tone. Their sequel, two *récits* entitled *La Scène capitale*, constitutes, as Starobinski says, 'sans doute le haut lieu de l'oeuvre narrative de Jouve'. In the final example of this narrative work, *Dans les années profondes*, Jouve succeeds in amalgamating in a single character of mythical proportions, Hélène de Sannis, elements drawn from a number of women who had played a role in his life. It is her *chevelure* that attracts the attention of the young Léonide when he first catches sight of her in a secret valley of the Engadine where he is on holiday. As soon as he has made her acquaintance, *la chevelure* becomes his obsession: 'Toujours plus belle, toujours plus mystérieuse, cette touffe, pleine de replis et de nuages, de reflets sanglants, de cavernes noires, dans laquelle mes regards se noyaient en éprouvant la volupté du plaisir de la mort.' The erotic adventure proceeding from this conjunction culminates in the death of Hélène in Léonide's arms at the climax of the sexual act. The theme of the interrelation between love and death that predominates throughout Jouve's writing never found better expression than here.

In 1946, Jouve opened a lecture (delivered in Oxford and London), 'L'Apologie du poète', by declaring: 'J'ai souvent pensé, tout au cours de ma vie, à une phrase d'Elizabeth Browning: "Le poète est celui qui dit les choses essentielles".' Alongside this indication of his lifelong aspiration should be placed a previous avowal of the fundamental aim of his later poetry: 'Obtenir une langue de poésie qui se justifiat entièrement comme chant: et trouver dans l'acte poétique une perspective religieuse – seul réponse au néant du temps.' Though brought up a Catholic, Jouve escapes all easy categorization as a religious poet. He recognized in himself a residual puritanism, referred to by one of his critics as Jansenist. The 1938 preface to a new edition of his earlier *Paradis perdu* is entitled 'La Faute', and this text, significantly, employs the expression *Deus Absconditus*. Underpinning all his more specifically religious poetry is what has now long been known as 'negative theology', and in all that he wrote, as in his character, asceticism is inseparable from sensuality. The mystical and the erotic constantly alternate or merge in his work, as in that of Georges Bataille, though never in so equivocal a fashion. Jouve regarded the writer's task as 'la transformation incessante de la matière personnelle', and the alchemy of this process as summarized by the term 'sublimation'. His objectivization of his personal experience – both of the vicissitudes of sexuality and of the spirit's wrestling for faith – often took the form in his poetry of an approximation to musical composition. The poems consist largely of inventions, of suites and of variations on themes, and one of the forms of 'personal matter' transformed by Jouve in this way resulted from an exceptionally acute response to the power of music. A frequenter from their inception of the Salzburg festivals, an admirer and friend of Bruno Walter, Jouve found inspiration for poems above all in the works of Mozart* and Alban Berg.

Both Jouve's full-length commentaries on operas (*Don Juan* and *Wozzeck*) are illustrated throughout by numerous quotations from the scores, and the second (*Wozzeck ou le nouvel opéra*) was written in collaboration with the musicologist Michel Fano. Both result from impassioned appreciation combined with a firm objective grasp of musical structure. Together they may well be considered an essential contribution to Jouve's total output; both are unfortunately excluded from the second volume of the *Oeuvre*, which in compensation makes available for the first time a suite of wholly uninhibited erotic notations dating from the 1930s, entitled *Les Beaux Masques*. This *inédit* is followed by a number of touchingly intimate fragments written after the death of Blanche in 1974.

The concluding 400 pages of Tome II are devoted to Jouve's work as a translator, and contain versions of work by a heterogeneous selection of poets: Tagore, Kipling, ('si curieusement brutal, religieux et fantaisiste à la fois'), Francis of Assisi, Hölderlin, Teresa of Avila, Góngora, Shakespeare (the Sonnets and 'The Phoenix and the Turtle') and even Montale and Ungaretti. A hypothetical further volume could reunite the translations of *Romeo and Juliet, Macbeth* and *Othello*, of Chekhov's *Three Sisters*, of Berg's reduction of Büchner's *Wozzeck* and of Wedekind's *Lulu* diptych.

One might consider that this edition of Jouve's *Oeuvre* is in some respects too complete, including material that might well have been reserved for a volume intended for specialists, and in others less complete than it might have been, had other priorities been preferred. Starobinski suggests that the present volumes should be followed by a third, which would contain not only the indispensable studies of *Don Juan* and *Wozzeck*, but also Jouve's commentaries on Baudelaire, Delacroix, Meryon, Courbet, Balthus and Artaud, which contain writing as characteristic of him as anything to be found in his poetry or fiction. He also produced eloquent politico-historical texts concerning Danton and de Gaulle, and if the existing two volumes reveal Jouve as being more essentially European than the majority of his contemporaries, the latter

---

* Editor's note: D.G.'s translation of Jouve's essay, *The Present Greatness of Mozart*, which first appeared in *Horizon*, has recently been reissued by the Delos Press, Birmingham (1996).

grandiose texts, together with his exegeses of paintings by Delacroix and Courbet, represent an intense but idiosyncratic patriotism – also apparent in the many poems in which he celebrated such places as Larchant, les Saintes-Maries-de-la-Mer and Dieulefit. But it is impossible not to be grateful to Mercure de France and Jean Starobinski for having honoured this writer's centenary by making available nearly 4,000 pages of ever more rewarding writings. It undoubtedly fulfils the desire Jouve expressed in the concluding lines of his 1960 *Proses* (subtitled 'La voix, le sexe et la mort'):

> Je ne veux de cloison avec l'oeuvre ni l'âme
> D'aucun son créateur au gouffre de mon temps.

VERNON WATKINS

A belated notice of this exceptionally rich and rewarding volume of nearly 500 pages of poetry may well begin, in view of the impossibility of adequately surveying in a few paragraphs the profuse variety of the book's contents, by saluting the courageous enterprise of the Golgonooza Press in producing it so opportunely and in such a suitably handsome format. Admirers of Vernon Watkins may well be astonished that his original publishers should, since the end of the Eliot era, seem to have lost interest in making his work available to the poetry-reading public.

In the words of Kathleen Raine, printed on the back flap of the cover, 'there have been poets in our century whose work embraces the whole of life, custodians to sacred values, who see humanity in relation to past and future, to our natural beginnings and our spiritual ends', poets who 'have profoundly understood and expressed some essential part of the human mystery. Vernon Watkins is such a poet.' With this statement, few significant poets of my generation could disagree. Unfortunately, current trends of criticism and appreciation appear to be incapable of arriving at a proper estimate of the lasting value of a poet of Watkins' stature. Anything like 'the bardic tradition' is apt at present to be regarded with misapprehension as representing an outdated mode of idealism. At no time either before or since his death could Watkins be thought of as a fashionable or popular poet. Perfection of diction, technical virtuosity and simple nobility of language and imagery such as he commanded are, however, of an order that is bound to achieve eventual recognition as long as there are readers able and willing to acknowledge their timeless value. To the nihilist the concept of timeless value is of course meaningless, and it is our affliction to live in an age of unconscious nihilists.

The most recent issue of *Temenos* (No. 8) contains many pages by and about Vernon Watkins (1906-67) that can provide a rewarding aid to fuller appreciation of the *Collected Poems*. Among them are a series of twenty-one letters to a close friend, the Frenchman Francis Dufeau-Labeyrie, to whom Watkins wrote in late 1937, ten years before the publication of the definitive edition of his first collection: 'you must know

---

'The last descendant of Taliesin', review of *The Collected Poems of Vernon Watkins* (Ipswich: Golgonooza Press, 1986), *Resurgence* 123 (July-August 1987), p. 42.

that a poet has only one need, that his poetry shall be loved'. Having written that Watkins could never be thought of as a popular poet, it occurred to me that in the very midst of his output are to be found eight ballads which, if they were available through anthologies, for instance, to the wider poetry-readership of those to whom his finest work might appear too recondite to be approachable, could easily become as popular (that is to say loved) as, say, the ballads of Charles Causley. The book under review begins and ends with two long and magnificent Ballads: 'of the Mari Lwyd' (Grey Mare), and 'of the Outer Dark', the second of which, dated 1966, was inspired by the dramatic production of the first in Swansea in 1948. Both are based on an ancient Welsh New Year's Eve tradition and equally deserve wider popularity than they may so far have received.

The same issue of *Temenos* also contains an invaluable twenty-four-page study of Watkins by his friend and translator the poet Roberto Sanesi (also the indefatigable translator of Shakespeare's sonnets, of Milton, Blake, Yeats, Eliot and Dylan Thomas). It seems sadly ironic that one of the first writers fully to appreciate the extent and depth of Vernon Watkins' learning and thought should be an Italian: the only detailed study of his work to have appeared in English so far is that by the critic Roland Mathias published by the University of Wales Press in 1974. The editor of *Temenos* has of course written about him in *Defending Ancient Springs*. But to be in possession of a truly European culture, resulting from a lifelong familiarity not only with the poets and thinkers of classical antiquity, but with the Bible, Dante, Michelangelo, Mozart, Goethe, Hölderlin, Blake and Yeats (to name only those figures alluded to in Watkins' hitherto unpublished poem of 1955, 'Moments') is today an achievement so rare in our British cultural environment that it risks going ignored.

'It is the hardest thing on earth to say what is simple, and unforgettable', wrote Watkins to his friend Sanesi in 1960, a sentence which aptly links him with the modern poet he most admired, knew and was influenced by, W. B. Yeats, who wrote unforgettably about 'the fascination of what's difficult'. Sanesi's recent essay is especially perceptive in focusing attention on Watkins' two central, interlinked themes: the figure of the bard/seer Taliesin with whom he increasingly identified himself; and the dimension of timelessness that transcends history and all 'the muddy vesture of decay'.

Kathleen Raine has said that Watkins 'is in a sense a poet's poet', and if I have any reserve about a certain amount of his work, that is because I find that at times he writes too many poems about other poets or poetry itself. No doubt Yeats and Eliot, Wordsworth and Keats, Hölderlin and

Heine provided him with subject-matter far better suited to his craft than the troubles, treasons and catastrophes of the actual world; but one may sometimes feel one has had enough literature about literature rather than about all the other topics with which literature is licensed though not obliged to deal.

It has not been possible in this review to refer in detail to any of the several hundred poems, the contents of ten volumes written during thirty years, collected in this large volume. Any expression of preference would inevitably be purely personal and subjective. But by way of conclusion I should like to quote in its entirety a brief poem from Vernon Watkins' 1962 collection *Affinities*. It represents an unanswerable refutation of the mild objection voiced earlier to poems about poetry, and may well be regarded as Watkins' poetic testament:

Demands of the Poet

I set my heart against all lesser toil.
Speak to me now more closely than the birds.
That labour done, on which I spent my oil,
Avails me nothing till you test the words.

How much the beating pulse may hold the years
Yet write the athletic wisdom on the page
You alone say. You bring the authentic tears
Which recognize the moment without age.

No lesser vision gives me consolation.
Wealth is a barren waste, that spring forgot.
Art is the principle of all creation,
And there the desert is, where art is not.

5

WRITINGS RELATING TO SURREALISM

PAUL ELUARD

In *Les Vases communicants* André Breton tells how he walked one evening through the streets of Paris offering a rose to every woman he met. That is probably the meaning of the title of Eluard's new book (for in one of the poems in it there is a stanza which apparently describes this admirable Surrealist gesture). But one would be disappointed if one sought for any similar references in Eluard's poetry; it is so pure and so concentrated that it requires no ideological framework, no explanation. Every line means exactly what it says: thus imagery becomes completely free of symbolism and refers to nothing but itself. This is a universal language, devoid of all particularities.

Paul Eluard is in the centre of an ever-widening circle. In *La Rose publique* he says what he has to say in a voice clearer than it has ever been. Each of his recent poems is an 'exhortation fervent as a brandished rose'.

'The Public Rose', review of Paul Eluard, *La Rose publique* (Paris: N.R.F., 1935), *New Verse* 13 (February 1935), p. 18.

ON SPONTANEITY

Mr Hugh Sykes Davies' *Petron* is cousin to de Chirico's *Hebdomeros*, and second-cousin-twice-removed to Lautréamont's *Maldoror*. The publisher's blurb mentions Beddoes and Julian Green; while Mr Herbert Read, in a recent article in *The New English Weekly*, has actually placed this work of Mr Davies' (and, even more boldly, Mr George Barker's *Janus*) in the Surrealist category. It is rather difficult to justify this classification. For though Mr Davies has obviously read the Surrealists and their predecessors most thoroughly, his method of writing is just as obviously different.

'If that which comes to me from down there has form, I will give it form,' wrote Rimbaud in one of his letters; 'if not, I will leave it formless.' And that is what any Surrealist would say. One cannot help wondering, then, whether Mr Davies really does *think* in language such as this:

> It is the serpent who has passed, the serpent who, so long twisted with the vulture in inextricable combat, has at last relaxed his hold, yet still relentless, makes his way to the mountains.

One cannot help wondering whether Petron genuinely is an 'interior hero', a projection of genuine obsessions and inner conflicts, or whether he is merely an ingeniously manipulated puppet, made to dance to a fantastic tune that Mr Davies once overheard in a library. Be that as it may, this is a curious and often exciting book, worth reading more than once.

There can be no question of premeditated style or imagery in *Facile*, the four most recent poems of Paul Eluard. No other living writer has achieved such perfect spontaneity. The emotion of love, so twisted and difficult a thing in the work of most contemporary poets, becomes verbal here without the least hesitation or constraint. *Facile est bien. Facile est beau sous tes paupières*: it is as simple as that. We cannot but accept such genuine clarity; it is only too rare a gift. The poems are accompanied by deliciously candid nudes by Man Ray, which form an integral part of the text, as Blake's drawings do in his prophetic books.

Review of Hugh Sykes Davies, *Petron* (Dent, 1935) and Paul Eluard, *Facile* (Paris: Editions G.L.M., 1935), *New Verse* 18 (December 1935), p. 19.

PROCESSION TO THE PRIVATE SECTOR

Author's Note

This scenario was originally written in the mid-Thirties in a notebook now belonging to the British Library. From a photocopy, I have now revised and corrected it, incidentally thereby making it seem slightly more up-to-date than the first draft. Notes in the margin of the MS suggest that I had originally intended a Surrealist-type poem* to be incorporated as spoken commentary at a certain juncture of the film; but I do not think I was ever able to produce a poetic text suitable for this purpose. As I am no longer capable of producing the type of poem that might be appropriate, I have selected three short texts (by Wittgenstein, Rimbaud and Nietzsche respectively) that a putative director could use should he consider they add interest to the film by clarifying what is for me its underlying significance, or leave out were he to decide that they would tend to create too portentous an impression. I have labelled the texts I have chosen 'Voice-Overs', and added them to the scenario as an appendix. I should like to complete this note by quoting two passages from Nicolas Berdyaev's *Towards a New Epoch* (Bles, 1949) which in combination seem to me to encapsulate the underlying implication of the film as I dimly saw it it at the time of its first conception, and to be at present even more relevant to what I should like the film to be thought of as fundamentally about than I could have imagined when I first outlined it:

> The theme of liberty is tragic, particularly for the cultural élite, which is passing through a serious crisis. If this élite is not penetrated through and through by the idea of service, if it remains imprisoned in self-satisfaction, despising those beneath itself, it

---

Version of D.G.'s *The Wrong Procession* (1936), taken from a notebook in the British Library and first published in Michel Rémy, *David Gascoyne, ou l'urgence de l'inexprimé* (Presses Universitaires de Nancy, 1984), pp. 157-74.

* Editor's note: I found the poem in 1992 out of place in the same notebook, and it has been incorporated into the text of the BBC Radio 3 production broadcast on 13 June 1998 in the series 'Between the Ears', adapted as a 'film for radio' by Sean Street and produced by Julian May, with music by John Surman, and with Simon Callow as the Camera.

will be condemned to disappear. Whatever may be the upshot the liberalism of the eighteenth and nineteenth centuries is finished and from now onwards impotent. The individualism which in former times was capable of being revolutionary has become nothing but a fruitless regret for the past. Economic liberalism particularly is becoming a reactionary force, the prop of capitalism at its last ebb. Liberal democracy is again equally played out. Attempts are, of course, made to keep it going, but it is an obstacle in the way of the social reform of society.

The future should not be conceived as if it were to be integrated and unified. It will always present us with a duality and spiritual conflict. This will doubtless be particularly acute when the social struggle is over. Then the spiritual problem, at present concealed beneath social disorders and contradictions, will come to the fore in its pure state.

May 1982

Foreword

It is difficult to give a precise 'précis' of a Surrealist film. Originally written in the mid-Thirties, when I was still an accredited member of the Surrealist movement in Paris as well as in London, it was to have been called 'The Wrong Procession'.* I gave it the updated title in 1981, when rewriting the scenario from a photocopy of the MS now in the British Library.

The subject-matter of the film derives, at least in part, from an authentic dream, which rightly or wrongly I considered at the time to be of collective as well as individual import. The stylized 'battle-scene' which constitutes the centre-piece of the film is not so much an anticipation of World War II, which at that time was beginning to seem inevitable, as a reflection of 'the class-struggle', or rather the conflict between the progressive and the reactionary forces in society. The story-line, in so far as there is one, concerns the vicissitudes of an amorous couple: the young 'protagonist' and his female counterpart, both intended as minimally personalized stereotypes. There are only two subsidiary characters of any importance; the rest of the cast consists of two initially contrasting groups of as many people as are needed to create the impression of a crowd. A modern dance group, or two working in collaboration, would be ideal, as their movements at certain moments ought properly to be choreographed. The key symbol in the second half is obviously sexual, but stands primarily for an ideological 'key to the problem of the world-crisis

---

* Editor's note: The title was also given in French: 'Le Cortège à tort'.

situation', which the 'protagonist' – representing the romantic liberal idealist 'in extremis' – deludedly imagines to have been entrusted to him. The author believes that many second-rate, banal but popular films often embody myths of authentic importance, which satisfy audiences which appreciate subliminally their possibly unintentional socio-psychoanalytic content. The ideas behind this film are now perceived by the author as serious, and possibly more pessimistic than he would have intended at the time of its conception. It is not, however, intended to be seen as solemn propaganda, but primarily to entertain on the level of fantasy. It contains elements of parody and send-up, as well as what may be considered a symptomatic reflection of twentieth-century man's essential dilemma and quest.

Spring 1984

PROCESSION TO THE PRIVATE SECTOR

– Surrealist film scenario –

Suggested Musical Background:
– Arnold Schoenberg: *Music for a Film Scene*
– Alban Berg: *Movement from 'Lyric Suite'*
– Edgard Varèse: *Ionisation*

The title and credits are superimposed on a background shot of rising clouds of heavy smoke, accompanied by a high-pitched whistle-note, which fades away and stops at the moment the titles end. The shot of smoke then dissolves into one of a long uphill street of suburban villas seen in the half-light of early morning. Beginning of music.

– A head lying on a crumpled pillow. At first only the mouth is seen. It gradually opens wide. The entire face is slowly revealed: it is that of a young man, with widely opened eyes and anguished expression, who appears to have just awoken from a nightmare. He rubs his eyes and turns to stare at the drawn window-curtains of a dingy, untidy room. Early morning light is beginning to penetrate them. The young man jumps out of bed and hurriedly starts to get dressed.

– Long-shot from the bedroom-window. The long deserted street. No-one in sight but a postman a few doors away. Shot of the front door of the house in which the young man has just awakened. Then the postman is seen approaching. He inserts a postcard into the letter-box, knocks hard and goes away.

– The top of the staircase. The young man emerges from the bedroom-door and hurries down the stairs, pulling on his jacket and straightening his tie as he goes. His hair is still dishevelled. He takes the postcard from the door and reads it. At first an expression of shocked dismay crosses his face, he claps a hand to his brow; then he begins to smile increasingly and ends by rocking with laughter.

– Close-up of the words written on the postcard: *Your home has been burnt to the ground and your wife is in the arms of a stranger:*
THE TRAIN LEAVES AT 8.30 A.M.

Still laughing, the young man puts the postcard into his pocket, shaking his head. He then immediately takes his hat and coat from the hall rack, puts them on, and hastily exits through the front-door, which he slams to behind him.

The next shot is of the garden-fence in front of one of the neighbouring houses, behind which an unshaven individual of brutal appearance is shown hiding. As the young man steps onto the pavement, this person emerges from his hiding-place and advances up the road to confront him. He is seen to be wearing some kind of black uniform. Without a word of warning, he knocks the young man to the ground with a punch on the jaw, kicks him, then runs away leaving him sprawled in the gutter.

The young man lying motionless at the edge of the road, a thread of blood running down his chin. Dissolve into shot of uprising smoke, as at the beginning.

Superimposed on the smoke, the following words:
YOUR HOME HAS BEEN BURNT TO THE GROUND ...

Smoke fades into a shot of a desolate piece of wasteland. In the foreground, a few scattered heaps of bricks covered with cinders and ash, some old clothes still burning, are lying about among newspapers and books and a miscellaneous debris of bric-à-brac. At the centre of the muddle stand a brokendown wicker chair still in flames and beside it a three-legged table supporting a small glass globe containing goldfish. From the misty distance, an old woman with her head covered by a black shawl and carrying a black umbrella advances towards the camera. Her clothing is shown to be covered with patches of white flour or powder. She hobbles up to the table and smashes the goldfish-bowl with her umbrella. The fish lie on the stony ground, wriggling among the ashes.

Further dissolve into rising smoke, superimposed with the words:
... AND YOUR WIFE ...

This time the smoke dissolves into a different interior. In it the old woman is seen again, with the back of her shawled head facing the camera. After a pause, she turns round, straightens up and throws off the shawl, revealing a beautiful, young and laughing blonde. Close-up of her face.

Dissolve into close-up shot of the (dark) back of a sofa. Superimposed on this background appear the words:

... IS IN THE ARMS OF A STRANGER.

The camera now pans round to confront the sofa. On it the young woman is seen going through the motions of making love with an invisible character. In doing so, she mimes a parody of the erotic contortions typical of an X movie, while avoiding as far as possible the appearance of indulging in 'solitary pleasure'. Her lips move, the expression on her face becomes ecstatic, she seems to be frantically caressing someone else. While this is happening, several eggs fall down, apparently from the ceiling, to break on the floor surrounding the sofa. She is too engrossed in her passionate activity with an unseen partner to pay any attention to this happening.

Exploratory shot of the room surrounding the young woman. It is a conventionally-furnished sitting-room, with open fireplace surmounted by a mantlepiece on which to one side of the clock stands an ornately-framed wedding photograph of the young woman holding a bouquet and the hand of the man seen in the opening sequence. A close-up of the broken eggs on the floor is followed by one of the young woman's now swooning face, which dissolves into the face of the mantlepiece clock: the hands mark 8.25.

The door of the room, seen for about thirty seconds before it bursts open to admit a group of a dozen or so drunken revellers in evening dress, wearing paper hats, false noses, dominoes, etc., and festooned with paper streamers. They rush wildly about the room, overturning articles of furniture, breaking vases and fighting one another. Among them, though he should not be immediately recognizable, is the character last seen lying in the gutter. The woman on the sofa appears to remain oblivious of the action taking place around her; she resumes caressing her invisible lover.

Second close-up of the clock-face: its hands have moved five minutes forward. Shot moves slowly up to the mirror above it. On its surface have been written with chalk or lipstick the words:

THE TRAIN LEAVES AT 8.30.

The disorderly intruders suddenly appear to become aware of the time, looking anxiously at the clock, nudging each other and consulting their wristwatches. The camera now focuses on the young man of the opening scene. In a state of evident agitation, he rushes to the sofa and starts tugging the woman's arm. She thereupon gives a violent start and appears to awaken as though from a trance.

– The revellers are now all rushing out of the room, followed by the principal man, dragging his supposed 'wife', whose face expresses dazed astonishment, after him. Last shot of the empty room, the door left open.

– A wide dimly-lit staircase, down which a confused herd of people are stampeding.

– Now follows a sequence of rapid, scrambled shots. – The revellers running down a street at accelerated speed. – Closeups of frantic, perspiring faces; running feet and legs. Revolving train-wheels. Traffic and railway signals. Intermittent clouds of smoke or steam. Blurred shots of clocks on public buildings. Postered walls rushing past.

– Shot of a railway-station platform, with a train first immobile, then beginning to leave.

– Revert to further shot of the group of people rushing through the streets.

– The empty station platform.

– The rushing crowd once more. Some of its members collapse in exhaustion, to be trampled underfoot.

– Shot of a train travelling at full speed through an open countryside. Repeat last shot of rushing crowd. Dissolve into shot of the façade of a Victorian Gothic redbrick railway-station. Camera swings to record the arrival into the forecourt of the small gasping, panic-stricken crowd.

– The station doors surmounted by an ENTRANCE sign. The next shot shows the same doors as seen from inside the station. They are violently pushed open and in rush the already dishevelled travellers, followed by the protagonist, dragging his fainting 'wife' after him with difficulty. Focus on the torn, stained, disordered appearance of the group's clothing, then on their wild, perspiring faces. Their expressions of anxiety abruptly change to looks of surprised astonishment and a different kind of alarm, as they gaze around them: what a strange building they are now in!

– Exploratory shots disclose an enormous, empty interior resembling a hangar, gymnasium or skating-rink, its lofty roof supported by metal scaffolding and rafters. At the far end of this hall, first shown in long-shot and then slowly approached, is to be seen standing a long trestle table, around and upon which is discovered a new group, or team, of curiously attired people. Their attitudes are grotesquely unconventional; some of them are lying on the table, some on the floor, some lying or kneeling on top of the others. Others are standing, some leaning to one side, with arms and legs twisted or stretched out wide. All are either wearing masks or have their faces painted white like clowns. Some of the men are naked except for a pair of briefs; others are dressed in some sort of uniform, in particular the loutish individual previously seen committing an assault on the protagonist earlier in the film. Some are draped in flags, some wearing cloaks, some are wearing tea-cosies on their heads; while a few of the women are attired in Victorian fashions or nuns' habits. Among them are what appear to be a priest, an admiral and a general; one is a gentleman sporting a frock-coat, top-hat and spats. All are at first shown perfectly motionless, like a group of statuary, during a shot lasting at least thirty seconds.

– The next shot is of the travellers at the opposite end of the hall, all of them apparently overcome with horror and consternation. At first, some of them are seen to be attempting to escape, but they discover the doors to be locked. The hall is devoid of windows. All of the members of this group next start to cower back against the wall behind them, and in so doing manage to upset a few of the baskets of flowers, fruit and other edibles that have been arranged at their end of the hall.

– Focus reverts to the motionless group opposite the travellers, at first in longshot, then after gradual panning towards them, in close-up. After a moment, all their faces begin to twitch rapidly and to display idiotic grimaces; then are abruptly frozen into immobility.

– Long-shot once more from the travellers' end of the hall. A figure among the group facing them emerges from his companions. He is dressed in sports-jacket and flannel trousers; over his head he is wearing a sort of sack or cushion-cover in which two slits have been pierced for the eyes. He runs swiftly and gracefully to the exact centre of the hall, where he sinks on one knee, his arms stiffly extended level with his shoulders. He is followed by two other representatives of his 'team' who are carrying a large placard between them, which they solemnly hold behind the kneeling figure's head.

– Close-up of the sack-masked head and of the placard behind it, on which are legible the words:

MAKE WAR NOT LOVE!

– Focus reverts to the revellers/travellers, and settles on the 'wife' of the protagonist. An expression of delighted surprise, quickly verging on ecstasy, transforms her face. Without hesitation, she rushes forward, flings her arms round the half-kneeling, motionless figure in front of the placard and attempts to embrace him. He remains with arms rigidly outstretched, then abruptly shakes her off with such violence that she falls back on to the floor. Behind him, the two placard-bearers change places, thus revealing the other side of the notice, on which is written:

THIS MEANS WAR!

– At this point, the statuesque group of figures at the far end of the hall comes to life and starts to prepare for the opening of hostilities. From behind the trestle table on and around which they have been posed, they begin to lift and expose to view on the table-top a previously concealed arsenal of miscellaneous articles: an alarm-clock, tins of sardines, rolls of paper, a shooting-stick, a violin, a crucifix, photograph-albums, plaster busts of famous composers, gloves, a frying-pan, chess-pieces, a transistor, a Rubik cube, plastic dolls, a weighing-machine, garden tools, bones, cups and saucers, coat-hangers, golf-balls, etc., etc. The placard-bearers have meanwhile turned, put the placard away under the table and taken out another, which they now proceed to carry forward and display to the opposing side. It reads:

WAR IS NOW INEVITABLE!

– The motley figures now start to fling their objects one after another into the centre of the hall.

– The protagonist's followers realize they must reply to this assault, and turn to pick up from the ground behind them handfuls of the flowers, fruit and vegetables they had scattered from the baskets that were standing at their end at the outset.

– Focus is now directed on the previously kneeling figure with a sack over his head. He springs up, takes a whistle from his pocket and starts to run about among the mêlée like a referee. The opposing groups rush at one another without restraint, throwing incongruous missiles in all directions. A situation of utter confusion and increasing violence ensues. Details of the struggle to be picked out momentarily by the camera include:

A figure wearing a pigtail, which repeatedly gets pulled by his opponents. – A nursemaid rushing about with a pram full of empty milk-bottles. – An elegantly dressed elderly woman with white hair, who after persistent attempts to observe what is taking place about her through a lorgnette, while being pushed from side to side, finally gets knocked down and trampled on. – The referee constantly consulting his wrist-watch. – Struggling couples on top of one another here and there. – A figure scattering confetti; another occupied in sprinkling the fallen with a large watering-can.

– Meanwhile, the faithless 'wife' is rushing about in every direction, continually attempting to embrace all and sundry and each time encountering a brusque rebuff.

– Throughout this scene, constituting for the most part a 'master shot', particular attention should be paid to the 'protagonist' figure who, when not trying to prevent his 'wife' from embracing their enemies, is chiefly engaged in dodging the loutish uniformed character who has previously attacked him and who now persists in chasing him from corner to corner of the set, armed with a dangerous-looking club. The scene should be rhythmically intercut with a number of apparently quite irrelevant shots: a firework display; a flying helicopter; the demolition of a building; armed guerrillas alongside corpses; carnivores in a zoo; one or two minimal extracts of footage from TV commercials such as 'Black Magic'; etc.

— By the conclusion of the preceding scene, all the participants are lying struggling with one another convulsively on the floor, and a state of chaos has been attained. Damaged or shattered heterogeneous objects are strewn about the writhing bodies. All movement is decelerated into immobility, while the musical accompaniment simultaneously diminishes into silence. For the first time the voice of the 'protagonist' is heard:
'*Is the end of the world at hand?*'

As he utters these words, an enormous sheet of gauze or muslin is shown floating slowly down from the roof, until finally it envelops the now motionless muddle on the ground entirely. Freeze for approximately thirty seconds.

— Dissolve, into a similar shot showing the same sheet of gauze/muslin covering a heap of bodies and objects, the shape of which must look as much as possible the same as at the conclusion of the previous scene. As the following shot recedes from the covered heap, the surroundings are revealed as having changed. They have in fact become the misty and derelict piece of wasteland on which the earlier scenes of the site of the supposed remains of a burnt home was shot. Next, feeble movement is shown disturbing the gauze. Gradually the disturbance travels towards the edge of the diaphanous cover, and finally the 'protagonist' emerges from beneath it. He is evidently in pain and looks in every way the worse for wear. He begins closely to examine the stony ground, on which a few derelict items of rubbish remain strewn. At last he discovers an unusually large, rusty-looking key fastened to the end of a long chain. He picks it up, giving the impression that it is unusually heavy; and the following shot shows him slowly trudging away towards the distance, dragging it after him at the end of its chain.*

— Brief frozen frame of the finally deserted landscape.

— Dissolve into long shot of an apparently endless empty corridor. Then the 'protagonist' appears in the foreground, and is next seen receding down the corridor, dragging the key behind him.

— The next shot explores a typical hotel entrance-lounge, focusing

---

* Editor's note: At this point in the MS there is a stage direction: *[Now the accompanying poem begins]*. The poem is reproduced on pp. 460–62 of this book.

finally on an elderly white-moustached gentleman seated in an armchair reading a newspaper. Swing towards a curtained archway at far end of set. The curtain is pushed aside, and the young man with a key emerges, looking anxious and down-and-out. He hesitantly approaches the hotel resident, carrying the cumbersome key and its chain in his hands. Then he leans over the old man's chair from one side, as though intending to address a question to him. The old man lowers his paper with a start, sits up to scrutinize the interloper and assumes an expression of outraged fury. The 'protagonist' holds out the key and chain towards him beseechingly, as though proffering an explanation of his intrusion. The old man's anger at once increases, he rolls up his newspaper and brandishes it with one hand at his interlocutor, while pointing with the other imperiously to the swing-doored entrance. After increased entreaty and correspondingly furious remonstrance between the two characters, the young man makes a disappointed retreat towards the entrance.

– There follows a brief episode involving the hotel swing-doors which should be treated in traditional burlesque manner. The attempted exit of the young man with the key, now in his hands and trailing its chain, is thwarted by the determined entry of someone from outside. Shot alternately from inside and outside the doors, the young man and the new entrant are shown engaged in increasingly desperate contest to get through the doors, one in, one out, hampered by the entanglement of the key-chain in the doors' central hinge. This is finally resolved by the young man's emerging in obvious discomfort into a busy street.

– Shot of the street, as seen from the kerbside about fifty yards from the hotel entrance, recognizable from the sign hanging above it: IMPERIAL HOTEL. The young man is seen tottering out on to the pavement, dragging the key he has succeeded in extricating from the revolving door. In the foreground, a young woman in smart attire is bending to pay attention to one of her shoes which is giving her trouble, incidentally displaying provocative portions of her anatomy. The young man is seen approaching her, his face wearing an expression of resigned disillusionment. She straightens up as he reaches her side, whereupon he proffers her the key. With a furious look of incredulous scorn, she slaps his face forcefully and hastens away towards the hotel. Holding the key pressed to his chest and trailing its chain, the 'protagonist' shrugs his shoulders and wanders sadly off out of sight in the other direction.

– The next shot reveals a stone bridge of medium size. The young man appears, slowly advancing from one end towards the middle. When he has reached it, he starts to fasten the chain he has been dragging around his neck; he then dangles the key over the balustrade. It becomes apparent that he is about to throw himself into the river beneath. Camera now swings to focus on the other end of the bridge, where the figure of a policeman is visible. As soon as he observes what the young man is doing, he comes racing towards him. He claps his hand on the would-be suicide's shoulder, shaking his head angrily; then, after a brief demonstration of remonstrance, he moves away in the direction of the end of the bridge at which the young man first appeared, holding his hands behind his back. The young man begins to move slowly in the other direction, dragging the key behind him again, his expression blank.

– The following scene represents a street-corner meeting. The young man with the key is seen approaching a crowd of people grouped round an orator who is haranguing them from a small rostrum draped with the Union Jack. The speaker is wearing a variety of medals and decorations and has a cleric's collar; his face is distorted and he is making increasingly impassioned arm-movements. The young man joins the outer fringe of the crowd and stands there listlessly for a while, trying to hear the speech. As he listens, he becomes visibly angry and indignant. Finally, his patience at an end, he takes up the key with both hands, unfastens it from its chain, and casts it with all his might at the speaker. It falls heavily to the ground at the speaker's feet, causing no damage, without even interrupting the oration. The members of the crowd pay no attention to the incident, with the exception of one business-suited individual who, having carefully picked up the missile, turns around and having without apparent difficulty identified its thrower, makes his way over to him and politely hands it back. With an expression of wretched resignation, the young man refastens the key to its chain and, dragging it behind him again, slowly leaves the scene.

Now ensues a sequence of street-scenes, each featuring the young man dragging his key behind him at the end of its chain. Three or four medium-range shots, of relatively brief duration, each showing a different, progressively less-populated street, should be sufficient. In each, the 'protagonist' will be seen slowly making his way, a lonely and incongruous figure, among pedestrians hurrying past without paying him any attention.

– The next shot after this peregrination sequence shows us a nondescript place on the outskirts of the town. The most outstanding feature of the shabby landscape is a high brick wall appearing to separate unkempt allotments from open wasteland. Zoom in on the wall to show, positioned against it, an elderly man with a long, bushy white beard, wearing a skullcap. He is apparently engaged in trying clumsily to lop off his beard with a pair of shears. (If a wall can be found with the creeping plant known as 'old-man's-growing', on it, the visual pun would considerably enhance the effect of this incident.) On the ground beside the old man lies a very large, awkwardly shaped brown-paper parcel; it is intricately tied up with string and cords. The size and shape of the parcel, and the fact that it momentarily jerks from side to side, suggest that it contains a living human body.

– The camera now swings to the left to record the shambling approach of the young man trailing his key from the direction of the nearby towns. Then, it swings to the right, showing the old man cutting off his beard for a passing instant before fixing the simultaneous approach from elsewhere of the young 'wife', or 'heroine', of earlier scenes. She is now clad in a swim-suit or bikini, and carries a beach-bag. The young man with the key greets her, she smiles dreamily, and they embrace with visible emotion. They then stand hand in hand, watching the eccentric activity of the old man at the foot of the wall for a while. He continues lopping off hanks of his beard, and now as he is doing so the young woman steps forward, stoops down, gathers up the scattered bits of shorn beard lying on the ground and stuffs them into her bag. As she does so, the mystery parcel at the old man's side begins to move convulsively, but the couple pay not the slightest attention to this phenomenon, of which they appear oblivious. Finally, having embraced once more, they go off together, without having addressed a word to the old man, the young man with his arm about his 'wife's' shoulders. They are walking along the wall away from the town.

– The following shot returns briefly to the old man, who by this time has nearly divested himself of his beard. He now turns to the mysterious parcel beside him and with the shears he has been using, cuts through the complicated entanglement of cords and string containing it; whereupon the personage concealed within bursts through the paper and reveals himself as an individual wearing black trousers, an open-necked white shirt and a domino mask, armed with a revolver. Facing the old but now nearly beardless man who has released him, he gives him a military salute, turns abruptly on his heel and bounds off in immediate pursuit of the departed couple, as fast as possible. The closing shot of this scene shows him from the rear, disappearing into the (blurred) distance.

– Dissolve into medium shot showing the reunited couple making their way along the foot of the wall, the young man dragging his key at the end of its chain behind him. Before long, they reach a massive door set in an archway in the wall. The door has a conspicuous keyhole. The young man detaches his key from its chain and approaches the door with it, applying it to the keyhole. Consternation: it is far too big to fit the hole. In exasperation, the young man drops the key. He is then seen looking down at it on the ground. Close-up of the key: it has noticeably diminished in size. The 'protagonist' then picks it up again with an astonished expression. He once more tries to fit it into the keyhole, but it is still too large. He at once drops it again. Second close-up of the key.

Its fall has again made it smaller. A further attempt is made to fit the key to the lock, only once more to meet frustration. A slow zoom in on the key on the ground now reveals it to be of normal size. The young man picks it up, fits it into the lock, turns it and triumphantly pushes the heavy door wide open. The couple pass through the doorway together, hand in hand, leaving the key in the lock and the door ajar.

– Shot of the back side of the wall, in close-up. On it gradually appear the superimposed words: THE ISLAND WAS COMPLETELY DESERTED.

– Long-shot of the couple crossing a wide stretch of open country. In the distance, a few factory chimneys and a gasworks are dimly discernible. Dusk is falling. The next shot discloses the edge of a gloomy wood, which the couple are approaching.

– The couple are next shown entering the wood and discovering with difficulty a narrow pathway through the trees. Dim lighting.

– The next shot zooms in to focus on a tree about fifteen yards further along and to the side of the path the couple are following. Shot shifts to the back of the tree, revealing the masked figure with a revolver seen previously being released from a mysterious parcel. This personage is now evidently in ambush. Shot returns to the couple advancing along the path. Intensify lighting. At the moment they reach the point on the path alongside which stands the tree concealing their would-be assailant, he steps into view, his revolver aimed at the couple. Close-up of the mouth of the weapon. Then of their shocked faces. Medium shot of the young man putting an arm round his companion's shoulders. The threatened pair stand perfectly still, while their faces assume an expression of complete calm. *[At this point, the Voice-Over quotation from Wittgenstein could begin, read slowly and distinctly in a neutral tone.]* As they stand staring unafraid at the masked figure, he slowly approaches them, his revolver ready to fire. At the moment he has reached lethally close range, the young woman suddenly lies down flat on her back in front of him. The young man then deliberately places one foot on her abdomen, at the same moment stretching out his arm at full length, directing an accusing forefinger at the weapon. Frame of the confrontation briefly frozen. Next, the menacing figure is seen to rip off his mask, revealing the face of the 'unshaven individual of brutal appearance' who featured in one of the opening sequences of the film. His visage now wears an expression of superstitious terror. He starts back, points his revolver to his own temple and fires. Half way through his fall to the ground, shot in slow motion, his body totally disappears.

– The next shots show the couple resuming their slow advance along the path through the wood. The lighting has become dim again, as before the hallucinatory murder threat episode. As they move forward, various figures are seen to step one by one from behind trees on either side of the path, and to begin to follow them, gradually forming a procession. They should be recognizably the same as the 'revellers' or thwarted 'travellers' who took part in earlier scenes. Finally, when the cast of the cortège has completely assembled, they all emerge from the obscurity of the wood, led by the young man and his companion. They are now seen to be wearing clothing that is similar, sober and simple. They are confronted by a further stretch of open twilit countryside.

– *[At this point, if it is used, the Voice-Over reading of a translation of the last paragraph of section IV of Rimbaud's 'Enfance' should begin, this time by a different, younger voice.]*

– The footpath through the wood continues through the country beyond it into the distance. On either side of it the camera, when not recording the slow progress of the procession, picks out details such as heaps of weedgrown stones, empty bottles, rusting cans, broken toys, an abandoned car chassis. From time to time, what appears to be a sprawling corpse left behind in this no-man's-land comes to life and totteringly joins the tail-end of the procession.

– At this point, the camera must focus for a time on the path, to show that it has by now become a disused railway-track, with grass and wildflowers sprouting between the lines (this flora should, if possible, include a clump of the broom, or gorse, mentioned in the Rimbaud poem quotation). The ground ahead is now seen to be sloping increasingly upward, till it reaches a quite steep gradient. The members of the procession have assumed the semblance of a team of explorers, struggling on doggedly towards some unknown goal, weary and worn but comradely. Some have joined hands, others are leaning on companions' shoulders. They persist in following the railway-track to the brow of the hill. At the top, against the skyline, a tattered flag hung from a broken pole, is to be seen.

– A sequence of concluding shots now show: first, the leading couple, he with his arms round his beloved's neck, their faces serene; next, one after the other, the companions who have rejoined them; and lastly, the resuscitated victims, in bloody and ragged clothes, who have joined the procession at the last moment. They are then seen from the rear, passing one by one over the brow of the hill and out of sight.

– Long shot of the empty, disused railway track leading uphill, the tattered flag, the dim gray sky beyond. Then, as the film closes, the sky begins to glow with radiant orange light. *[If the Voice-Over extract from Nietzsche is used, a voice should recite it as the glow begins and increases.]* As the last shot fades, a distant echo of the high-pitched whistle with which the film opened should be heard.

(Possible Voice-Over texts from Wittgenstein, Rimbaud and Nietzsche appended.)

I

VOICE-OVER:

If someone says, only the *present experience* has reality, then the word 'present' must be redundant here, as the word 'I' is in other contexts. For it cannot mean *present* as opposed to past and future.
– Something else must be meant by the word, something that isn't *in* a space, but is itself a space. That is to say, not something bordering on something else (from which it could therefore be limited off). And so, something language cannot legitimately set in relief.

The present we are talking about here is not the frame in the film reel that is in front of the projector's lens at precisely this moment, as opposed to the frames before and after it, which have already been there or are yet to come; but the picture on the screen which would illegitimately be called present, since 'present' would not be used here to distinguish it from past and future. And so it is a meaningless epithet.

Ludwig Wittgenstein
(Philosophical Remarks)

II

VOICE-OVER:

The flag makes its way to the foul landscape, and our jabber drowns the sound of drums.

In the town-centres we shall maintain the most cynical prostitution. We shall suppress logical revolts with slaughter.

To the syphilized and softened lands! – in the service of the most monstrous industrial or military exploitations.

Good-bye to here, no matter where. Conscripts to good-will, ours will be a ferocious philosophy; uninformed with regard to science, shrewd whenever comfort is concerned; bust-up for the world in progress. That's true advance. Forward, march!

Arthur Rimbaud
(Translation from 'Democratie', No. 37 in *Illuminations*.)

(To precede or replace the above)

The tracks are rugged. The hillocks are covered in broom. How far off are the birds and the springheads! This can only be the end of the world approaching.

Arthur Rimbaud
(From the end of 'Enfance', IV, No. 2 of *Illuminations*.)

III

VOICE-OVER:

– The real world – unattainable? Unattained, at any rate. And if unattained also *unknown*. Consequently also no consolation, no redemption, no duty; how could we have a duty towards something unknown?

(The grey of dawn. First yawnings of reason . . .)

– The 'real world' – an idea no longer of any use, not even a duty any longer – an idea grown useless, superfluous, *consequently* a refuted idea: let us abolish it!

(Broad daylight; . . . all free spirits run riot.)

– We have abolished the real world: what world is left? the apparent world perhaps? . . . But no! *With the real world we have also abolished the apparent world!*

(Mid-day; moment of the shortest shadow; end of the longest error; zenith of mankind; INCIPIT ZARATHUSTRA.)

FRIEDRICH NIETZSCHE
(From: *How the 'Real World' at last Became a Myth*,
in *Twilight of the Idols*.)

HISTORY OF THE WOMB
or NINE MONTHS' HORROR

The first part of the film takes place beside the sea. Some remote and uncultivated spot should be chosen for the shooting of these scenes, preferably Dungeness or Portland Bill.

The opening shot is of a stony, deserted beach. A grey sea washes against the shore. There is no sign of vegetation or human life.

– After a few minutes, a naked woman dashes across the scene and out of sight. She is followed by a naked man. We only see their backs. –

After they have gone, we continue for some time to watch the sea lapping against the stones of the shore.

Now a large old woman appears, with a forlorn, sulky-looking little boy (about eight years old) following at her heels. The old woman is wearing voluminous fusty black garments, shawls, a white mobcap covers her copious black hair which is coiled at the back of her head; she is carrying a heavy work-bag. Slowly and painfully she lowers herself into a sitting position on the stones.

OLD WOMAN: *Don't you dare to talk, or I'll beat you.*

She opens her work-bag, taking out some needlework with which she begins to busy herself. The wretched little boy sits down on the stones behind her. We see her back.

At first, the boy tries to play some games with the stones. Then he gets up and puts one leg over the old woman's shoulder.

LITTLE BOY: *I want to stand on your eye-lids!*

She turns upon him angrily, her hand raised.

Film scenario (c. 1936). Transcribed by Roger Scott from D.G.'s Notebook Add. MS 56040 in the British Library. Previously unpublished.

Editor's note: In November 1995, when I showed him the script I had found in one of his Notebooks in the British Library, D.G. told me the inspiration behind the scenario was a specific painting by Salvador Dalí, *The Weaning of Furniture-Nutrition* (or *Furniture-Food*) (1934), a reproduction of which was included in his *A Short Survey of Surrealism*, and in his translation of Salvador Dalí's *Conquest of the Irrational* (New York: Julien Levy, 1935), plate 29.

OLD WOMAN: *Keep quiet, or I'll brain you!*

The child sticks his tongue out at her behind her back. She goes on with her work.

Far away out at sea, a rowing boat has appeared; there are two figures in it.

The child soon gets tired of piling stones one on top of the other; they always topple over. He creeps softly up behind the old woman's back, and without her noticing it, apparently, removes the mobcap from her head. Then, taking out her hairpins one by one, he unwinds the enormous black coil of her hair. There are yards and yards of it; it falls down her back and out across the stones behind her. Still she appears to be too engrossed in her needlework to notice what is happening. The child bends close over her head, seized with a violent curiosity..

Close-ups of the old woman's head. Tangled in the hair on top there are a number of small objects: a model ship, a wheel from a toy train, a flat slip of wood on which a mouth has been drawn, a dry star-fish, and lastly, a large mint humbug, very sticky. It is this last which chiefly attracts the little boy: he wants to eat it.

He quickly untangles the various other objects and sets them down among the stones he has been playing with; but when he comes to remove the humbug, he finds that it is so inextricably stuck to the surrounding hair that he has to give it a sudden violent tug.

With a piercing and uncanny scream the old woman now swings round upon him like a rock. We see that her face is the face of a hyena, covered with bestial hair and with long slavering carious teeth, her eyes red coals. With one claw she clutches the child's arm, biting into its flesh, with the other she brutally beats him down upon his back. The child howls, screams, picks up handfuls of stones and flings them at her. A horrible battle ensues.

While all this has been going on, the rowing-boat we saw in the distance just now has been coming nearer and nearer to the shore. Now it approaches the edge of the beach and we see in it a young man and woman dressed in eighteenth-century costume. The young man is carrying a large piano-accordion slung over his shoulders on a strap. He gets out of the boat and wades ashore, dragging the boat after him and beaching it. The young woman jumps out after him. They sit down on the stones not far from the edge of the sea, their backs to the fighting nurse and child (she has now half-killed him by this time) whom they totally ignore. The young woman unpacks a picnic-basket and spreads a cloth over the stones, and her companion starts playing his accordion.

At the first notes of the music, the old woman's human face returns.

The child stops throwing stones. The old woman looks red in the face and still rather angry, but now she only slaps the child's hand, tidies her hair and returns to her needlework.

The little boy wanders away from her towards the eighteenth-century couple, but they take no notice of him.

LOUIS ARAGON

The first enquiry most non-Parisian readers want to make about Louis Aragon nowadays concerns the question of whether or not he is still an ardent Communist Party member and undeviating Stalinist. As time was too brief during a recent trip to the French capital, I was unable to attempt, as I had intended, to visit his apartment opposite the Soviet Embassy in order to interview him, and so I am afraid I am unable to furnish those eager to hear about Aragon's present political stance with any authentic utterance on the subject straight from the old war-horse's mouth. As to current popular French opinion, I think my Paris bookseller's answer, when asked whether this writer was still to be considered an unrepentant Stalinist, 'Ah! le M. Aragon d'aujourd'hui est surtout fantaisiste', may be taken as a fairly symptomatic comment.

It is now possible to describe Aragon as old without fear of offensive inaccuracy, since he was born in 1897. A poem called 'Statue' in his earliest collection, *Feu de joie* of 1919, ends with two lines that may be once more today to some extent true, or may be thought of as a premonitory comment on his by now abundant output of poetry and prose of many kinds:

> Un homme à la mer Encre
> A la dérive.

The political Aragon, who broke with his formerly close friend André Breton in 1930, after a famous row, may also be thought of as a man who joined the Party and threw in his lot with the capable and astute novelist Elsa Triolet, who was of Russian birth but after 1919 a Parisienne of decidedly Left inclination, in order firmly to put a stop to his own innate tendency to drift without much thought for the morrow. It seems legitimate to speculate as to whether or not his friendship with the intransigently rebellious Nancy Cunard may have had some influence on his decision to sever connections with the revolutionary-minded but impractical Surrealists; though I would have thought the tough British

---

'The art of embroidery', review of Louis Aragon, *Aragon: le mentir-vrai* (Paris: Gallimard, 1980), *Times Literary Supplement* (23 January 1981), p. 75.

beauty too much of an individualist ever to have handcuffed herself to any sort of barbed-wire Party line.

Aragon as a young man may well have been pleased to have been considered a nonchalant womanizer. Indeed, the third story in the present collection, dated 1926, which seems to be far more a chapter of autobiographical reminiscence than a *nouvelle* in the strict sense, not only constitutes a fascinating evocation of Paris by Night nearly sixty years ago, but contains a lyrical confession of how much his youthful frequentation of prostitutes meant to him. These particular pages illustrate well this side of the early Aragon (also to be found reflected in an amusing book of his Surrealist period, *Le Libertinage*, which its author apparently no longer finds satisfactory: 'Je crois que j'ai eu besoin des femmes comme pas un. D'autres les ont sans doute aimées davantage. J'en ai eu besoin. Et non pas d'une. De toutes les femmes . . . Du tableau indéfiniment mobile de leurs possibilités.' 'Dignes, honorables, belles, vertueuses, honnêtes putains, reprenez-le, l'argent, qui vous vient par les hommes, restituez-le à la grande vie métaphysique d'où les hommes l'ont fait sortir.'

However, despite this initial taste for dissipation, soon after meeting Elsa Triolet in 1928 Aragon became an adoringly one-woman man, mythologizing his companion in a number of poetic works, and using her name almost as a symbol for the new revolutionary woman, a sort of reincarnation of Marianne as depicted by Delacroix. Breton, the great friend of his youth, after severing all connection with him, published his treatise on the Surrealist doctrine of love, *L'Amour fou*; much later, in 1963, Aragon produced *Le Fou d'Elsa*. In a way it is sad that political disagreement should so completely have separated from one another two men who had more than a little in common.

The 138 pages which make up the first section of *Le mentir-vrai*, presumably devoted only to pre-war writings (the chronological order of the pieces contained in the volume is not always easily determined), contains one item in particular which is equivocal both in being classified as a *nouvelle* and in its content. 'La Sainte Russie', a highly entertaining and quite possibly true story concerning a vaguely dotty mistress of Tsar Alexander the Second and her passionate devotion to dogs, ends with her bequeathing the remains of her small fortune to the foundation of a canine cemetery on the Riviera, a subject that Elsa Triolet conceivably suggested. But this is followed by 'Le souris rouge', which can no longer truly be called a *nouvelle* at all, representing as it does a typical piece of Communist polemic about the deplorable state of poetry in pre-war France, facile and disputable in the extreme, like a bad article in our own *Left Review* of that period.

The first piece, which gives the book its title, is dated 1964; it might be subtitled 'Défense et illustration de l'art romanesque d'Aragon'. In it he alternates passages of quasi-autobiographical memoir, told in the first person with appropriately typical colloquialisms, relating his transition from early boyhood to adolescence, with passages explaining to the reader just how such a writer as Aragon converts the initial *données* of more or less hazily distant memory into more or less straightforward fictitious narrative. The expression 'le mentir-vrai' could be described as what we would call 'embroidering'. These forty introductory pages constitute a document that is as entertainingly readable as it is skilfully written and informative. Here is an unusually interesting extract from one of Aragon's explanatory asides:

> Hors de propos, de nos jours on chante sur un air de Léo Ferré, un poème du moi qui est devenu une chanson de lui, et je n'ai jamais compris pourquoi cela fait rire les gens quand les vers disent: *J'aimai déjà les étrangères – Quand j'étais un petit enfant.* . . . Mais c'est d'un effet comique assuré. Je ne le dirai pas à Pierre (i.e. Louis), ça lui donnerait un coup. Pierre est un petit garçon beaucoup plus simple que moi dans ce domaine. Je veux dire *alors* . . . car que serait-il devenu? Vous le voyez au dernier trimestre, mai, juin, juillet, les romans ne me suffisaient plus, ni les poèmes: j'avais beau en écrire tant que je ne savais plus où les cacher, il me fallait inventer d'autres miroirs à mes folies.

The whole text is such as to lead one to reformulate a famous old logical puzzle: Aragon says writing fiction is a sort of lying. He writes fiction founded on fact. Does that make him a liar?

The eight short stories near the middle of the book, grouped under the heading 'Servitude et Grandeur des Français: Scènes des années terribles', constitute its most nourishing meat. In them one can find Aragon the authentically patriotic Frenchman performing his rôle as imaginatively realistic storyteller in an exemplary manner. In varying ways each of these eight wartime stories illustrates his technical expertise as well as his gift for compassionate empathy with a wide spectrum of socially disparate characters. Even the psychology of the typical petit-bourgeois collaborationist is presented convincingly because of its gently understanding insight in a story which ends abruptly with a single sentence of horrible pathos. 'Les jeunes gens' shows us succinctly just what it must have been like to have had to grow up in France during the Occupation, and here again the blend of humane perception and bitter irony is memorable. The final story of this section, entitled 'Le droit romain n'est plus', is followed by a brief rider, appended in 1964, which appears almost to apologize for the hatred it displays against the Germans. Considering how dispassionate these particular stories are on the whole, the expression of such an emotion seems the most venial of lapses; and this final story represents such a display of virtuosity – switching as it does between the Nazis' inner ruminations, the character sketch of a wholly believable German equivalent of one of our WAACs, ordinary personal narrative and a surely not distorted picture of the warped conception of justice that was an inevitable concomitant of Hitlerian ideology – that it can hardly be considered to have been spoilt by depicting the military Fräulein as an unspeakable bitch.

After these eight *nouvelles* there follow thirty-four pages devoted to what one is informed by a note really constitute the opening chapter of a not yet completed novel, the title of which Aragon has still to decide on. The fragment is provisionally entitled 'Les rencontres romains', and leads one greatly to hope that the whole novel will by now have been completed and will appear before too long. It should prove to be quite as striking a piece of period reconstruction, based on historical and intrinsically fascinating characters, as *La Semaine sainte*. This new novel should have an especial appeal for English readers, being apparently above all concerned with the still fundamentally mysterious, in certain ways undoubtedly pathetic, figure of George IV's reviled, rejected and exiled Caroline of Brunswick, during her involuntary sojourn in Rome, and her relationship with a young French sculptor, Pierre-Jean David, friend and protégé of Ingres and the son, presumably, of the great Jacques-Louis.

There remain fourteen more stories which I have not the space to discuss in detail. In the main they are delightfully amusing, some even frivolous for a supposed Party-liner; but most of them provide one with a bonus in the way of some item or other about twentieth-century French history and *mœurs*. In 'Damien ou les confidences', a bachelor on the verge of middle age attempts to bridge the generation gap by giving his niece a complete history of the different types of tooth-brush he has known during his lifetime, and encounters in the girl the usual exaggerated sophistication of today's young, mingled with the kind of naive seriousness which prompts her to tell him that when talking of toothbrushes one does not necessarily have to refer to the Marxist theory of production. 'L'inconnue du printemps' incidentally draws attention to the French passion for pullovers, while 'Shakespeare en meublé' is a captivating example of Aragon's sympathetic understanding of youth and shows at the same time how adept he can be at telling a short tale, resuming certain features of a given period, in the form of a monologue rich in typical colloquialisms. But I must add that Aragon's view of today's junior citizens can also be mordant, as he shows in 'Les Histoires'.

In considering the diversified output and career of Louis Aragon, one is forced to conclude that in his end are to be found many reminders of his beginning. As to the Stalinist label, I believe Aragon only wore it temporarily, for reasons of expediency above all, no doubt, and was probably as relieved as anyone when de-Stalinization became official. Aragon is certainly one of the most prolific writers of his generation and may today well be one of the most widely-read. It seems fair to say that though what the bookseller told me about his being above all a *fantaisiste* nowadays was probably far from misleading (his observation was borne out by what several Paris informants told me about a rather ridiculous television appearance last year during which Aragon insisted on wearing a paper-bag mask and refused to listen to, or more probably could conveniently no longer hear, any of the interviewer's questions), in the end the renown of Louis Aragon will be that of a poet, novelist and critic who tried his best to give Communist writing in France a human face.

RENÉ CHAR

Enshrined this year in the Pantheon of the Bibliothèque de la Pléiade, René Char, born in 1907, is the most recent of eight twentieth-century French poets to be accorded such an accolade and the only one still living. Despite the common assumption that Char is an obscure poet, it is now to be presumed that his work, which he would vigorously defend against the charge of being élitist, will at last reach a much wider public than that which appreciates most contemporary poetry. Though this edition may attract the mortician's trade of academic exegesis, its outstanding virtue is that of revealing that Char's work, when viewed in its entirety, is not only charged with exceptional vitality but has a hitherto seldom recognized unity and coherence.

The most commonly accepted opinion with regard to Char has been that he is an abstruse, even esoteric poet. He would seem to be fully aware of being a hard knot to untie: 'Le poète, on le sait, mêle le manque et l'excès, le but et le passé. D'où l'insolvabilité de son poème . . .'

Here the latent ambiguity of the key-word, *insolvabilité*, mingling insolvency with insolubility, typifies one of the commonest difficulties with which Char's readers may find themselves confronted. Reflecting on how to comment most appositely on the variety of problems facing even the best-informed student of Char, I ran through the titles of his numerous collections in search of a suggestive clue, and came across *La nuit talismanique qui brillait dans son cercle* of 1972. *Talismanique* at once awoke an echo which before long brought George Steiner's *On Difficulty* (1978) to mind. In this collection, the words 'talisman' and 'talismanic' are employed in a context touching closely on the question of Char's supposed obscurity; and Steiner's title-essay may be recommended to anyone desiring to attain a proper appreciation of how Char may most profitably be approached. Steiner alludes to Dada and the Surrealists in this essay, though never specifically to Char; but perhaps the most salient of his applications of the term 'talismanic' occurs in his examination of the work of Paul Celan, who happens to have been the most notable of Char's German translators.

'Between lack and excess', review of René Char, *Oeuvres complètes* (Paris: Gallimard, 1983), *Times Literary Supplement* (14 October 1983).

It may come as a surprise to some to learn that one of the most remarkable of Char's English-language translators was William Carlos Williams, described in the Pléiade edition's chronological notes as a faithful friend of the French poet and of his work. Williams's 1944 collection *The Wedge* contains 'A Sort of Song', consisting of twelve lines which begin by presenting the image of a sleeping serpent (viz, 'A la santé du serpent'), and conclude with the words: 'Saxifrage is my flower that splits/the rocks'. It is hard to see mere coincidence in the fact that Char was later to publish an item entitled 'Pour un Promethée saxifrage: En touchant la main aeolienne de Hölderlin', or that this prose-poem starts by asking 'La réalité sans l'énergie disloquante de la poésie, – qu'est-ce?' American energy allied to constant questioning regarding the nature of reality seems as characteristic of Williams as his invocation of the saxifrage is akin to the implicit rock-breaking force involved in Char's 'Le poème pulvérisé'.

It would hardly be possible to present his poetry without some reference to Char's early association with the Surrealist movement; indeed, it is likely that his reputation outside France is above all that of the Surrealist poet who inspired Pierre Boulez's still frequently performed *Marteau sans maître* of 1955. In fact, however, his adherence to the movement, though never officially terminated, was of no more than ten years' duration. After 1936, while remaining as responsive as ever to the flux of the feelings and of oneiric phenomena, his transcription of the objective world and of contemporary history becomes simultaneously more personal and more impersonally documentary. When the whole of his strictly Surrealist production was republished by José Corti in 1945, a leaflet accompanying the collection stated: 'La clé du "Marteau sans maître" tourne dans la réalité pressentie des années 1937-1944.'

Char's involvement with the Provençal Resistance began almost immediately after his demobilization in 1940. By 1945, the reputation of 'Capitaine Alexandre', a hefty one-time rugby player as he must have been regarded by many of his comrades who were not assiduous readers of poetry, had become deservedly legendary, as an example of courage, pertinacity, cunning and contagious idealism. This period of the poet's life, undoubtedly the most crucial in his development, is commemorated by the *Feuillets d'Hypnos* of 1943-4, dedicated to Albert Camus, a series of 237 notations, some of them tightly knit apothegms, others resembling factual diary entries, demonstrating the interdependence of poet and man of action in a way probably without parallel. A poem written at this time, 'Affres, détonations, silence', is one of the most moving, because so compactly reticent, of all elegies prompted by the ravages of that era.

Though it would clearly be equivocal to suggest that much of Char's post-war poetry could be specified as regionalist, it is nevertheless undeniable that it is uniquely redolent of the still comparatively unmarred enclave situated between Apt and Avignon, and in particular the Vaucluse. The Ventoux and the Lubéron mountains, together with the flora, fauna and indigenous insect-world familiar to Fabre, provide Char with innumerable images, and the very title of the 1972-5 collection, *Aromates chasseurs*, is evocative of the atmosphere of his hereditary region. The title of Jean Roudaut's excellent introduction to the Pléiade *Oeuvres* is 'Les Territoires de René Char', but though Roudaut draws due attention to the environmental factor in Char's accomplishment, he is mainly concerned with its thematic zones.

The questionable term 'Post-modernism' has recently established itself in the currency of criticism, and though personally averse to it I can see that an attempt to pigeon-hole Char's enterprise under such a heading might well be thought justifiable. *La crise du concept de littérature* was opportunely defined by Jacques Rivière in an essay published fifty years ago. What he then saw as having emerged from Romanticism was a trend that had become increasingly conspicuous in French writing since Rimbaud, who, after Baudelaire, was the first to insist on the exigency of the modern. 'Tu as bien fait de partir, Arthur Rimbaud!' is the title of a poem in a collection Char published soon after the Liberation. And in 1956, referring to Rimbaud's *Génie*, Char wrote: 'Comme Nietzsche, comme Lautréamont, après avoir tout exigé de nous, il nous demande de le "renvoyer".'

The centennial crisis in literature propounded by Rivière is one that appears to have affected British writing only minimally, owing to our innate pragmatic mistrust of such notions as the mantic function of poetry, of poetry as an emanation of the demiurge or involved in the quest for ultimate Being. This being the case, I have long maintained that 'poetry' can be a deceptive translation of the word *poésie*. *Poésie* such as Char's may be said to have become in the strictest sense a transliterary phenomenon. Similarly, the word *parole*, employed so frequently by Char, as it has been by innumerable French authors during the past hundred years, has no satisfactory English equivalent. The *words* central to semantically orientated British thought obviously bear little or no relation to the *parole* evoked in the following gnomic pronouncement: 'Les dieux sont de retour, compagnons. Ils viennent à l'instant de pénétrer dans cette vie; mais la parole qui révoque, sous la parole qui déploie, est réapparue, elle aussi, pour ensemble nous faire souffrir.' *Les dieux* evinced here are recognizably as closely allied to the deities all of which, according to Blake, 'reside in the human breast', as they are to the gods of Hölderlin and Heidegger.

An allusion to Heidegger is bound to lead to some comment on the relationship that developed between the poet and the philosopher after their first meeting near Paris in 1955, under the auspices of Jean Baufret, the addressee of Heidegger's 'Letter on Humanism' (*Ueber den Humanismus*, 1946). Before visiting France that year, Heidegger had intimated that he would be particularly glad to make the acquaintance of Georges Braque and René Char. Six pages of the appendix to the Pléiade volume are devoted to an account of this encounter of the German thinker with the poet whose work he found specially interesting. A mutual passion for the pre-Socratics, perhaps above all for the thought of Parmenides and Heraclitus, predisposed them both to the possibility of dialogue. To designate Char's mature poetry as basically philosophical would be an evident misrepresentation; but in a significant area of his output the poetic and the noematic can nevertheless be seen to converge.

In the summer of 1968, Heidegger took part at Char's invitation in what were to become known as 'les Séminaires du Thor', at a location near the poet's native Île-sur-Sorgue, and between 1950 and 1964 Char wrote a series of reflections representing his 'hommage de respect, de reconnaissance et d'affection à Martin Heidegger', which appear here under the title of 'Impressions anciennes'. On the day of the philosopher's death in 1976, Char wrote a brief epitaph entitled 'Aisé à porter'. It should not be overlooked that at the time of the development of Char's friendly and profitable exchanges with Heidegger, the latter was still overshadowed by the anathema resulting from his undeniable and never retracted connivance with Nazism, while Char's attitude remained one of implacable resistance to the tyranny and human degradation epitomized by Hitler's reign of terror. The crux of the Char/Heidegger connection should probably be sought in the concluding paragraph of Heidegger's disquisition on 'Hölderlin and the Essence of Poetry', in which he predicates the poet's potential value in a time of distress and extols his perseverance in the face of nothingness and night in order to weld truth for posterity, authentically though vicariously, in the utmost solitude of his vocation.

Even in this metaphrasis the passage in question will have a forbiddingly portentous ring to the average English reader of poetry, if he or she exists. But Char's poetry demands to be regarded in the light of what is commonly called 'high seriousness', exemplifying as it does the use of language at its most ambitious, where each 'raid on the inarticulate' represents a risk. Such poetic utterance is characterized by a singular tension between density and transparency. The words of a typical Char poem appear to have come together according to some law of magnetic interaction, and the meaning of the ensuing product to elude all paraphrase.

The rule of 'letting-be' applies both to the process whereby the poem is produced and to the way in which the ideal reader should allow its words to affect him. Subsequent glosses may yield much that is immediately intelligible, but repeated reading of the text will be rewarded by the kindling of an awareness of themes intrinsic to Char's poetry: the human condition, nature, dawn and dark, love and wrath, death and the astonishing enigma of existence itself.

ANDRÉ BRETON and PHILIPPE SOUPAULT

Although André Breton's first *Manifeste du surréalisme* was not to appear until the Autumn of 1924, the first collection of texts that can accurately be categorized as 'Surrealist' had already been published under the title *Les Champs magnétiques* in 1920, the year when the Dada movement which had earlier erupted quasi-simultaneously in Switzerland, New York and defeated Germany began its invasion of Paris. The claim that this joint production of Breton and Philippe Soupault, presented here in its first English translation, was epoch-making can hardly be considered exaggerated. Surrealism, which virtually predated French Dada, was to develop into one of the most significant and seminally creative movements of the century, while the nihilistic manifestations of the Parisian Dadaists were to peter out in futile squabbles within a few years. An attempt to include in this preface an adequate historico-literary survey of the circumstances surrounding the first known resort to purely automatic writing has to be curbed for the sake of brevity. Yet the most cursory synopsis of these texts' background is obliged to contain certain initial references. The first of these should obviously be to Guillaume Apollinaire who, having coined the term *surréalisme* in the Spring of 1917, subtitled his play *Les Mamelles de Tirésias*, performed just before his death the following year, *Drame surréaliste*. It was in fact Apollinaire who first introduced Breton to Philippe Soupault at his 125 Boulevard St Germain apartment, meeting-place for most of the significant avantgarde figures of the day. Mention must just as obviously be made of Jacques Vaché, the lucidly anarchic dandy of Nantes, to whose memory the result of their experimental collaboration is dedicated by the authors at its conclusion: he had died as the result of an apparently deliberate overdose of opium in January 1919, but continued to operate a determining influence on Breton's outlook for many years. Within a month of his death, Tristan Tzara in Zurich received a letter from Breton expressing enthusiasm for his Dada Manifesto of the previous year, which initiated a lively correspondence that was to continue until Tzara's arrival in Paris in 1920. Louis Aragon, who happened to have been attending

---

Introduction to D.G.'s translation of André Breton and Philippe Soupault, *The Magnetic Fields* (Atlas Press, 1985), pp. 7-21.

the same 'auxiliary medicine' course at the Val de Grâce hospital as Breton, encountered him for the first time in 1917 at the *Maison des amis des livres* founded by Adrienne Monnier in the rue de l'Odéon two years previously; in the same bookshop two years later Breton was to declare to the proprietress, after reading her some early extracts from *Les Champs magnétiques*, 'If that's genius, it's easy'. In *Nadja* (1928), Breton recounts that it was at about this time that he made the acquaintance of Paul Eluard, who more than a decade later was to collaborate with him in a more premeditated series of texts, *L'Immaculée Conception*.

In March 1919 the first number of the review *Littérature* made its appearance, to be followed by eleven monthly issues and then – after a break – by a new series of thirteen dating from March 1922. Breton, Aragon and Soupault, who had by now begun to meet constantly, having become bonded by a passionate common rediscovery of Lautréamont, decided to launch a periodical in which work representative of the latest tendencies of post-war writing could reveal what was their 'common denominator'. Their original intention was to call it *Le Nouveau Monde*, but when this title was pre-empted by a new daily paper, the trio adopted the suggestion of Paul Valéry (whom Breton had first begun to frequent in 1914) that they should call their publication *Littérature*, thus no doubt evoking Verlaine's line 'Et tout le reste est littérature'. The initial number, brought out less than six months after the Armistice, is scarcely distinguishable from other literary reviews of its kind, its contents page featuring such names as Gide, Valéry and Jean Paulhan, with Aragon and Breton bringing up the rear as comparative novices. It was not until No. 7, six months later, that it began to contain extracts from what we now know as *Les Champs magnétiques*, the first being entitled simply *Usine* (now part of the section with the overall title *Ne Bougeons Plus*, translated by me as 'Let's Move no More'). After the contributions to earlier numbers of poets such as André Salmon, Max Jacob and Léon-Paul Fargue, this item must have struck a note of startling originality. The last text from the then still unnamed collection to appear separately in a magazine was a poem from the *Le Pagure Dit*: series, 'Détour par le Ciel' ('Bypass through the Sky'), published by Eluard in the 4th issue of his *Proverbe* in April 1920.

While there is no doubt that the notebooks containing the exercises in automatic writing which provided the material for *Les Champs magnétiques* were filled by Breton and Soupault during the late Spring and early Summer of 1919, it would scarcely be possible to assign exact dates to the beginning and ending of its composition. In Breton's *Manifeste du surréalisme* of 1924 there occurs a passage in which, while describing how he first became aware of the possibilities of automatic writing, he refers to 'one evening' when, just as he was about to fall asleep, he became aware of the formation in his mind of an *assez bizarre* ('pretty unusual') sentence, which appeared to have nothing to do with the current events of his life, a sentence so intent on entering his consciousness that it appeared to be 'knocking at the window-pane'. Breton goes on to explain that he was unable to note down this sentence word for word, but it was something to do with there being 'a man cut in two by the window'. In *Les Pas perdus*, published earlier in 1924 than the *Manifeste*, when referring to the time when he first began to be seriously preoccupied with the phenomenon of spontaneously irrupting autonomous phrases, Breton simply names the year 1919. 'Later on,' he writes,

> Soupault and I formed the intention of deliberately reproducing in ourselves the state out of which (such sentences) emerged. In order to do this all that was necessary was to disregard the context of the external world, and it was thus that they made their way to us, during a period of two months, soon following each other without interruption so rapidly that we had to resort to abbreviations in order to note them down. *Les Champs magnétiques* represents only the first application of this discovery: the only reason for ending each chapter was the coming to an end of the day when its writing had been undertaken and, from one chapter to another, only the changing of speed brought about slightly different results. *(L'Entrée des médiums)*

In 1919, according to Henri-Jacques Dupuy,[1] the medical student André Breton went nearly every day to fetch Soupault at the Petrol Commisariat in the rue de Grenelle where he was then still working and take him back to the Hôtel des Grandes Hommes alongside the Panthéon where he was himself staying at the time in order to carry on discussions with him concerning the question of poetic spontaneity, with which Soupault was evidently exceptionally gifted. As a result of the experiments leading from these conversations *Usine*, the first to be published of their joint productions, appeared in October of that year, as has been noted, in the review *Littérature*. Louis Aragon, in an article ('L'Homme coupé en deux') published in a literary periodical in 1968, declared that it was on his return to Paris after being demobilized towards the middle of April following the Armistice that Breton, in a St Germain café called La Source, read to him 'in a confidential voice' the first four chapters of an 'unprecedented book'. On 29 July, according to Michel

---

[1] *Poètes d'aujourd'hui 58: Philippe Soupault* (Paris: Seghers, 1957).

Sanouillet,[2] Breton announced to Tristan Tzara the appearance in September of a book consisting of 'a hundred pages of prose and verse' written by himself in collaboration with Philippe Soupault. The book must in fact have been virtually complete by the end of July; and the eventual title must have been decided on at much the same time, as Breton refers to it as *Les Champs magnétiques* in a letter to Paul Valéry dated 5 September. It appears that the authors had previously thought of calling it *Les Précipités*, possibly after a sentence in *Eclipses*, in which this has the sense of chemical precipitates, though it is difficult to exclude the ambiguous double sense implying speed, since the question of varying speeds at which the texts were written seems to have constituted their chief distinguishing factor. Aragon, in the article already referred to, alludes to a certain amount of rearrangement and addition of material, parts of which had in some cases been personally signed by one or the other of the collaborators prior to the establishment of the definitive texts and the choice of their overall title. There even exists a letter from Breton to Paul Valéry, dated 26 December 1919, in which he writes of having produced with Philippe Soupault 'a sequel to *Les Champs magnétiques* (in a manner of speaking)', and suggests he might bring it with him in order to read a fragment of it to the older poet.

In Breton's 1924 Manifesto there is a passage explaining that his collaboration with Soupault came about in the wake of his medico-psychiatric training during the War, when he was wholly under the influence of Freudian theory. While referring neither to Janet nor his own mentor, nor to the hospital at Saint-Dizier where in all probability the most influential of his contacts with mental patients occurred in 1916, the passage specifies that these wartime experiences led him to the conclusion that their most essential feature when related to poetic adventure consisted in the attempt to capture and fix *spoken thought* of the kind that analysts encourage their clients to produce in the form of rapid, spontaneous, unselfcritical monologues. Having confided in Soupault his desire to explore the possibilities opened up by attempting to track down in writing such products of uncontrolled thought as the sentence about a man cut in half by a window that had obsessed him, he persuaded him to 'blacken paper' with him, 'with laudable disdain as regards the literary quality of the results'. In his reminiscent article of 1968, Aragon expressed doubt as to whether Breton would ever have been capable of producing a work such as *Les Champs magnétiques* alone, since the undertaking entailed a then virtually unprecedented confrontation with the unknown,

---

[2] *Dada à Paris* (Paris: Pauvert, 1965).

in the dark depths of the human mind, where horrors and wonders might be encountered that could endanger the sanity of any one individual on his own. Fifty years earlier, Rimbaud had abandoned his *Alchimie du Verbe*, a not dissimilar experiment; and in 1916 Breton, writing to a friend, confessed that rereading *Illuminations* had scared him, on remembering that Rimbaud had said: 'My health was endangered. Terror assailed me'. Lautréamont's incredible feat in writing *Les Chants de Maldoror* in complete solitude might not have come about, according to at least one commentator, without his resorting to the use of belladonna as a stimulant; and he reacted against this wholly irrational first outpouring by producing a short second book of sober and logical maxims (*Poésies*, first republished by Breton and Aragon in an early number of *Littérature*). Breton and Soupault were both of sound mind, and unaddicted to any drug such as the opium that Breton's friend Jacques Vaché had been in the habit of using, when by mutual consent and compatability they embarked on the sessions of tandem composition that before long brought *Les Champs magnétiques* into existence.

In the fourth of his interviews with André Parinaud broadcast by what is now RTF in the Spring of 1952,[3] Breton declared that the results of his collaboration with Soupault constituted

> indisputably the first *Surrealist* (and in no sense Dada) work, since it is the fruit of the first systematic use of automatic writing . . . The daily practice of automatic writing – on occasion we would devote ourselves to it continuously from eight to ten hours a day – entailed on our part observations of considerable portent but which were only subsequently to achieve coordination and permit inferences to be drawn from them. It is none the less true that we lived at that time in a state of euphoria, almost in the intoxication of discovery. Our situation was that of anyone who has just excavated a vein of precious metal.

For many recent readers of this pioneering work the question of who wrote which sections and passages of it and who the others is one that has aroused much curiosity. This curiosity should be satisfied as fully as possible when the Bibliothèque de la Pléiade edition of André Breton's complete works makes its appearance next year, and with it what Mme. Marguerite Bonnet announced as *l'édition critique* in her scrupulously researched and documented study of 1975: *André Breton et la naissance de l'aventure surréaliste*.[4] By far the greatest part of the evidence illuminating

---

[3] A. Breton, *Entretiens (1913-1952) avec André Parinaud, etc.* (Paris: NRF/Gallimard, 'Idees', 1969).

[4] Librairie José Corti.

the question of which poet was responsible for which sentences or portions of the amalgamated texts is to be found in two of the 300 copies of the 1920 Au Sans Pareil edition. The first of these is the copy given at the time of its appearance by Breton to Simone Kahn, whom he married the following year, and in which in 1924 he underlined for her all the passages he remembered writing himself. The second is the first of the five special copies on rice-paper belonging in 1930 to Valentine Hugo, when Breton added to it a number of manuscript annotations, noting on a spare page; 'This copy of *Les Champs magnétiques* is the only one containing these additions, none of which have been copied by the author. A.B.' This is confirmed by a note signed by Soupault. On two and a half pages of small, closely-spaced handwriting Breton explained the book's genesis and provided its key, specifying his own share in the collaboration, and above all indicating the varying speeds at which the various passages were written. On many pages there are also marginal notes, commenting on or explaining details. With a green pencil, Breton underlined all the sentences and paragraphs he had written himself; in the margins he indicated in red pencil the passages to which he had always wanted special attention to be drawn, and with a grey line he encircled such as both authors had at the time of writing them agreed were the most satisfactory.

The annotations made on the No. 1 de luxe paper copy of the book belonging to Valentine Hugo in 1930 were first divulged in 1970 in the 7th issue of the review *Change* by Alain Jouffroy, author of the brief foreword to Gallimard's reprint of *Les Champs magnétiques*, the first since 1920, published three years earlier with two Dada 'playlets' of the same period, also apparently written in collaboration. It is not easy to decide which of the many items of information regarding the composition of the work under discussion disclosed by these notes have the greatest relevance to the purpose of this Introduction. It is satisfying to know for certain that it was André Breton who was chiefly responsible for arranging the order of sequence of the texts. There were originally to have been eight sections. If one counts the last three pages (the first of which I have left untranslated as *La Fin de tout*) as the final section, then the book can now be said to consist of ten parts. The sixth, 'Let's Move No More', was apparently added when the book was in proof stage, which is curious when one considers that it contains as a subsection the first extract to appear in print, 'Factory'; it would seem in fact to consist of an amalgam of loose ends refractory to categorization. Breton would appear generally to have admitted Soupault's relatively random addition of title-headings to certain sections only with reluctance. The notes in Valentine Hugo's copy make it clear that all the principal titles except the fourth (which seems intended to evoke Jules Verne) were decided on by Breton. It may be surprising to learn that the first, which I have translated as 'The Unsilvered Glass', derives from the title of a painting by Matisse, *La Glâce sans tain*. The word *tain* may literally be rendered as 'foil' or 'tin-foil', an equivalent of which might be 'silver-paper'; a dictionary defines it as an amalgam of tin or mercury applied to the back of a piece of glass to make it reflect light. Had I preferred to make a more purely literary translation, I might well have adopted the suggestion that this title should become 'The Transparent Mirror' in English. It is possible that it has an implicit reference to an invisible barrier separating the objective world from subjectivity, or external reality from oneiric reflections of it. It is in any case clear from Breton's 1930 notes that he regarded this section as being imbued with the ubiquitous underlying feeling of despair rife among young survivors of the Great War during the year following the Armistice.

It is similarly certain that the first of the concluding poem-sequences headed 'The Hermit-crab Says:' was written entirely by Breton, the second by Soupault. Here again the title may be interpreted as having a predetermined meaning. Towards the end of 'White Gloves', the text preceding these sets of poems, occurs the following passage:

> Whatever is inhabiting our two friends gradually emerges from its quasi-immobility. It gropes its way forward obtruding a fine pair of stalked eyes. The body in complete phosphorus formation remains halfway between the day and the tailor's shop. It is connected by delicate antennae to the sleep of children.

The mysterious creature obtruding a fine pair of stalked eyes and groping its way forward from within 'our two friends' is unmistakably a crab: the hermit-crab. What it says might well be said to represent an equivalent of the utterances of the *bouche d'ombre* transcribed, in however vastly different a manner, by Victor Hugo some seventy years earlier. In his preface to the recent Gallimard *Poésie* edition of the work, Philippe Audoin refers to the hermit-crab *(pagure)* as the totem-animal of the *Champs*, which 'declares itself, amidst the luxuriant flora and fauna the Fields' climate engenders, to be nothing short of oracular.'

To return to the second section, 'Seasons' constitutes, according to Breton's 1930 notes, a narrative of confused recollections of his childhood. The title arose from his recent preoccupation with Rimbaud, echoing one of the latter's best-known lines, 'Ô saisons! Ô châteaux!' 'Fôret Noire', one of the nine poems making up Breton's *Mont de Piété*, his first collection published in 1919, is based on a factual incident in the life of Rimbaud after he had abandoned poetry and is therefore, despite its apparently random construction, a poem recounting a consciously chosen subject, just as 'Seasons' was predetermined by Breton's decision to recapture a few of his earliest memories. The first paragraph refers to the first four years of his life, when he was being looked after by his maternal grandfather in Brittany at Saint-Brieuc, in a house containing a lithograph representing the Ages of Man (sentences 5 and 6). The puzzling sentence about the pronunciation of what would normally be *château* proves to be simply a transcription of local Breton accent. Later paragraphs go on to evoke the period following his parents' move to Paris at the turn of the century, and in the margin of the passage referring to a feminine presence opposite the narrator in a railway-carriage, the shape of a heart containing the name Alice was subsequently drawn, a reference one might suppose to a childhood sweetheart.

But it is by no means necessary to show that behind all the inconsequent irrationality of these texts there is a basis of lived experience. The psychoanalytic operation is intended to bring mysteries to light in order to explain them. The purpose of automatic writing is to discover the marvellous but not to fabricate it deliberately. *Les Champs magnétiques*, unquestionably inspired by the development of the psychoanalytic method, is not a series of exercises intended to demonstrate the results of this method, but arose above all from the application of a distinctly new type of literary discipline, and the application of a deliberate experimental principle concerning the factor of varying speed when writing spontaneously.

The discipline to which Breton and Soupault submitted themselves in order to perform the task they undertook in 1919 was of possibly unparalleled novelty. It would be impossible now to say to what extent Rimbaud and Lautréamont rewrote, tidied up or altered the first drafts of *Illuminations* or *Chants de Maldoror*. The first principle ruling the production of *Les Champs magnétiques* was that none of its words, phrases or sentences, once having found their way to paper through the authors' intermediary, were to be in any way altered or improved. This is hardly the place to analyse Breton's earliest poems or to enumerate the influences discernible in them; but it should be said that they display considerable technical proficiency, and that it is obvious that he was conscious in 1914 of emerging irresistibly from the accomplishments of *symbolisme*, or more precisely of poetry as conceived by Mallarmé, Vielé-Griffin and Valéry, whose control of rhyme, metre and form was as consciously consummate as possible. Having become aware of the extempore nature of certain Apollinaire items such as *Zone* and *Lundi rue Christine*, and made the acquaintance first of Jacques Vaché, then of Aragon and Soupault, he went on completely to jettison the technical apparatus he had cultivated at the time of his first attempts to write poetry, in favour of a quite different ideal of purity, an anti-poetry, in a sense, to be distinguished by its freedom from conscious aesthetic control. The source of poetry, in other words, was to be sought in an id no longer subservient to a superego. A more complete summary of the turning point in French poetry at this time would be bound to take account of the austere aesthetics of language and image being independently developed by Pierre Reverdy, for whom Breton was repeatedly to evince his admiration, but adequately to do so would involve too complex a digression.

The discipline involved in automatic writing is that of vigilantly resisting the temptation to interrupt the stream of consciousness, or rather of the theoretically subjacent consciousness, or to interfere with or in any way alter *post facto* the results obtained 'with laudable disdain as regards their literary quality'. The other factor I have referred to as being of capital concern to the authors during their collaboration is that of the range of varying speeds at which the dictation of the subconscious may be registered. In Breton's annotations occurs a passage of some twenty lines in which he specifies the degree of rapidity determining each of the eight texts he had produced with Soupault. His indications are schematized by the use of the letter v (for *vitesse*, speed) and the addition to it, up to four times, of the sign ', denoting the range of acceleration manifested during the different sessions of co-operation. In the first section, v at the outset stands for very great speed, corresponding to the urgency of the need to communicate a certain mood. 'Seasons' is somewhat confusingly accorded v', this being said to indicate a comparatively diminished speed, roughly a third of that of the first text, though far greater than that at which a man would normally attempt to recount his childhood memories. The next, 'Eclipses', is marked v'', and this is explained as representing a speed even greater than v, intended in fact to be the fastest possible, the kind of eclipse announced by the title is 'of course' that of specific subject-matter. It might be thought, in view of a sentence like: 'Stiff stems of Suzanne uselessness above all village of flavours with a lobster church', that the speed at which this chapter developed led to ellipses as well as the eclipse of subject, as in few other places in the work does straightforward syntactic structure give way to something like telegraphese. 'In 80 Days', written almost entirely by Soupault and described by Breton as representing the memories of a man seeking escape from his memories in an imaginary voyage, is marked v''', representing half way between v and v''. 'Barriers' is a dialogue undertaken at medium Surrealist speed, which is about that represented by v': it might be thought to represent the solipsistic breakdown of conversational exchange, that characteristic phenomenon of the age, made familiar fifty years later by, for instance, Jean-Luc Godard. 'White Gloves' is meticulously marked v'''', as the text is compared by Breton to an express train gradually slowing down on reaching the station at the end of its journey.

In the article he published in 1968, Aragon wrote: 'From *Barrières* onwards, immediately after *En 80 Jours*, a considerable curiosity, of an order quite different from that accompanying my initial surprise, was aroused in me by the abandoning of the Maldororian style, to put it simply, of the whole opening. The modifications to be seen in the writing of the *Champs* are,' Breton says, 'essentially due to variations in the speed of writing. Philippe's testimony makes it clear that from the junction referred to (*Barrières*) till the end such modifications were made in ever accelerating order.'

The two series of 'Hermit-crab' poems, the title of which suggests, according to Aragon, that both authors wished to disown all personal responsibility for them by attributing their words to the dictation of some shared parasitical organism, were written at slightly varying speeds, in each case much faster than that normal for poetry. All twenty poems contain verbal play verging on the pun, difficult to translate at all closely other than literally word for word. They would appear, in any case, to represent a dissolution of all previous styles of poetry by means of travesty and derision. Breton was to call the continued use of lines as a requisite for the writing of poetry into question altogether as from this time, though he never abandoned it, and in 1930 seems to have regarded his ten 'Hermit-crab' poems with scant enthusiasm.

The last three pages of 'The Magnetic Fields' say almost nothing yet express a great deal. 1919 was a year of liquidation, the end of everything, but also of paroxysmic death-birth, incubating seeds of renewal. For a proper explanation of what the notice 'Wood & Coal' (*Bois & charbons*) meant to Breton at this time one should turn to a passage in *Nadja*, too long to be transcribed here, in which the author describes himself wandering about Paris with Soupault and continually finding himself confronted, to his increasing annoyance, by placards displaying this announcement, until he began to feel himself able to predict its next appearance. There was a time when one used to see this notice outside or in the windows of *bistros*, owned usually by Auvergnats who happened to specialize in dealing in domestic fuel as a sideline. The penultimate page suggests that at the time of completing their joint literary venture, which at the same time they regarded as an anti-literary gesture, the collaborators shared a longing to disappear into the quasi-anonymity of running an obscure little back-street establishment, rather as Arthur Craven had enigmatically vanished in the Gulf of Mexico not long before, or as

Rimbaud had abandoned all literary ambition fifty years earlier to adopt the guise of a trader in Abyssinia. The simple dedication of the work to the memory of Jacques Vaché, who had killed himself less than a year previously, and whose *Lettres de guerre* he decided to publish as soon as *Les Champs magnétiques* had appeared, must have been inspired by Vaché's integrity in refusing to indulge in literary activity which could have been taxed with a kind of seriousness entirely at odds with what he called *umour* and defined as being inseparable from 'a sense of the theatrical (and joyless) uselessness of everything'. To ask what Vaché would have thought of the publication of his letters, and the subsequently highly productive career of his principal admirer, is not unlike asking what Kafka would have thought of Max Brod's divulging his unfinished, unpublished works to the world, although manifestly Breton and Brod are in no other way comparable.

Few readers of Kafka today can fail to feel grateful for Brod's betrayal, if such it was; nor would many reproach Breton for having preserved for posterity the name of Vaché, by no means a European genius but whose letters certainly have value as documents of an exemplary disgust with the bourgeois civilization that had culminated in the unbridled carnage and mendacity castigated by Karl Kraus in *Die letzen Tage der Menscheit*. The post-1918 phase of revolt against all that respectable 'literature' can stand for what was undoubtedly a healthy purge, and the kind of writing that can perhaps sententiously be described as the nourishment without which the human spirit would soon wither away can but benefit from intermittent outbreaks of such 'anti-literature' as the international Dada period produced.

It was not to take Breton long to recuperate from the mood of desperate disillusionment that appears temporarily to have prevailed over his innately protagonistic aspirations, for within six years he had launched the first three of at least a score of works of prose and poetry constituting an *oeuvre* of which the style alone can now be said to possess an idiosyncratic sumptuosity and elegance unrivalled by that of almost any other French writer of the twentieth century. No doubt he would himself prefer to be regarded not merely as a great stylist but far more as a polemical iconoclast and instigator. Nevertheless it is as literature in the least pejorative sense that his writings are about to be consecrated by their inclusion in the 1985 Bibliothèque de la Pléiade edition.

There might seem to be a certain irony in the fact that Philippe Soupault, though still referred to in the Surrealist Manifesto of 1924 as 'rising with the stars', had within ten years of the publication of *Les Champs magnétiques* gradually parted company with the combative confrères of his youth, having tacitly severed connections with the group in order to devote himself mainly to novel-writing, journalism and travel, so that his name does not appear among the signatories of the 1930 Manifesto. Today he remains the sole living survivor of both Dada and Surrealism, and his entire output is at last being enthusiastically rediscovered by generations still unborn at the time of his adventurous creative début. We are glad to take this opportunity to salute and thank this protean poet and veteran freedom-fighter for giving his consent to this first English translation of a work which would never have existed without his participation, and his time to the signing of forty copies of it.

Since I began to write this Introduction, the December 1984 issue of the *Magazine littéraire*, devoted mainly to the celebration of '60 Years of Surrealism', has made its appearance. Two of its sixteen special features are devoted to Breton alone, and one to *Soupault le magnétique*. In the latter, M.-J. Hoyet Marsigli writes: 'in *Les Champs magnétiques* verbal associations proliferate, sudden and surprising images abound, and Soupault's specially distinctive writing, "immunized against all compunction" according to the expression Breton applied to it, comes into its first flower'. Accompanying this article are six paragraphs (by Marc Dachy) devoted to one of the first reviews of *Le manuscrit des champs magnétiques*, which has just been published by Lachenal & Ritter. Anyone interested in verifying or comparing the details given earlier regarding the composition of the work here presented in English can now consult a facsimile of its original manuscript, believed for half a century to have been lost. 'The authors themselves believed the manuscript to be irrecoverable,' says the *Magazine littéraire*, 'since all trace of it had been mislaid in the hands of the director of *Au Sans Pareil*, René Hilsum. Here it is in facsimile, plunging the reader of today into the source of nascent Surrealism. What the text loses in secrecy regarding its common composition by two hands it gains in authenticity, in adventurous and poetic voltage.' Later in the review, the author adds: 'the manuscript is very close to the published edition made from it. A few corrections in Breton's handwriting transform in Soupault's part of the text the first person singular into the plural, perhaps in order to increase the osmosis between the authors. Elsewhere, the transcriptions reveal a number of unpublished texts that Breton, through severity with himself, crossed out and would not have type-set. These texts of the first water reappear today thanks to the rediscovery of the manuscript and its publication has been closely supervised by Philippe Soupault himself.'

By way of conclusion, a brief reference must be made to certain specific problems that I have tried to resolve in my translation of *Les Champs magnétiques*. On the one hand, Breton's various comments on the nature of the enterprise he persuaded Soupault to undertake with him leave no doubt that for him the intention of bringing the *sub-* or *un-*conscious to light (no place here to debate the theoretical distinction to be drawn between the two terms) considerably predominated that of creating a novel literary work. On the other hand, it must not be forgotten that both collaborators were poets by nature and vocation, however greatly Breton may have initially been influenced by his early psycho-medical training. Above all, I have tried to maintain a balance between literalness and literacy, and whenever possible to allow the *visual* images to emerge as accurately and distinctly as possible. Since translation can seldom hope to render adequate aural equivalents of French verbal felicities, while necessarily missing many pun-like *jeux-de-mots*, I have wherever possible resorted to such devices as alliteration, and often altered the syntax when this did not entail a betrayal of the substantive meaning of the phrase. Now and then problems have arisen that I have been unable to settle satisfactorily, in some cases deriving from expressions that may, I suspect, have been current in French vernacular at a time when I was three years old and can hardly therefore be expected to be familiar with (what, for instance, is or was what I have rendered as 'Botot water'?) Should a translator be aware of the definition of a *dicton de Saint-Médard*? In the early eighteenth century, there occurred in the cemetery at Saint-Médard a series of phenomena comparable only to the goings-on in the previous century at Loudun (recounted by Huxley, Whiting, etc.): mass hysteria producing at first ecstatic convulsions, eventually effusive utterances deemed to be prophetic.[5] The word *bifur* in the penultimate poem in the second 'Hermit-crab' sequence is printed in roman rather than the contextual italic lettering of these poems, and I have decided to leave it untranslated since, though aware that it is an abbreviation for forked or branching, implying a turning-point that requires a decision to be made, I am unable to vouch for whether or not it was at one time used as a road-sign: ten years later, at least, the word was to become the title of a neo-Surrealist periodical. Other such details might be somewhat tediously discussed, but as this Introduction is by now quite long enough, I will forego further enumeration of them.

---

5 See Catherine-Laurence Maire, *Les Convulsionnaires de Saint-Médard, miracles, convulsions et prophéties à Paris au XVIIIe siècle* (Paris: Coll. Archives/Gallimard Julliard, 1985).

ARCHIVES DU SURRÉALISME

These two volumes, brought out simultaneously with the first *tome* of the Pléiade edition of André Breton's *Oeuvres complètes*, appear with exemplary introductions, editing and notes (though both would have benefited from the addition of an index) under the auspices of the association whose acronym is ACTUAL. For some time now this has been compiling and annotating for posterity a vast amount of material appertaining to some sixty years of Surrealism's history, with the complementary intention of establishing in Paris a permanent centre of documentation on the movement.

It might be supposed that the Surrealist group was formed in 1924, the year of the publication of Breton's *Premier Manifeste*. In fact its origins go back to the confused disruption of Dada two or three years earlier, by which time Breton, Louis Aragon and Philippe Soupault were already well acquainted with one another and united in their enraged disgust with all the established values they believed to have been rendered null by the war in which they were only recalcitrant young participants. The *Bureau de recherches surréalistes* opened its doors to the public at 15 rue de Grenelle on 11 October 1924. It continued to be open every afternoon between 4.30 and 6.30 until the end of January 1925. Among its contents was an attendance ledger, the *Cahier de la permanence*. Members of the group took turns, two at a time, to preside at the office, see to the enquiries or suggestions of visitors, attend to business connected with the first issue of *La Révolution surréaliste*, which was due to appear in December that year, and make notes of the day's incidents in the ledger.

The entries on the ledger's first page, for the Bureau's opening day, consist of only four lines, the first of which refers to a letter to be written to a certain Pierre Morhange forbidding him to pronounce the word 'surrealism'. To infer from the initial entries in the *Cahier* that it was devoted mainly to daily trivialities would be misleading, yet not wholly without foundation. One could select at random numerous memos, amusing in themselves or of interest to the cultural or social historian of

---

'Revolution inside and out', review of *Archives du Surréalisme*, 2 vols., ed. Paule Thévenin and Marguerite Bonnet (Paris: Gallimard, 1988), *Times Literary Supplement* (7-13 October 1988), p. 1126.

the post-1918 decade. On 17 November, for example, it was the turn of Breton and Aragon to be in attendance. They noted that Man Ray came to lend a chessboard that had been exhibited at the Independents in 1921 and brought photographs of Picasso and himself. Aragon was busy making final notes for the group's forthcoming *revue* and fetching the first proofs of its illustrations. 'Crevel is coming tomorrow with two friends. Ask Paul Eluard to make him wait for me,' signed A.B. The following day Eluard and Péret were on duty. They noted principally that Artaud's photograph had been received, and that Miss Cunard had called with René Crevel. It can safely be assumed that this visit led to the 'close attachment' of many years between Nancy Cunard and Aragon.

Already, however, early in the previous month, someone had inserted on a verso page of the ledger the following observations: 'We're becoming idiotic. Nobody cares a damn about Surrealism. Nobody works any more. They collect autographs. Only Aragon and Breton work. As to the others . . . !' And from then on, until the end of the year, occasional similar hints of individual disaffection continue to appear. On 17 December, when 1,000 copies of the initial number of the review arrived for distribution, Pierre Naville took the opportunity to propose that the Bureau should be closed between 25 December and 1 January, adding: 'A week's reflection will perhaps restore to the Surrealists that mental activity of which for some time past this ledger no longer bears any trace.'

At about this time Breton, whose private personality was always quite distinct from his public persona, which as a rule effectively concealed his more intimate concerns, appears to have been going through a period of temporary disappointment. If he was dissatisfied, it would have been not so much with public reaction to his recently published *Premier Manifeste*, as with the results of the principles it announced being put into daily practice by the multifarious and varyingly compatible members of the group that surrounded him. There was also something else disturbing him. Only recently had he begun to be fully aware of the existence in his orbit of a powerful character with an unpredictable potential for demoralization and revolt that set him in a category of his own. Breton had begun to appreciate Antonin Artaud.

By mid-1924, Artaud, already well known as an actor in avant-garde theatrical circles, could announce in a letter that he had 'got to know all the Dadas, who would gladly include me in the crew of their latest Surrealist boat, but nothing doing – I'm far too Surrealist for that'. By the end of January of the following year not only Breton but the whole group had reached the conclusion that Artaud seemed indeed to be the very incarnation of all that they believed Surrealism was striving to become. A *Cahier* entry for the 24th of that month records a general meeting that had taken place the previous evening, uniting eighteen adherents, who had unanimously agreed that the *Centrale* had demonstrated its inability to achieve the ends for which it had been set up, and that in order to remedy the situation it was necessary to hand over directorship to Artaud – *avec tous pouvoirs*. A few days later, it was decided that from then on the *Centrale* would no longer be open to the public.

The period during which Artaud controlled the rue de Grenelle headquarters of Surrealism is recorded in the official ledger by a notably reduced number of entries, and seven of its remaining twenty pages were left completely blank. Page forty-four was cut out with scissors following an incident involving Naville and Breton on 25 March. Naville had put up a poster commenting on Breton's non-participation in the *Centrale*'s affairs in terms which the latter considered insulting, and after deploring the fact that neither Aragon nor Artaud had torn this placard down, Breton wrote that in such conditions *nothing* in the Surrealist revolution interested him any longer.

The first volume of the *Archives du Surréalisme* also contains twenty-five pages of *Annexes*, consisting of certain texts indispensable for an adequate understanding of the brief but crucial initial phase of the movement's development which includes the period of explicitly political debate covered by the second volume. Of these ten documents, by far the most remarkable must surely be the personal letter addressed by Breton to Artaud on 27 March 1925. Exactly two months previously, on the occasion of his assuming complete control of the *Centrale*, Artaud had issued a declaration in which he proclaimed, among other things, that: 'We have nothing to do with literature, but we are very capable, if needs be, of making use of it like everyone else.' 'SURREALISM is not a new or easier means of expression, nor even a metaphysics of poetry; it is a means of totally liberating the mind' (*l'esprit*: the ambiguities of the French word have led to endless and immemorial misunderstandings). Breton's letter to Artaud written at the end of March, following the unpleasantness of the incident involving Naville, begins *Mon cher ami*, and is a confidential expression of Breton's worst doubts at that time with regard to the future outcome of the Surrealist adventure.

> I ask myself sometimes if it's really necessary to endure this sort of thing: someone reads you a poem one hasn't the least desire to hear and that gets lost in a cloud of similar poems, another tells you what he's done at night, when he might have been sleeping. Lucky for you if you don't have to discuss publishing concerns, travelling projects or other nameless imbecilities.... During my complete absence of late, I have left it entirely to you to safeguard a certain number of principles which I believe would

otherwise have been *very hypocritically* trampled under foot. . . . I am not, as it pleases you to pretend, the raison d'être or the mainstay of Surrealism! However much I question and examine myself, I can find nothing to justify this allegation. Let's put it that I'm happy to know you, to know Masson, that's all . . . . In the light of what I've been feeling for nearly two months, I only know that nothing I normally put up with can find any further favour. On the contrary, what I see of you reassures me, touches me, prevents me from losing myself very completely. I beg you therefore once more to *be on the watch* . . . and avoid subordinating in any circumstance the immediate interest of the mind to political or other necessity.

Breton's confidence in Artaud was destined to be short-lived. The third issue of *La Révolution surréaliste*, April 1925, for which Artaud was largely responsible, contains some of the most inflammatory texts ever to appear in the review ('Open the prisons, disband the army!'), open letters to the Pope, the Dalai Lama, the rectors of European Universities, the psychiatric directors of lunatic asylums. Breton, alarmed by a sudden realization that Artaud was compelled to carry all his undertakings to extremes, assumed editorship of the review for is nine succeeding numbers. A definitive parting of the ways between Artaud and the by now 'orthodox' members of the group occurred two years later.

During the summer of 1925, whenever the Surrealists met there were heated discussions about what exactly they meant when employing the term Revolution. For Artaud it continued to mean above all, and before long only, an inner revolution, that of *l'esprit*. The group surrounding Breton soon came to the conclusion, prompted by the colonialist war then being waged by the French in Morocco, that if they seriously desired to 'change life' by 'transforming the world', they would have to acquiesce in the Marxist doctrine of 'the primacy of matter over mind'. The turning-point for Breton was his reading of Trotsky's short book on Lenin, written immediately after the latter's death the preceding year. Trotsky's views came as a revelation to him, and having communicated his enthusiasm to Eluard, he wrote a three-page article on the book.

The rapid development of political awareness, and indeed acuity, in Breton and all those closest to him (Artaud apart) during the comparatively brief period following July 1925, is the principal disclosure yielded by the documents assembled in the second *tome* under the heading 'Vers l'action politique'. A unanimous antagonism among the Surrealists to France's colonialist policy in Morocco fostered their contact with three groups of contemporary intellectuals of Marxist-revolutionary tendency, associated respectively with three reviews: *Clarté* (originally connected with Barbusse), *Philosophies* and the short-lived Belgian *Correspondance*. Between mid-October and 20 November, ten committee meetings were held, following the inaugural general assembly of 5 October, in the premises occupied by *Clarté*, also used for a while as a temporary Surrealist gallery. The second volume of Surrealist *Archives* consists mainly of the reproduction *in toto* of the scrupulously drawn-up minutes of the proceedings.

The sobriety, coherence and discipline characterizing the many motions, resolutions and communiqués reported during the course of the meetings are such as to astound and confute all those still inclined to think of the Surrealists as a group intent above all on flabbergasting the bourgeoisie with their eccentric antics. The topics they discussed were, in the main, typical of what were to be the central preoccupations of would-be revolutionary intellectuals for the following forty years. The arguments involved may appear confusing to many today, but though complex and sometimes subtle they are not confused. It may come as a surprise to some readers to learn that the name of Raymond Queneau is also to be found among those of the participants in these political debates of late 1925.

A third volume of *Archives du Surréalisme* is in preparation, to be designated *Adhérer au parti communiste?* The interrogative form of this provisional title reflects what has been described as Breton's 'equivocal' three-year adhesion to the PCF. He was eventually to find himself consigned to a cell obviously unsuited to him, and by 1930 had definitively separated himself from all forms of Stalinism. It is perhaps the most striking of the ironies in which the history of Surrealism abounds that Aragon, who was to become the most orthodox of literary Communist Party-liners, should have referred, prior to 1925, to 'doddering Moscow' and described the Bolshevik Revolution as 'a vague ministerial crisis'; but in those days, of course, it was Aragon who was most noticeably endowed with *esprit*, in the sense most different from that which Artaud intended the word to convey.

FRANCIS PICABIA

I wonder how many of those who have undertaken to make a study of twentieth-century art would agree with me that most, or should I say many, contemporary critics and art historians – those engaged by the BBC to address Open University students seem to me specially typical – appear to be obsessed above all with the desire to label and classify all artists who come under the 'modernist' rubric as neatly as possible according to clearly established movements, schools and tendencies. Francis Picabia is the figure most likely to give such critics a headache if the time at their disposal is limited.

Picabia was pre-eminently a Proteus, who made up his own movements and fashions as he went along. The two-page entry under the heading *Picabia* to be found in the *Dictionnaire général du surréalisme et de ses environs* of 1982 ends by concluding: 'Marked by his powerful personality, the work of Francis Picabia escapes from the category Surrealism as it does from that of Dada. If the Surrealists could never quite accept him as one of their own, neither did they ever reject him as foreign to their concerns: in fact, if Francis Picabia could never have remained shackled by the serious aspect of Surrealism, his revolt nevertheless proceeded from the same state of mind that had brought the movement into being, and his poetic and pictural researches often rejoin those of the Surrealists.'

Of all those who may legitimately be regarded as the father-figures of the 'modernism' considered for at least a decade to have been superseded by a *post* appendage of disputable definition, Picabia is surprisingly the senior (with the sole exception of Wassily Kandinsky, born in 1866). Picabia was born in 1879, as was Paul Klee, but though Picabia must have been well aware of Klee's existence and work, there does not appear to be so much as a passing allusion to him in the copious occasional writings of his exact contemporary. Both however were Picasso's senior by two years and Braque's by three, while Marcel Duchamp was by eight years their junior. By the time Picabia met the prodigious Duchamp family in 1911 he had already been married for two years to Gabrielle Buffet, and had not only exhibited youthful paintings at the Salon d'Automne and the

---

Lecture *Francis Picabia: Funny-guy* given at the Royal Scottish Academy, Edinburgh, 1988, to accompany the exhibition *Francis Picabia (1874-1953)*, 28 July – 4 September. Previously unpublished.

Indépendants, but had established himself as a well-known Impressionist and held a successful one-man show at the Galerie Haussmann. And by the time he first met Duchamp, he had begun to be dissatisfied with the ideals and aesthetics left over from the nineteenth century that are characteristic of his earliest period. This encounter with Duchamp aroused all the aggressive iconoclasm and inventiveness that had been latent in his nature. About fifty years later, Duchamp presented an unexceptionably sober and factual account of Picabia's career in this introduction written for the catalogue to a late Picabia retrospective:

> Picabia's career is a kaleidoscopic series of art experiences. They are hardly related to one another in their external appearances but all are definitely marked by a strong personality.
>
> In his fifty years of painting Picabia has constantly avoided adhering to any formula or wearing a badge. He could be called the greatest exponent of freedom in art, not only against academic slavery, but also against slavery to any given dogma.
>
> As a lad of fourteen he joined the Impressionists and showed a great talent as a young follower of an already old movement. About 1912 his first personal contribution as an artist was based on the possibilities of a non-figurative art. He was a pioneer in this field alongside Mondrian, Kupka and Kandinsky. Between 1917 and 1924 the Dada Movement, in itself a metaphysical attempt towards irrationalism, offered little scope for painting. Yet Picabia in his paintings of that period showed great affinity with the Dada spirit. From this he turned to paint for years watercolours of a strictly academic style representing Spanish girls in their native costumes.
>
> Later, Picabia took great interest in the study of transparency in painting. By a juxtaposition of transparent forms and colours the canvas would, so to speak, express the feeling of a third dimension without the aid of perspective. Picabia, being very prolific, belongs to the type of artist who possesses the perfect tool: an indefatigable imagination.

At this point I hope I may insert without too obvious irrelevance some account of how I came to be acquainted with the art and anti-art of Francis Picabia. In my early teens I came into contact through a family friend with Harold and Alida Monro, who were then running the Poetry Bookshop just off Great Russell Street in front of the British Museum. Since the early 1920s they had been known for their publishing of broadsheet poems illustrated by well-known graphic artists of the period, and of a regular periodical known as *The Chapbook*, each issue of which was devoted to a special theme or group. I was able to acquire several back numbers of these Chapbooks, and the one I found by far the most exciting was published in 1921 and consisted of an essay by the Imagist poet F. S. Flint in which he attempted to convey to English readers some idea of what Dada, then the latest and most outrageous of Continental movements, was all about. It contained a considerable amount of information and translations of typical Dadaist poems as well as small reproductions of works by Picabia and Arp. In this way I first became aware of such other names as André Breton and Philippe Soupault, Louis Aragon and Tristan Tzara, Man Ray and Ribemont-Dessaignes. By the time of my first visit to Paris, where I spent my seventeenth birthday, I had obtained and become familiar with the contents of the special Surrealist number of the Anglo/French review *This Quarter*, edited by André Breton and published the previous autumn. One of the features of this mini-anthology of translated texts which specially intrigued me was a resumé of Duchamp's complex, enigmatic and best-known masterpiece, *La Mariée mise à nue par ses célibataires, même* ('The Bride Stripped Bare by her Bachelors, Even'), accompanied by some of the fragmentary notes written in connection with it. I mention this simply because of all Duchamp's works this is probably the closest in spirit to what appears to be the most salient aspect of Picabia's production during at least a decade. During the last three months of 1933, which I spent in Paris, there was an exhibition of Picabia's work at the Galerie Vignon which I do not remember visiting, though I managed to obtain some ephemeral publication connected with it, unfortunately long since lost, which contained some typically Picabiaesque aphorisms and a few reproductions of the transparency-type pictures Picabia had by then been producing for some time. I confess that these did not then particularly appeal to me, and no doubt I considered them inferior to the recent Mirós I had been shown at Pierre Loeb's rue de Seine Gallery, or to the works Max Ernst showed me when I was sent by Jeanne Bucher to see him in his rue des Plantes studio, and less accomplished even than the works which Pavel Tchelitchew was producing at the time, not all of them wholly dissimilar to Picabia's transparencies but more obviously meticulous in technique. When a couple of years later I returned to Paris specially to meet Breton and the Surrealist group, in order to collect from them material to document the book Cobden-Sanderson had commissioned me to write on the movement and which was to appear that autumn under the title *A Short Survey of Surrealism*, it would have been impossible for me to meet or interview Picabia, as at that time he was wholly absorbed in his life as a wealthy, yacht-owning playboy on the Riviera. Among the paintings by Picabia which formed part of André Breton's collection at that time were *The Double World* of 1918, and

After Rain of 1925, and I may have seen them on the couple of occasions I had of visiting Breton in his rue Fontaine apartment, but this was packed with other objects and pictures, such as de Chirico's extraordinary *Le cerveau de l'enfant* ('The child's brain'), more likely to have captured my fascinated attention when I was not paying it to Breton. Eluard also possessed in his smaller collection a 1914 Picabia watercolour, called simply *Animation*, but I do not recall his pointing it out to me. All these three works of Picabia, together with three from another collection, were among the 380 items displayed at the International Surrealist Exhibition at London's New Burlington Galleries in June and July of the following year, 1936.

One of the chapters of my potted history of Surrealism was to be devoted to Dada, and I set out to collect as much information on the subject as I could. Among those who were particularly helpful in this respect were Eluard and Georges Hugnet. Eluard gave me some numbers of his by then already exceedingly rare series of *Proverbe* leaflets, and other Dadaist ephemera; Georges Hugnet, ten years my senior in 1935, was nevertheless too young to have participated in the heyday of Dada, but was engaged in producing one of his several historical studies of the movement which denied that it was a movement, and was a great help in providing me with Dadaist data and documentation. No doubt it was he who presented me with the number of Picabia's periodical *391* which contains on one of its large folded pages a reproduction of a superb splash of ink, entitled simply *La sainte vierge*, a masterly prototype of the products of the short-lived post-1945 movement known as *tâchisme*. With scant appreciation of the value of this rarity, I stuck it up with drawing-pins on the wall of my room at home in Teddington, when I returned to England to write and publish my *Short Survey*.

In the Dada chapter of this book there are many references to Picabia. After a paragraph describing his association with Duchamp in New York in 1917, and referring to the latter's well-advertised disgust with Aaart, his invention of the ready-made and addiction to chess, which became before long his principal preoccupation, on the next page I wrote and quote:

> Francis Picabia, a somewhat less interesting person than Duchamp, was a great asset to the Dada movement on account of his wealth of humour – a bitter and obscure sort of humour, to be sure, but nevertheless *humour* – and his indefatigable zest for bringing out reviews. In January 1917, he left New York for Barcelona, and there brought out the first number of *391*, twelve numbers of *291* (title derived from the number on 5th Avenue of the Stieglitz Gallery) having already appeared. From Barcelona

he went on to Geneva, where he brought out a few more numbers of his review (which, for the most part, he wrote and illustrated himself) and also one or two small books of poems and drawings. [Though I may not have known it in 1935, I was referring here to *Fille née sans mère, L'Athlète des pompes funèbres, Rateliers platoniques* and *Poésie Ron-Ron*.] And then, at last, he went on to Zurich, met Tzara and his friends and merged into the Dada movement proper. He was known to the others as the Anti-painter, just as Tzara was known as the Anti-philosopher. He soon brought out the eighth number of *391*, a completely Dada number this time, containing poems and prose by himself and Tzara, a manifesto by Gabrielle Buffet, Picabia's wife, and illustrations by Arp and Alice Bailly. On the cover was printed this terse little verse by Picabia:

> I have a horror of the painting
> of Cezanne
> it bores me stiff

Little could I have dreamt at the time of writing this chapter that thirty years later I should become a close friend of Gabrielle Buffet, after she had been one of Picabia's three widows for only two years. During the summers I spent in her company in the 1950s as a fellow-guest of Meraud Guevara at the Tour de César just outside Aix-en-Provence, Gaby occasionally told the story of her chance meeting during the War with the one-time Surrealist poet René Char, known by then by the code-name of Capitaine Alexandre. Returning from one of her expeditions as a guide leading escaped or stranded British air-force pilots across the Pyrenees, while crossing the Vaucluse region she ran unexpectedly into the local Resistance leader. '*Gaby, par example!*' exclaimed Char. By the time I got to know Gaby Picabia, I no longer had any copies of my little treatise on Surrealism left to show her, but had I been able to point out to her the reference to her in the Dada chapter, I can well imagine her exclaiming '*Ça, par example!*' She would no doubt have been amused by the *naïveté* of a passage a page or two later in which I explained Duchamp's once supremely subversive version of the Gioconda, reproduced in 1920 in the twelfth number of *391* and provocatively displayed by André Breton to the audience at the Dada matinée at the Palais des Sports that year, in the following terms:

> a large printed reproduction of the Mona Lisa with a handsome pair of moustaches painted on to her face and bearing underneath the inscription: LHOOQ (phonetic, perhaps, for 'Look!', since Duchamp knew English quite well).

The truth is, I'm afraid, that in 1935 I still knew French considerably less well than I thought. The five letters stand for *Elle a chaud au cul*, meaning 'She has a hot arse', or as Roland Penrose explained to me as soon as the book appeared, 'She's a hot bit of tail'.

It should not be supposed from the anecdote associating Gabrielle Buffet-Picabia with her Resistance activities that she was in the habit of reminiscing even to her friends about her wartime exploits, about which she was in fact extremely reticent. That she should be regarded as a heroine embarrassed her deeply, as she regarded all admiration of such a kind as absurd. She may well have wondered what the editor of *391* would have thought of her receiving the Legion of Honour, badge of shame in the eyes of devout Dadas and Surrealists. That she should also have accepted from the State the token award of managership of a tobacconist's was more likely to have amused him.

But this is perhaps the place to explain how I came to get to know Gaby Picabia in her late seventies and what I was doing in her company at Aix. Our hostess was Meraud Guevara, to whom I was first introduced, shortly after returning from a reading-tour in the States, by Mrs Mary St John Hutchinson, about whom I can say no more than that to talk about her now would be an unwarrantable digression. Meraud, who had come to London in connection with an exhibition of paintings by her husband Alvaro (better known as Chili) Guevara, whose portrait of Edith Sitwell could then still be seen at the Tate, was accompanied by a charming young man called Jeannot, who was actually Swiss and lived at the Tour de César. At the end of the lunch party Meraud said to me: 'If you're ever in Aix, do come to see us'. In the summer of 1954 I managed to get down to Aix for the first time, to spend a couple of months with a group of American friends, among them the painter Sam Francis. I went up to call on Meraud Guevara at the Tour de César, she came down one evening to supper with the Americans, and before I left Aix she had told me that if I were to return there the following summer, I would be welcome to stay at the Tour. In the end I was to spend eight summers at her house with its perfect view of the Montagne de la Sainte Victoire, and the same number of winters at her Paris apartment in the rue de Lille. In case you are wondering what this autobiographical discursion is doing in a talk on the subject of Picabia, I should hasten to explain that though to begin with I knew next to nothing of Meraud's connection with Picabia – or for that matter with Gertrude Stein, André Salmon, Blaise Cendrars or Joseph Delteil – it was not long before I discovered that she had known him well for many years and that his first wife was among her closest friends. Her rue de Lille apartment was and still is on the top floor of a building belonging to her family, the banking

Guinnesses, and had originally been that allocated to the *chambres de bonnes*. From the entrance door at one end to the studio at the other runs a narrow corridor, the walls of which are entirely covered with rows of pictures, mostly but not all by Meraud. Half-way down on the left side hung for many years a large photo by Man Ray of Picabia apparently hugely enjoying himself at the wheel of the latest of his 127 *voitures*, a *décapotable* sports-car, the photo set against the middle of a larger bare canvas and entitled *The Merry Widow*. Not only that, on a wall of the small *salon* adjacent to the studio there hung for a long period an early work by Picabia in a style at first unfamiliar to me: the more I saw of it the better I liked it. It is a wonderful picture to live with, and is reproduced in colour on page 56 of the catalogue of the current Picabia exhibition. It dates from 1913 and is entitled *New York*.

It may be of interest to learn what Picabia himself was actually saying about painting and the state of the arts at the time of his stay of 1913 in New York, which he visited with Gabrielle in order to attend the opening of the epoch-making Armory Show. In February of that year, the *New York Times* published an interview headlined: PICABIA, ART REBEL, HERE TO TEACH NEW MOVEMENT. Asked what he hoped to accomplish and what was his purpose in coming to America, the painter declared:

> France is more or less finished as far as art is concerned. I believe that it is in America that the theories of the new Art will take root with the greatest tenacity. I am here to ask the American people to welcome the New Movement in Art in the same spirit as that with which they have welcomed political movements towards which they may at first have felt antagonistic but which their true love of freedom of expression in all domains has led them to treat with a rare openmindedness. If the paintings I am going to exhibit provoke the same hostile and antagonistic criticism they encountered in France, I would appeal to that love of free expression in every department of activity that characterizes the American people.

Here we have an early demonstration of Picabia's lifelong mastery of publicity and the manoeuvres of P.R. Later in the interview, asked what distinguished him from the Cubists and why, he ended by referring to a painting he had just finished and that may well be the one now on show in Room 7, and that (after having hung for a while in a rue de Lille apartment in the 1950s) finally found its way to the Centre Pompidou as the result of a legacy.

> 'As for me,' said Picabia to his interviewer, 'I don't try to reproduce the original. You won't find a trace of the original in my

paintings. Take for example a picture I painted the other day. Did I paint the Woolworth Tower or the Empire State Building? Have I painted the impression made on me by the skyscrapers of your great city? No, I tried to render the feeling of those who drove themselves to build the Tower of Babel – the desire of man to attain the heavens, to reach the infinite.'

Intended only for a mass newspaper audience, it is notable that this sort of declaration has little in common with the bombast of the Futurist Marinetti or the pugnacity of the Vorticist Wyndham Lewis. In reasonable tones, Picabia told his interviewer that the Cubists had committed a great fault, the Impressionists likewise, and modern French art in general, in spite of its many achievements, was also at fault. He identified this fault with artists' outworn ambition to *represent* subjects or impressions of visually experienced objects. He spoke of the New Art, claiming to represent it, without intending any reference to the decorative tendency of the *art nouveau* of two decades earlier and also ignoring the stylistic and symbolist/expressionist novelties introduced by the Austrian Secession and its affiliated movements in the rest of Europe at about the turn of the century. It was at just about the same date as this interview that Kandinsky was elaborating, in his treatise on *The Art of Spiritual Harmony*, a defence and illustration of non-figurative painting; but in his approach lay an implicit belief in an immaterial reality behind appearances. Between 1913 and 1917, a rapid transition took place in Picabia's art, as he moved from the starting point of his rejection of all recognizably figurative forms of representation towards what before long became a series of absurdist assemblages of incongruous mechanical parts to which were added provocative word salads in capital letters. Number 6 in the present exhibition is representative of the earlier stage of this development. It is obliquely inscribed *Gabrielle Buffet, elle corrige les moeurs en riant* ('she laughingly corrects or counterbalances habits') and depicts with austere simplicity what the mammoth catalogue* to the Hayward Gallery Dada/Surrealist Exhibition of 1978 described as 'a portrait of Picabia's wife symbolized as a car windscreen (or shield)'. Its title seems to result from a private joke, and it can hardly be worth bothering today as to whether *moeurs* should be understood to mean morals, manners or habits, or whether these *moeurs* are those of the Picabias' New York café-society milieu of 1915, or of the by then war-convulsed Old world. To this phase of the artist's so-called mechano-morphic period belong often

---

* Editor's note: *Dada and Surrealism Reviewed*, by Dawn Ades, with an introduction by David Sylvester and a supplementary essay by Elizabeth Cowling (Arts Council of Great Britain).

simple and meticulously exact representations of machine parts – a hub, a ratchet-wheel, a screw propellor, for instance – or, in the case of *Fille née sans mère* (number 10 in the present exhibition) part of a metal wheel apparently accompanied by piping, a piston and cylinder, tastefully coloured in green, black and white against a metallic background. The severe, quasi-classical item ambiguously dubbed *Prenez garde à la peinture* (simply translated in the present catalogue as 'Wet Paint') is another notable example of this type of machine-inspired picture. In the first number of his *291* series of publications, Picabia explained works like this in terms of blatantly tongue-in-cheek irony:

> So as to express the spiritual realities of this world, Francis Picabia is resolute in borrowing symbols only from the repertoire of exclusively modern forms. An extremely intelligent censor was recently mistaken in thinking he recognized in pictures which represented variously Love, Death and Thought, something like the plan of a compressed air brake.

For some time from 1917 onwards, Picabia produced innumerable caricatural amalgams of stereotypical machine parts accompanied by a plethora of written names and facetious captions. The increasingly careless futility of his designs of this type is obviously deliberate and intended to play an important part in the Dada campaign to deride and discredit the entire solemn enterprise of artistic expression as licensed by outworn bourgeois aesthetics.

It becomes difficult to draw a line at this point between fascinated admiration of machines and the inventiveness of their designers, and revulsion against the ever increasing mechanization of a society obsessed with the mass-production of armaments, machine-guns, tanks and fighter planes; and their successors the great industrialist dynasties of America have all owed their vast fortunes and social supremacy entirely to the use of machines and the concomitant advance of technology.

At this point I must turn back for a moment to complete what I began to say earlier about the 1913 picture entitled *New York*. In 1975 and 1978 Pierre Belfond published in his series *Les bâtisseurs du XXe siècle* two thick volumes of Picabia's *Écrits*, the first containing texts written between 1913 and 1920, the second those belonging to the period between 1921 and 1953, the year of his death. I have read you a quotation from an interview given by Picabia to the New York press in 1913 which is to be found in the first volume, where it is preceded only by a few brief paragraphs representing Picabia's reply to an enquiry sent in 1907 by *Le Gaulois du Dimanche* to a group of noted landscape painters of that period, *la belle époque* in fact. The reply is earnest in tone and contains at least one sentence that I cannot resist quoting in passing, so demonstrative is it of the immeasurable gap separating the young painter from Picabia *le loustic*, the wag, the funny-guy, incorrigible farceur and blagueur that he became during the first Great War, for whom nothing, least of all Art, was sacred: 'Il ne faut pas vouloir "épater le public" comme font beaucoup de jeunes; le Salon d'Automne est un example très malheureux', he told the pre-war Sunday newspaper. But what to my regret is missing from Picabia's complete writings is any discussion or even mention of the period between 1912 and 1914 which produced the five outstandingly remarkable pictures with which the present Picabia exhibition opens; including *La source, Danseuse étoile et son école de danse, Chanson nègre I, Je revois en souvenir ma chère Udnie* as well as the *New York* already referred to. However, William Camfield (with Michel Sanouillet among the most devoted of Picabia's chroniclers) maintains, in his preface to the catalogue to an important Italian retrospective, that 'Abstrac-tion was the dominant style when Picabia first became a major avant-garde artist'; and he refers to 'a group of paintings in which Picabia, moving from a background in Cubism, developed a form of abstract art capable of holding its own in the contemporary company of Kandinsky, Delaunay, Mondrian and Kupka.' Camfield then goes on to discuss at considerable length the variety of styles and interpretations appertaining to the whole of Picabia's 'machinist' output, having first quoted from a letter of 1913 from Picabia to Alfred Stieglitz, proprietor of the Photo-Secession Gallery of 291 Fifth Avenue, which explains that *Udnie* is a nostalgic memento of his trip to New York for the Armory Show, '– a memento dealing with American girls and an exotic dancer he met on the voyage to America.' The cryptic title itself may be, appropriately according to Camfield, an adaptation of that seductive water sprite Undine. Anyone inclined to believe in the concept of a collective unconscious and Jung's related idea of synchronicity will find this reading of Udnie as a faulty anagrammatic version of Undine will be likely to associate it with the Surrealists' later preoccupation with the related fable of Melusine, or conceivably with Apollinaire's Lorelei. The rare works of Picabia produced during the 1912-14 period that I have seen impress me as being the work of a major twentieth-century artist, one who has developed a pictural language entirely his own and is gifted with a power of architectural construction as individual as his austere blend of colours. *New York* is perhaps the most buoyant and glowing of this group of Picabia's compositions. By the time he had become wholeheartedly involved in the spontaneous combustion of international Dada, Picabia had turned his back once and for all on any desire he may once have had to continue working the rich vein of his first mature style and approach, and was carried away by his apparently equally innate gift for iconoclastic gesture, ridicule, parody, invective and scandal. By 1920, a full realization of what had happened to civilization during the 'war to end all wars' had sunk in, and the amusing experiments of *391* had become fodder for Picabia the Dada Cannibal:

> Dada feels nothing, it is nothing, nothing, nothing
> It is like your hopes: nothing
> like your paradise: nothing
> like your idols: nothing
> like your political men: nothing
> like your heroes: nothing
> like your artists: nothing
> like your religions: nothing.
> Whistle, catcall, smash my jaw, then what, what then? I'll tell you once more you're all a lot of mugs. In three months' time my friends and I will sell you our pictures for a few francs

It is typical of Picabia that at about the same time that he was delivering himself of this expression of disgusted nihilism he should have begun to produce a series of line drawing portraits of himself and his avant-garde contemporaries that are of a classic simplicity and represent recognizably good likenesses while suggesting a backward look to the suave outline of Ingres. When Alistair Brotchie of the Atlas Press decided in 1985 to publish my translation of André Breton's and Philippe Soupault's proto-surrealist automatic texts *Les Champs magnétiques* of 1919, he designed an excellent cover design for the book representing the lines of force typically produced by magnetic fields, against which he intended to inset, on the front and back, two drawings of 1919 by Picabia, one portraying Breton, the other Soupault. The copyright association SPADEM demanded so excessive a fee for the right to reproduce these drawings that photographs of the same epoch of the poets had to be substituted. It should not be forgotten that at about the same period, Picasso also was producing numerous line drawing portraits of outstanding contemporaries such as Apollinaire, Max Jacob and Cocteau, Stravinsky, Diaghilev and Satie, which cannot be dissociated from Picasso's unconcealed predilection for Ingres at that time. I believe that to consider Picasso's portrait drawings superior to Picabia's is more the result of objective judgement than of prejudice. Historical coincidence or deliberate competition on the part of Picabia: it would be impossible now to decide. It is not difficult to understand Picabia's frequent expressions of irritation at the increasing adulation of 'the other Spaniard' (Picabia's father was Cuban), the other Pic.

I cannot resist at this point an impulse to express a distinct feeling that it may be necessary to pronounce a word of warning against what appears today to be a strong concerted tendency to sanctify Picabia as the preeminent precursor of what a recent related strong concerted tendency has succeeded in establishing under the all-embracing rubric of *post-modernism*. In all fairness it must be pointed out that Picabia has many rivals equally or even better qualified to claim this sort of distinction. As has been observed in the present Picabia Exhibition catalogue, the overriding international importance accorded to Duchamp after the War until a decade or so ago has led to an apparent, if not actually total, eclipse of Duchamp in the esteem of contemporary artists (and even more so, of art historians). This only proves that over-emphasis on the significance of any single father-figure leads before long to a backlash. The history of twentieth-century reputations teaches a rebarbative lesson that certain Picabia enthusiasts seem to prefer to ignore.

Already, the poem 'Magic City', dated 1913-14 and published in the early collection *52 Miroirs*, opens with the words: 'a dangerous and alluring wind of sublime nihilism pursues us at a prodigious speed', and goes on to qualify the passions then manifested by men and women everywhere as *sterile*: 'Opium. Whiskey. Tango'. Anti-religion, anti-philosophy, anti-art are already by implication designated as the opium of the avant-garde élite — let us democratically leave it to the masses to decide by ballot-poll what their favourite alternative to religion is today.

Another poem, published in the short-lived magazine *Rongwrong* in 1917, sounds much the same note. If my translation is rapid it is at least, I hope, appropriately so:

> Filth. Silence. Void. Ennui.
> Sudden music laughter noise.
> Lack of opium, lack of meat,
> Lack of poetry, lack of joy
> Great shindy, great tumult,
> Enormous hunger, enormous void,
> Cold chicken, iced water,
> Frightful beasts, pretty women,
> Charming looks, vanished hunger,
> That's Pharamousse, that's America (for you)
>   signed: Marquis de la Torre.

This last pseudonym is explained by its resemblance to the name of his paternal grandfather, which his youngest daughter Marie adopted after becoming seriously unbalanced in the late 1950s. Among the numerous sobriquets adopted by Picabia throughout his life, the one that strikes as being — what shall I say? — the most crucially revealing? is *Francis le raté*.

To *épater* is to flabbergast. To be a *raté* is to prove to have been only a flash-in-the-pan. For me these are the two keywords to the secret drama of Picabia's output and career after the breakup of his marriage to Gabrielle Buffet. I should not wish to suggest that what one admires or deplores about the later works of Picabia can be directly related to the end of his first marriage, only to point out that the appearance of the most distinctive features of these works corresponds chronologically with the end of his life with Gaby, together with whom he had 'used up both pleasures and quarrels'. Gabrielle Buffet has often been described by those who knew her as a Voltaireian spirit, sophisticated, tolerant and shrewd. She was primarily interested in music and there was never any question of rivalry between her and Francis on the professional plane. There was never a time when she and Francis could no longer see one another because a permanent acrimony had developed between them. Gabrielle Buffet-Picabia lived to a great age and was well over a hundred when she died. She had climbed to the top of the Montagne de la Sainte Victoire on St John's Eve with me and our Swiss friend Jeannot when she was getting on for eighty. Finally she became confined to her modest studio-apartment on the rue Chateaubriand, overlooking the back entrance to the Lido. It was there that I last saw her on two or three occasions after I'd begun returning to Paris about ten years ago. Once, after lunching with her, my wife and I went on to see a Picabia retrospective that was being held in the Gallery that forms part of the complex at La Défense.

Luc-Henri Marcié sums up Picabia's relationships with his wives, mistresses and women in general in one of the 209 notes appended to *Caravansérail*, Picabia's autobiographical novel of 1924, posthumously published thirty years later with the approval of Germaine Everling:

> If Picabia always cheated on his wives and mistresses, he nevertheless carried off the tour de force of never seriously quarrelling with any of them. Women appreciated his 'vitality', his humour and his conversation, a flow carrying away pell-mell a mixture of *bon mots*, paradoxes, platitudes and pertinent reflections impertinently expressed.

This quotation prompts me to make a further one that will lead me back to the subject of Meraud Guevara, from whom I learnt most of what I knew until recently about Picabia. A note referring to the first chapter of Picabia's obviously autobiographical, apparently unfinished novel quotes a letter to Germaine Everling that he wrote in 1933, headed: 'At the Coupole, nine o'clock in the evening'. After informing Germaine that in the course of a busy day he had had a picture bought by the Luxembourg (in those days the only State-supported Gallery of Modern Art in Paris), he goes on:

2) De Monzie has decorated me with the Legion of Honour, it's unbelievable. I beg you not to talk too much about all that. 3) I've exchanged my Austin for a sturdier one. 4) André Breton and Duchamp are against me, the GBFP [Gabrielle Buffet / Francis Picabia] business, delicious friends aren't they? Breton, that doesn't surprise me, seeing that he's bought twelve pictures from Gabrielle.

Then, after referring to various legal and business affairs, he adds: 'Meraud (misspelt) is well, but what a life, poor thing, Guevara is drunk from morning till night . . .'

I personally met Chili Guevara on only one occasion, some time before I'd even heard of Meraud's existence. He was then cultural attaché at the Chilean Embassy in London, and I had been invited to a party given there in honour of Gabriela Mistral, the Chilean woman poet who had been awarded that year's Nobel Prize, and after it was over we went out together. I certainly would not then have suspected him of being an alcoholic. My friendship with Meraud dates from the year after his death. Of all her infrequent reminiscences of her husband, I do not recall any that implied she had reason to complain of his being over-fond of the bottle. Chili Guevara may not have been an altogether ideal husband but his widow has remained as loyal to his memory as Gabrielle Buffet was to Picabia's, and she used fondly to preserve a few rare examples of his work. Today, paintings by both of them are to be seen hanging next to each other in a basement gallery of the Tate.

Though she once introduced me to the then still well-known art critic Waldemar George, who had written enthusiastically about a post-war exhibition of her work, Meraud never referred to or showed me the preface that Picabia wrote for the catalogue of her first Paris show at the Van-Leer Gallery in 1928. The young painter was then still known as Meraud-Michael Guinness. The preface has an epigraph of two verses:

> Elle a des yeux
> Pleins de soupirs

which go rather well into English: 'She has eyes / Full of sighs'. The heading is in capital letters with an exclamation-mark: *ENCORE UNE!* Or perhaps less fortunately: 'Yet one more!' *Pourquoi diable fait-elle de la peinture, elle est si riche!* (Why on earth does she paint when she's so rich!) But you will forgive me, I hope, if I renounce further translation, to save time and the effort to render some equivalent of Picabia's personal way of expressing himself.

> Eh bien, c'est justement à cause de cela!
> Ecœurée, dégoûtée des milieux où l'argent joue le premier rôle elle s'est refugiée en elle-même; dans cette retraite, prenant conscience de son moi, elle a compris que sa véritable expression ne pourrait exister que dans la joie égoïste de l'Art.
> L'antisepsie que dégage le grand monde est une glace tres belle mais la vie y est impossible pour les êtres vibrants.
> Meraud Guinness aime la vie, la vie libre et indépendante: elle a renversé jusqu'aux plus petites frontières des conventions morales c'est pour cela que l'on peut croire en elle, attendre d'elle des possibilités infinies de le domaine de l'invention. Ses tableaux sont déjà des oeuvres extrêmement personelles dont la bourgeoisie est exclue. Il y a des tableaux chauds, des tableaux froids: les siens sont chauds. Pour vous en assurer, prenez-les entre vos mains, fermez les yeux pour mieux voir . . .

I find it hard to imagine Meraud ever caring to have her family's fortune drawn attention to in this way. By the time I knew her, her share of it had considerably diminished, and what remained to her she dispersed in continually unstinting but unobtrusive forms of generosity. Picabia's observation that her pictures are extremely personal works from which the bourgeoisie is excluded remains perfectly true, and probably explains why they remained for so long unappreciated by more than the restricted circle of her friends. When I got to know her, I believe I detected something of Picabia's influence in her lasting dislike of 'ghastly good taste'. She shocked me at first by sticking artificial flowers in the plots of soil on the terrace of her house at the Tour de César though later she developed an enthusiastic interest in gardening real flowers. When she undertook completely to redecorate her attic-floor rue de Lille apartment, she not only decorated the walls of the two main living-rooms by painting on them her own improvised irregular abstract designs in refreshing colours, she made new curtains for them by obtaining a selection of varicoloured dish-clouts from the nearby Bon Marché store and stitching them together. This resulted not only in attractively unusual pairs of curtains which would surely have appealed to Picabia, but also in extremely long-lasting furnishings which I believe are still in use today; as is a knobbly book-shelf / étagère or whatnot of the kind to be found in junk-shops, touched here and there with gilt and painted to match the walls. Though Meraud knew a number of writers intimately and enjoyed the company of poets, she seldom read anything but detective stories, preferably American: we shared for a while a preference for Rex Stout. When she once tried to read *Les Fleurs du mal*, having heard her friends refer to Baudelaire so many times, she found it remarkably bad and failed to understand how intelligent people could continue to revere its author. But her passion for painting and creating attractive objects was unabatable, and occupied her inner life and imagination completely.

The 1913 Picabia painting known as *New York* did not hang on the wall above the drinks table in her salon because she owned it, however. She was glad to have it there because it gave pleasure and reminded her of an old friend of her youth; but actually she was only giving it temporary house room, because its present owner or custodian had nowhere to put it in his mother's flat where he was living and did not wish to consign it to a warehouse. I have already mentioned the fascinating possibilities of exploring the provenances of Picabia's picture. The unquestionably odd, ambiguous and ultimately mysterious one-time proprietor of *New York* who eventually bequeathed it to the Centre Pompidou collection, was Doctor Robert Le Masle. The son of a notable venereologist of the *belle époque*, he had adopted his father's profession as a way of earning a living.

Max Ernst arrived from Cologne to hold his first Paris exhibition in 1921; and the following year he painted a group-portrait entitled *Au rendez-vous des amis*: against a suitably oneiric background a company of sixteen figures are assembled, among them Ernst himself. (It is of some significance that Picabia is conspicuous by his absence from this group portrait, as he had been from the opening of Ernst's first Paris show.) Perhaps the most unusual feature of the picture is that in the midst of it is to be distinguished a figure, with Ernst sitting on his right knee, with the bearded visage of Dostoievsky. In the third row behind him, looking like an up-to-date lady, Raphael's Uffizi self-portrait is to be seen, as enigmatic as Leonardo's Gioconda, while to the other side Gala looks back over her shoulder. Dostoievsky's position in the midst of this gathering of neo-nihilists is no doubt due above all to his being the author of *Notes from the Underground* which exemplifies not only Ernst's wide-ranging literary but also his occasionally acute prophetic intuition. The novel now known as *The Devils*, formerly as *The Possessed*, contains the most keen-sighted presentation in nineteenth-century literature of the results of the discovery of God's death: all things are possible, there is no longer any foundation for absolute standards restraining men's obedience to their most destructive instincts. *Crime and Punishment* had already demonstrated Dostoievsky's foresight into the type of mentality that can ultimately treat human beings as rival units to be disposed of or eliminated without sentimental compunction. By 1922 most Dadaists had begun to foresee that unmitigated nihilism would lead them before long into monotonously futile repetitiveness; and out of his reaction against the prospect of getting stuck in such a boring rut came Breton's initiative to instigate a Congress of Paris that would enquire into the possible definition of what constituted the 'modern spirit' in the post-1918 era. This plan to discuss rationally the current tendency to denounce and exploit the breakdown of civilized rationalism provoked the irritated derision of Tristan Tzara in particular, and was treated with typically sardonic scepticism by Picabia. Breton's determination to salvage something positive from Dada's chaotic irrationality led within two years to the launching with his First Manifesto of the Surrealist movement.

When Max Ernst reached Paris in 1921, leaving behind him the supremely subversive German Dada manifestations of 1919, Picabia was firmly established as the sole Parisian Dada painter of any importance. One can imagine how *boring* (his own word in this connection at the time) he found the enthusiastic reception by the younger Dadaists of the first exhibition of this latest recruit from across the Rhine. A letter from Breton to André Derain written in October of that year explained the inventive novelty of Ernst's personal use of collage techniques, adding that all this was sufficient to make Picabia *mourir de dépit* – die of spite, resentment, vexation – what term would Picabia's erstwhile admirer have employed had he been English?

To describe Breton as Picabia's 'erstwhile admirer' in1921 is however misleading. At the climactic Dada Festival at the Salle Gaveau in May 1920, it was Breton who, looking solemn in imitation spectacles, appeared displaying like a sandwichboard-man a placard signed Francis Picabia on which, above and below a large circular target, were inscribed in capital letters the words (I paraphrase): 'In order to appreciate something you must first have seen and heard it for a long time bunch of clots'. Breton's relations with Picabia were subject to inevitable fluctuations, but fundamentally he remained ever faithful to his earliest admiration of Picabia (who was, it should be remembered, seventeen years his senior). His 1924 collection of prose pieces, *Les Pas perdus* ('Waiting-room') contains not only an enthusiastic appreciation of Max Ernst – 'who projects under our eyes the most captivating film in the world', 'we do not hesitate to see in Max Ernst a man of infinite possibilities' – but also six pages devoted to a penetrating appraisal of Picabia, which ends by asking:

> And how could the majority of men be expected to notice that painting was becoming for the first time a source of mystery after having been for long no more than speculation on mystery, or that with this art devoid of model, neither decorative nor symbolic, Picabia has no doubt succeeded in reaching the highest rung of the ladder of creation.

Thirty years later Breton was to pronounce in the cemetery of Montmartre Picabia's funeral oration, entitled when printed the following year:

Adieu ne plaise ('Heaven forbid farewell', as one might translate the punning phrase), which began by quoting Apollinaire's words at Jarry's funeral, saying that it was as unsuitable an occasion for tears as were the burials of Folengo, Rabelais or Swift. I had intended to translate the entire text of this oration, but in a talk that is already quite long enough it would not be possible to quote it all. Breton recalled having been fascinated in his youth by such poems as those collected in *52 Miroirs* and *Pensées sans langage*. He referred to Picabia's most recent collections as 'd'admirables plaquettes bien trop peu connues – tirées à bien trop petit nombre', saying 'so much the worse for those whose ears are not attuned to such accents' before quoting extracts from *Fleur montée* of 1952. He also spoke of a certain *aura* on account of which a few people regarded as beyond comparison the monumental *Udnie* of 1913 as well as the *Printemps* of 1938 (if he mistook the date by three years, this might be item 39 in the present exhibition) – an aura that was and will continue to remain eternally Picabia's. Breton ended his speech with these words:

> My dear Francis, would you believe that in one of yesterday's papers I was said to have influenced you? We both know very well that exactly the opposite is true. You have been one of the two or three great pioneers of what is called, for want of a better term, *the modern spirit*. This has been conditioned to a major degree by your movements, and nothing can change the fact that, even after the distressed salutation I address you, you will remain the magnetized tip of this spirit. *Nous aurions honte, que dis-je, nous aurions peur de vous quitter.*

Breton's allusion to Picabia as having been one of the two or three great pioneers of what he still thought best referred to as *l'esprit moderne*, prompts one to speculate as to who else should be considered worthy of this distinction. The first two names to occur to me in this context are those of Guillaume Apollinaire and Marcel Duchamp. Picabia was in Lausanne in 1918 when he learnt that Apollinaire had died a victim of that autumn's notorious flu epidemic in Paris on 9 November. 'You can imagine what a shock this was to me,' he wrote soon afterwards,

> we had been very close for many years . . . His death seems to me impossible. Guillaume Apollinaire is one of the rare men to have followed the whole evolution of modern art and to have completely understood it, he defended it bravely and honestly because he loved it, as he loved life and all new forms of activity. His was a rich, even sumptuous spirit, supple, sensitive, proud and childlike. His work is full of variety, *esprit* and invention.

It was of course Apollinaire who first applied the term 'orphic-cubism' to the work of Picabia's first important pre-war creative period. The invention of Apollinaire's that may seem most closely connected with Picabia's subsequent development is that of the *Calligramme*, the pictorial disposition of written or printed words on the page. In Apollinaire's posthumous collection *Le Guetteur mélancolique*, two pages reproducing words, names and phrases arranged so as to represent figures, a bottle, a tree, the café Dôme, and so on, corresponding to the twelve letters spelling MONTPARNASSE, immediately precede the poem entitled 'Francis Picabia':

> Praxiteles is a bandage-maker
> Your right big toe
> Has hurled abuse
> At the horseman who in Venice has three
> In Asia Minor or in maybe Champagne
> Where the deer-stags bring their antlers
> For you know which gentlemen
> And if you dance the tango
> Noli me tangere

This charmingly inconsequential piece cannot be precisely dated, but was probably written, like most of Apollinaire's *Calligrammes*, in or soon after 1914, which makes it more or less contemporary with Picabia's *52 Miroirs*, which it closely resembles in style. At about the same date, words, names and phrases begin to form an integral part of an increasing number of Picabia's Dada-period constructions, painted and graphic.

Whereas Guillaume Apollinaire may be said to have expressed in his work a struggle between melancholy fatalism and a finally optimistic joie de vivre, Duchamp's nonchalant ribaldry at the expense of Art, his elaborate hoaxes, obsession with puns and expressed preference for idling, gambling and chess, conceal a reticent but fundamental pessimism. It should not be forgotten that as a painter, Marcel Duchamp was by far the most gifted of an exceptionally gifted family, or that the *Nude Descending a Staircase*, the sensation of the New York Armory show of 1913, when he was twenty-six, was already one of the say half-dozen most outstanding masterpieces of early twentieth-century painting, when he began to express his sardonic rejection of all previous conceptions of art and aesthetics. The 'large glass' first undertaken in 1914, known in English as *The Bride Stripped Bare by her Bachelors, Even* and described by Breton as a 'mechanist, cynical interpretation of the phenomenon of love', was intended to be broken, but posterity has insisted on reconstructing it and continued to regard it as an even greater masterpiece than the *Nude*, even though it rendered such a conventional category as masterpiece obsolete. Duchamp the 'salt merchant', was and remains the embodiment of what Americans still call 'cool'. To give expression either to pessimism or to optimism would have struck Duchamp as absurdly uncool. The point I want to make with regard to Duchamp and Picabia, with whom he was closely associated in New York before and during the first War, has, I find, conveniently been made for me by Hans Richter in his 1964 study of *Dada Art and Anti-art*, in the chapter devoted to New York Dada 1915, under the heading *Nihil*:

> In opposition to Art, as represented by the *Venus de Milo* or the *Laocoön*, Duchamp set up Reality as represented by his readymades. His purpose was to administer a strong purgative to an age riddled with lies – and to the society which had brought it into being – an age of shame for which he found a counterpart in the shape of a Mona Lisa with a moustache.
>
> All that Picabia had argued, passionately, in every line, every poem, every drawing, every manifesto in *391* was now reduced to a precise formula. With Picabia the words 'Art is dead' seem always to be followed by a faint echo: 'Long live Art'. With Duchamp the echo is silent. And that is not all: this silence renders meaningless every further enquiry after art.

Duchamp remained faithful for the rest of his life to the conviction he had reached by the time he was thirty that the history of Art is finished, the tradition of easel-painting over. The attitude of ironic flippancy he adopted remained consistent to the end; which to my mind gives him a definite superiority over Picabia, though I realize that comparisons are often invidious. Duchamp's sphinxlike smile may appear gently amused, but the riddle he propounded can prove lethally corrosive. Picabia's progress, on the other hand, from the frenetic days of *Cannibale* to the period of the late abstracts which most frequently consist of round coloured dots or spots on impastoed grounds, is distinguished above all by its inconsistency. *L'Instantanéisme*, launched in number 19 of *391* in 1924, in defiant rivalry with Breton's launching of Surrealism with its first Manifesto published that year, announces the most consistent attitude of Picabia's middle age and later. Instantaneism wanted neither yesterday or tomorrow, it believed only in today, in life, in freedom for all, in perpetual motion, and it recognized no great men. It also claimed to be exceptional, cynical and indecent. Dawn Ades tells us in the exhaustively researched foreword she wrote to the catalogue of the Dada / Surrealist Exhibition at the Hayward Gallery in 1978, that when Picabia was asked towards the end of his life about *391*, he was astonished that anyone remembered it. 'Picabia presented himself accurately as an instantaneist', comments Ades, 'for he never looked back.'

The *Animal Trainer* of 1923, reproduced in the publicity sheet for the present exhibition, seems to set a precedent for the style of some of the best poster designs of the mid-century; but I am unable to regard it as vastly superior to the work of, for example, Cassandre at his best. The latter's pseudonymous signature, however, could never be claimed to confer on his work the value that Picabia's, with its anachronistic date, vouchsafes his *Dresseur d'animaux*. By the time Picabia had begun to produce a large number of pictures of this type he was already installed on the Riviera, based at the *Château de Mai* he had built himself at Mougins and absorbed in a lifestyle of luxurious hedonism involving fast sportscars, yachts and casinos. In other words Funny-guy had now become one more wealthy cosmopolitan playboy on the Côte d'Azur between the wars, and his compulsion to continue painting had become subordinate to his determination to have fun at all costs. In one chapter of *Caravansérail*, the autobiographical novel of 1924, he had referred to 'this life of ruolz, so far from everything that still gives me pleasure'. Luc-Henri Mercié explains that *ruolz* is a silver-plated metal, then much employed in Art Deco and representative of the period's taste for the artificial, the substitute and the ersatz, adding the comment that for Picabia real life became a succession of Rolls, or Delage *décapotables*, in which he could easily snap his fingers at his hard-up little one-time Dadaist friends. The pictures of this period which evoke the Riviera in ingenious assemblages of feathers, macaroni or drinking-straws, tooth-picks, corn-plasters and so on, are best qualified as charming and amusing; they hardly represent a startling technical breakthrough, and express nothing of the meridional sensuality that inspired Bonnard and Matisse – maybe an unfair comparison that if it misses one point does however I think make another valid one.

We have observed Marcel Duchamp fulfilling the role of Sphinx of Anti-art. I confess that I find Picabia in the rôle of fashionable portraitist and painter of pinup-type nudes far more enigmatic, indeed ultimately inexplicable. Many of the pictures of this period seem ideally suited to a market intended to appeal to undegenerate Nazi connoisseurs. It has been said that by the time of the Occupation, Picabia had squandered the bulk of his fortune and needed to make money to live on by selling his work to a wily dealer in Algiers. But a notable forerunner of the work of this period is Picabia's portrait of the singer and cabaret owner Suzy Solidor, which is dated 1933, that is ten years previously.

Duchamp's calculated undermining of the standards which claim to distinguish good (either bourgeois or proletarian) from bad (either proletarian or bourgeois) taste cannot excuse the kind of kitsch perpetrated by Picabia during the early 1940s by pretending that it represents a deliberate and provocative caricature of kitsch. The question as to how the commemorator of his dear Udnie could end by celebrating these antiseptic, not even truly erotic, nude females is an unsurmountable challenge to critical comprehension.

If challenged to define *kitsch*, which means literally *trash*, I should resort to a term borrowed from existential thinkers: the inauthentic. If this severe qualification is ever applicable in Picabia's case, it is so only in so far as it is a by-product of his innate inconsistency. A text dated 1939 but published by Picabia during the year at the end of which he died, is headed in capitals YES / NO / YES / NO / YES / NO. This four-page fragmentary poem begins:

> Painting music literature
> hot-house flowers
> yes no

Later it observes:

> Serious people
> have a slight odour
> of carrion

And it ends disarmingly:

> Now if you don't mind
> let's talk about my painting
> for I am perhaps the disciple
> of myself.

To conclude from occasional quotations of maxims from Nietzsche to be found in Picabia's later writings that he seriously thought of himself as his disciple would be absurdly naive. Luc-Henri Mercié refers to Picabia's admiration for the prophet of the Superman, but asserts that he had read only a few pages of his voluminous writings. Considering the dislike of great men professed in Picabia's Instantaneist manifesto, it is obviously unlikely that he could have sustained this admiration for long. What he disliked more than the kind of figures admired by Breton and his fellow Surrealists – Rimbaud, Lautréamont, Picasso, for instance – was what he regarded as the personality cult devoted to them. He had no objection to a cult devoted to himself, to the enjoyment of life and of the sun. The philosopher to whom he seems closest, if it is not offensive to his memory to make a serious comparison, is Max Stirner. Admittedly

I am ill-qualified to speak of this neglected nineteenth-century thinker, scarcely heard of in Britain, but I have at least read in French translation a sufficient number of selected passages from his masterwork, *The Unique and his Property* (meaning what is appropriate to him as much as what he owns) to recognize how much it might have appealed to Picabia if he had ever had the time or the inclination to study this Hegelian systematization of self-justified egotism. How could he not have felt himself to be a kindred spirit of the Stirner who declared:

> Not only is it not out of love for you, it is not even out of love of (the) truth that I express what I think. No.
> I sing as the bird sings
> Living among the leaves.
> The very song my voice brings forth
> Is my salary, and a royal one.

I referred earlier to a secret drama to be discerned behind all Picabia's post-1920 output, and proposed two keywords to explain it: *épater* and *rater*. To these I think should be added a third, which is *cafard*, the chronic affliction of twentieth-century man divested of all positive faith and so faced with an ubiquitous void – the bleak restless boredom to assuage which one is driven ever onwards in quest of new inventions, new distractions, new isms and ideologies, or failing these, new narcotics. And the key phrase which I would suggest best explains the Picabia phenomenon is, slightly to alter Milan Kundera's well-known title without radically distorting its meaning, 'The unbearable emptiness of being'.

By way of antidote to the unwonted solemnity of this conclusion, I should like to quote Tristan Tzara's encomium of Picabia's achievements, written when the argument as to who should be credited with having originated Dada was still in full swing:

> Funny-guy invented Dadaism in 1889, Cubism in 1870, Futurism in 1867, and Impressionism in 1857. In 1867 he encountered Nietzsche, in 1902 he remarked that he was only the pseudonym of Confucius. In 1910 a monument to him was erected on the Czechoslovakian Place de la Concorde, for he steadfastly believed in the existence of geniuses and the beneficial advantages of love.

GALA ELUARD

Helena Diakanoff Devulina, known since early youth as Gala, died at an advanced age in 1982 in the solitary Catalan castle of Púbol, to which she had withdrawn as the result of ultimate estrangement from Salvador Dalí, having devoted the previous half-century to serving the cause of his genius. After her decease, Dalí installed himself in the castle in which she lay buried. Two years later a disastrous fire broke out in this retreat, and the octogenarian painter was rescued from it so badly burnt that he was not expected to recover – especially as by then he was suffering from malnutrition resulting from his inability to swallow food since Gala's death. Tim McGirk, an American journalist, was sent by *The Sunday Times* to cover the story. Had it not been for this assignment, he explains at the outset of *Wicked Lady*, he would never have become intrigued by Gala. His initial realization that no adequate estimate of Dalí's enormous and unequal output could be made without taking full account of the paramount role his wife played in his life led McGirk to undertake her biography. The author declares in his preface: 'I went through stages of hating Gala. She was, I thought, a woman of genuine evil. She was greedy and cruel and vicious. Her amorality repelled me. Yet there is also much to admire about her.'

Gala's career as a muse began in 1917 when she married the budding poet Eugène Grindel, soon to become known as Paul Eluard, whom she had first met before the First World War in a Swiss sanatorium for consumptives where they were both undergoing treatment. She was highly strung, cultivated and intelligent, and her love for the future Surrealist was at first as passionate as her appreciation of Tolstoy and Dostoevsky; but in the angrily selfish resentment she displayed when her adored *dorogoï maltchik* ('dear boy') had himself transferred from a safe hospital job to service at the front with an infantry regiment McGirk sees an early illustration of the fierce and obstinate side of her character. Eluard survived the war safely, however, and before the Armistice Gala had given birth to their daughter Cécile, though her muse's temperament was soon to prove incompatible with the least display of maternal concern.

'A mercenary Madonna', review of Tim McGirk, *Wicked Lady: Salvador Dalí's Muse* (Century Hutchinson, 1989), *Times Literary Supplement* (14-20 April 1989), p. 393.

In 1921, Eluard's admiration for the early collages of Max Ernst prompted him to seek his collaboration as illustrator of the collection he was then preparing, and the following year Paul and Max immediately became firm friends. Eluard did nothing to discourage Ernst's subsequent infatuation with Gala, which she reciprocated, apparently seeing herself as Katarina Ivanovna torn between the brothers Karamazov. Ernst abandoned his wife and child in order to return with the Eluards to France, where for a time they formed a *ménage à trois* in their new villa at Eaubonne. This was when he painted the group-portrait *Au rendez-vous des amis*, in which Gala is shown turning her back on a dozen nascent Surrealists, while Eluard appears alongside the head of Dostoevsky, on whose knee Ernst has depicted himself seated. McGirk's account of Gala's relations with Eluard's partners in Surrealism and their authoritarian leader, André Breton, suggests that she cultivated a noticeable aloofness from the movement and its activities.

Fortunately for Eluard, his father was a successful property developer, which meant that during the post-war decade the poet remained more prosperous than most of his friends, and thus was able to assuage the financial anxiety that Gala shared with her exiled compatriots of that period, while indulging her taste for luxury and fashion. But by 1929, the Eluards' marriage appears to have reached a stage of tacit disenchantment and, as McGirk puts it, 'the time was ripe for a new romance'. During the summer of the year of the Great Crash, Gala accompanied her husband on a visit to Cadaquès to investigate the work of a young Catalan painter who had just completed with his friend Luis Buñuel an astonishing short film, *Un Chien andalou*. The story of Gala's first encounters with Dalí in the rocky setting now made so familiar by his pictural use of it is recounted by McGirk in all its quirky complexity, and without undue sensationalism. Eluard was eventually obliged to return to Paris without Gala, while she remained to inspire the most creative period of Dalí's production, more convinced of his genius than he was himself.

Though not officially divorced until 1932, Gala had by then become Dalí's constant companion, who succeeded in reorganizing the practical side of his life, promoting his work with dealers and wealthy clients and becoming virtually his sole protector and guide at the moment when his career was at its lowest ebb. (Her care of him was interrupted by serious health problems in 1931, when she had to undergo a couple of operations, the second to remove a uterine tumour, which left her sterile.) One June day in 1935, Eluard took his daughter Cécile to lunch with her mother and new stepfather in their atelier-flat near the Porte d'Orléans. Half-way through the meal, he asked: 'Do you know which are the finest love-poems I have ever written?' then went over to a shelf and brought back to the table a book from which he read aloud an impassioned extract from *Nuits partagées*, a series indisputably inspired by Gala. Dalí's reaction was to pay a more obsessed attention than usual to the *baguette* of bread he was nibbling. Shy, seventeen-year-old Cécile was evidently touched by this tribute to the spell of the mother for whose affection she longed in vain. Gala accorded scant comment on the incident other than one of her rare smiles of gratification. I was present on account of being at the time the translator of a text of Dalí's,* intended for the catalogue of his forthcoming second New York exhibition, and felt I had witnessed an impressive demonstration of Gala's simultaneous ascendancy over two men of undoubted genius. It did not occur to me then that she might one day come to deserve the designation of 'wicked lady', though I could understand her being already referred to by many dealers and younger Surrealists as 'Gala la gale'.

Gala continued to hoard Eluard's letters to her until 1948; the last of the 272 now printed concludes: 'Embrasse le petit Dalí pour moi. J'ai vu des photos de très beaux tableaux.' By this time she had spent nearly ten years unremittingly promoting Dalí's fame and more particularly fortune in America. McGirk chronicles this period with a wealth of detail attesting to the ruination of whatever integrity Dalí had possessed, and the rapid deterioration of his muse into a hardened mercenary virago. One of his more amusing anecdotes reveals Anaïs Nin overcome with grudging admiration for an even more manipulative 'entrepreneuse' than herself. But the shrewd, avaricious business woman is not the only side of Gala well documented in *Wicked Lady*. The concluding chapters contain plenty of information regarding her apparently prodigious erotic capacity in later life, as well as her addiction to gambling. One of the photographs in the book is baldly captioned: 'Dalí's fears excluded all sexual activity but masturbation. He was a voyeur repelled by physical contact with women.' McGirk reasonably concludes that Gala was increasingly driven to compensate for what he calls 'the unhappiness involved in sharing Dalí's bed' by having affairs with a constant succession of young men unrepelled by her age, of Spanish fishermen and even rent-boys. She reminded Max Ernst's son Jimmy of an 'unchaste Diana of the Hunt after the Kill . . . in constant wait for unnamed sensualities'. In her late seventies she was conducting a protracted affair with the actor who had played *Jesus Christ Superstar* on Broadway; nor was this infatuation the last. Dalí liked to claim that these habitual infidelities stimulated his creativity. They certainly did not deter him from transforming Gala's

---

* Editor's note: *Conquest of the Irrational* (New York: Julien Levy, 1935).

features into those of the many Madonnas of his late Catalan period, one of which is said to have evinced the admiration of the Pope.

The rancorous break-up of the long Dalí/Gala partnership, involving warring entourages and physical violence between the couple, finally became inevitable, and provides an unedifying chronicle with a bitter conclusion. In the Dalí Teatro Museo at Figueres there is a late portrait of Gala wholly unlike any of his previous representations of her. It is not reproduced in McGirk's book, which is a pity, as it proves that the painter at last achieved a tragically disillusioned vision of what had become of his muse. Entitled *Portrait of Gala against the Light* ('Retrato de Gala a contraluz'), it shows her framed by a window against a menacing sky, her face the colour of gun-metal and wearing an expression of malignity reminiscent of Arletty's in the role of an emissary of the Devil at the beginning of Carné's *Les Visiteurs du soir*. The Chanel bow that became an inseparable feature of Gala's coiffure during her last decade appears indistinguishable from a brutal pair of horns.

LEONORA CARRINGTON

Leonora Carrington is little known in England, the country she left for good in 1937, when she was nineteen. By 1977 she had had four books published in France, and her reputation as a painter has already been well established abroad for many years: her fresco *The Magic World of the Mayas*, for instance, was commissioned by the Mexican National Museum of Anthropology in 1963. Marina Warner's sympathetic and informative introduction to *The House of Fear* begins by sketching in Carrington's family background and her début as a Surrealist *femme-enfant en fleur*. The daughter of a Lancashire textile magnate and his Irish Catholic wife, Leonora emerged from the chafing tutelage of nannies and nuns to be 'finished' at a Florentine Academy, returning to be presented as a débutante at George V's court during the season of 1936. She then insisted on becoming enrolled as a student at the art-school Amédée Ozenfant had just set up in London.

This was the summer of the great International Surrealist Exhibition at the New Burlington Galleries: her visit to it spellbound the student. The following year she found herself being introduced to her fellow-guest, Max Ernst, at a dinner-party given by the architect Erno Goldfinger, the father of another Ozenfant pupil. Ernst was then having his first one-man show in Mayfair. He was forty-one. Shortly afterwards, Leonora accompanied Ernst back to his Montparnasse studio. According to the version of what happened then that Roland Penrose subsequently relayed to me, when Ernst's wife Marie-Berthe went to the door to welcome her husband home, Leonora sweetly explained to her: 'Max wants me to live with him now, so I'm sure that if you want him to be happy you'll find somewhere else to stay, otherwise things might be awkward!'

Marina Warner clearly feels that first readers of Leonora Carrington's tales and writings will be unlikely fully to appreciate their idiosyncratic quality without some knowledge of the equally extravagant real characters and events which generated them. She recounts in some detail the circumstances of Leonora's elopement and subsequent settling down to

---

'Tasteful snatchings', review of Leonora Carrington, *The House of Fear: Notes from down below*, trans. Kathrine Talbot and Marina Warner (Virago, 1989) and *The Seventh Horse and Other Tales*, trans. Kathrine Talbot and Anthony Kerrigan (Virago, 1989), *Times Literary Supplement* (4-10 August 1989), p. 836.

live with Ernst in a Provençal village in the late summer of 1937. It is plain that the young refugee from conformist bourgeois platitude must eagerly have embraced the influence of Ernst, master of unbridled fantasy in the tradition of Hoffmann and von Arnim, while he in turn saw in her the embodiment of some of his most cherished obsessions, 'bride of the wind', 'the nymph Echo', 'Perturbation my sister'. An immediate result of this period of Carrington's life was the writing, still in English, of the arrestingly original and accomplished novella 'Little Francis', which occupies seventy pages of *The House of Fear*. The tone of the opening passage reminds one at first of Ronald Firbank:

> 'Musical instruments are bodies out of space', said the father. They were under the dome in the Salle Liszt. The orchestra had got half through the fifth Brandenburg Concerto.
> 'Like God?' said Amelia.
> 'No, not like God . . . They're like stars and planets.'
> 'Reverend Mother says, "Honour thy father and thy mother". How can I obey her when you tell such wicked lies?'
> 'You are becoming a little prude.'
> 'Father, I shall scream.'
> 'Scream then.'
> Silence.

Comparisons between the style of a work and the various others of which it may remind one might be rewardingly prolonged in the case of Carrington, if most often misleadingly. Though it is far from unlikely that an omnivorous reader, catholic in both senses, would have come across Firbank at an early age, it is impossible to say with any certainty that the author of 'Little Francis' was familiar with his work in 1937. What one can say is that nothing written by her can conveniently be fitted into the category of 'camp', even though according to Warner's reading of this often playfully told narrative the theme of androgyny is central to it. There is a vein of toughness, even ferocity, close to the surface of all Carrington's writings, of a kind that repudiates the self-defensive mask of send-up. Attention is, however, drawn in the introduction to one source that Carrington had already encountered at the time when 'Little Francis' was being written, and that is Alexandra David-Neel's *With Mystics and Magicians in Tibet*, which had then just been printed as a Penguin paperback. This links the young Carrington with another Surrealist woman poet fourteen years her senior, Roland Penrose's French wife Valentine, who had been for years a close friend and disciple of Mme David-Neel.

An absorption in magic and mysticism, alchemy and the cabbala runs through the most outstanding of the twenty-six novellas and tales brought together in these two collections of Leonora Carrington's writings. It is especially predominant in 'The Stone Door', written in 1946, the year she married the Hungarian photographer Imre Weisz, who had found refuge in Mexico City soon after Carrington had settled there. The centre-piece of *The Seventh Horse and other tales*, 'The Stone Door', 'transforms her husband's story, his poverty and his wanderings', to quote Marina Warner's introduction, 'into a parable about a young seeker — Zakarias — who absorbs into himself the wisdom of Jewish cabbalistic mysticism'. It is a richly complex narrative, combining the element of initiatory quest with a zodiacal allegory and such unexpected symbolism as that of 'a stick of cinnamon, a skein of black wool, and five iron nails'. It first appeared in 1976 as *La Porte de pierre*, translated by Henri Parisot, who later became the definitive translator of the complete works of Lewis Carroll. When the original English version made its appearance the following year in New York, Jane Miller observed in the *TLS* that 'in spite of all its waywardness and intimations of profundity . . . its eclectic, not to say magpie, snatching at bright detail and unexplained incident is controlled by a tastefulness and sense of design which are old-fashioned and charming rather than portentous'.

Marina Warner reports Carrington once saying that 'dailiness' is very important to her, and that the making of art is like 'making strawberry jam – really carefully and well'. This prompts reference to another preoccupation of Carrington's, as characteristic of her output as her concern with alchemy and magic, and probably inseparable from it: the culinary arts. André Breton was so impressed by her preparation of hare served with oysters that he referred to it in his *Anthologie de l'humour noir*, which contains the early tale translated in *The House of Fear* as 'The Débutante'. Commenting on her 1946 painting of *The Temptation of St Anthony*, she wrote of the figure of a bald serving-maid in it: 'you will notice that she is engaged in making an unctuous broth of (let us say) lobsters, mushrooms, fat turtle, spring chicken, ripe tomatoes, gorgonzola cheese, milk chocolate, onions and tinned peaches.' 'The Sisters', an early tale first written in French, concludes with this pungent paragraph:

> Meat, wine, cakes, all half eaten, were heaped around them in extravagant abundance. Huge pots of jam spilled on the floor made a sticky lake round their feet. The carcass of a peacock decorated Jumart's head. His beard was full of sauces, fish heads, crushed fruit. His gown was torn and stained with all sorts of food.

An account of Carrington's writing would be incomplete without some allusion to the equally abundant contents of her bestiary. Horses, dogs, cats (most often feral), cows, sheep and goats are the most commonplace of the creatures frequenting her stories. Rabbits and jaguars, peacocks, parrots and insects of every description endow her prose with something of their pulsating energy. But animals contribute little to the special interest distinguishing 'Down Below', the last text in *The House of Fear*. This is the account which Pierre Mabille, a surgeon and intellectual on the fringe of the Surrealist circle, persuaded Carrington to give him of the crucial period of her life, beginning in 1940, when she went out of her mind and underwent horrifying treatment in a Madrid asylum.

After the outbreak of war in Europe, most of the Surrealists began planning emigration to the United States. Max Ernst, an enemy alien despite seventeen years' residence in France, was arrested and sent to a camp. After frantic attempts, Leonora succeeded in procuring his release. A year later, he was imprisoned again. Soon after the beginning of Carrington's account, recollected two years later when she and Mabille were both camping in Mexico City, she tells him:

> I begin therefore with the moment when Max was taken away to a concentration camp for a second time, under the escort of a gendarme who carried a rifle. I was living in Saint-Martin-d'Ardèche. I wept for several hours, down in the village; then I went up again to my house where, for twenty-four hours, I indulged in voluntary vomitings induced by drinking orange-blossom water and interrupted by a short nap.

After three weeks, two old friends arrived in the village. Leonora was in a state verging on nervous breakdown, and by now harbouring strange obsessions and delusions. Convinced that only perfect health would enable her to survive, she agreed to accompany her friends in their attempt to cross the frontier into Spain. After Perpignan and Andorra, leaving one friend behind on the way, she managed to reach Barcelona, and eventually Madrid. All the way, Leonora's sanity had been progressively deteriorating, and by now she was demented. She made contact with a sinister character claiming to be an agent of her father's business connection (Imperial Chemicals) and offering to help her to reach Lisbon. Some time towards the end of August 1940, Leonora awoke in a tiny room with no outside windows, believing herself to be the victim of a car accident. She was in fact incarcerated as a supposedly incurable patient in the mental hospital of Dr Morales, one of the pavilions in the ground of which was known to the inmates as 'Down Below'.*

---

* Editor's note: Carrington was rescued by her nanny, sent out to Spain by her parents, and travelled to Lisbon where she met Ernst again.

Marina Warner ranks 'Down Below' as 'a testimony to the horrors of psychosis and evidence of medical treatment and convulsive therapy, beside autobiographical fiction like Antonia White's *The Sugar House*, Sylvia Plath's *The Bell Jar* and Janet Frame's *Faces in the Water*'. (Virago have also reprinted *The Shutter of Snow*, by Antonia White's American friend Emily Holmes Coleman, a masterly and neglected record, published in 1930, of a sojourn on the borderlands of insanity, that is of comparable literary quality.) Needless to say, Carrington made a rapid recovery after reaching Mexico City in 1942. She married twice, has two sons, and has led a life of singular creativity, active as an artist, writer and feminist in New York and Chicago as well as Mexico. It is time that England duly acclaimed her. Octavio Paz paid her fitting tribute when he declared: 'Romantic heroines, beautiful and terrible . . . come back to life in women like Leonora Carrington.'

MAX ERNST and MAN RAY

When Man Ray from Manhattan and Max Ernst from Cologne arrived in Paris to settle there seventy years ago, both had already been actively involved in the explosively subversive Dada movement, generally supposed to have started in Zurich about half-way through the First World War. Man Ray had been a friend and ally of Marcel Duchamp and Francis Picabia since taking part with them in the proto-Dada Armory Show of 1913. In that year, Max Ernst made his first brief visit to Paris, where he encountered Guillaume Apollinaire, who originated the term *surréaliste* four years later: and he first met Hans Arp in July 1914. In 1946, Man Ray and Max Ernst married their last wives in Hollywood on the same day, witnesses to each other's weddings. Both died in Paris in 1976, Man less than a year older than Max. If the fact that exhibitions of works by both of them are being held in London during the early months of this year is a coincidence, it is surely a happy one.

As indicated by its subtitle, 'The Bazaar Years', the Man Ray show at the Barbican is devoted only to his photography, and for the most part to the plates he contributed to *Bazaar* (soon incorporated with *Harper's*), and occasionally to *Vanity Fair*, *Femina*, Paris *Vogue* and a few other such magazines. These are interspersed with portraits of people like Gertrude Stein and Picasso, but more particularly of such figures as the vicomtesse Marie Laure de Noailles, Mrs Daisy Fellowes, Lady Abdy, Nancy Cunard and Peggy Guggenheim, representatives of the High or café society most influential in the world of fashion between the wars. Mostly anonymous models are shown displaying dresses designed by Poiret, Patou, Paquin, Vionnet, Lanvin and Lelong. There are portraits of some of the designers themselves: Schiaparelli, Mainbocher and Chanel. As an image of timeless and archetypical twentieth-century chic, the picture of Coco Chanel in 1935, wearing a simple black dress and small hat, wristbangles and many chains of pearls or beads, in profile and with a cigarette in her mouth, against a white background which happens to be part of a large Giacometti sculpture, must surely be unsurpassable.

'Loplop and his aviary: the Surrealist visions of Max Ernst and Man Ray', review of *Man Ray: the Bazaar Years* (Barbican Art Gallery, London) and *Max Ernst* (Tate Gallery, London), *Times Literary Supplement* (8 March 1991), pp. 14–15.

Perhaps the most interesting question the show prompts one to ask is how it was possible for Man Ray and the intransigently anti-bourgeois Dada / Surrealist group to reconcile their commonly shared principles with an evident tolerance of a way of life and standards of elegance exclusive to an opulent élite. Elusive and ambiguous though answers to this question may be, it should be remembered when considering them that, before leaving New York in July 1921, Man Ray collaborated with Duchamp, already one of his closest friends, in the production of the cover-design for the only issue of the *New York Dada* magazine: a spoof perfume advert for *Eau de Violette: Belle Haleine*, featuring a scent bottle with a label surmounted by the head of Marcel made up as a mascaraed 'sphingine' vamp. The coolly derisive attitude to the beauty market and *la mode* that this item clearly demonstrated was one the fashion-photographer no doubt covertly preserved throughout his subsequent career. It is similarly significant that it should have been Francis ('Funny-guy') Picabia's first wife, Gabrielle Buffet, who should have instigated this career in 1922, after the commercial failure of Man's first Paris show of paintings, rayograms and provocative objects, by introducing him to her husband's old friend, the art-collecting *haut couturier* Paul Poiret. This Dior of his day at once recognized and encouraged the young Ameri-can's potential as recorder and propagator of his creations, and it was not long before his many rivals began to seek Man's services, thus freeing him to paint and pursue other visual researches without financial anxiety.

He soon became sufficiently well off to own a country place and a car smart enough to rival one of Picabia's. In the introduction to the Barbican catalogue, *Man Ray in Fashion*, there is a reference to the 'dichotomy of Man Ray's life, his activities in the world of the Parisian avant-garde and his work as a commercial photographer'. One of the most striking apparent resolutions of this dichotomy occurred in 1925, the year of the still famous International Art Deco Exhibition, when in July the cover of the fourth number of *La Révolution surréaliste*, of which Breton had just assumed the editorship, featured a Man Ray photograph of a wooden mannequin displaying a Poiret evening gown, a photo actually taken at the foot of a staircase in the Pavillon de l'Elégance of the Grand Palais. The picture was flanked by the words LA GUERRE / AU TRAVAIL. A month later, a group of similar Man Ray photos appeared in Paris *Vogue*. As 1925 was also the year when Breton's group, disturbed by the French colonial war in Morocco, began to take a serious interest in revolutionary politics, the cover of their official organ at that date was indicative of a singular approach to the class war, while at the same time demonstrating how much more indulgent Breton and his fellow ideo-logues always were towards Man Ray than they were, for instance, towards Ernst and Miró when they accepted a commission from Diaghilev to produce décors for his ballet *Romeo et Juliette*, a collaboration denounced in the next issue of the Surrealist review as 'giving arms to the worst partisans of moral equivocation'. One may be a little surprised to find banal photos advertising Pond's Cold Cream and Wrigley's Chewing Gum represented at the Barbican, but these were either tacitly ignored by the Surrealists as 'bread and butter' work, or considered not deserving of high-minded condemnation. Towards the end of his life, Man Ray declared to an interviewer: 'I never had rows with the Surrealists: I trusted them and they trusted me.'

It is notable that Man Ray's magazine photos fall on the whole into two distinct categories. The work devoted to straightforward promotion of the latest fashions is impersonal and relatively austere, eschewing the use of broken plinths, swathes and gauze and bizarre bric-à-brac resorted to at the time by English photographers such as Angus MacBean or even Cecil Beaton. On the other hand, this exhibition contains a considerable number of overtly erotic studies of women and of the female nude. Most notable are the legendary Kiki (usually referred to as *de Montparnasse*), the photographer's acknowledged mistress during the 1920s, and the stunning Lee Miller who lived with Man Ray for three years, often modelled for him and was taught by him to become an outstanding photographer herself. Then there is the seemingly fragile Alsatian beauty always known as Nusch, the second wife of Paul Eluard, shown modelling jewellery, and also nude in the illustrations to Eluard's poem sequence *Facile*, the words of which appear on the page alongside the outlines of the beloved's slender body. The Swiss artist Meret Oppenheim, as attractive as she was gifted, creator of the celebrated fur tea-set, also inspired many seductive studies, of which three are shown. Finally, Juliet Man Ray appears in 1945 with her head in a tight-stretched silk stocking which fails to disguise enticing features.

A portfolio commissioned in 1931 by the Electricity Company of France contains photographs demonstrating how the appeal of a nude female torso can be enhanced by the addition of white streaks of simulated lightning. There are some studies of bodies striated by cords, unmistakably suggestive of bondage; while others more clearly display an element of SM, especially evident in the kinky accoutrements commissioned for his wife by William Seabrooke, a writer once well known for his research into Haitian voodoo and the results of prolonged sensory deprivation.

In three photographs, one of Man Ray's best-known paintings appears as a background. The models stretched out beneath the frieze-like *A l'heure de l'observatoire – les amoureux*, a canvas in which a huge pair of perfect lips hovers in the sky above a dusky landscape, show how long are the painted lips above them. At the International Surrealist Exhibition at the New Burlington Galleries in 1936, and later the same year at the New York Museum of Modern Art's show of *Fantastic Art, Dada, Surrealism*, this picture was perceived as dominating all the others, not on account of its size alone but because the public found in it such a compellingly memorable icon, even though many critics considered it inferior to most of the works surrounding it. The inspiration of this painting is the subject of the simplest photo at the Barbican; it represents the lips of Lee Miller in 1930, an enduring emblem of ephemeral passion.

The comprehensive Max Ernst retrospective at the Tate contains 250 works representative of a production spanning fifty years. As a teenager on my first visit to Paris, I acquired from José Corti's bookshop at the foot of Montmartre a copy of Ernst's *La Femme 100 têtes*, his first collage 'novel', published four years previously in 1929; and soon after was able, through an introduction from Jeanne Bucher, to visit the artist in his studio-apartment south of Montparnasse, and buy from him at an absurdly low price a gouache, *Oiseau en forêt*. After further encounters with Ernst and, briefly, with Marie-Berthe (Aurenche), Leonora Carrington and Dorothea Tanning, and having seen many Ernst works of all periods in London, Paris and New York, I felt this artist's world had become familiar to me. But at the Tate, confronted once more with such powerful exhibits as *L'Eléphant Celebes, La Révolution la nuit*, the *Histoire naturelle* frottage series first published by Jeanne Bucher as a portfolio in 1926, the terrifyingly rampageous *L'Ange du foyer*, the *Jardin gobe-avions* group, *La Nymphe Echo*, and *Europe after the Rain*, I realized that these pictures will always astonish one with the novelty of their individuality, that they always make one feel one is seeing them for the first time, while recognizing them as already enigmatically familiar. This is hardly a surprising reaction to the works of an artist who once described himself as 'a difficult character, hopelessly complex, obstinate and with an impenetrable mind ("he is a nest of contradictions" they say), transparent and full of enigma at the same time'.

Anyone encountering Ernst's work in bulk for the first time at the Tate will be bound soon to become aware of a number of obsessions, and in particular an obsession with birds. It appears that the question most often asked by visitors is: Who, or what, is Loplop? In the *Dictionnaire abrégé du surréalisme* compiled by Eluard and Breton in 1938, the entry under ERNST (Max) reads: 'born in 1891 – "Loplop, le supérieur des oiseaux". Painter, poet and surrealist theorist from the origins of the Movement till today.' It strikes me that current translation of the sobriquet as simply King or Superior of the birds may be missing a relevant point. From one of the autobiographical notes Ernst prepared for the catalogue of the 1951 exhibition of his work in his home town of Brühl, one learns that in 1894 'little Max's first contact with painting was when he watched his father painting a watercolour called *Loneliness*. It showed a monk sitting in a beech-wood, reading a book.' The pious Catholicism of Ernst's early upbringing is undoubtedly a capital predeterminant. When I first visited him in the rue des Plantes in 1933, he showed me his father's portrait of him as the five-year-old Infant Jesus with a sardonic amusement evidently not unmixed with a certain pride. In his collage novels of the 1920s and 30s, particularly *Rêve d'une petite fille qui voulut entrer au Carmel*, religious orders having Mothers and Fathers Superior are a significant feature. Loplop is the Superior of a monastic aviary. Like all the other creatures and personages in the Ernstian mythology, birds of every sort are polyreferential. Loplop is most obviously Ernst's *alter ego*, or his Id with a beak and wings. The order to which he belongs is an erotically sacrilegious one; and Hermes, winged messenger of the gods, is surely its primary patron.

Many critics and commentators are agreed that the imagery to be found in Ernst's work is demonstrably of an emblematic nature. The emblems that seem to bear an unmistakable resemblance to those in many of Ernst's compositions belong to the pictorially rich hermetic tradition, and in particular to that of alchemy, its symbols and processes. Earth, water, fire and air, for instance, play a major part in the collage portfolios known as *Une Semaine de bonté* (1934); and the American M. E. Warlick has pointed out that their association reflects the classical symbols and processes of alchemy, whose ultimate goal is the attainment of spiritual purity. Similarly, says Evan Maurer in his essay 'Images of Dream and Desire', in *Max Ernst: Beyond Surrealism – A retrospective of the artist's books and prints* (1986),

> Ernst's repeated references to marriage, sexual union, the joining of terrestrial and celestial entities, violence, death and decay mirror the essential metaphors of alchemical theory, and his three most frequently used animal symbols, the lion, the bird and the dragon, are associated with many aspects of alchemical procedures. . . . It was because Ernst recognized the kinship between magic and art that he compared the technique of collage to the alchemical process, calling it 'something like the alchemy of the visual image'.

This formulation irresistibly recalls the 'Alchimie du Verbe' evoked in the second section of Rimbaud's *Une Saison en enfer*: 'I loved idiotic paintings, panel-friezes, decorative graining, backdrops for tumblers, inn signs, popular coloured prints, out-of-date literature, church latin, badly spelt erotic books, old folk novels, fairy tales, little books for children. . . .' Rimbaud's prodigious development culminated in his concept of the poet's role as *seer*; and Ernst continued the aspiration abandoned by Rimbaud fifty years earlier by becoming the personification of the seer as artist. 'Seeing was my favourite occupation', as he once declared of his youth. According to Joë Bousquet, quoted by Werner Spies in the splendid Tate catalogue edited by him, 'Rimbaud's experience could only be thought through and continued by a painter. . . . A poet had shaken the notion of poetry so thoroughly as to suggest a new definition of language. Max Ernst, himself a great poet and, moreover, an artist of exceptional genius, gathered together all the means of painting and turned them against it, incessantly.' This refers to the anti-art attitude Ernst carried forward from Dada, expressive of the anti-individualism characterized by Lautréamont's maxim so often cited by the Surrealists: 'Poetry should be produced [*faite*] by all, not by one.'

While recognizing that the argument 'against interpretation' may well be valid in any discussion of the Ernst *oeuvre*, as a variety of interpretations are possible and no single one adequate, the analogy with alchemy seems to me nevertheless to be the most satisfactory, even if accepted with some reservations. The triumphant painting of 1948 entitled *Chemical Nuptials*, which probably refers to the hermetic treatise attributed to Christian Rosencreuz, can be seen as confirming this exegetical hypothesis. It is relevant here to observe that the Milanese Surrealist expert, Arturo Schwarz, has even succeeded in finding alchemical archetypes in the work of Picabia, and in Marcel Duchamp has seen *L'Alchimiste mise à nu chez le célibataire, même*.

Though Breton and the Surrealists in general venerated Freud and acknowledged their debt to him, it was in fact Jung, the principal dissident from Freudian orthodoxy, who first, with the exception of Herbert Silberer, recognized the unmistakable parallel between the archetypes and profuse symbols in which the multiple texts of the age-old canon of alchemy abound and those encountered during what he formulated as the process of individuation, or the integration of the personality, the ideal aim of the type of analysis practised by him. Despite Breton's increasing recognition in middle age of the importance of gnosticism, magic and the hermetic tradition to his continuing Surrealist quest, the deep-rooted and unwavering materialism of his outlook never permitted him to recognize Jung's later theories and studies as other than suspect and aberrant. The year 1938 had seen the beginning of an inevitable estrangement between Breton and Ernst, though they seem to have become briefly reconciled during their wartime American exile. There is no evidence of their having discussed the question of the relevance of alchemy to Surrealist research. But it is unlikely that Ernst would at any time have disagreed with the following passage from Breton's Brussels lecture of 1934 (*Qu'est-ce que le surréalisme?*):

> I can now say that Surrealism, launched fifteen years ago by a discovery [i.e. that of the method of automatic writing] that seemed at first only to concern poetic language, has in pursuit of its course spread tumultuously not only in art but in life; that it has provoked new states of consciousness and overthrown walls behind which it had from time immemorial been impossible to see; that it has modified sensibility, and taken a decisive step towards the unification of the personality, of that personality it had found undergoing a process of ever more profound dissociation.

This is what Surrealism is really all about; and any presentation of writing or painting properly classifiable as Surrealist that ignores this fundamental aim is bound to be superficial and obscurantist. That aim is to change the way we live and thereby the world we live in by increasing our self-awareness and altering our limited idea of reality.

Of all Surrealist painters, Ernst was probably the best educated and most widely read. He had studied philosophy and psychiatry as well as art history at Bonn before 1914. He became familiar early on not only with Goethe, Hölderlin, Lichtenberg, Novalis, Grabbe, Arnim, Kleist and Heine, but also with Hugo, Rimbaud, Lautréamont, Jarry and Apollinaire, while Shakespeare, Blake, Poe, Coleridge, Whitman and Carroll were among his favourite English-language writers. He thought of Cologne, near his birthplace, as being 'still haunted by the spirit of the great magician Cornelius Agrippa, and by that of Albertus Magnus, who lived and died there'. He would seem to have been influenced by acquaintance with Paracelsus and Boehme, as with the 'doctrine of signatures'. To make such claims for the wealth of his cultural background may well seem to reinforce an idea of Ernst as above all a 'literary' artist, whose works are meant to be read rather than looked at. But while awareness of the eclectic diversity of his interests and influences will undoubtedly enhance appreciation of the content of Ernst's work and recognition of its underlying coherence, it ought not to lead to an underestimation of its purely painterly qualities, the compelling disposition of form and colour always evident in it, or of the masterly virtuosity of *facture* and *métier* it displays.

Throughout his career from 1919 onwards, Ernst developed at least four individual techniques, all designed to 'intensify the irritability of the mental faculties', as he put it, in the service of the imagination. All can be thought of as basically related to the common experience of seeing faces, objects or landscapes in stains on the ceiling, passing cloud formations or the embers of a dying fire. The meticulously assembled early collages present incongruous juxtapositions of assorted ready-made images culled from such sources as commercial catalogues or popular magazines: Ernst defined this sort of collage as representing 'the exploitation of the chance meeting of two distant realities on an unfamiliar plane, the culture of systematic displacement and its effect – the spark of poetry that leaps across the gap as the two realities converge'. This spark can be seen burning brightly in the pages of *Répétitions* (1921-2), the first of Ernst's collaborations as illustrator with Paul Eluard, with whom he shared a special predilection for old saws, proverbs, clichés and other oddities of the vernacular. The more famous large pictures of the early 1920s are in fact paintings of such collages blown up to seemingly monumental proportions.

In 1925 came the discovery of the different but complementary technique known as *frottage*. This is akin to the process of brass-rubbing applied to almost any uneven surface. One day, Ernst became fascinated by the scrubbed wooden floor in a small hotel room. After placing sheets of paper on the floorboards, he rubbed them with a piece of soft graphite, and found that the striations and variegated textures that appeared as a result spontaneously suggested a number of fantastic creatures and shapes, which he then accentuated by outlining them with a few added strokes of the pencil. He went on to use other materials than floorboards, such as wickerwork, string, sea-shells, leaves and bark. Thus the portfolio of thirty-four collotype plates entitled *Histoire naturelle* came into existence, to be published by Jeanne Bucher the following year. From then on, the results of *frottage* were continually incorporated in new series of paintings, particularly of forests haunted by birds. Towards the end of the 1920s, the method of enriching the surfaces of oil paintings known as *grattage* was developed. Werner Spies says of this technique that it 'led to astonishingly innovative imagery. . . . The dramatic force of these paintings, the richness of their scintillating colour, made them high points of imaginative Surrealist art in the late 1920s.'

Between 1929 and 1934, the three collage sequences already referred to as novels made their appearance. They comprise hundreds of plates made up of figures and backgrounds from thousands of steel-plate engravings taken from late nineteenth-century magazines and popular novels of a melodramatic nature, with the addition of illustrations from scientific and medical journals. Only a small number of these can be represented in the exhibition. They can be properly enjoyed only when pored over repeatedly in their entirety. They were republished in their original format in America by George Braziller about ten years ago. Are they really considered too disturbing to tempt the present art-book-buying British public?

Not long before the outbreak of war in 1939, the Surrealists had begun experimenting with another pictural technique, known as decalcomania, after the French word for what children call transfers. It consists in placing a sheet of paper or glass on a painted surface and then peeling it away, producing a result not unlike 'marbling' but richer and more varied. By developing this technique during his exile in America during the war, in Arizona during the years following his encounter with Dorothea Tanning and marriage to her, Ernst evolved the depiction of a mysterious matter, a seeming amalgamation of sponge and fungus, petrified foam, coral, lava and decayed vegetation, undergoing constant metamorphosis into the most enigmatic of all Ernst's landscapes, peopled with reincarnations of the phantasms, fauna, monsters and nymphs that haunted his earlier work. *Europe after the Rain*, now belonging to a collection in Hartford, Connecticut, may well be thought to be the masterpiece of this particular series, but it was followed by a number of even more astonishing creations, which means that many visitors will find the last three rooms of the exhibition, containing one *tour de force* after another – *The Antipope, Le déjeuner sur l'herbe, Surrealism and Painting, Flute of Angels, A Swarm of Bees in the Palace of Justice* – perhaps the most exciting and demanding of all. The titles alone give some notion of the exotic diversity of Ernst's final period. *The Temptation of St Anthony*, painted for a Hollywood film in 1945, a lurid and obvious parody or pastiche of Grünewald, alone seems unworthy of it – an opinion I share with George Melly, who has recorded a succinct and helpful tape that may be hired by bewildered visitors in need of elucidation.

It now seems incredible that Ernst should have already written, in autobiographical catalogue notes published forty years ago, referring to his memories of the year 1906: 'Excursions into the world of prodigies, chimaeras, phantoms, poets, philosophers, birds, women, magi, trees, erotica, stones, insects, mountains, poisons, mathematics, etc'. All these phenomena are to be found inhabiting most of his final pictures, in particular the last-named item, in the form of Euclid and the geometric lines and rhomboids making up certain disturbingly alien late figures. Another note tells us that 'Max Ernst died on 1st August 1914. He returned to life on 11th November 1918, a young man who wanted to become a magician and find the central myth of his age.' The Tate exhibition surely provides ample proof of his having succeeded in many ways. In his 1981 *Scrapbook*, Roland Penrose described as follows a picture that once belonged to Paul Eluard, then to him and now to the Tate:

> *Celebes* is a haunting image, defiantly pessimistic and terrifying, but in which the vitality of the imagery triumphs over the hollow echo of a possibly doomed civilization. . . . 'Art here rejoins myth' and, I would add, the dream elucidates reality.

Ernst's at first sight private world constantly reflects what has been going on in the labyrinthine underworld of the collective unconscious of our age. One of the last pictures in the Tate exhibition is simply entitled *The Twentieth Century*. In it, above a sombre, chaotic and apparently calcinated scene arises, wan and ghostly still, a huge white circle representing one of the most potent alchemical symbols of all, the Sun at Midnight, testifying to the persistence of an impossible hope.

ANDRÉ BRETON

André Breton, who dominated Surrealism in France between the wars, died in Paris in September 1966, already a quarter of a century ago. Presumably this lapse of time provided a conventional pretext for organizing the exhibition that has been drawing international crowds to the Centre Pompidou in Paris from the end of April until this week. It was consecrated to his memory and to his extensive personal collections of paintings, drawings, photographs and *objets*. Its rubric, 'La beauté convulsive', derives from the characteristically peremptory concluding words of *Nadja* (1928): 'La beauté sera CONVULSIVE ou ne sera pas'. Breton defined what he meant by 'convulsive beauty' in an essay anticipating the opening pages of *L'Amour fou* (1938) that appeared in an early number of the de luxe review, *Minotaure*: 'In my opinion, there can be no beauty – convulsive beauty – except at the price of the affirmation of the reciprocal relationship that joins an object in motion to the same object at rest. I am sorry to be unable to reproduce here a photograph of a very handsome locomotive after having been abandoned for many years to the fever of a virgin forest' (translation published in number 43 of Fabers' *Criterion Miscellany*, 1936).★

The persona of Breton, mythical as it had become in his lifetime, may now be seen more impartially, as the man behind the mask begins to emerge in his intrinsic human complexity. Two emblematic images suggest themselves to represent the way he himself might most have liked to be thought of. First, the Great Anteater, selected by Breton as his heraldic beast and appearing as such on the *ex-libris* plate Dalí designed for him soon after their first encounter, symbolizing an insatiable and ever-alert appetite for the least morsel of the swarming *insolite*. (Breton's indefatigable exponent, Mme Marguerite Bonnet, has succeeded in tracing

---

'Alchemist of the spirit: Breton's esoteric treasure hunt', review of four Breton publications: *La Nouvelle Revue Française – Avril 1967: André Breton 1896-1966, Hommages, Témoignages, L'Oeuvre* (Paris: Gallimard, 1990); André Breton, *Je vois, j'imagine: poèmes – objets* (Paris: Gallimard, 1991); *André Breton, la beauté convulsive* (Paris: Centre Georges Pompidou, 1991); André Breton and Gérard Legrand, *L'Art magique: Une histoire de l'art* (Paris: Phébus, 1991). *Times Literary Supplement* (23 August 1991), pp. 14-15.

★ Editor's note: D.G. is referring to his translation of Breton's *What is Surrealism?*

the patent of this animal back to a passage in Browning's 'Mr Sludge "The Medium",' beginning: 'Open-mouthed like my friend the anteater, / Letting all nature's loosely-guarded motes / Settle and, slick, be swallowed!' This poem was included in a selection of translations from Browning published in France in 1922, the year when Breton produced the essay *Entrée des médiums*, his account of the pre-Manifesto 'period of sleeping-fits'.) More conventional than the anteater is the silhouette traced by Julien Gracq at the end of his long 1945 essay on Breton, whom he likens to a knight errant, with absent gaze as in Dürer's engraving, forever in quest of the great adventure – a figure in whom, Gracq declares, the posterity to which he paid no heed will not fail to recognize one of the heroes of our time.

At the end of last year Gallimard republished a group of back numbers of the *Nouvelle Revue Française* that first appeared after the deaths of four of the century's most influential French writers (all of them, incidentally, from the Gallimard stable): Proust, Gide, Sartre and Breton. The issue for April 1967 devoted to the latter provides an appropriate preface to what has become, in effect, a year of Breton commemoration. It contains some forty homages and *témoignages*, and is introduced by three pages of Jean Paulhan, the revue's editor since 1925, headed 'Un Héro du Monde Occidental', no doubt with Synge's *Playboy* in mind (Breton had included an extract from the play in his *Anthologie de l'humour noir*, banned by the Vichy government) rather than the conclusion of Gracq's monograph. Among the contributors' names that attract most immediate attention today are those of Raymond Queneau, Octavio Paz, Philippe Soupault, Roger Caillois, Michel Butor, Philippe Jacottet and Maurice Blanchot. The temptation to quote from several of these encomiums must be resisted, but I feel obliged to mention how grateful I was to find Octavio Paz asserting that the magnetic power Breton exercised over those who frequented him had nothing to do with the fear or respect commonly accorded to a superior, 'though I think', adds Paz, 'that if there are certain superior men, then Breton was one of them. Never did I see in him a chief, even less so a pope, to use the ignoble expression popularized by a few *goujats* [oiks]'. A phrase by an Italian critic, Piero Brigongiani, can aptly be set beside this testimony from Paz: Brigongiani describes 'the subtle Doctor of surrealism' as being 'gifted with an incredible facility of biblical biliary explosions when confronted by the century's impostures and betrayals'. Queneau sees Breton's dictatorship as tempered by a humour best described as lucid and direct rather than black.

Octavio Paz opened his 1967 *NRF* tribute with the affirmation that it is impossible to write about Breton in other than passionate terms. The preface he has written to introduce *Je vois, j'imagine*, the handsome album containing colour-plate reproductions of all the *poèmes-objets* Breton ever made – some fifteen in all – begins with the observation that Breton was no recluse, his two grand passions being friendship and love. For the rest, however, its style is that of an erudite poet coolly assessing the history and significance of heraldic and emblematic imagery in baroque and mannerist art, and its parallel development in Renaissance period poetry. This tradition included poems printed in the shape of objects (an isolated but typical English example is provided by George Herbert's 'Easter Wings') and the genre culminated in Apollinaire's *Calligrammes*.

Breton defined the *poème-objet* that he virtually pioneered in the 1930s as 'a composition tending to combine the resources of poetry and plastic art and to speculate on their power of mutual exaltation'. According to Paz: 'The poem-object embodies a contradictory double impulse: graphic signs tend to be transformed into images and images into signs'. And further: 'The emblem and the poem-object both present us with visual enigmas: deciphering them requires us to read them and so convert images into signs'. The poem-objects elaborated by Breton can be described as having evolved from the rebus once such a popular feature of children's annuals. The book takes its title from an example that is itself untitled. Above five lines of poetry written in Breton's immaculate rounded hand, signed and dated '12.1.35', are affixed with string to a rectangular card mounted on wood, a little pair of greenish wings that might once have been part of a mantlepiece ornament, what appears to be about half of a smashed dark glass slide, and a china egg inscribed with the words JE VOIS / J'IMAGINE. Assembling the most complicated of the works reproduced must have occupied most of Breton's spare time during the first unhappy year of his wartime New York exile. Headed *Un bas dechiré*, it has a small pin-up photo of a smiling brunette in elbow-length black gloves and frilled panties stuck to the top left hand corner to make clear from the start that the composition belongs to the category that Breton designated *érotique-voilée*. Beneath it are arranged at least twenty objects of varying sizes, interspersed with twelve neatly written fragments of text. To one side of the top half is fastened an abundantly leaved stem, to the other a whisk-like bunch of twigs, amongst which two cigarettes, one with a red tip, have been inserted; while in the lower half are to be found two large hanks of white silk thread surrounded by numerous smaller objects, the most noticeable of which is a jumbo-sized fishing float like an elongated yellow pear surmounting a screw propellor.

To describe the whole thing adequately would require many long further paragraphs and any attempt at interpretation even more. Interpretation would in any case defeat the primary object of the exercise, which is the stimulation of the viewer's suggestibility and faculty of mental association, not the transmission of a message, secret or otherwise. The first object-poem in the book, reproduced only in black and white, is entitled in capital letters 'Portrait de L'Acteur A. B. dans son rôle mémorable l'an de grâce 1713', and is accompanied by three pages of explanation which make it none the less mysterious. The date turns out to derive from a distortion of the initial letters of Breton's name, and to involve references to Diderot, the peace of Utrecht, Cardinal de Retz, Port Royal, Pope Clement XI (*vieux chien*), Pascal and Racine. This item alone suffices to demonstrate that Breton's preoccupations were often far from being limited to the discreetly or provocatively erotic.

The reproduction in *Je vois, j'imagine* are not only of Breton's *poèmes-objets* but also of his entire extra-literary output: collages, photo-montages, paintings and drawings. They are accompanied by an anthology of some fifty selected extracts from his poetry and prose. Breton would not have claimed to be more gifted in the graphic domain than the average amateur, but all his pictural productions manifest evident proficiency and a strong sense of unifying composition. No matter how heterogeneous and disparate the objects combined with the texts of his poem-objects may be, they immediately impress one as belonging to one another, parts of a whole suggested but never defined or confined by their verbal accompaniment. Among the other reproductions in the book is a large photo-montage assembled about 1937, when Breton was compiling the *Anthologie de l'humour noir* that was almost unobtainable until 1950 but is now available in *livre de poche* format. At the top appear Picasso's head, Sade's signature and the buck-goat horns of a Goya Satan, and here and there down to the bottom row in which the face of Jacques Vaché has its privileged place, portraits or photos of Dalí and Artaud, Duchamp and Desnos are to be discerned, followed by De Quincey, Harpo Marx and Hans Arp, while adjoining images of a swan, a comb and a miniature map of County Galway, the eyes of Rimbaud, the heads of Jarry and Charles Cros appear, and Freud looks out severely from the top of a huge capital N dominating the right-hand lower part of the montage. No commentary is necessary to convince one that this is the group-portrait of a clandestine brotherhood, a legendary lodge united by a tacit resolve to discredit the conventional norms of artistic expression.

Je vois: the most distinctive feature of Breton's particular genius is the eye with which he saw things in the world about him, an eye that caught the special, the vivid, above all the marvellous. From his earliest writings onward, his vocabulary contained an ever-increasing number of names of birds, common and exotic, of animals and insects, flowers and plants, crystals and gems. His poetic vision constantly fed on what he had seen of Nantes, Paris and Prague, and later of the landscapes of Mexico,

Canada and Teneriffe. His perpetual pursuit of eye-opening analogies was paralleled by a lifelong treasure-hunt that led to his amassing the fabulous collections epitomized by this year's exhibition at the Centre Pompidou. The catalogue produced to mark this occasion contains overwhelming evidence for Breton's eye as the most acutely perceptive, with regard to modern art, of his time (after that of Apollinaire, whose role he inherited), and his taste as the most decisively influential.

He purchased an Easter Island fetish-object as early as 1913, when he was seventeen. His first enthusiasms were for Matisse and Derain. On first visiting Apollinaire's apartment when on leave from the military psychiatric hospital of Nantes in 1916, he succumbed to an enduring fascination for the painting of de Chirico, and saw works of Rousseau, Picasso and Braque surrounded by 'primitive' carvings and masks. Not long after Apollinaire's death and the Armistice, Breton made contact with the wealthy couturier Jacques Doucet, and entered his employ as adviser and agent in the accumulation of an exemplary collection of early twentieth-century books, manuscripts and above all paintings. This decisive episode in the history of Breton's own development as a collector is the subject of one of many valuable articles to be found in the catalogue. Another deals with the de Chirico painting, *The Child's Brain*, that for many years dominated Breton's Montmartre studio-apartment at 42 rue Fontaine. Two further articles are devoted to this studio, into which Breton moved with his first wife Simone on New Year's Day, 1922, and in which Mme Elisa Breton, his third wife and widow, lives to this day. The walls, shelves, tables and desk-tops of the two rooms of this modestly proportioned dwelling have from the start been covered by a prodigious number of paintings, drawings, carvings, objects, cases of butterflies and of fishing-hooks, for instance, arranged and juxtaposed in such a way as to make their complementarity apparent. This double *cabinet de merveilles* has appeared to some like a grotto, so much did it suggest a natural phenomenon. After Breton's five years of wartime exile, the *atelier* was moved down a floor and reassembled, this time enriched by a large number of Hopi Indian dolls and examples of Eskimo carving, while certain works of Picasso and Miró, Tanguy, Picabia, Masson and Man Ray remained constant companions among them, now joined by examples of Matta, Gorky and Lam.

The catalogue's value is augmented by notes on Breton's activities and encounters during every year of his life, material for an ideally impartial biography. The notes for the ten years preceding the appearance of the *Premier Manifeste du surréalisme* constitute a timely reminder that prior to 1924, nominally Surrealist painting had no existence. Only three painters of former times, Uccello, Seurat and Gustave Moreau, are referred to in the *Premier Manifeste* as having anticipated a Surrealist mode of vision. Breton had begun by acclaiming de Chirico, Picasso, Picabia and Duchamp as pioneers in painting of the *esprit moderne* he sought to define, but all four subsequently avoided declaring formal allegiance to the Surrealist (or any other) movement. Though the *Premier Manifeste* was illustrated by a frontispiece by Max Ernst, its nineteen signatories were all poets and writers; it was, however, followed in 1928 by Breton's *Le Surréalisme et la peinture*, illustrated by seventy-seven works by Arp, Braque, Masson, Miró, Picabia, Man Ray, Tanguy and others. The *Second Manifeste* of two years later contains scarcely any reference to painting as such, being mainly devoted to caustic and arid excoriations of the many original members of the movement who had failed to maintain the standards of integrity expected of them. (Even Rimbaud and Duchamp are berated in this document for having abandoned their youthful achievements.) In a note prefacing its 1946 republication, Breton admitted that it contained certain 'fallible elements' due to the special circumstances of the time when it was written. One might be tempted to regard 1930, the year of the *Second Manifeste*, as the 1793 of the Surrealist Revolution; and that the movement survived the virulent purge of this period so successfully may be seen as proof of the essential potency of its first principles.

The publication this year in a sumptuous new format of *L'Art magique*, originally written to commission for a limited edition restricted to members of the *Club Française du Livre* and virtually inaccessible to 'the general public' or even Breton's most ardent readers since 1957, sheds new light both on Surrealism's basic principles and on the significance of the *Second Manifeste*. In a passage at the centre of the latter text occur key references to alchemy (Nicolas Flamel), magic (Cornelius Agrippa) and even astrology, accompanied by a peremptory command for 'l'occultation profonde, véritable du surréalisme'. Even in the *Manifeste* of 1924 there are pages headed 'Secrets de l'art magique surréaliste'. The title of the book Breton wrote in Canada in 1944, *Arcane 17*, is the name of the seventeenth card of the Tarot, the Star of Hope, and from then till the end of his life Breton's dominant preoccupation was with spiritual alchemy and the esoteric in general.

The first few pages of the opening section of *L'Art magique* are to be found in *Perspective cavalière*, a posthumous miscellany of introductions and articles published in 1970, but these gave little indication of the grandiose scope of the volume planned as the first of a series of five, the whole somewhat vaguely conceived by Marcel Brion as 'Formes de l'art'. Eventually it became what may best be described as Breton's account of his vision of the entire field of art, from pre-history to mid-twentieth century. To 256 pages of text and over 300 illustrations, two thirds of these in colour, are appended a further 90 pages of answers from a wide variety of authors to an inquiry consisting of five questions, concerning eleven small black-and-white reproductions of works ranging from a design in the Egyptian Book of the Dead to Kandinsky's frontispiece to his 1912 treatise *On the Spiritual in Art*.

The impossibility of summarizing such a work here is immediately obvious, but it should be specified that it cannot strictly be categorized either as a history of art or as an essay in hermeneutic iconography. Neither can it be said to be supported by anything like a conclusive synopsis of the theory and practice of magic. *L'Art magique* is undoubtedly, however, an erudite work, however remote Breton's persona may seem from the conventional image of the scholar or professor. Among authors and source material referred to are Freud, whose *Totem and Taboo* of 1920 is mentioned at the outset, J. G. Frazer, himself acknowledged by Freud and C. G. Jung, while Huizinga and Eliade are later accorded passing allusion. It is clear that the philosopher whom Breton read more often than most was Hegel: the notable frequency with which the turn of phrase *il n'en est pas moins* recurs in Breton's prose is surely indicative of a grounding in Hegelian dialectics.

L'Art magique is as magisterial in tone as most of Breton's previous exegetical writings, if to begin with a little less peremptory than usual. His real authority derived from a passionate and lifelong exploration of and familiarity with what most concerned him. The book may be read as much for what it tells us about Breton's elective affinities and antipathies as for its account of art, magic and their innumerable conjunctions. Its main theme is the interdependence of visual representations or images and totemism, shamanism and sympathetic magic, which eventually, from the earliest civilizations onwards, evolved into the quasi-universal tradition known variously as hermetic, gnostic, cabbalistic or esoteric, involving most notably the doctrine of signatures and correspondences, as expounded by Paracelsus, Boehme and Swedenborg. Breton was early convinced that Surrealism represented the twentieth-century continuation of this tradition, influentially recapitulated in 1860 by Eliphas Lévi.

There are reproductions from and discussions of, among others, Hieronymus Bosch, a painter still strangely neglected sixty years ago by Parisian critics and cognoscenti; Brueghel, Uccello, Piero di Cosimo, Dürer, Grünewald, Altdorfer, Holbein, Arcimboldo, Caron, Monsu Desiderio, Blake, Fuseli, Goya, Friedrich, Böcklin, Gauguin, Moreau, Henri Rousseau and de Chirico, though in far from chronological order. Despite Breton's avowed distaste for works of the Italian Renaissance, exception is made for Leonardo's *Virgin and Child with St Anne* (largely on account of Freud's discovery in it of the phantom of a vulture), and for Giorgione's *The Tempest*. Five plates are devoted to works by Antoine Caron, signal representative of the recently 'rediscovered' sixteenth-century Ecole de Fontainebleau, whose subject-matter is eminently mysterious and esoteric, though presented in a style that would once have been regarded by conventional standards with scant enthusiasm. A subsection of the text is headed: 'D'Antoine Caron à Ingres: le contenu secret de la "Beauté" classique'. From Breton's comment on the Ingres he has chosen to reproduce, the superb *Thétis implorant Jupiter* to be seen at Aix-en-Provence, it is clear that it was the master's profound intuitive understanding of 'the eternal feminine' that particularly captivated him.

That Breton should focus attention on the perennially astonishing and obscure so-called Monsu Desiderio might well have been expected. It would have been more surprising had he *failed* to surprise the reader with certain dismissals from his pantheon: *le pâle Rembrandt*, for instance, along with *le triste Rubens*. Baudelaire's over-estimation of the value of Delacroix is found 'consternant'; Paul Klee is finally qualified as 'un fertile amuseur'. Kandinsky, on the other hand, is acclaimed for opening a way out for painting towards the future, and is shown to have been, like Mondrian, mistakenly supposed to be a partisan of pure non-figuration. Breton, incidentally, succeeds here in making the old distinction, opposing the abstract to the figurative, seem illusory and outdated. His comments on Franz Marc also succeed in making this painter's achievement seem far more lastingly significant than has hitherto been realized.

Towards the end of *L'Art magique*, a whole chapter is devoted to pairing Gustave Moreau and Gauguin. Though perfectly aware of the sophisticated disdain with which Moreau was regarded even by his less typically decadent *fin de siècle* contemporaries, Breton retained all his life his youthful admiration for this solitary visionary devoted to reviving a poetic mythology on which the now celebrated painters of his time had all resolutely turned their backs. Perhaps before dismissing Moreau as a Byzantine bazaar merchant (who, according to Degas, 'put watch-chains on the gods of Olympus') one ought at least to make the effort to visit the usually deserted Musée Gustave Moreau near the Gare St Lazare, once his house and studio, where it is possible to form a fairer evaluation of him and better understand how he came to win Breton's lasting approbation. The pages devoted to the appreciation of Gauguin as a poet-magician in paint – 'more fecund than the splendid dreams of Gustave Moreau' – are far more convincing.

I have not sufficient space to convey an adequate idea of the richness and range of the reproductions of prehistoric and 'primitive' art, of masks and artefacts, with which the pictures already referred to are interspersed: the earliest known wall-paintings, the products of the Australian dreamtime, of Polynesia, Melanesia, New Guinea, Borneo, of North American Indians and Eskimos, of Mexico, Egypt and pre-Roman Gaul, Easter Island and Stonehenge. *L'Art magique* has the potential to transform the historic museum-plan view of art into the prospect of a timeless continuum wherein Duchamp's *Nude Descending a Staircase* is neighbour, without the least incongruity, to the shapes of the beasts galloping across the walls of the caverns of Lascaux.

Breton opens his meandering disquisition on magic by quoting Novalis: 'Love is the principle that renders magic possible. Love's action is magical.' When Marcel Duchamp was asked by the wartime New York magazine *View* to define his conception of magic, he replied simply: 'ANTI-REALITY'. In an interview given just after Breton's death in 1966, the same Duchamp declared: 'I've never known a man who had a greater capacity for love. Breton loved as a heart beats. He was a lover of love in a world that believes in prostitution. That was his sign.' The photo of Breton prefacing *Je vois, j'imagine* shows him sitting on the ground at the foot of a headless sculpture in the park surrounding de Sade's ruined château at Lacoste. The famous leonine profile emanates a calm, unselfconscious resignation to imprisonment in his own innate nobility. If the capacity to recognize greatness and nobility has not yet withered away, perhaps proper awareness of Breton's true stature has only just begun.

6

ADDITIONAL UNCOLLECTED WRITINGS

BLIND MAN'S BUFF
(Fragments from an unpublished Notebook)

Not until the blindfold is removed does one begin to realize that one is forever blind.

★
★ ★

Trouble. – A man grows up with an open mind, not knowing what life is going to turn out to be. Maybe happiness is not rare, or again it may be a deception. He earnestly seeks to find out. He discovers that the normal condition of man is something far more atrocious than he had ever imagined, but that nobody talks about it. Being innocent and unprepared, he suffers with more intensity than some men would be able to bear. His suffering would be intolerable to him were it not that there is something in him that reacts to it in the same way that the substance in the oyster reacts to 'trouble'. The expression which he gives to his anguish, the articulation of his despair, becomes a pearl: a 'black' pearl, perhaps, but which compensates him to a certain extent for the groaning labour of its bringing forth.

★
★ ★

The English. – Particular horror of living in these islands. How the English evoke in one at times the desire to kick and bite them! It is because they present an unparalleled example of spiritual virginity: girdle of chastity permanently padlocked against the intrusion of the least idea that might start an interior process of disturbance. 'England our cow!' (Auden). Moral bombs and dynamite are of no use whatever; the island's damp climate extinguishes the fuses.

But this complacency *shall* be shattered sooner or later. Nothing could be more desirable or more edifying than the violent dissolution of the British Empire.

★
★ ★

Excess. – There are some who are born with an excess of spirit, and who never rest in their search for an alleviation of the discomfort caused

---

The Booster, 3me année, No. 9 (November 1937), pp. 34-6.
Editor's note: These passages are all that remain of the original Notebook, irretrievably lost many years ago.

by this excess, which is like that suffered by a woman whose breasts are overflowing with milk but who has no child to suckle her. Violence, tension, insatiability.

St Teresa of Avila and the Marquis de Sade are alike in that they both possess a certain quality of which one can only say that the less one has of it, the greater one's spiritual mediocrity.

★
★ ★

Confusion. – 'In the beginning' was chaos. The mistake is to imagine that there has ever been an end to the beginning. The blind, the frightened, believe in order: (blind to the essential confusion, frightened of the gulf beneath their feet). They seek to escape from the first, the inescapable condition of man.

The most highly ordered state one can imagine would be no more than confusion 'raised to a higher plane'. It would not even be an ordered *surface* above chaos, but still an integral part of chaos (in extension).

★
★ ★

No wisdom without ambivalence. We cannot surpass futility until we have accepted it. The most desirable state: not order, but to be 'illusioned' and disillusioned both at once. The tightrope-walk.

★
★ ★

Chance. – The positive term of our inescapable ambivalence, the 'instinct which we cannot repress and which lifts us up', that which prevents us from pulling the irrevocable trigger: the Irrational. The tormenting trust in chance, the desire to know what will happen when we are not there, curiosity –.

Ought not our childish trust in chance to have been destroyed once and for all by the fact that it is precisely the reign of *chance* instead of *justice* that gives us reason to despair?

★
★ ★

Despair, madness, death: *the domain of tragedy*. It is into this domain that all search for the absolute leads: all other absolutes are temporary and dissoluble: they are all doors leading one by one into this labyrinth which is *safe* at last, *but endless.*

Despair, the one firm foundation. And the one supreme virtue, courage. Courage, which is the antithesis of the underlying fear to be discovered in everything which is most disgusting in the modern world: courage to build one's life on the foundation of despair.

Despair, and the courage to live it out, are alone capable of restoring grandeur and significance to existence. (Even though despair *denies* grandeur and significance).

★
★ ★

Religion. – Mere atheism, free-thought, etc.: nothing to do with religion. (Why Nietzsche hated David Strauss.)

The Communist: 'Religion, the opium of the people: pie in the sky. We have to transform the imaginary consolations of heaven into real consolations on earth'.

This sort of argument has not the slightest relevance to the religious problem.

What sort of freedom is that which is the 'knowledge of necessity'? The freedom of the slave to contemplate the chains which bind him hand and foot and which he drags with him everywhere he goes. – Similarly, what sort of consolation for the horror of existence could there be in *any* form of society?

The Communist (no doubt): 'Your argument is that of a neurasthenic bourgeois.' – 'C'est bien le fait d'un paresseux nerveux!'

Fortunate to be able to convince oneself so easily that uncomfortable problems do not exist.

★
★ ★

With happily smiling faces, the Communist League of Youth marches past in the Red Square, the People's Leader smilingly returns their gay salute. Everything is for the best in the best of all possible worlds. The factories are all working faster and faster, science is on the march, materialism is triumphant, les Soviets partout, the glorious and invincible Red Army shows its strength, – everyone is healthy, contented, well-fed, well-clothed, well-educated, well-exercised, well –! In such conditions how can one possibly talk about 'the horror of existence'?

Alas, we do not spend all our time parading in the public square. When the festivals and demonstrations are all over, everyone goes home, goes to bed, turns out the light. And then?

What about the 'opium of the people', now? And what about the story of 'The Emperor's New Clothes'?

The Emperor was not foolish because he paraded without clothes, but only because he insisted that he was dressed.

One must be absolutely naked. (But we are already: we are all Emperors.)

CHORUS

Is this the final coast
Between the dark land and tomorrow's sea
Home friends and lover lost
Is this the cost
Wandering aimlessly
And questions asked
Unlock the monster's jaws at last

Now he has come
Into a foreign hall
Which is not home at all
Now he is here
The cross-word puzzle fan
Looks up but does not hear
Or answer our lost man.

In the unfriendly street
Wings of the pavement beat
About the bright bowed head
No questions answered no
Encouragement, and so
Best beat a swift retreat
Before the signals change from green to red

And now the answer's plain
Stand and stare down again
Where water flows
Biting the town in half –
Unlock death's easy jaws
Fall like a stone
And disregard the frown

Editor's note: This unpublished poem was transcribed from one of D.G.'s Notebooks in the British Library. It is intended to be an integral part of the Surrealist film scenario *The Wrong Procession* (later renamed *Procession to the Private Sector*), according to p. 25 of the Notebook. See pp. 357-72.

But men conspire
The desperate to cheat
Street after street
Our wanderer
Seeks for a lock to try
He wants to die
But does not dare

Here will he hear
Another's angry voice
Teaching the crowd to fear
God and the State –
Hurl then the heavy mace
Although it may fly too far
And fall too late

Away again away
The phrase repeat
Day after day
Follows these weary streets
Searching forgotten joy
No stone commemorates
Who did not dare to die

Till the town's furthest bound
Cements its bond
With lonely ruined fields
Desolate acres spanned
By a forbidding wall
Whose shadow shields
No-one at all

But this old clumsy clown
Last remnant of the past
See how his beard falls down
See on the ground
His unknown captive squirm –
Fear an old fool at last
And the silk worm

Now a familiar face
Appears when all hope seemed lost
Joy with a summer grace
Come like a welcome ghost
To save what mattered most
Lovers embrace
Making the past a jest

If out of sight be out of mind
Then leave this place
If love be blind
Happy then not to see the clown's grimace
Together advance once more
Along the wall set out to find
The certain door

Though landscapes lie beyond
Tragic as those once passed
Now they go hand in hand
The terrors still ahead
Seem but their journey's last
Warning lest too great a speed
Should rob them of their land.